REPRODUCTION,
ETHICS,
AND THE LAW

Reproduction, Ethics, and the Law

Feminist Perspectives

Edited by Joan C. Callahan

INDIANA UNIVERSITY PRESS

Bloomington and Indianapolis

The paper used in this publication
meets the minimum requirements of American National Standard
for Information Sciences—Permanence of Paper
for Printed Library Materials,
ANSI Z39.48-1984.
⊗™

Manufactured in the
United States of America

Library of Congress Cataloging-in-Publication Data

Reproduction, ethics, and the law : feminist perspectives / edited by Joan C. Callahan.
p.   cm.
Includes index.
ISBN 0-253-32938-8 (cl : alk. paper). — ISBN 0-253-20996-X (pa : alk. paper)
1. Human reproductive technology—Moral and ethical aspects.
2. Human reproductive technology—Social aspects.   3. Human
reproductive technology—Government policy.   4. Feminist theory.
I. Callahan, Joan C., date.
RG133.5.R44   1995
176—dc20   95-13722

1 2 3 4 5 00 99 98 97 96 95

FOR

JENNIFER

Contents

Contents

Acknowledgments

Thanks to the University of Utah Press for permission to adapt material from Joan C. Callahan and James W. Knight, *Preventing Birth: Contemporary Methods and Related Moral Controversies* (Salt Lake City: University of Utah Press, 1989); to the editor of the *Journal of Clinical Ethics* for permission to adapt material from Joan C. Callahan, "The Contract Motherhood Debate," *Journal of Clinical Ethics* 4:1 (1993): 82–91, and Joan C. Callahan, "Feminism and Reproductive Technologies," *Journal of Clinical Ethics* 5:1 (1994): 75–85; to the American Section of the International Society for Philosophy of Law and Social Philosophy (AMINTAPHIL) for permission to adapt material from Joan C. Callahan and Patricia Smith, "Liberalism, Communitarianism, and Feminism," in Noel Reynolds, Cornelius Murphy, and Robert Moffat, eds., *Liberalism and Community* (in progress); and to the editor of the *Journal of Social Philosophy* for permission to adapt material from Rosemarie Tong, "The Overdue Death of a Feminist Chameleon: Taking a Stand on Surrogacy Arrangements," *Journal of Social Philosophy* 21:2–3, (1990): 40–56, and Joan C. Callahan, "Let's Get the Lead Out: Or Why *Johnson Controls* Is Not an Unequivocal Victory for Women," *Journal of Social Philosophy* 25:3 (1994): 65–75.

Windy Knoll Farm
December 1994

REPRODUCTION,

ETHICS,

AND THE LAW

Editor's Introduction:
Reproduction, Ethics, and the Law:
Feminist Perspectives

Joan C. Callahan

Reproduction is the locus of some of the most pressing conceptual, moral, and legal quandaries in contemporary society. In recent years, we have seen stunning advances in technologies that limit reproduction and even more spectacular advances in those that assist it. We have witnessed court cases that assign legal parenthood to genetic progenitors of children borne by women genetically unrelated to them, and court cases that pass over genetic mothers or fathers to assign legal parenthood to individuals only socially related to the children involved. Alongside developments in medical and surgical interventions for fetuses, we have seen an increasing number of court cases that hold women responsible for causing prenatal harm, as well as a landmark Supreme Court decision that might well release industry from liability for causing prenatal harm in the workplace. We've recently seen the development of a technology that allows postmenopausal women to bear children, while other technologies permit scientists to sustain younger and younger fetuses independent of women. Physicians can perform prenatal diagnosis that may encourage elective abortions; can deploy tissue taken from aborted fetuses in the hope of assisting persons afflicted with progressive, debilitating disease; can fertilize and implant in women's wombs eggs harvested from aborted female fetuses; and can sustain infants with no hope for characteristically human lives long enough to make their organs available to other infants in vital need.

All of these developments raise difficult questions of the utmost moral urgency, and how those questions are answered in custom and policy has profound effects on the position of women and children in society. The purpose of this collection is to add to the explicitly feminist dimension of the public discussion of how these questions should be answered.

Each of the papers in this collection is written from a feminist perspective. But since feminism is not a monolithic view or theory, the feminist perspectives that are reflected in the papers represent only some of the various positions found among contemporary feminists on the questions that occupy the authors here. The collection, then, is not presumed to be exhaustive of feminist perspectives on any of its topics, nor is it presumed to offer "the" definitive feminist position on any of its topics. Rather, the collection is meant to serve as a "state-of-the-art" contribution by a variety of committed feminists to the public discussion of puzzling and troubling conceptual, moral, and policy questions concerning human reproduction in contemporary society

The introductory essays to the book's four parts are meant to do several things—namely, to introduce the papers in those sections; direct the reader to related work by the book's contributors; touch on facets of the issues discussed in the section which are not taken up by the authors; draw in alternative feminist perspectives on the issues under discussion; and make substantive contributions to the public discussion of these issues. Since there is considerable confusion these days about what counts as a characteristically feminist perspective, I want to preface this collection with some conceptual mapmaking—laying out, at least in broad strokes, the geography of contemporary feminism as it engages questions in value theory and, in particular, questions regarding reproduction, ethics, and the law.

As I indicated earlier, there are a great variety of feminist theories and feminist perspectives on all sorts of topics, and it would be a mistake to think that feminists will always (or even usually) agree on how particular questions should be answered. That being the case, the first question to be asked is what features all views that are rightly considered feminist views share. I'll commence my cartographic housekeeping, then, by offering an account of what it means for a view or a theory or a perspective (in any domain) to be a feminist one. Next, I'll look quickly at various forms of feminism and where some of these forms most substantially disagree with one another. I'll finish with some reproductive technologies, sketching some feminist perspectives on them, according to the common features and differences among feminists that I've identified. I encourage corrections to my conceptual map of the feminist terrain; it is the nature of developing areas of inquiry to invite disagreement on how to envision their organization, and such conceptual work will not be completed in any single place. What I offer here is a way to think about feminism which is, I believe, coherent with the most precise work that has been done on this question, yet does things just a little differently from the suggestions I have so far seen.

Feminine and Feminist Perspectives[1]

The first distinction that needs to be made is between what have come to be known as *feminine* and *feminist* perspectives in any domain. I'll use ethics as an example, relying substantially on Rosemarie Tong's excellent work in *Feminine and Feminist Ethics*, even though my articulation of the distinction is slightly different from Tong's.[2]

In a well-known and extremely influential book, social scientist Carol Gilligan suggested that many women and girls have an approach to ethical questions that is quite different from the approach taken by most men and boys.[3] Gilligan's work unfolded as a critique of the work of one of her teachers, Lawrence Kohlberg, who had argued that there are six stages of moral development, proceeding from simply deferring to authority to operating from self-chosen, universal principles of justice.[4] Gilligan pointed out that Kohlberg's studies had used only male subjects, and that when women and girls are subjects, quite a different picture emerges. When asked to struggle with moral problems, Gilligan's female subjects appealed to "a network of connection, a web of relationships that is sustained by a process of communication,"[5] as opposed to appealing to the hierarchical arrangement of values advanced by Kohlberg that has come to be known as the "justice perspective in ethics." The problem was that if a Kohlbergian framework were used, the responses of women and girls to moral quandaries would be deficient, because the women and girls Gilligan studied did not attempt to resolve moral problems by deducing their solutions from abstract, universalistic principles, particularly principles of justice.

Gilligan concluded that the moral trajectories of many women are just different from those of most men. Women, she suggested, speak in a different, but *not* a deficient, voice. She offered a characterization of this moral perspective, which she described as comprised of six stages that include three levels of development. Movement is from the preconventional stage, with a preoccupation with survival, to the highest stage, where tensions between self and others are dissipated and a principle of care for self and others is embraced.[6]

Relationships at the highest stage are understood to require the participation and interaction of an integrated self—not a wholly self-sacrificing self, which marks an earlier stage. In Gilligan's stage 6, care becomes a chosen principle, and what will count as care will be highly context dependent. Interdependence of self and others is recognized and exploitation and hurt are condemned. The self in Gilligan's stage 6 is understood, essentially, as self-in-relation, and the moral mandate is to care.

This is crucially different from the Kohlbergian model, where the self is conceived atomistically and the moral mandate is to respect the rights of others. The Kohlbergian model emphasizes the individuality of and differences among persons. Persons are thought of as being, in an important way, antagonistically related. Rights are conceived as laying out moral spaces encompassing individuals—spaces that must not be crossed without permission. The emphasis is on respecting and negotiating these highly independent moral spaces. Gilligan's model, on the other hand, emphasizes the similarities and interdependencies among persons. Rights need not be wholly abandoned, but the emphasis is on preventing hurt and maintaining relationships. Rights take a back seat, at best, to care.

It is in this way that the so-called ethics of care emerged from Gilligan's observation that the received view of moral development failed to take into account the experiences and responses that she found in her female subjects. And it is that emphasis on the experience of women that marks what has come to be known as a characteristically *feminine* perspective or *feminine* consciousness. We can say, then, that a characteristically *feminine* approach to any question will display two features: (1) it will emphasize the inclusion of women's experience(s); and (2) it will focus on care, or some of what have traditionally been considered feminine virtues, in particular, nurturance and compassion, which issue in caring behavior. Thus it is that classically feminine approaches celebrate many of the traditional so-called feminine virtues and the experiences that are peculiar to women, such as pregnancy, labor, childbirth, and nursing.

Feminist perspectives, on the other hand, characteristically involve these three features:

(1) a recognition that women as a group have been and are oppressed;
(2) an account of the source or sources of that oppression; and
(3) suggestions for how the oppression of women can be overcome.[7]

Particularly in the work of feminists of color, feminist approaches also frequently include

(4) an account of the ways in which women have resisted oppression.[8]

Notice that the first three features of this characterization, which I take to be definitive of *feminist* approaches, make no direct appeal to the experiences of women, nor does this characterization put forward an ethics of care. However, this definition of the *feminist* perspective is fully compatible with both of those features of what I have called *feminine* theories or approaches to issues. Some theorists offer characterizations of feminism which combine the features of both feminine and feminist consciousness. An example is Canadian philosopher Christine Overall's articulation of the feminist perspective, which helps to illuminate the shared features of feminist views and theories and the basic differences between characteristically feminist views and nonfeminist views. Explaining that a feminist perspective involves understanding and incorporating women's experiences into the analysis of the issue(s) in question, Overall further explains that a characteristically feminist analysis pays attention to the ways that oppression of women has been maintained under patriarchy (the system of male dominance).[9] In her account, feminist proposals on issues will be guided by the determination to avoid perpetuating that oppression and by a commitment not only to contribute to the dissolution of sexual inequality but also to attend to the welfare of women (and children).[10] What I find attractive about Overall's characterization of the feminist perspective is that in addition to its focus on the position of women as a group, it also incorporates close attention to the actual experiences of individual women, which can vary greatly across ethnicities, classes, (sub)cultures, sexual orientations, physical abilities, educational backgrounds, ages, and so on. Although we can separate these two features of Overall's characterization, with one belonging essentially to feminist consciousness (or perspectives) and the other belonging essentially to feminine consciousness (or perspectives), in practice, most feminists are concerned to take the actual experiences of women into account, as is Overall. Thus, feminist perspectives, in fact, generally incorporate the first feature of feminine perspectives.

Pure Feminine Perspectives

Before leaving pure feminine approaches behind, it should be made explicit that pure feminine approaches as defined here do not perceive women as oppressed, and a feminine consciousness or perspective can be perfectly consistent with the most traditional treatment of women.

Thus, for example, someone like Phyllis Schlafly can argue—on grounds that take at least some of the experiences of many women into central account—that things for women should remain as they were. Or a book such as Marabel Morgan's *The Total Woman*, which celebrates the subordination of women to men, could be construed as taking a feminine perspective.[11] Women's being in subordinate, dependent roles is fully consistent with a pure feminine perspective. But such subordination is, emphatically, *not* compatible with a feminist perspective, since, by definition, feminist perspectives begin with seeing women as oppressed and have removal of that oppression as their goal.

Examples of Contrasts among Feminist Perspectives

Since feminist perspectives have the three features outlined above, and often the fourth, they all share the view that women as a group are oppressed; but they can disagree in their accounts of the oppression's sources and/or of methods for its removal. Let me illustrate with a quick (and grossly oversimplified) characterization of just a few out of many feminist perspectives that embody such disagreements.[12]

Consider, first, *liberal feminism*. Views known as "liberal feminist" were the first to recognize women as a sexual class (i.e., to recognize women as in a collective and disadvantaged position in relation to men). As Zillah Eisenstein has pointed out,

> . . . liberal feminism is not feminism merely added to liberalism. Rather, there is a real difference between liberalism and liberal feminism in that feminism requires a recognition, however implicit and undefined, of the sexual-class identification of women as women.[13]

Liberal feminism is so called because it shares the fundamental insights and commitments that bind characteristically feminist views, while also sharing the fundamental metaphysical and moral commitments of liberalism—commitments that postliberal feminists have rejected. For example, like liberals *simpliciter*, liberal feminists assume that persons are radically individualized autonomous agents, that the uniqueness of human beings is located in the capacity for rationality and autonomy, and that the protection of individual autonomy is the keystone of a morally well-ordered society.

The metaphysical and moral commitment to individual autonomy that informs liberalism and liberal feminism tends to issue in a morality of rights. In addition to being the source of later feminisms,[14] the great contribution of liberal feminism has been in its insistence that a political structure that protects the interests of men but not of women will not bear moral scrutiny. Although there are certain differences among liberal feminists, all liberal feminism presupposes that either social structures (especially informal social structures) are not barriers to individual action and decision or, if they are barriers, they can be overcome (ultimately) with sufficient individual effort, just as long as legal rights are equally recognized for men and women.

It should also be recognized that many liberal feminists are pragmatists—that is, many liberal feminists argue for protection of equality, autonomy, and rights, for neutrality and noninterference by government, not on the ground that our institutions are, in fact, neutral and unbiased, but rather on the ground that it is too dangerous to adopt any other position. With all the disadvantages that have burdened women throughout history, some liberal feminists argue, we are better off with identical treatment of men and women in law, since special treatment of women has always been used to women's disadvantage. Thus Nadine Taub and Wendy Williams, for example, argue against a special-treatment approach to women even as applied to pregnancy leaves in equal protection cases under Title VII of the 1964 Civil Rights Act.[15] They ask us to recall protective labor legislation of the past that barred women from many occupations, restricted their hours and their ability to compete, even in markets from which they were not barred. Another example they cite is the Mann Act of 1910, which forbade the transportation of women across state lines "for immoral purposes" and which was supposedly enacted to protect women from "white slavery," but was in practice used to prosecute women. And statutory rape laws, ostensibly protective of young girls, have been used to repress women and prosecute deviation of young women from accepted societal norms. Furthermore, they argue, any special treatment labels its beneficiaries as different from "normal" members of that class of persons, and, therefore, a burden. Women have always paid more than they have received for special treatment. This is why Taub and Williams argue against any sort of legal recognition of differences between men and women, despite the disadvantages that women will still bear under conditions of formal equality.[16]

The demand that women not be disenfranchised has been, is, and always will be a significant feature of all feminist views. But insofar as liberal feminists have limited their focus to a concern for equal legal rights for men and women within existing legal, social, and cultural structures, their feminist critics have pointed out that they have failed to attend to important social and cultural dimensions of the contexts within which women find themselves, including dimensions of ethnicity, class, sexual orientation, physical ability, age, and so on, which contribute to women's oppression. Other feminists argue that we need critiques of the formal institutions and informal social structures that liberalism leaves intact, for example, marriage, home, family, religion, law, education, capitalism. The mere granting of equal legal rights to women will not genuinely "liberate" women—we need, according to these feminists, profound changes in society and, according to some, profound changes in our very understanding of what women are.

One form of feminism that sharply differs from liberal feminism is *Marxist feminism*. Marxist feminists believe that the source of women's oppression lies in the classed nature of society and the introduction of private property. The argument is that inegalitarian systems of class lead to exploitation and imperialism—the domination of the have-nots by the haves, both at home (including the household) and abroad. According to the Marxist feminist, when the classed society is abandoned and no one is economically subordinate to anyone else, women will no longer be oppressed.

For example, theorists such as Margaret Bentson and Mariarosa Dalla Costa and Selma James have argued that women constitute a single class of workers who produce use-values for home consumption. It is here, according to these theorists, that the oppression of women is rooted, and this oppression will only be overcome when the domestic work done by women is transformed. In some accounts, the transformation is to be achieved by the full socialization of domestic work; in other accounts, by making domestic work a form of wage labor whereby women are paid for the child-rearing and housework they do.

The main criticism of such analyses, however, is that in treating women as a single laboring class, Marxist feminists miss the fact that women come from *all* economic classes and that women's oppression spans *all* economic classes, even if it is true that women's oppression is not precisely the same across classes. As Nancy Holstrom has pointed out, working-class women are doubly exploited—in their wage work on the job and in the domestic sphere. And, in comparison to upper- and middle-class women, they have less access to abortion, contraception, and child care. At the same time, oppression of women does extend across economic classes, and Marxism is unable to explain this. Gail Rubin makes the point sharply:

No analysis of the reproduction of labor power under capitalism can explain foot-binding, chastity belts, or any of the incredible array of Byzantine, fetishized indignities, let alone the more ordinary ones, which have been inflicted upon women in various times and places (163).[17]

As another example, in the 1990s in the West, economically independent women have not been fully relieved of oppressive features of their cultures. It is uncontroversial that women who are as highly educated and capable as men are still paid less than men for precisely the same work and that they still find opportunities far less available to them than to their male counterparts. Systems of male dominance are found everywhere—not just in capitalistic societies. Indeed, as Marxism itself as a political movement organized around the globe in this century, men (again) dominated as political leaders.

For these reasons, Marxist feminism has been challenged by other feminists—including *radical feminists*, who hold that Marxism simply doesn't get at the true source of women's oppression. Radical feminists insist that the system of male domination is what oppresses women. Capitalism, in this view, is merely a tool of patriarchy, and the destruction of capitalism is, at most, a necessary condition, but not a sufficient one, for the liberation of women. As against both liberal and Marxist feminists, radical feminists hold that neither women's lack of equal legal rights nor women's economic position provides an adequate explanation of women's oppression, and they deny that merely leveling out legal and economic positions will root out women's oppression. We need, in the radical feminist view, revolutionary changes at all levels of society, from the most obvious legal arrangements that disenfranchise women to the most hidden and fundamental institutions and practices that shape our lives and which systematically devalue women.

Mediating Marxist feminism and radical feminism is *socialist feminism*, which attempts to incorporate the main insights of Marxist feminism and radical feminism, while avoiding the lack of adequate gender analysis in Marxist feminism and the emphasis on women's biology that tends to inform much of radical feminism. Combining these insights, socialist feminists hold that we need to rethink institutions as basic as marriage and the family. Indeed, we need to reconsider not just our economic and legal arrangements, but our language, our science, our technology, our way of practicing medicine, the accepted canons in our academic disciplines, our academic disciplines themselves, our art, our music, our accounts of human history, our heterosexual biases—in short, the changing must go to our deepest roots. Such theorists emphasize the interlocking nature of ethnic, class, gender, heterosexist, ableist, ageist, and other oppressions. And they contend that the very fabrics of our private and public lives need to be unwoven and reassembled in a way that gives up even the dichotomy between the private and the public, just as it gives up the familiar dichotomies between mind and body, reason and emotion, thought and action, and a host of others.

Feminist Perspectives on Reproductive Technologies

That little bit said about only a handful of feminist perspectives, it should be evident where feminists might disagree on how we should think about reproductive technologies. One example of feminist disagreement occurs with the issue of contract or gestational motherhood, which will be taken up in more detail in part I. Liberal feminists have argued that if these contracts are not enforced, this will only be used against women. One of the most thoughtful and articulate proponents of this view is attorney Lori Andrews, who argues that failing to hold contract mothers to their agreements treats women as less able than men to make promises and keep them. Women end up being construed as pushed around by their feelings, which then get tied to their biology. According to Andrews, we need to be done with the biology-is-destiny mythology; but exempting women from their contracts because they want to keep the children they have gestated pushes us right back into the myth.[18]

Other feminists, however, have argued that enforcing or even allowing certain forms of gestational motherhood arrangements contributes to the commodification of both women and children, which is already rampant in our society and which is certainly bad for both women and children. It is particularly bad for poor women and for women of color, who are likely to be the most exploited in these arrangements. The whole notion of contract, according to these theorists, is inappropriately deployed in reproductive matters, and we should do nothing to support its use here, let alone enforce it legally. The most demanding of these views contends that the state should not only refuse to enforce these contracts, but should forbid them altogether.[19] Between this and the liberal view is a range of other feminist views, such as Rosemarie Tong's, offered in part I, which support non-commercial forms of these arrangements and argue for a modification of adoption laws to govern them.

Feminists also disagree on other forms of assisted reproduction, such as artificial insemination, in vitro fertilization and embryo transfer, gamete intrafallopian transfer (GIFT), zygote intrafallopian transfer (ZIFT), and so on. More liberal feminists tend to emphasize women's autonomy and reproductive choice, and they argue that if women want children genetically related to themselves and/or their partners, these options should be open to them and other feminists should not criticize women for seeking them. Barbara Berg provides an extremely sensitive articulation of this position in her paper in part I.

For various sorts of reasons, other feminists tend to oppose the development and deployment of most or all of these technologies. One reason is that the reproductive technologies perpetuate the common emphasis on genetic rather than social connections between persons—an emphasis that these feminists find squarely rooted in patriarchy and its preoccupation with the male seed.[20] Joan Mahoney's paper in part I offers such a view.

Feminists also disagree on when women should and should not reproduce. For example, some feminists argue that genuine concern for children dictates that one should not reproduce if it is predictable that a child with some sort of significant disability will be born. In part III, Laura Purdy argues for this position.[21] But other feminists, taking what is known as "the disability perspective," have argued that such views encourage pressuring women into trying to produce perfect babies, and that they contribute to what are already extremely worrisome attitudes toward persons who are disabled.[22] Thus, even among those feminists who share a normative perspective that accepts care as a fundamental moral commitment, they can, and often do, disagree on what care implies for practices such as abortion and extensive prenatal screening.

Feminists even disagree on the question of contraception. For example, many of us have received in the mail a flyer from the Feminist Majority Foundation, a group founded and directed by Eleanor Smeal, former director of the National Organization for Women. The flyer urges its recipients to do all they can to help make the abortifacient drug RU 486 available to women in the United States. Smeal's position, which is best characterized as a liberal feminist position (traditionally the dominant form of feminism in the National Organization for Women, although that is now changing), is that U.S. women should have maximal choices in available contraceptive technologies. RU 486 is construed by this group to be a technology that will help to take pregnancy termination out of the hands of the medical profession and put it in the hands of women, where it belongs.[23] Other feminists, however, such as Janice Raymond in her contribution to part III, have taken a very different stance. Raymond and her coauthors elsewhere argue that we need to be highly suspicious of this technology, just as we need to be suspicious of *all* technologies that are applied to women's reproductive capacities.[24] According to these feminists, RU 486's putting pregnancy termination into the hands of women is itself a myth, perpetrated by those who developed and are marketing the drug.

Conclusion

In the area of reproduction, as in so many other areas, the great contribution of feminism is to bring a perspective that takes seriously the lives and conditions of those who have been systematically, and often subtly, left out of consideration. Feminism began with bringing women and children into central consideration. Today, feminists have expanded our analyses to bring into central consideration other groups that have been left out in the structuring of our world by the dominant perspectives—from our theories, to our laws and public policies, to our formal and informal social institutions, to the design of our living spaces and workplaces, to our very language. The purpose of this collection is to add to that contribution.

Notes

1. Portions of this discussion are adapted with permission from Joan C. Callahan and Patricia Smith, "Liberalism, Communitarianism, and Feminism," in Noel Reynolds, Cornelius Murphy, and Robert Moffat, eds., *Liberalism and Community* (in progress), and from Joan C. Callahan, "Feminism and Reproductive Technologies," *Journal of Clinical Ethics* 5/1 (1994): 75–85.

2. Rosemarie Tong, *Feminine and Feminist Ethics* (Belmont, CA: Wadsworth, 1993), chapter 1.

3. Carol Gilligan, *In a Different Voice: Psychological Theory and Women's Development* (Cambridge, MA: Harvard University Press, 1982).

4. Kohlberg's stages are: (1) simply deferring to authority; (2) satisfying one's own needs and some of the needs of others; (3) seeking others' approval by conforming to stereotypical roles; (4) augmentation of conformity with a sense of the value of maintaining the social order and of the contribution of dutiful conduct to that order; (5) the association of morality with rights and standards endorsed by society as a whole; and (6) operating from self-chosen, universal principles of justice. See Lawrence Kohlberg, *Essays on Moral Development*, vol. 1 (San Francisco, CA: Harper & Row, 1981), pp.

409–12. See also the introduction to Eva Feder Kittay and Diana T. Meyers, eds., *Women and Moral Theory* (Savage, MD: Rowman and Littlefield, 1987), to which my articulation of Kohlberg's stages is indebted.

5. Gilligan, p. 33.

6. Gilligan's trajectory: (1) the preconventional level, which is marked by orientation toward survival; (2) the second stage, marked by a conceptualization of the first stage as being selfish. This is the transitional stage from self-centeredness to awareness of and care for others; (3) the conventional stage, marked by conformity and a desire to please others. Caring for others is seen as good, and goodness is frequently identified with self-sacrifice; (4) a stage in which the self-sacrifice of stage 3 becomes felt as disequilibrium, and the focus moves from a concern with goodness to a concern with truth. In stage 4, the individual realizes that inequality between herself and others is illogical; (5) a stage involving a focus on relationships that moves away from the tension between self and others that was realized in stage 4; (6) a stage where the dissipation of this tension is complete. This articulation of Gilligan's view is indebted to the introduction to Kittay and Meyers, eds.

7. Compare Tong, pp. 10–11, explaining Alison Jaggar's view that a feminist approach to ethics seeks

    1. to articulate moral critiques of actions and practices that perpetuate women's subordination;
    2. to prescribe morally justifiable ways of resisting such actions and practices;
    3. to envision morally desirable alternatives that will promote women's emancipation.

    See Alison Jaggar, "Feminist Ethics," in L. Becker and C. Becker, eds., *Encyclopedia of Ethics* (New York: Garland, 1992), pp. 361–370.

8. See, e.g., Patricia Hill Collins, *Black Feminist Thought: Knowledge, Consciousness, and the Politics of Power* (Boston: Unwin Hyman, 1990; reprinted New York: Routledge, 1991).

9. "Patriarchy" is, perhaps, most thoroughly characterized by Rich as "the power of fathers: a familial-social, ideological, political system in which men—by force, direct pressure, or through ritual, tradition, law and language, customs, etiquette, education and the division of labor, determine what part women shall or shall not play, and in which the female is everywhere subsumed under the male." Adrienne Rich, *Of Woman Born: Motherhood as Experience and Institution* (New York: Norton, 1976), p. 57.

10. Christine Overall, *Ethics and Human Reproduction: A Feminist Analysis* (Boston: Allen and Unwin, 1987), introduction.

11. Marabel Morgan, *The Total Woman* (Old Tappan, NJ: F. H. Revell, 1973).

12. For extended discussions of variations in feminist thought, see, e.g., Alison

M. Jaggar, *Feminist Politics and Human Nature* (Totowa, NJ: Rowman and Allanheld, 1983); Josephine Donovan, *Feminist Theory: The Intellectual Traditions of American Feminism* (New York: Frederick Unger, 1985); and Rosemarie Tong, *Feminist Thought: A Comprehensive Introduction* (Boulder, CO: Westview Press, 1989).

13. Zillah R. Eisenstein, *The Radical Future of Liberal Feminism* (New York: Longman, 1981), p. 6.

14. See Eisenstein, who argues this in detail.

15. Nadine Taub and Wendy Williams, "Will Equality Require More Than Assimilation, Accommodation, or Separation?" *Rutgers Law Review: Civil Rights Developments* 37 (1985): 825, referring to the Civil Rights Act, Title VII, 42 U.S.C. Sect. 2000e et seq. (1964). For an account of how the care perspective has been used against women in a recent Title VII case, see Joan Williams's discussion of *EEOC v. Sears, Roebuck & Co.* (628 F. Supp. 1264 [N.D. Ill. 1986], affd., 839 F.2d 302 [7th Cir. 1988]) in "Deconstructing Gender," *Michigan Law Review* 87 (1989): 797. Accused of discriminating against women in its relatively high-paying commission sales positions, Sears successfully used the work of writers such as Gilligan to argue that women's focus on relationships caused them to lack interest in highly competitive positions with long hours, such as its own commission sales positions.

16. Taub and Williams are opposed to the law's taking men and women to be different, and then constructing policy to recognize such differences. More precisely, they are opposed to views which argue for the accommodation of women, who are marked as "different" when the hidden norm is a male norm. However, they are not opposed to asking whether certain policies or practices have disparate effects on members of different groups. Where there are such disparate effects, policies and practices are to be changed to avoid them. Their point here is that an accommodation model allows women (or anyone else who is different from what the norm assumes) to be treated as a problem, a burden; a disparate-effects model, on the other hand, takes the policy or practice in question to be the problem.

17. Margaret Bentson, "The Political Economy of Women's Liberation," *Monthly Review* 21/4 (September 1969): 13–27; Mariarosa Dalla Costa and Selma James, *The Power of Wisdom and the Subversion of the Community* (Bristol, England: Falling Wall, 1972); Nancy Holstrom, " 'Women's Work,' the Family, and Capitalism," *Science and Society* 45/2 (Summer 1982): 186–211; Gail Rubin, "The Traffic in Women: Notes on the 'Political Economy' of Sex," in Rayna R. Reiter, ed., *Toward an Anthropology of Women* (New York: Monthly Review Press, 1975), pp. 157–210. For extensive discussions of Marxist feminism, radical feminism, and socialist feminism see Donovan; Jaggar (who is a leading socialist feminist), *Feminist Politics and Human Nature*; and Tong, *Feminist Thought*.

18. See, e.g., Lori B. Andrews, "Surrogate Motherhood: The Challenge for

Feminists," in Larry Gostin, ed., *Surrogate Motherhood: Politics and Privacy* (Bloomington: Indiana University Press, 1990), pp. 167–182. For another liberal feminist discussion of contract motherhood, see Christine T. Sistare, "Reproductive Freedom and Women's Freedom: Surrogacy and Autonomy," *The Philosophical Forum* 19/4 (Summer 1988): 227–240. For a more detailed discussion of feminist disagreements on contract motherhood, see Joan C. Callahan, "The Contract Motherhood Debate," *Journal of Clinical Ethics* 4/1 (1993): 82–91.

19. See Christine Overall, "The Case Against the Legalization of Contract Motherhood," in Simon Rosenblum and Peter Findlay, eds., *Debating Canada's Future: Views from the Left* (Toronto: James Lorimer, 1991), pp. 210–225.

20. For a discussion of the connections between patriarchy, capitalism, and technology and how our concern with genetic ties figures into these connections, see Barbara Katz Rothman, *Recreating Motherhood* (New York: Norton, 1989).

21. See also Laura M. Purdy, "Genetic Diseases: Can Having Children be Immoral?" in John J. Buckley, Jr., ed., *Genetics Now: Ethical Issues in Genetic Research* (Washington, D.C.: University Press of America, 1978), reprinted in Thomas A. Mappes and Jane S. Zembaty, eds., *Biomedical Ethics*, 3rd ed. (New York: McGraw-Hill, 1991), pp. 488–495.

22. See, e.g., Adrienne Asch, "Reproductive Technology and Disability," in Sherrill Cohen and Nadine Taub, eds., *Reproductive Laws for the 1990s* (Clifton, NJ: Humana Press, 1989), pp. 69–124.

23. There are also other probable uses of RU 486, including treatment for certain forms of cancer. For a discussion of the potential uses of RU 486, see James W. Knight and Joan C. Callahan, *Preventing Birth: Contemporary Methods and Related Moral Controversies* (Salt Lake City: University of Utah Press, 1989), chapter 6.

24. Janice G. Raymond, Renate Klein, and Lynette J. Dumble, *RU 486: Misconceptions, Myths and Morals* (Cambridge, MA: Institute on Women and Technology, 1991).

PART I:
RECONSIDERING
PARENTHOOD

Introduction[1]

Joan C. Callahan

The essays that follow, by Joan Mahoney, Rosemarie Tong, Barbara J. Berg, and Patricia Smith, raise a number of questions regarding the recognition of parenthood in fact and in law, the legitimacy of deploying reproduction-assisting technologies, changing conceptions of parenthood and, more generally, changing conceptions of the family.

Reconceptualizing Parenthood

Joan Mahoney's paper sets the stage for the others that will follow in this section. Mahoney develops and defends a functional definition of parenthood that would establish nurturers as parents, independent of whether they are genetically connected to a child or legally connected through adoption or by marriage to a child's legal parent. She traces the history of the concept of parenthood in law, pointing out that using genetic links to determine parenthood is outdated, inadequate, and wrongfully focused on the interests of adults rather than those of children. The nurturing model of parenthood she proposes would expand the category of parent to encompass an indefinite number of persons who have been involved in a child's care, including the prenatal care provided by gestational mothers in so-called surrogate motherhood arrangements where a woman gestates a fetus which may or may not be genetically related to her.

The pervasive emphasis on genetic parenthood in our society has led to some questionable practices and technological developments. For example, at the time of the Gulf war, the popular media reported that a number of departing servicemen banked their sperm so that their wives could be inseminated with it, letting them "father" children posthumously if they were lost in battle. In another development, post-menopausal women are now able to bear children who are genetically related to their male partners.[2]

Most recently, attempts are being made to inseminate HIV-negative women with "cleaned" sperm from their HIV-positive male partners. A study published by a team of Italian doctors in late 1992 indicated success in a sperm "washing" technique, with none of the 21 women inseminated with the processed sperm having seroconverted more than six months after the inseminations.[3] Despite the Centers for Disease Control's position that no technique can, at this point, reliably completely remove all traces of HIV from sperm, HIV-discordant hetero-sexual couples (seropositive man, seronegative woman) around the country have been clamoring for availability of the Italian method in the United States. In one case in Virginia, a woman seroconverted to HIV positivity following an insemination with her partner's sperm which had been processed in a manner similar to the process used in the Italian study. It remains unclear whether the woman's seroconversion was caused by the insemination, but it is known that "a fairly significant number" of women have been infected by HIV in attempting to have children genetically related to their seropositive male partners.[4]

That the genetic model as the primary model of parenthood should be abandoned has been suggested by a number of feminists. Barbara Katz Rothman, for example, argues that the emphasis on genetic ties captures a patriarchal concern with possession and domination, which we should reject:

> Genetic connection was the basis for men's control over the children of women. The contemporary modification of traditional patriarchy has been to recognize the genetic parenthood of women as being equivalent to the genetic parenthood of men. Genetic parenthood replaces paternity in determining who a child is, who it belongs to. I believe it is time to move beyond the patriarchal concern with genetic relationships.[5]

This "contemporary modification" of the emphasis on genetic ties is clearly demonstrated in the case of *Anna J. v. Mark C.*[6] As both Mahoney and Rosemarie Tong explain, Anna Johnson was the gestational mother of a child who was the genetic offspring of the couple who contracted her, Mark and Crispina Calvert. When Anna Johnson decided she wanted to keep the child, it was held by the court that the genetic progenitors were the legal parents, and that she had no legal claim whatever to parenthood of the child. In the famous case of *Baby M*, the New Jersey Supreme Court acknowledged the maternity of Mary Beth Whitehead, based on her genetic relationship to the child.[7] But a statement by Judge Harvey Sorkow in the lower court decision indicates how a man's genetic connection to a child can be more commanding than woman's. In response to Whitehead's claim that giving the baby to William Stern would constitute baby-selling (a claim with which the New Jersey Supreme Court agreed), Judge Sorkow replied:

> The fact is . . . that the money to be paid to the surrogate is not being paid for the surrender of the child to the father. . . . The biological father pays the surrogate for her willingness to be impregnated and carry his child to term. At birth, the father does not purchase the child. It is his own biologically related child. He cannot purchase what is already his.[8]

Judge Sorkow's argument supports Mahoney's contention that establishing parenthood on the basis of genetic ties commodifies reproduction. Stern is construed by the Court as owning the child, much as he might own a house or an automobile. (At the same time, Whitehead's genetic connection to the child is ignored by Judge Sorkow, even though she is the other genetic progenitor of the child.) As Sara Ann Ketchum has observed,

> Terms such as "surrogate mother" and "renting a womb" are distortions—the surrogate mother *is* the mother, and she is giving up her child for adoption just as is the birth mother who gives up her child for adoption by an unrelated person. This language allows the defenders of paternal rights to argue for the importance of biological (genetic) connection when it comes to the *father's* rights, but bury the greater physical connection between the mother and the child in talk that suggests that mothers are mere receptacles (shades of Aristotle's biology) or that the mother has a more artificial relationship to the child than does the father or the potential adoptive mother.[9]

The emphasis on genetic ties establishing parenthood has precluded legal standing even to be heard in court for persons who have been intimately involved in the raising of children. In a case discussed by Mahoney, for example, a lesbian couple who had lived together for several years decided to have a child. Virginia M. was artificially inseminated; she had the child; and she, her partner, and the child all lived together for two years. The couple separated, but Virginia's ex-partner,

Alison D., had the child for regular weekly visits for the next two years, while she paid child support and mortgage payments to Virginia. Virginia then decided to limit contact between Alison and the child. When she moved to foreclose all contact between Alison and the child, Alison went to court seeking a judgment that would allow her to continue visiting the child. Not only did she fail to get that judgment, the trial court held that since Alison was neither a genetic nor an adoptive parent, she was no parent at all, and had not even the right to be heard in court. Her case was dismissed by the lower court and the dismissal was upheld by the high court.[10] One of Mahoney's purposes is to argue for standing for people such as Alison D.—people who have clearly functioned as parents, even though they have no genetic or legal ties to a child through which this standing would normally be afforded to them. Such a development would let them at least make an argument in court for continuing the relationships they have established with children.

We are beginning to see some changes that point toward the law's recognizing a de facto parent/child relationship as establishing legal parenthood. A recent Kentucky case is an example. In 1985, Pam Troklus, then married to Robert Troklus, gave birth to a girl, Amanda. The couple divorced in 1987. In 1988, Pam married Jerry Taylor. Jerry and Pam had been having an affair at the time that Pam became pregnant with Amanda. From the beginning, Jerry believed that he was the child's father. At his request after he and Pam were married, he, Pam, and Amanda underwent Human Leukocyte Antigens (HLA) blood tests. The tests were done in late 1988 and the results, confirmed in February of 1989, showed the probability of Jerry's paternity at 96.93%. In April of 1989, he filed an action for a declaration of paternity. The action was dismissed by Judge John W. Potter in December of 1989, on the ground that the action was really a motion to modify the divorce judgment.[11] Judge Potter advised Jerry to file for an intervention in the original divorce case, in which Robert Troklus was granted visitation with Amanda on the basis of the ordinary legal presumption that the husband of a birth mother is the child's father. In January of 1990, Jerry filed an action to intervene in the divorce case, which had been handled by Judge Ellen B. Ewing.

Judge Ewing denied Jerry's motion to intervene on the ground that the motion was brought too late to be considered. Amanda had been born in August of 1985, and the Troklus divorce action was filed in August of 1987. Jerry knew that questions regarding custody of and visitation with Amanda would have been decided in the divorce decree, yet he did not seek intervention while the Troklus divorce action was pending. Judge Ewing also reasoned:

One of the factors to be considered when determining whether to allow an intervention is the question of prejudice to the respondents. . . . Under the facts of this case, Respondent [Robert Troklus] has always treated the child as if she were his biological child. The child will be five years old this month. During those five years, a parent/child bond has been established between [Mr. Troklus] and the child. [Mr. Troklus] has also supported said child and has continually maintained contact with the child. Obviously, [Mr. Troklus] will be adversely affected if Mr. Taylor is allowed to intervene and prove that he is the child's father.[12]

The judgment that Robert Troklus would remain Amanda's legal father was unanimously upheld by the Kentucky Court of Appeals.[13]

Judge Ewing's decision against allowing Jerry Taylor to intervene in *Troklus* was based in part on an appeal to Robert Troklus's interest in maintaining his relationship with Amanda. This was necessitated by the law's allowing formal consideration only of the interests of parties in the case, which did not permit the court to consider Amanda's interests.[14] However, were the major consideration (or a significant one) in such cases the best interests of the child, as Mahoney suggests, the decision would not need to have been taken on the technical ground of failure to request intervention in a timely fashion, but could have been reasoned on the ground of Amanda's investment in maintaining her well-established parent/child relationship with Robert Troklus. Mahoney's view, with its emphasis on relationships rather than rights rooted in genetic connections, seeks to formally and explicitly protect by law precisely that kind of nurturing relationship.[15]

Gestational Motherhood

The so-called surrogate mother cases introduced by Mahoney are the focus of Rosemarie Tong's paper. In an important departure from her previous position,[16] Tong suggests that even though there has been no consensus among feminists on these arrangements, the most basic concerns of feminists can best be addressed by assimilating *all* forms of gestational motherhood into properly modified adoption laws. To show this, Tong traces the main feminist positions that have been forwarded on so-called surrogacy arrangements, which run from the position that all of them should be prohibited by law to the position that virtually all should be enforced by law, with a variety of positions in between.

As would be expected, the disagreements among feminists on gestational motherhood arrangements have centered on what is really in the best interests of women and children. Standard (i.e., non-feminist) arguments for enforcing gestational motherhood contracts have been based on rights, including rights to noninterference and equal rights of the infertile to have children. Attorney John Robertson, for example, argues that noncoital means of reproduction should have the same protection under the law as coital means, and that only demonstrable, serious harm to others—harm that is not avoidable by less restrictive means—can justify state interference with noncoital means of reproduction. Says Robertson,

> The values and interests that undergird the right of coital reproduction clearly exist with the coitally infertile. Their interest in bearing, begetting, or parenting is no less than that of the coitally fertile.[17]

On its face, this seems to take equally seriously the interests of *all* individuals in "bearing, begetting, or parenting." But a closer look at Robertson's argument shows that this is not the case. Just after the passage cited above, Robertson goes on to say,

> It follows that restrictions on noncoital reproduction by an infertile *married* couple should be subject to the rigorous scrutiny that would be accorded elsewhere [emphasis added].[18]

Thus, only the reproductive interests of the married are to be considered. And elsewhere he says:

> Noncoital reproduction involving embryos, gamete donors, children and surrogates [sic] enables infertile *married* couples to rear children *who are biologically related to one, if not both rearing partners* [emphases added].[19]

But this is an argument for protecting the reproductive interests of the *fertile*, not the reproductive interests of the infertile at all. That is, a concern to enable (married, heterosexual) couples to have children who are genetically related to at least one of them cashes out to a concern to see to the interests of those whose genetic heritage can be passed on, often in the ordinary way. Robertson's view, then, is not what it might seem. It does not defend the protection through enforceable contracts of some fundamental right of the infertile to "have" and rear children. Rather, it ascribes that right only to the married (and in the United States, necessarily heterosexual) fertile individual with an infertile partner or, as in the *Baby M* and *Anna J.* cases, a fertile partner who is unable to *carry* a child. Such individuals, of course, are fertile *men*. Indeed, in all the gestational motherhood cases discussed by both

Mahoney and Tong that have involved legal intervention, white fertile men were attempting to acquire children genetically related to them.

Such considerations have moved George Annas to argue that gestational motherhood arrangements not only do not speak to egalitarian concerns, but that their "core reality," he asserts, "is both classist and sexist."[20] Annas contends that gestational motherhood arrangements provide white males with a method of obtaining children genetically related to them and, he argues, it does this by exploiting poor white women. He further points out that even though

> black couples are *twice* as likely as white couples to be infertile, . . . [gestational motherhood] is not promoted for black couples, nor has anyone openly advocated covering the procedure by Medicaid for poor infertile couples.[21]

When we put all of these considerations together, it becomes obvious that while these arrangements protect the reproductive interests of fertile, married, heterosexual, well-off white men, they do not protect those of infertile, unmarried, homosexual, poor, or non-white men, or women of any color.

Although it has not been noticed that *fertile* men are typically served by the practice of gestational motherhood, feminists have taken seriously the issue of who is not served well by these arrangements. Christine Overall, for example, argues that

> . . . insofar as the best interests of the child are achieved through contract motherhood, that goal is a side-effect, at best; . . . it is the best interests, as defined by him, of the hiring father—inevitably a wealthy and privileged individual—that are the overriding goal of the practice. . . . In the practice of contract motherhood, only the longings of the wealthy infertile seem to count. None of the defenders of this practice seem very concerned about the unhappiness of poor and working-class persons—who may, in fact, suffer from higher rates of infertility, often through greater exposure to reproductive hazards and contaminants. For the most part, also, no one is very concerned about single persons, lesbian couples, people of color, or disabled persons who may "want" a child just as much as do the wealthy, white, heterosexual couples who are able to buy a child through existing contract-motherhood arrangements.[22]

Overall argues against the state's endorsement of the practice by enforcing these arrangements on the grounds that this would be tantamount to the state's "fostering the work of women as breeders" and that the practice is not compatible with a state commitment to reproductive freedom and non-exploitative employment for women or with "the vision of women as equal, autonomous, valued members of [the] culture."[23] With a number of other feminists, she takes commercial gestational motherhood arrangements to involve baby-selling. She contends, moreover, that in addition to sexism and racism, the practice reinforces ableism, betraying "a eugenicist's desire to obtain not just a baby, but the best possible baby."[24]

On the other side of this debate, liberals have argued that failure to hold women to gestational motherhood agreements serves to undermine the autonomy of women and will only be used against them. For example, Ruth Macklin contends that feminists

> . . . who oppose surrogacy presume to speak for all women. But what they are really saying is that those who elect to enter surrogacy arrangements are incompetent to choose and stand in need of protection. . . . [T]he feminist charge that the practice of surrogacy exploits women is paternalistic. . . . [T]he charge of exploitation contradicts the moral stance that women have the ability and the right to control their own bodies.[25]

This is just one articulation of the often-heard claim that feminists who oppose contract motherhood arrangements are either parentalistic or inconsistent—feminists cannot hold that women are capable, competent moral agents and then deny that they should be free to enter into these arrangements and be held to their word.

But anyone who opposes these arrangements need not hold that women entering into them are incompetent to make such judgments for themselves, nor that women require some sort of special protection. In general, at least, it is acceptable to select public policies which attempt to limit the activities of *exploiters*, even if fully competent people might choose to be exploitees.[26] That is, it can be argued that such arrangements should not be permitted or (minimally) should not be enforced, not because they exploit incompetent women, but because they enable exploiters, and because they contribute to societal attitudes toward and general treatment of women and children that simply ought not be encouraged by the state. Such a view is neither parentalistic nor inconsistent with the view that women are fully competent agents.

The other strain of argument favoring state recognition of gestational mother contracts comes from pragmatist liberal feminists, such as Lori Andrews, who urge that contracts in these arrangements should be enforceable. Otherwise, say these feminists, we make an exception in contracts for women that will eventually come back to haunt them, much as other policies purportedly designed to protect women's interests became tools for oppressing women.[27] More specifically, Andrews argues that the rationales some feminists have put forward for proscribing and regulating gestational motherhood arrangements can easily undermine the gains feminists have made in the contexts of abortion, contraception, non-traditional families, and employment.

These rationales fall into three general categories: symbolic harm to society, risks to women, and risks to children. The symbolic harm rationales include much pejorative language. For example, the description of contract motherhood as "baby-selling" is, in Andrews' view, dangerous because much the same might be said of paying a physician to "create" a child through in vitro fertilization for a woman who cannot conceive her own child. Similarly, Andrews suggests that rejecting commercial gestational motherhood arrangements because they involve women's selling their parental rights implies that men should not be required to terminate their parental rights when they donate sperm for artificial insemination by a donor (AID).

Like Macklin, Andrews contends that the arguments from potential harm to women are often demeaning to women. By emphasizing biological bonds and hormonal changes during pregnancy and consequent emotional bonds between gestational mothers and their offspring, these arguments, she asserts, not only raise the specter of biology-is-destiny; they also concede that government, not individual women, should decide what risks a woman will be allowed to take—in particular, what risks regarding agreements that might be regretted later. Christine Sistare argues similarly, casting the issue in terms of women's freedom, and contending that neither a consent model

> which precludes the possibility of consent nor the mystifying representation of maternal feeling as a primal urge too potent to admit of rational control can provide grounds on which to *violate the right of all women* to be the dispositors of their own reproductive capacities. Women are not and should not be treated as a special subclass of adults by virtue of their reproductive capacities or their parental feelings.[28]

On the question of exploitation, Andrews suggests that this problem is to be avoided, not by disallowing these arrangements, but by ensuring that all women have equal access to the labor market. In addition, says Andrews, there should be sufficient social services available to poor women with other children at home to ensure that such women will not feel compelled to take on gestational motherhood agreements in order to support their other children.

In response to these considerations, Joan Mahoney has illustrated in another paper the moral repugnance of the law's requiring specific performance in these cases. This provides another non–parentalistic argument for nonenforcement, both as regards a woman's conduct during a contract pregnancy and as regards relinquishment of a child after birth.[29] Mahoney also distinguishes genetically related and non–genetically related gestational mothers. Women who "donate" oocytes, she argues, are analogous to sperm "donors," but such "donors" are *not* analogous to women who carry pregnancies to term; hence the law should not treat gestational mothers as analogous to gamete providers who do not participate in gestation.[30] In Mahoney's view, then, refusing to enforce an agreement to relinquish parental rights of a gestational mother does not constitute the kind of special treatment for women that pragmatic liberal feminists such as Andrews worry about, since the involvement of a gestational mother in the birth of a child is far more extensive than the involvement of a sperm "donor." Using several precedents in labor law, Mahoney argues that precluding gestational mothers from contracting away their parental rights amounts to just one more provision among many that restrict the freedom of employees. Under this kind of analysis, the fact that only women can get pregnant does not imply that women are in any way less competent and more in need of protection from their decisions than are men.[31]

Rosemarie Tong's paper offers a view that attempts to address all of these feminist concerns and bridge these positions by asking just what legal treatment of gestational motherhood arrangements (commercial or not) will serve most kinds of women best. While rejecting a ban on these arrangements, she argues that the contract model should be rejected in favor of an appropriately modified adoption approach.

Tong's paper takes seriously the feminist objections to gestational motherhood arrangements (e.g., those of Mahoney and Overall); arguments, such as Andrews's and Sistare's, that support them; and the desires of women on the initiating side of these arrangements—the Betsy Sterns and Crispina Calverts—who, for one reason or another, are not in a position to bear children. In taking these latter concerns so seriously, Tong's paper sets the stage for a discussion of infertility, which is taken up by Barbara Berg.

Infertility

In an interesting and illuminating paper, Naomi Pfeffer has argued that we need to lift the stigma associated with infertility.[32] She asserts that even though many people might regret their infertility as a loss of potential, the assumption that infertile people are necessarily desperate for offspring is certainly inadequately defended and cannot be used to justify the Western concentration on developing reproduction-assisting technologies. Pfeffer notes that people seeking infertility interventions often have unrealistically high hopes of success, which are then used by the developers and appliers of these technologies to justify additional research. The concentration of research efforts on spectacular interventive technologies detracts from research on the causes and possible treatments of infertility, an omission which, by implication, leaves the infertile as they were—and directly dependent on the medical community for assistance each time a pregnancy is desired. Similarly, Lesley Doyal has pointed out that although the arguments for the development of these technologies purportedly rest on a concern to serve the involuntarily infertile, the sincerity of such arguments is questionable when they are offered by those who have so much to gain in the way of professional prestige and financial reward from the development and application of these technologies and, in comparison, so little to gain from basic research into the causes and prevention of infertility.[33]

Despite these objections and the objection that gestational motherhood arrangements have so far tended to serve the interests of fertile, white, well-off males, many women do share the investment in raising children genetically related to them and/or their partners. Consider, for example, Christa Uchytils. Christa was born with intact ovaries, but without a uterus. In 1991, eggs taken from Christa's ovaries were fertilized by her husband's sperm and implanted into her 42-year-old mother, Arlette Schweitzer, who bore twins in her place. This recalls the South African Anthony case discussed by Tong, where a 48-year-old woman gave birth to triplets conceived by her daughter (who needed her uterus removed).[34] Cases like these are not open to the concerns attending cases involving fees for gestational mothers and for "surrogacy brokers," and they are instances of women providing for their daughters what their daughters, under ordinary circumstances, would be able to achieve on their own with their mates.

Although Barbara Berg is skeptical about gestational motherhood, she writes as a psychologist dealing with infertile couples, and she urges that more serious consideration be given by feminists to the actual experiences of the women she sees in her practice. She allows that not all infertile women or women with infertile or subfertile mates are desperate for children; but she is concerned that instead of advocating for the infertile, feminists too often speak for them, and the result is that women who seek help in conceiving or bearing children genetically related to them and/or their partners are presented as mindless dupes of a pronatalist patriarchy. Aware of the problems feminists have raised regarding the emphasis on genetic links, Berg also argues that a woman's desire to gestate a child is often not so much based on a desire to reproduce her (or her partner's) genes as it is to have the experience of pregnancy, childbirth, and nursing. Certain forms of assisted reproduction (e.g., AID, in vitro fertilization [IVF], and embryo transfer [ET]) make possible experiences that would otherwise be impossible for these women, be they heterosexual women in infertile couples, single women, or women in lesbian couples who are prepared to parent a child together.

Despite Berg's skepticism about the acceptability of gestational motherhood arrangements, it can certainly be argued on the kinds of grounds she puts forward that arrangements which genetically connect a child to one or both parents provide some women with an opportunity for the legitimate pleasures other genetic parents experience. Berg is concerned that those who cannot reproduce in the ordinary way are being held to higher standards than those who can, and she presents the genetic bond between parents and children as one additional bond which allows parents to face the strains which invariably accompany parenthood.

Although Berg acknowledges the virtue of adoption as an alternative to reproduction-assisting technologies, she points out that adoption is not always easily accomplished or well supported in our present society. Moreover, she observes that the unwillingness of potential parents to take on a child with special needs may not be simply the result of bias or selfishness, but the result of an honest sense of self that issues in the realization that they may not cope well with the additional challenges brought by adoption of an older child, a child with serious disabilities, or a child of another race. On this last point, Berg observes that adoptive parents are often in a double bind—urged to adopt children of racial/ethnic origins other than their own, but then subject to criticism for not being able to steep those children in their own heritages. The message of her essay is that feminists must not ignore the experiences of individual women who may ardently desire to rear a child they have helped to create and have nurtured from the beginning—an experience simply there for the taking for most women.

Reconceptualizing Parenthood Revisited

Patricia Smith concludes this first section with a reflection on changes in motherhood in Western European and North American societies. As we talk about parenthood and the desire to parent, Smith reminds us that within our own culture motherhood has undergone profound changes in the last century. Following Berg's paper, which focuses on certain constants in genetic and gestational motherhood, Smith's paper focuses on a cultural revolution that has swept away features of motherhood that were constant for centuries. Indeed, Smith's account suggests that motherhood has been so profoundly transformed that it is barely recognizable as the same role played out by our grandmothers. Concerned though many feminists might be about male domination and patriarchal attempts to control women by controlling reproduction, Smith points out that, in much of the West at least, far more reproductive control is in the hands of women now, and that this has made a revolutionary difference for all women. Despite the fact that many women want and will continue to want to be mothers, it is no longer plausible to argue or to even think that women's nature and value are tied to reproduction. Even women's consciousness has been transformed in a way that makes it impossible for us to fully grasp what the subservience of our foremothers was really like. The paradigm has shifted. Just what this means for motherhood, says Smith, is still open; but it does mean that the future has arrived and will stay—despite the efforts of traditionalists, there is no going back. In short, and whether we realize it or not, we are, according to Smith, seeing the end of the world as it was known for all of history.

Notes

1. Parts of the following discussion have been adapted with permission from Joan C. Callahan, "The Contract Motherhood Debate," *Journal of Clinical Ethics* 4/1 (1993): 82–91.
2. See Patricia Smith, "Selfish Genes and Maternal Myths: A Look at Postmenopausal Pregnancy," in *Menopause: A Midlife Passage*, ed. Joan C. Callahan (Bloomington: Indiana University Press, 1993), pp. 92–119.
3. A. E. Sempini, P. Levi-Setti, et al., "Insemination of HIV-negative Women with Processed Semen of HIV-positive partners," *Lancet* 340 (1992): 1,317–1,319.
4. "Sperm Washing Study Encouraging But U.S. Researchers Leery of Risks," *AIDS Alert* 8/4 (1993): 53–56.
5. Barbara Katz Rothman, *Recreating Motherhood: Ideology and Technology in a Patriarchal Society* (New York: Norton, 1989), p. 39.
6. *Anna J. v. Mark C.*, 286 Cal. Rptr. 369 (1991).
7. *In the Case of Baby M*, 217 N.J. Super. 313 (1987), rev'd in part, 525 A.2d 1128, 1988 WL 6251, Slip Op. A-39–87, dec'd February 3, 1988.

8. "Excerpts from the Ruling on Baby M," *New York Times*, April 1, 1987, p. 13.

9. Sara Ann Ketchum, "Selling Babies and Selling Bodies," *Hypatia* 4/3 (1989): 116–127, 125, n. 2, emphases in original. See also James W. Knight and Joan C. Callahan, *Preventing Birth: Contemporary Methods and Related Moral Controversies* (Salt Lake City: University of Utah Press, 1989), p. 265, n. 7; and Rosemarie Tong, "The Overdue Death of a Feminist Chameleon: Taking a Stand on Surrogacy Arrangements," 21 *Journal of Social Philosophy* 2/3 (1990): 40–56, 53, n. 1.

10. *Alison D. v. Virginia M.*, 77 N.Y.2d 651 (Ct. of Appeals, 1991). For a detailed discussion of the case, see Martha Minow, "Redefining Families: Who's In and Who's Out?" 62 *University of Colorado Law Review* 269 (1991).

11. *Jerry W. Taylor v. Pamela M. Taylor and Robert A. Troklus*, 89CI-02691 (Jefferson Cir. Ct., Div. 7, Louisville, KY, 1989).

12. *Pamela Marie Troklus v. Robert Anthony Troklus*, 87CI-06354 (Jefferson Cir. Ct., Div. 16, Louisville, KY, 1990).

13. *Jerry W. Taylor v. Pamela Marie Taylor and Robert Anthony Troklus*, 90-CA-002176 (Ky. Ct. of Appeals, 1992).

14. In this case, the Court was faced with the narrow question of whether to allow the intervention at all. Had it been decided that Jerry Taylor could intervene in the Troklus divorce case and attempt to have the divorce decree modified, the court would then have had to consider the substance of the proposed modification itself, at which point Amanda's best interests could have been brought into consideration. It is not at all clear, though, that, had Jerry Taylor's case gotten that far, he would not have succeeded in getting the divorce decree amended, since Kentucky law presumes that genetic parents are legally entitled to custody of their children. Absent a custody judgment necessitated by a divorce, depriving a genetic parent of custody is not even considered unless a parent is found to be unfit. Abandonment can be used to argue that a parent is unfit; but it is not clear in this case that such an argument could have justified a denial of a valid motion for intervention in the divorce decree (the motion through which Jerry Taylor sought to have Robert Troklus's parental rights terminated). It should be noticed, however, that there are also problems with the best-interest-of-the-child standard, at least as it has been used by the courts. For a discussion of problems with this standard for determining custody decisions, see Mary Shanley's paper in part II.

15. See also *Matter of Robert O. v. Russell K.* (80 N.Y.2d 252 [1992]), discussed by Mary Shanley in part II.

16. Tong, "The Overdue Death of a Feminist Chameleon."

17. John A. Robertson, "Procreative Liberty and the State's Burden of Proof in Regulating Noncoital Reproduction," in Larry Gostin, ed., *Surrogate*

Motherhood: Politics and Privacy (Bloomington: Indiana University Press, 1990), pp. 24–42, p. 26. For a more extended discussion, see John A. Robertson, *Children of Choice: Freedom and the New Reproductive Technologies* (Princeton: Princeton University Press, 1994).

18. Robertson, "Procreative Liberty," p. 26.

19. Robertson, "Procreative Liberty," p. 25.

20. George J. Annas, "Fairy Tales Surrogate Mothers Tell," in Larry Gostin, ed., pp. 43–55, p. 43.

21. Annas, p. 45, emphasis in original.

22. Christine Overall, "The Case against the Legalization of Contract Motherhood," in Simon Rosenblum and Peter Findlay, eds., *Debating Canada's Future: Views From the Left* (Toronto: James Lorimer, 1991), pp. 210–225, 214, 217–218.

23. Overall, p. 221.

24. Overall, p. 223.

25. Ruth Macklin, "Is There Anything Wrong with Surrogate Motherhood? An Ethical Analysis," in Larry Gostin, ed., pp. 136–150, 141.

26. See, e.g., Joan C. Callahan, "Paternalism and Voluntariness," *Canadian Journal of Philosophy* 16/2 (1986): 199–219.

27. Lori B. Andrews, "Surrogate Motherhood: The Challenge for Feminists," in Larry Gostin, ed., pp. 167–182. See also Nadine Taub and Wendy Williams, "Will Equality Require More Than Assimilation, Accommodation, or Separation?" *Rutgers Law Review: Civil Rights Developments* 37 (1985): 825, which is discussed in the introduction to this volume.

28. Christine Sistare, "Reproductive Freedom and Women's Freedom: Surrogacy and Autonomy," *The Philosophical Forum* 19/4 (1988): 227–240, 231.

29. Joan Mahoney, "An Essay on Surrogacy and Feminist Thought," in Larry Gostin, ed., pp. 183–197.

30. It does need to be pointed out, however, that women who provide "donor" eggs (unlike men who provide "donor" sperm) do so by means of medical/surgical interventions that involve significant risks and discomfort for them. See, e.g., the description of oocyte retrieval in Robyn Rowland, *Living Laboratories: Women and Reproductive Technologies* (Bloomington: Indiana University Press, 1992).

31. Again, see Taub and Williams (discussed in the introduction), who argue that policies or practices that disadvantage women (i.e., have burdensome effects on women that are not shared by men) can be disallowed in order to preclude disparate effects.

32. Naomi Pfeffer, "Artificial Insemination, In-vitro Fertilization and the Stigma of Infertility," in Michelle Stanworth, ed., *Reproductive Technologies: Gender, Motherhood and Medicine* (Minneapolis: University of Minnesota Press, 1987), pp. 81–97.

33. Lesley Doyal, "Infertility—A Life Sentence? Women and the National Health Service," in Michelle Stanworth, ed., pp. 174–190.

34. Ellen Goodman, "Carrying Daughter's Baby: There Are Doubts," *Lexington Herald Leader*, August 11, 1991, p. F2; and J. Madeleine Nash, "All in the Family: How Does That Gutsy South Dakota Grandma Feel about Being Pregnant with Her Daughter's Twins?" *Time*, August 19, 1991, p. 58.

Adoption as a Feminist Alternative to Reproductive Technology

Joan Mahoney

The idea that a family consists of one man, one woman, and the children they produce together is both a fairly recent concept and one that is prevalent primarily in Western middle class culture. Families at other times and in other places are multigenerational, sometimes involve multiple spouses, and include raising children who may or may not be genetically related to either parent.

In fact, the ideal nuclear family is not the only model in our own culture. Given the high incidence of divorce, many people have more than one spouse in the course of their lives, although we tend to wed our spouses serially rather than simultaneously, in contrast with polygamous cultures. Some of our families consist of same-sex couples or opposite-sex couples who remain unmarried. Some people choose not to have children, and others choose not to reproduce and add children to their families through adoption. Other couples (or single people) find that they cannot produce a biological child within their family situations, and they either forego child-raising or resort to one of a number of available solutions. These include adoption, contract motherhood, and—either alone or in conjunction with another arrangement—the use of reproductive technology, such as artificial insemination or in vitro fertilization.

Many of these techniques are painful, intrusive, and expensive. Some—such as contract motherhood—arguably involve the commodification of both women and children.[1] And, in cases involving a number of these alternative methodologies, difficult legal questions have arisen when the couple who has produced a child, or is attempting to do so, breaks up; or the contract with a third party breaks down; or both.

When these alternative arrangements have resulted in litigation, courts have attempted to define parenthood as the way to resolve the disputes before them. The results have been diverse and somewhat confusing; but, in general, courts have tended to look at the genetic connection as defining parenthood. It is true that in some instances a genetic connection may be deemed insufficient to create ties of parenthood.[2] Moreover, states may, by law, create parental rights in those who are not genetic parents—typically, through laws regulating and recognizing adoption, but also in making presumptions regarding the paternity of the mother's husband, for instance.[3] However, there are few cases in which courts have recognized the parental rights of those with no genetic connection to a child in the absence of state law establishing the bond.

The problem, or one problem, with this approach is that it focuses on the rights of the parents—or those people deemed to be parents because of their genetic connection with the child—rather than on the needs of the child. Although the litigation is generally between those parties who are claiming to be the parents and who are fighting over such things as custody and visitation, the interests of the child (if a child has been born before the litigation occurs) often are critical; yet they appear to be legally irrelevant.

In the Anglo-American legal system, children were deemed to be the property of their fathers until the late nineteenth century, and only in extraordinary cases were fathers denied custody in the event of divorce or separation.[4] This changed during the Victorian period, in which women in general and mothers in particular were often idealized. The Victorian vision of women led to custody of children, at least those of "tender years," being given to their mothers.[5] Only in the mid-twentieth century have courts begun to look at the best interests of children, rather than the "rights" of parents as automatically determined by their gender, when deciding custody. In many states, the best-interests standard has now been adopted by law.[6]

Nonetheless, when deciding questions of custody and visitation in extraordinary cases in which the contesting parties include both those who are genetically related and those who are not (such as lesbian parents or gestational surrogates), courts turn not to the best interests of children but to the rights of genetic parents, as if we had gone back to the concept of ownership of children that existed prior to the twentieth century.

The Nonmarital Fathers Cases

The first line of cases in which courts were called upon to define parenthood involved questions concerning the rights of nonmarital fathers. The issue was generally not whether the man in question was in fact the father of the child or children but whether the fact of his genetic paternity created enforceable constitutional rights. In *Stanley v. Illinois* (1972),[7] the Supreme Court rejected the action of Illinois in terminating Stanley's right to his children. He had lived with the children's mother for eighteen years prior to her death, although they were not married. Following her death, the children were declared wards of the state, and Stanley was denied a hearing on his fitness as a parent. The Court held that the denial deprived Stanley of both due process and equal protection.

In *Quilloin v. Walcott* (1978),[8] however, an unmarried father who had not attempted to legitimate his child was denied an opportunity to prevent the child's adoption by the mother's husband. The next year, in *Caban v. Mohammed*,[9] the Supreme Court struck down a New York law in order to uphold the rights of an unwed father. The law would have permitted adoption without his consent, which the Supreme Court found invalid, presumably because in this case the father had lived with the mother for several years.

Relying on *Stanley* and *Caban*, the father in *Lehr v. Robertson* (1983)[10] argued that he had an absolute right to notice and opportunity to be heard before his daughter was adopted by her mother's husband. Although he had lived with the child's mother before the child was born and had visited her in the hospital, the parents had not lived together after the birth and Lehr had not paid support. The majority rejected Lehr's argument, holding that the genetic connection alone was not sufficient to establish a parental relationship protected by due process. It may be necessary in most instances to establish a genetic tie to be deemed a parent legally (unless a *legal* tie has been established through adoption) and thus be entitled to the legal protection of parenthood, but genetics is not enough.

Based on this line of cases, it would have been perfectly reasonable for Michael H. to have assumed that his attempt to secure visitation with the child he had apparently fathered and also lived with would have been upheld.[11] Michael[12] had an affair with Carole while she was married to Gerald. After the child, Victoria, was born, Carole told Michael he might be the father, and blood tests confirmed a high likelihood of paternity. For the next several years, Carole and Victoria lived alternately with Michael, Gerald, and another man, but while they were living together, Michael referred to Victoria as his child and thought of her in that way. After Gerald and Carole reconciled, they decided that Victoria should no longer have contact with Michael, and Michael went to court both to establish paternity and to seek visitation.

The California court rejected his claim, based on a state statute that presumes that the child of a married woman is her husband's child, unless certain conditions are met that were not present in this case.[13] On appeal, the Supreme Court of the United States affirmed. There was no majority decision, but the plurality opinion of Justice Scalia indicates that while a genetic tie may help to establish legal paternity, California is free to decide who a child's legal father is, unless their decision violates an interest traditionally protected by our society.[14] Since we have not traditionally protected the rights of "adulterous" fathers, Michael had no grounds to object to the California law.

The Court takes very little time to dispose of Victoria's interest (which receives considerably less attention than Michael's claim), holding that Victoria has no right to maintain relationships with two fathers. Justice Scalia states, "This assertion merits little discussion, for . . . the claim that a State must recognize multiple fatherhood has no support in the history and traditions of this country."[15]

Although the *Michael H.* case appears to be dealing with a new issue, the rationale for the decision would seem to require reversal of all of the previous unwed father cases. It is certainly not clear that our traditions protect the paternal rights of any unmarried fathers. Indeed, at common law, nonmarital children were *filii nullius*—they *had* no fathers. What Scalia seems to be saying in *Michael H.* is that genetic paternity is enough to establish legal paternity, if there is also a social connection, but only insofar as a state chooses to recognize that person as a father. That doctrine would leave unmarried fathers at the mercy of state law.

Legal issues regarding paternity are nothing new. Indeed, before blood tests to determine paternity became widely available, it was reasonable to establish legal presumptions like the one California adopted, because of the impossibility of establishing genetic paternity with any certainty. Many of our social mores (such as the value placed on virginity for women, and the greater penalty for adultery by women than by men[16]) derived both from the role of marriage as a vehicle for the transmission of property from one generation to the next and from the inability to know for certain what man fathered what child, unless the mother of the child were known to have had sexual relations with only one man. (And, of course, only the woman could know or verify this.)

On the other hand, until recently, and until the development of modern reproductive technology, there was rarely any comparable question about maternity. Unless a baby was abandoned at birth, it was clear who had given birth to a child, and the person who gave birth was both in law and in fact the child's mother. Because we can now separate motherhood into three components—genetic, gestational, and social[17]—courts have had to determine which of those connections (if any) are both necessary and sufficient to establish maternity.

The Contract Mother Cases

Although there may well have been instances over the years of women bearing children for other women to raise, it is only with the modern development of contract motherhood that courts have been called upon to determine maternity when there is a dispute between those carrying out different portions of the maternal role. The earlier form of contract motherhood—such as in the *Baby M* case, in which the genetic/gestational mother carries a baby intended to be raised by the genetic father and (usually) his wife—should probably not have raised any unique legal issues. After all, these cases are not that different from the standard case of the genetic and gestational mother who contracts to give up a baby for adoption and then changes her mind. The peculiarity of contract parenthood, however, is that the "adoptive" father is also the genetic father.[18] Perhaps, then, genetic contract motherhood cases should be treated as a cross between the nonmarital father situation and the adoption model.

That was, in fact, how the California Court of Appeals treated the first contract motherhood case that reached it. In *Adoption of Matthew B.*,[19] the child's birth mother, who was also the genetic mother, tried to withdraw her consent to the child's adoption by the genetic father's wife. The court did not rely on the contract, but looked at the birth mother's consent, and the circumstances in which it was given, to determine whether the consent should be set aside. Finally, the court evaluated the adoption based on the best interests of the child (who had lived with the adoptive parents since his birth) and upheld the finding of the lower court that Matthew's bonding with the adoptive mother should lead to approval of the adoption.

Unlike the California court, the New Jersey trial court in the *Baby M* case[20] treated the dispute between the contracting couple, William and Elizabeth Stern, and the genetic/gestational mother, Mary Beth Whitehead, as a unique legal arrangement. The court upheld the contract, terminated Ms. Whitehead's parental rights, and allowed the adoption by the genetic father's wife to proceed. On appeal, the New Jersey Supreme Court rejected much of the lower court's opinion, finding that so-called surrogacy contracts were a form of baby selling and were therefore unenforceable. On the other hand, the Supreme Court upheld the custody determination made by the trial court, allowing the Sterns to retain custody on the grounds that it was in the child's best interests. Ms. Whitehead, however, had her parental rights restored and was allowed visitation.

More recently, California was faced with a case in which the gestational mother was not the genetic parent of the child she had carried for a couple who were the genetic parents.[21] During the pregnancy, Anna, the gestational mother, had become attached to the child, and, following his birth, tried to have the agreement set aside. Although the Uniform Parentage Act[22] provides that the relationship between a child and its "natural" mother may be established by proof of her having given birth to the child, the trial judge instead analogized to the standard for determining fatherhood, and held that since blood tests established that Anna was not the genetic mother, she was not the legal mother (or *a* legal mother) either. Because the contracting father could establish paternity by blood tests, the court held that it would be sex discrimination to deny the contracting mother the right to establish maternity by the same means. What the court refused to consider, of course, is the fact that women become biological mothers by two different means—genetics and gestation—and that therefore it is quite possible for a child to have two biological mothers.

The Frozen Embryo Case

The separation of genetics and gestation made possible by in vitro fertilization also creates possible legal complications regarding rights of preembryos before they are implanted. It was just such a dispute that led to the widely known case of *Davis v. Davis*.[23] Mr. and Mrs. Davis had attempted to resolve their fertility problems through in vitro fertilization. Several attempts at implantation had failed, and seven cryogenically preserved (i.e., "frozen") embryos remained at the fertility center at the time that the marriage dissolved. Mrs. Davis originally wanted "custody" of the embryos so that she could attempt to implant them, while Mr. Davis took the position that he did not want to father any children by Mrs. Davis and, therefore, that he had a right to have the embryos destroyed.

The trial court found that there was no such thing as a "preembryo," but that human life begins at the moment of conception and the embryos were, therefore, human life.[24] Mrs. Davis was awarded custody for the purpose of implantation. Had the positions of the parties on the disposition of the embryos been reversed, the trial court would presumably have awarded custody to Mr. Davis, so that he could either have donated the embryos to another couple or found a woman willing to carry the embryos to term.

On appeal, the Tennessee court reversed, indicating that embryos do not become persons at the moment of conception but in fact develop and acquire both legal and moral rights over time. Therefore, both parties were given joint control over the embryos, with equal rights to determine their disposition. Both courts, at the trial level and on appeal, seemed to have difficulty distinguishing between the preembryos as property and as children, perhaps because they are neither.

The *Davis* case does not fit neatly with the others that have been discussed, since it is not a case about who *is* a parent, but is concerned with who has a right to become, or not become, a parent, and who gets to make decisions about the disposition of genetic materials when they exist separate from the bodies of either of the originators of that material.

On the other hand, some recent decisions concerning custody and visitation disputes between lesbian parents has everything to do with who is a parent and whether there is some factor other than genetics that gives rise to parental rights.

The Lesbian Parent Cases

Two of the recent lesbian parent cases involved couples in which one member had given birth through artificial insemination. In *Alison D. v. Virginia M.*,[25] the two women had lived together for some time when Virginia was artificially inseminated and gave birth to a child. The child was given Alison's last name as his middle name and Virginia's last name as his last name. Both women acted as parents to the child until they separated, at which point Virginia kept custody and Alison had visitation. About four years later, Virginia terminated contact between Alison and the child, and Alison sued. The trial court found that Alison was not the child's parent and that she was therefore not entitled to either custody or visitation. Both the Appellate Division of the Supreme Court and the Court of Appeals of New York affirmed. The court refused to apply the concept of "de facto" parent and also refused to expand the definition of those who are entitled to seek visitation to include those who have developed a relationship with the child or the child's parent.

In *Nancy S. v. Michele G.*,[26] there were two children born during the course of the relationship, a son and a daughter. Nancy was the biological mother of both children, and Michele was listed as the father on their birth certificates. When the two women separated, each kept one child, although the children spent a lot of time with the other parent and with each other. When Nancy sought to change the arrangement and Michele refused, Nancy brought legal proceedings to determine that she was the only parent. She sought custody of both children, denying visitation to Michele.

The trial court held that Michele was not a de facto parent under the definition of the Uniform Parentage Act and that, even if she were, the court could not award custody to her unless the "natural" mother were unfit. The Court of Appeals upheld the lower court, expressing a fear that if the definition of parent were expanded, they would have to adjudicate claims of "childcare providers of long standing, relatives, successive sets of stepparents or other close friends of the family."[27]

What is remarkable about both of these cases is that, in each, a child's parent had terminated a long-standing relationship with a person that the child obviously considered a parent (in the California case, Michele had had custody of one of the children for a period of several years). The court's concern in both cases seems to be solely with the rights of the biological parent to decide who gets to associate with the child. No one seems to be worried about what harm will be done to the children in these cases when they lose the right to live, visit, or talk with people they have long considered parents. The children are treated as property and the biological parents as the owners of the property.

The case of *Sporleder v. Hermes*[28] involved an adoption, rather than artificial insemination. After attempting to have a child by artificial insemination, and after living with Sporleder for eight years, Hermes applied to adopt a child. The child was placed in their home in March 1988, and Sporleder provided the primary care until the two women separated, in October 1988. The women entered into an agreement regarding custody and visitation either just before or after they separated (the facts were in dispute on this issue), but Hermes completed the adoption and denied visitation to Sporleder.

The court refused to honor the agreement, finding it void as against public policy, and then went on to determine that Sporleder had no rights to the child, since she was neither a biological nor an adoptive parent. Again, as in the previous cases, the court expressed the fear that recognizing Sporleder's rights would open the floodgates to "parental" claims by multiple parties, leaving children subject to multiple custody and visitation arrangements.

Reconceptualizing Parenthood

Looking at these cases taken together, we can conclude that neither genetics nor nurture creates parental rights that are protected by the Constitution as it is currently interpreted, but that essentially parenthood exists as it is defined by state law. Those laws generally define parenthood through either genetics or adoption, except in extraordinary cases, such as the presumption that a mother's husband is the father, and the assignment of paternal rights to the mother's husband in cases involving artificial insemination by an anonymous donor. Neither legislatures nor courts seem to be eager to expand the definition of "parents" to include other people who may be closely associated with a child and who may be viewed by the child as a parent, nor to legally acknowledge nonstandard parental entitlements in such alternate arrangements as gestational surrogacy and same-sex parenting.

It seems clear from most of the decisions of the last several years in which courts have attempted to grapple with definitions of parenthood that they are getting it wrong because they are asking the wrong question. If one starts from the point of view of the parents and then tries to determine who has a "right" to the child—to live with the child, make decisions about the child, determine who else gets to associate with the child—then parenthood cannot help looking like ownership. But the property model of children is no longer relevant or defensible at a time when questions of property and succession are less socially pressing and when that model in fact militates against children's interests. That is, given the multiplicity of family arrangements, the ownership model just doesn't help in determining parenthood, and it tends to lead to the commodification of children.[29]

In Western society, families used to need children in order to keep their property (i.e., land holdings) intact. When children are the conduit through which property is passed, it is necessary to exercise control over them, to keep them in the parents' possession, so that the children themselves are viewed as property. Today we tend to have less landed property to pass on and we are less concerned with continuing an estate, in both the literal and the legal senses of the term. But while families no longer need children as property, children still need families. The human child is unable to provide for itself physically or emotionally for some time; and babies clearly need a caretaker, preferably one or more continuous caretakers over the course of the first 15 or 20 years of life.

If parents no longer need children as property, presumably there must be some reason why children continue to be valued, other than an unquestioning continuation of social tradition. Watching parents and children together, it seems clear that adults gain something from nurturing, just as children gain from being nurtured. If, then, we need children to love, perhaps we can begin to define parenthood in those terms, rather than in terms of ownership.

There have been a number of recent attempts to redefine parenthood, often in the context of reproductive technology and/or changing family structure. While many courts still seem to be focusing on the genetic connection, several commentators have looked instead at the intent of the parties. Marjorie Maguire Shultz, for example, has argued that "Within the context of artificial reproductive techniques, intentions that are voluntarily chosen, deliberate, and bargained-for ought presumptively to determine legal parenthood."[30] At least as between several biological progenitors, John Lawrence Hill would also determine legal priority in favor of those who intended to be parents.[31]

Carmel Shalev describes our changing conceptions of the family as moving from one based on status to one based on contract, as can be seen, for example, in our modern acceptance of adoption. Based on the contract model, she then argues for the acceptability of surrogacy, and, in addition, for the enforcement of surrogacy contracts.[32]

The problem with these theories is that the move from a genetic basis for parenthood to a contract basis seems to increase, not decrease, the commodification of children, and, in contract motherhood arrangements, of women as well. Most states have attempted to limit, if not prevent, what amounts to the sale of babies, by refusing to enforce consent to adoption by birth mothers given before birth or until a certain period after the birth, and by restricting the amount of money that can change hands at the time of the adoption.[33] If genetics does not determine parenthood, then the fact that one or more of the contracting parties is also genetically connected to the child should not result in approval, or indeed encouragement, of what would otherwise be forbidden.

Hill argues that if contract mothers are not defined as parents, the transfer of the child for money cannot be baby-selling[34]; but he seems to be engaging in circular reasoning. If we say the gestator of a baby is not the mother, she is not engaged in baby-selling, since she cannot sell what she doesn't own; but she is nonetheless taking money for waiving parental rights to a child whose mother she would have been but for the contract saying she is not. Hill's prototype hypothetical, in fact, concerns a man and woman who are both infertile obtaining a sperm donor, an egg donor, and a contract gestator, who agrees to carry the implanted embryo for a fee. The intention in this case occurs before conception, and neither the contracting couple nor the gestating woman are genetically related to the child. Nonetheless, given the lack of genetic connection by the contracting couple, this case is almost the same as the case of a couple who make contact with a pregnant woman and pay her to carry the child to term for them. Yet the latter arrangement is prohibited by state law, while Hill is arguing that the former should be permitted, if not encouraged.

A second problem with the contract theory of parenthood is that it appears to continue to rely on the notion that children may only have one parent of either sex and, therefore, it does not help to resolve the problems that arise when children have had more than one person of either sex acting in a parental capacity, or more than one biological parent of either sex, and the courts are called upon to resolve disputes between them. Shultz specifically adopts the one mother–one father model as a basis for her attempt to determine which of two women is a child's mother in a gestational surrogacy case. She says: "Perhaps, then, the child in question should have two biological mothers. Such an approach is unconventional, and therefore unlikely to be imposed."[35] Looking at intent may make it possible to reduce the number of same-sex parents in a contract motherhood case, but not when both intended parents are either male or female, or in cases in which children have had successive stepparents.

Finally, moving from a genetic/ownership model to a contract model of parenthood still constructs parenthood in an essentially masculine, rights-oriented way. A feminist approach to families would be constructed, instead, on relationships rather than rights.[36] This is not to say that a concern with legal rights is never relevant, nor that such a concern is always anti-feminist. Indeed, feminists have relied for a number of years on rights-enforcing doctrines, such as antidiscrimination laws. My point is that in the context of the family itself (perhaps as opposed to the relationship between the family and the state), relationships are more important than rights.

The emphasis on relationships rather than rights requires us to revise our concepts of families. To begin with, we need to understand that children are not entitled to one, and only one, parent of each sex. Such a construct may be necessary in law when we need to determine the legal rights of some persons as opposed to others seeking the same rights, such as stepparents or contract mothers, although even then, as the cases show, the construct is not very useful. But if we are instead looking at the needs of children for relationships and the needs of those who have been involved in a child's life to continue relationships, then it is clear that parenthood need not be exclusive.[37]

Certainly in the case of families created by two lesbians involved in a long-term relationship, the one mother–one father model makes it all too possible to deprive a child of one of the mothers he or she has related to, perhaps for years, and allow that mother to be shut out of the child's life.[38]

Further, if we look at parenthood as based on relationship, or nurture, then it is clear that neither a sperm donor nor an egg donor is a child's parent *without more*. That is, they may well become parents, and they may even have a priority interest, as against the interests of a person who is both a biological stranger and non-nurturer in the child's life; but they do not become parents based solely on the genetic connection. On the other hand, it is clear that a gestator, whether or not she is also a child's genetic mother, is a parent, as is the lesbian mother who has nurtured the child since birth, even if she did not give birth.

If we accept this construction of parents, courts or legislatures will have to alter the approach they have taken. Instead of looking at the genetic connection first, or attempting to sort out conflicting claims as to who *the* parent is, the definition should be expanded to include all those people who have played a parental role in the child's life. Recognizing more people as parents does not automatically give them the right to control over a child's life, but it does give them the right to be *heard* on questions of custody and visitation, as well, perhaps, as on questions of education and medical care.

Bartlett, for example, would allow nonparents to exercise parental status if the relationship with the natural or legal parent has been interrupted, if the claimant had had physical custody of the child for at least six months, and if the relationship began with the consent of the legal parent or pursuant to court order (as would be the case with most foster parents).[39] Although her standard is a welcome move away from the concept of exclusive parenthood, it still defines parents on the basis of biology or adoption, and precludes others who have functioned as parents from seeking custody or visitation unless the nuclear family has failed. The non-biological lesbian parent would seem to be left out under this standard, unless she had had custody, and the stepparent who had lived with a biological parent and child would similarly have no rights to a continuing relationship with the child.

Rather than expanding the rights of nonparents, Polikoff would alter the definition of parenthood itself, to include those with whom the child has had a parent/child relationship.[40] She has urged courts to redefine parenthood to include "anyone in a functional parental relationship that a legally recognized parent created with the intent that an additional parent-child relationship exist."[41] Although her suggestion does not require that the relationship with the legally recognized parent be disrupted, as Bartlett's does, and would therefore presumably include stepparents as well as non-biological lesbian mothers, it is not clear whether she would include a non-genetic gestating contract mother as a parent, since the legally recognized parent would not have intended to include her.

I would include all of those who have played a parental role in a child's life as parents, whether or not the nuclear family has broken down and whether or not any other legally recognized parent intended to include him or her. This standard, it is true, answers only the first question—who is a parent?—rather than the next, and perhaps ultimate question—who will have responsibility for and control over the child's life? However, we already have standards to determine custody and visitation, and once we recognize the various individuals who may need to be heard on that issue, the needs of the child can be provided for according to the standards now in existence. Simply because we recognize a stepparent, lesbian partner of the genetic mother, or gestating contract mother as a parent does not mean that the person *will* be awarded either custody or visitation. It means only that the biological parent will not have the ability to shut the other person out of the child's life unless it is determined that the best interests of the child would be served by terminating the relationship. It also seems clear that, despite the alarms raised by courts about opening the floodgates to claims from neighbors and babysitters, there is a clear line that can be drawn between those who have been concerned with a child and provided some nurturing, and those who have acted as parents and, more often than not, will have lived with the child.

Some feminists have suggested that the problem with moving to a de facto parenthood model is that it opens the way for abusive male companions to seek custody of or visitation with the children of the woman he has lived with and abused.[42] I see no way to draw a principled line that allows courts to recognize claims by lesbian partners but refuses to consider the claims of male partners. The answer seems to be that we will simply have to rely on courts to sort out the claims that would be in the best interests of the children involved from those that would not.[43]

The shift from an ownership model to a nurturance model of parenthood not only comports with feminist theory but also with the fact that women, as a rule, have tended to be less concerned with owning children and more concerned with nurturing them.[44] After all, until the last century, married women did not own property, so they were less concerned with children in terms of passing on their estates. And it was fathers, not mothers, who were entitled to the profits of their children's labor and entitled to custody in the event of divorce or separation.

If women bond with the children they nurture, then the way those children come into their lives becomes less relevant, if not irrelevant. The genetic link only matters if our children are our products, not if they are the people we happen to cherish and care for.[45] Acceptance of the nurturing model of parenthood not only changes the way we resolve disputes between people claiming to be parents, but should also lead to changes in the way we evaluate methods of becoming parents.

Most people do not think of adoption as a method of reproduction. Instead, adoption is seen as second best—a way of adding children to a family if one cannot have children of one's "own" (or children that one owns)—while reproduction means adding children by birth. But valuing nurturing over genetics means that the way our children become members of our families is less important than the relationship that develops once they are here, and adoption becomes not only a viable alternative but a morally preferable alternative to some of the other available forms of reproduction.

The decisions in which courts have recently defined parenthood and the articles in which scholars have grappled with the same issue have tended to look at one situation (e.g., contract motherhood, in vitro fertilization, lesbian parents) and then propose a definition of parenting to fit that situation. What I would like to do instead is to look at the nurturing model of parenthood and apply it to various methods of reproductive technology in order to evaluate them from a feminist perspective.

The oldest method of reproductive technology, and one that in fact requires little in the way of technology, is artificial insemination. A woman may choose artificial insemination as a way of becoming pregnant in preference to sexual intercourse, in which case she may obtain sperm from an anonymous donor or from someone she knows.[46] It may also be used by a couple in which the man is infertile or subfertile, in which case the couple almost always seeks an anonymous donor.

If (1) the sperm donor is unknown; (2) both the woman becoming pregnant and her partner (if she has one) are intending to be parents; and (3) both become involved in parenting the child once it is born, then under the model proposed, both the woman and her partner should be recognized legally as parents and the sperm donor should not. If, on the other hand, the sperm donor is known to the woman and acts as a parent (for example, if a gay man and a lesbian decide to have a child together), then both the biological father and the mother should be recognized as parents.[47]

The advantages of artificial insemination are that it is simple and inexpensive (there are those who have carried out the process at home without medical intervention) and that it allows the woman who carries the child to begin the nurturing role before birth instead of after, as she would be limited to doing in the case of adoption. The use of donor sperm does not result in the exploitation of men, since the process of donation is not painful and the supply is not limited, and the use of the sperm of the intended father is only a slight variation on coital reproduction. Use of the nurturing model of parenthood, therefore, would neither lead to a rejection of artificial insemination as a means of reproduction nor require extraordinary revisions in our current definition of parenthood, except in those cases where the intended non-biological parent is not the woman's husband.

In vitro fertilization, on the other hand, is neither easy nor cheap. When it is used by a woman who intends to become a mother (not, that is, in the contract motherhood situation), it does have the advantage of allowing her to begin nurturing sooner than she would if she adopted a child. Moreover, whether the egg and sperm come from her and her partner or from donated genetic material, there is very little question raised about who the parents are, since under the nurturing model the provision of genetic material, taken alone, does not give rise to claims of parenthood.

The negative aspects of in vitro fertilization are the cost, the intrusive medical procedures (especially if the woman is using her own eggs and is subject to the procedure to retrieve the eggs as well as the implantation of the fertilized preembryo), and the small likelihood of success. Most medical insurance plans do not cover IVF,[48] and the cost for each attempt can be very high. The success rates vary widely from one clinic to another, but on average, the chances of each attempt at IVF working are between 10 percent and 15 percent. In order for IVF to succeed, especially when a woman is using her own eggs, it is necessary for the woman to arrange her life around her menstrual cycle and her attempts to get pregnant.

It is understandable why a woman who has never been pregnant might subject herself to the IVF process in order to have the experience of pregnancy. But if she has already had a child, the value of the extra period of nurturance seems hardly worth the monetary, physical, and psychological costs. Other motivations for trying IVF involve genetic considerations. Some people believe that intelligence and personality are largely hereditary, in which case they might prefer IVF to adoption (assuming they also believed they had good genes). Others might simply enjoy watching a baby develop physical characteristics or talents that were reminiscent of others in the family. On the other hand, adoptive parents can watch a child develop habits and traits similar to those of the family the child has joined. In any case, the costs of IVF seem to be a high price to pay for the pleasure of seeing one's great-aunt's smile on the baby.

In vitro fertilization allows a woman to bear a child when she is either unable to produce eggs and/or is unable to become pregnant by sexual intercourse. IVF may also be used by a couple to allow a contract mother to gestate a child that will be genetically related to one or both of them. On the other hand, the earlier form of contract motherhood, and the form that is still less expensive and more prevalent, is that in which the contract mother (the "surrogate") becomes pregnant through artificial insemination with the contracting father's sperm.

If parenthood is based on nurturing rather than genetics, contract motherhood has few advantages over adoption. When contract motherhood is carried out commercially, rather than by a family member or close friend performing a service out of concern for the intended parents, it is expensive and arguably leads to the exploitation of women and the commodification of children.[49] In addition, if we adopt the nurturing view of parenthood, the gestational surrogate is defined, under this standard, as the child's mother, whether or not she is the genetic mother. Once the child is turned over to the contracting couple, assuming the gestational mother *does* follow through on the agreement, both parties become parents, whether or not the contracting mother is also the genetic mother.[50] In other words, almost from the start, surrogacy involving a contracting couple creates a situation where there are at least three parents, and possibly more.

Using the nurturance model, once the genetic father's partner begins caring for the child, he or she has all the rights of a parent, so that if the couple separates before he or she has completed adoption proceedings, it would not be possible for the genetic father to exclude his partner from the child's life. Similarly, if the gestational mother chooses to remain involved with the child, unless and until she has signed a release allowing adoption by the genetic father's partner, she is entitled to seek either visitation or custody, and the determination would be based on the best interests of the child, not on priority of "ownership."

The major disadvantages of adoption as means of adding children to a family are that it delays nurturing until after the birth of the child, and, as in the case of foreign adoptions, possibly for some time after that. And it can be expensive and time-consuming. In addition, because of the agency investigation involved, many people find the process demeaning and intrusive. (No one checks to see if we are good housekeepers before we give birth, so having someone check the house before the adoption is approved seems to unfairly set a higher standard for adopting parents.[51]) Finally, because there seem to be fewer available healthy white infants than prospective parents for them, adoption may also lead to the commodification of children.

On the other hand, adoption requires no intrusive physical processes. It allows opposite-sex couples, same-sex couples (assuming that an agency is willing to deal with a same-sex couple and that state law would allow a same-sex couple to adopt), and single people to become parents without having to hire someone to carry out all or part of the physical processes. And adoption gives children homes without increasing the population. That is, adoption provides children for those who want to nurture and parents for children who might not otherwise receive the kind of consistent care they need.

The old model of adoption, in which the adoptive parents were substituted completely for the birth parents and no further contact between the birth parents and the child was allowed, has slowly been giving way to the concept of open adoption, in which there is contact between the birth parents and the adoptive parents before, and possibly after, the birth. In addition, adoptive children are being told more about their families of origin and being given access to identifying information so that they may make contact, if they so choose, with their birth parents. In fact, open adoption is one of the first practices that has recognized the non-exclusive nature of parenthood, and it may serve nicely as a model for other forms of shared parenting.

I am not suggesting that adoption is the only form of noncoital reproduction that should be acceptable to feminists. But I am suggesting that it is a method of creating families with children that avoids some of the legal and ethical dilemmas posed by other alternate means of reproduction. If the purpose of reproduction is to have a child to love, then the best method of bringing a child into a family may vary from one situation to another. But the *best* method will, at least, avoid exploiting either women or children in the process.

Notes

1. Christine Overall, *Ethics and Human Reproduction: A Feminist Analysis* (Boston, MA: Allen & Unwin, 1987), pp. 199–200.

2. See *Lehr v. Robertson*, 463 U.S. 248 (1983).

3. See *Michael H. v. Gerald D.*, 491 U.S. 110 (1989).

4. A. H. Manchester, *Modern Legal History* (London: Butterworths, 1980) p. 390.

5. Manchester, p. 392.

6. See, e.g., *Missouri Revised Statutes*, Section 452.375.

7. *Stanley v. Illinois*, 405 U.S. 645 (1972).

8. *Quilloin v. Walcott*, 434 U.S. 246 (1978).

9. *Caban v. Mohammed*, 441 U.S. 380 (1979).

10. *Lehr v. Robertson*, 463 U.S. 248 (1983).

11. *Michael H. v. Gerald D.*, 491 U.S. 110 (1989).

12. In order to protect the parties' anonymity, many of these cases refer to the parties by pseudonyms or by using their first names and a last initial. For the sake of clarity, it is easier to use first names when discussing the cases than to refer to Ms. D. or Mr. H. This usage is not meant to indicate a lack of appropriate respect for the parties involved.

13. *California Code of Civ. Proc.* § 1962(5) provides that the "issue of a wife cohabiting with her husband, who is not impotent, is indisputably presumed to be legitimate." Cited in *Michael H. v. Gerald C.*, 491 U.S. 110, 117 (1989).

14. 491 U.S. 110, 125 (1989).

15. 491 U.S. 110, 131 (1989).

16. Until 1923, for example, men in Britain could obtain divorces based solely on their partner's adultery, while wives had to establish misconduct in addition to adultery to obtain a divorce. Manchester, p. 381.

17. Because men cannot gestate babies—at least not yet—we can only divide paternity into two components, genetic and social.

18. If a woman agreed to carry a child for a man who was infertile or subfertile, through donor artificial insemination, and she was the genetic as well as gestational mother, it is likely that a court would treat the case like any other adoption in which the birth mother has a change of heart, assuming the agreement broke down. If the contracting father had no genetic connection to the child, he would have no special relationship likely to be legally recognized. Therefore, in discussing contract motherhood, I have assumed a genetic connection between at least one intended parent and the prospective child.

19. *Adoption of Matthew B.*, 284 Cal. Rptr. 18 (1991).

20. *In the Matter of Baby M.*, 217 N.J. Supr. 313 (1987), aff'd in part and rev'd in part, 109 N.J. 396 (1988).

21. *Anna J. v. Mark C.*, 286 Cal. Rptr. 369 (1991).

22. The Uniform Parentage Act is incorporated in California law as *California Civil Code* §§7000–7021.

23. *Davis v. Davis*, No. E-14496, slip op. (Tenn. Cir. Ct. Sept. 21, 1989), rev'd, C/A No. 180, slip op. (Tenn. Ct. App. Sept. 13, 1990).

24. The trial court judge specifically rejected the accepted medical terminology, and, as summarized by the Court of Appeals, held that "The term 'preembryo' is not an accepted term and serves as a false distinction between the developmental stages of a human embryo." No. 180, slip op., p. 2 (Tenn. Ct. App. Sept. 13, 1990).

25. *Alison D. v. Virginia M.*, 77 N.Y.2d 651 (Ct. of Appeals, 1991).

26. *Nancy S. v. Michele G.*, 228 Cal. App. 3d 831 (1991).

27. 228 Cal. App. 3d 831, 841 (1991).

28. *Sporleder v. Hermes*, 162 Wisc. 2d 1002 (1991).

29. See Margaret Radin, "Market Inalienability," 100 *Harvard Law Review* (1987), p. 1925, for a discussion of commodification.

30. Marjorie Maguire Shultz, "Reproductive Technology and Intent-Based Parenthood: An Opportunity for Gender Neutrality," 1990 *Wisconsin Law Review* (1990), p. 323.

31. John Lawrence Hill, "What Does It Mean to be a 'Parent'? The Claims of Biology as the Basis for Parental Rights," 66 *New York University Law Review* (1991), p. 357.

32. Carmel Shalev, *Birth Power* (New Haven, CT: Yale University Press, 1989), pp. 18–20.

33. Because contract mothers are generally required to hand over the baby in order to collect their fees, they are clearly not being paid for services but for the product they deliver, the baby itself.

34. Hill, p. 356.

35. Shultz, p. 332. It does seem odd that in an article arguing in favor of contract motherhood (hardly a conventional idea), Shultz rejects one possible resolution of the situation out of hand as unconventional.

36. See Carol Gilligan, *In a Different Voice* (Cambridge, MA: Harvard University Press, 1982) for a discussion of women's tendencies to look at relationships rather than rights, or connections rather than hierarchy.

37. See Katherine T. Bartlett, "Rethinking Parenthood as an Exclusive Status: The Need for Legal Alternatives When the Premise of the Nuclear Family Has Failed," 70 *Virginia Law Review* (1984), p. 879 et seq.

38. See Nancy Polikoff, "This Child Does Have Two Mothers: Redefining Parenthood to Meet the Needs of Children in Lesbian-Mother and Other Nontraditional Families", 78 *Georgia Law Journal* (1990), p. 459 et seq.

39. Bartlett, pp. 946–7.

40. Polikoff, p. 472.

41. Polikoff, p. 572.

42. Sheila James Kuehl, Director of the Southern California Women's Law Center, raised this concern in a talk at the Women in Legal Education

Luncheon, Annual Meeting, Association of American Law Schools, January 5, 1992.

43. Martha Minow has also expressed concern about problems that could arise when the state adopts a functional view of the family. See "Redefining Families: Who's In and Who's Out," 62 *University of Colorado Law Review* (1991), pp. 279–281.

44. Although it is hard to find evidence to support this suspicion, I am not alone in making the assumption. Christine Overall states in *Ethics and Human Reproduction* (p. 149), "Indeed, the need for a genetic connection with one's offspring seems to be of particular importance to men."

45. There is an additional argument in favor of raising our genetic children, based on the modern version of eugenics, but the strength of that argument varies with the emphasis on nature or nurture that is popular at any given time.

46. The term "donor" when used to describe the provision of sperm anonymously is in fact misleading. Most sperm donors are paid for their services (product?), and most would presumably not provide sperm if they were not paid.

47. There are a number of other alternatives to the example used here. If, for example, a gay man and a lesbian have a child together, both act as parents, and either has a partner who also act as a parent, then the child would have three parents (or four, if both of the biological parents had partners).

48. Nor does the National Health Service cover IVF in Britain.

49. There are feminists who defend contract motherhood (see, e.g., Shultz), but although they argue that it should not be prohibited, I assume they would not argue that it is preferable to other forms of reproduction. See also Lori B. Andrews, "Surrogate Motherhood: The Challenge for Feminists," in *Surrogate Motherhood: Politics and Privacy*, ed. L. Gostin (Bloomington, IN: Indiana University Press, 1990), pp. 167–69.

50. If the contract is between a man (who contributes the sperm) and a genetic/gestational mother, the child will have only two parents from the start, and all the contract will have done is to determine custody.

51. I would imagine that the intrusiveness of the home study is resented more by the infertile, who may see adoption as, in any event, a less worthwhile way of reproducing, than by those who are fertile but have chosen to adopt as what they see as a better way of adding to their families.

Feminist Perspectives and Gestational Motherhood: The Search for a Unified Legal Focus

Rosemarie Tong

The topic of surrogate motherhood probably needs no introduction. The media have aggressively covered the Stern-Whitehead, the Malahoff-Stiver, the Calvert, and the Anthony cases, to mention some of the most publicized examples of surrogacy arrangements so far. The Stern-Whitehead case involved a 40-year-old biochemist, William Stern, and his wife, Elizabeth, a 40-year-old pediatrician suffering from the effects of multiple sclerosis. Because Elizabeth felt that she could not risk a pregnancy, she and William contacted the Infertility Center of New York. The Center arranged for them to contact Mary Beth Whitehead, a young married woman with two children of her own, to be artificially inseminated by William Stern. As a result of the artificial insemination, Whitehead became pregnant and agreed to carry the fetus to term for $10,000 and to give it up after birth to the Sterns.

After giving birth to the child, whom she named Sara, Whitehead felt that she could not go through with her agreement. Since the Sterns were unwilling to accept her change of heart, they secured a court order to gain temporary custody of the baby, whom they decided to name Melissa. Realizing that her baby was going to be taken away from her, Whitehead fled out of state with the baby and the rest of her family. Within days, however, the police tracked down the Whiteheads and recovered the baby.

Since the Sterns' legal custody of the baby was only temporary, they as well as the Whiteheads appealed to the New Jersey court to decide on a permanent home for Sara/Melissa. In granting custody to the Sterns, Judge Harvey R. Sorkow ruled that gestational motherhood arrange-

55

ments were legally binding, despite the fact that no state specifically authorized such contracts.[1] On appeal, the New Jersey Supreme Court voided the contract between Mary Beth Whitehead and the Sterns as against public policy, holding that such transactions are illegal baby-selling[2] under New Jersey adoption laws as well as "perhaps criminal and potentially degrading to women."[3]

In the Stiver-Malahoff case, a married woman, Judy Stiver, was inseminated with the sperm of a then single man, Alex Malahoff, under a contract arranged by a surrogacy broker. The child was born with microencephaly and a strep infection. Malahoff asked the hospital not to treat the child, but the hospital secured a court order to do so against Malahoff's wishes. When this happened, Malahoff denied paternity and refused both to take the child and to pay Stiver's fee. A court later determined that the child was in fact not sired by Malahoff but by Stiver's husband. The Stivers then sued Malahoff, claiming that the child's defect was not congenital but caused by a virus from Malahoff's sperm. Not only was the suit unsuccessful, the Stivers were told in no uncertain terms that the child was their responsibility. Within a short time, the Stivers had the child institutionalized.[4]

In the Calvert-Johnson case, Crispina Calvert and her husband Mark contracted Anna Johnson to bear their genetic child. Because Crispina Calvert had previously undergone a hysterectomy that removed her uterus but left her ovaries intact, she was capable of providing genetic material but not of gestating a child. Johnson agreed to an in vitro process in which she would gestate the Calverts' embryo, which was genetically unrelated to her. In her seventh month, Johnson changed her mind and sued for custody of the unborn child. After the child was born, Johnson shared visitation rights with the Calverts; however, California Supreme Court Judge Parslow quickly ruled that custody belonged with the Calverts. He argued that Johnson was a "genetic stranger" to the child, accusing her of filing suit in order to make money from book and movie rights. He further declared that gestational surrogacy transactions involve the selling not of babies but of "pain and suffering" (the pain and suffering being that of pregnancy and labor).[5]

Finally, in the Anthony case, a woman in Johannesburg, South Africa, had a hysterectomy. However, before she underwent surgery, she conceived naturally using a fertility drug. Through the process of uterine lavage, her embryo was flushed into the womb of her mother. Nine months later, her mother gave birth to her own three grandchildren whom she immediately, and apparently with great joy, gave over to her very happy daughter and son-in-law.[6]

Given the differing circumstances of these births, it is no wonder that the public is deeply divided about the morality/legality of surrogate motherhood, which I prefer to term "gestational motherhood." After all, one of the questions at stake in such arrangements is the identity of the baby's *real* mother. Is she the child's genetic mother (the ovum donor), the child's gestational mother, and/or the child's social mother? To term the child's gestational mother, who may or may not also be the child's genetic mother, the "surrogate mother," is to imply that she is not the *real* mother of the child when it is precisely her claim to "motherhood" that is at stake.

What I wish to examine in this paper, however, is not the semantics of what I will term "gestational motherhood."[7] Rather I wish to determine whether there is enough of a feminist consensus on the *ethics* of gestational motherhood to warrant a unified recommendation about the appropriate legal remedy for it. I will argue that although feminists have not achieved total consensus about the harms and/or benefits of gestational motherhood, the guiding principles of feminist ethics suggest that all forms of gestational motherhood might best be assimilated into *properly modified adoption laws.*[8]

Legal Responses to Gestational Motherhood

At least four legal responses have been proposed for gestational motherhood. They are: (1) the non-enforcement of all surrogacy arrangements, commercial or non-commercial; (2) the criminalization of commercial surrogacy arrangements, but not non-commercial ones; (3) the enforcement of commercial, surrogacy arrangements through contract law, but not non-commercial ones; and (4) the assimilation of non-commercial surrogacy arrangements, and perhaps also commercial ones, into either traditional or modified adoption law. Before presenting a set of primarily feminist arguments both for and against these legal remedies, it is important to understand what they each promise to do. Only then will we be in a position to determine which of these remedies best resists those actions, practices, and states of affairs that "perpetuate women's subordination."[9]

Non-Enforcement of Gestational Motherhood

In overturning Judge Harvey R. Sorkow's ruling in the original Baby M case, the New Jersey Supreme Court observed that contracts for gestational mothers are a disguised form of baby-selling that may also lead to the exploitation of financially needy women.[10] Since such contracts are clearly against public policy, the Court ruled that they are legally unenforceable. No state should recognize agreements that egregiously violate the rights of human persons—especially vulnerable ones.

Calling a contract for a mother unenforceable means that if either the gestational mother or the contracting couple breaches the contract, the state will leave the parties as it finds them. So, for example, if the contracting couple fail to pay the gestational mother her fee, the state will not help her collect it. Or if the contracting couple refuse to take the child from the gestational mother, the state will not force them to do so. Instead, the state will require the gestational mother either to maintain her parental relationship with the child or to put the child up for adoption. In the former case, she may be entitled to child support from the genetic father; and in the latter case, she may be entitled to his financial assistance.

Alternatively, if the gestational mother refuses to give the child to the contracting couple, the genetic father will not be able to secure custody based on the *contract* he and his wife made with her. Nor will he and his wife be able to legally force the gestational mother to waive her abortion right or to maintain a program of proper diet and exercise during pregnancy.[11] However, because the state has a great deal of concern for the child of a gestational mother and a contracting couple, it does not leave them as it finds them. Rather the state will use the "best interest of the child" standard—the custody test that is employed in divorce cases— to determine whether the gestational mother and/or the contracting couple should raise the child to adulthood.

Criminalizing of Gestational Motherhood

Some legal theorists, equating commercial surrogacy with a disguised form of baby-selling, argue that criminalization—rather than non-enforcement—is the most appropriate remedy for the problem. In 1985 the United Kingdom passed the Surrogacy Arrangements Act, which bans commercial but not non-commercial surrogacy. Stating that it is not in the best interests of a child to be born of parents "subject to the taint of criminality,"[12] the House of Lords decided to penalize neither contracting couples nor gestational mothers. Instead, the people who serve as the "brokers" in commercial surrogacy negotiations—lawyers, physicians, and social workers—face fines and/or imprisonment if they

    (a) initiate or take part in any negotiations with a view to the making of a surrogacy arrangement,

(b) offer or agree to negotiate the making of a surrogacy arrangement, or

(c) compile any information with a view to its ease in making, or
negotiating the making, of surrogacy arrangements.[13]

In addition, publishers, directors, and managers of newspapers, periodicals, and telecommunications systems are subject to fines and/or imprisonment if they accept ads such as "womb for hire" or "couple willing to pay royally for host womb."[14] Interestingly, several United States
jurisdictions have expressed a readiness to follow the United Kingdom's
lead.[15] In fact, Michigan has already passed a law making it a felony to
serve as a "surrogate broker," with a maximum penalty of a $50,000 fine
and five years in prison.[16]

Enforcement of Commercial Gestational Motherhood through
Contract Law

Unconvinced that contracts for mothers go against public policy, some
legal commentators urge that these contracts be recognized as collabo-
rative-reproduction agreements. All disputes between gestational mothers and contracting couples should be regarded as breaches of contract
to be remedied either by a specific performance or damages approach.[17]

1. *Specific Performance*: Because specific performance forces the parties to a contract to fulfill its terms, it eliminates the kind of uncertainty that characterizes less formal human arrangements. Uncertainty
is always difficult for human beings to handle, particularly when their
most precious dreams are at stake. For a contracting couple to wait nine
months for a child, not knowing whether the gestational mother will
finally relinquish him or her to them, is agonizing. So too is it agonizing for a gestational mother to carry a child for nine months, not knowing whether the contracting couple will accept him or her upon "delivery."

Significantly, specific performance is not the preferred way to enforce
personal service contracts. For example, if David Letterman refuses to
come on stage and perform, no court is going to force him to do his
monologue. Under such circumstances, he is not apt to be very funny.
Analogously, a contracting couple will achieve less than optimal results
if they force a gestational mother to follow "doctor's orders" during her
pregnancy; to carry the fetus to term (unless doing so endangers her
life); and/or to surrender the child to them no matter how much she
loves him or her. Still, since a child exists apart from the gestational
mother in a way that David Letterman's humor does not exist apart

from David Letterman, supporters of the contract approach maintain that issues of optimum good aside, it is not only feasible but desirable for the State to force the gestational mother to relinquish the child to the genetic father. Since the genetic father contributed the same amount of genetic material as the gestational mother,[18] and since he can feel just as badly about losing access to his child as she can, the promises a gestational mother knowingly and willingly made to the contracting couple arguably work to tip the custodial scales in their direction.[19]

2. *Damages Approach*: Unconvinced that specific performance is the appropriate remedy for breach of a personal service contract, other legal commentators stress the advantages of a damages approach. Imagine, for example, a gestational mother who "gets religion." As a result, this "born-again" woman reneges on her contract, viewing it as the foreign act of a former, false self—an unborn Christian who led her true self astray. Since specific performance of her promise to serve as a gestational mother would force her to confront her old unredeemed self repeatedly, the State should, on this view, permit her to make good on her contract another way—namely, the paying of damages.[20] What the supporters of the damages approach offer the parties in a contract for motherhood, then, is a choice. They may honor the contract, but do violence to their sense of self on the one hand; or breach the contract and pay damages, but emerge with their sense of self intact on the other hand.

*The Assimilation of Non-Commercial and Perhaps Commercial
Gestational Motherhood into Properly Modified Adoption Law*

Since there is arguably little difference between making arrangements to adopt a baby shortly before or shortly after conception,[21] some legal theorists argue that the kind of rules that govern adoption negotiations should also govern surrogacy arrangements. Although most of these thinkers maintain that gestational mothers should be paid, but only for their reasonable medical expenses, others maintain that contracting couples should be permitted to pay gestational mothers an additional "fair fee" for their extraordinary services, provided that they attach no exploitative strings to these fair fees. In fact, several years ago philosopher Peter Singer and physician Deane Wells proposed the establishment of State Surrogacy Boards. Anyone wanting a gestational mother, or wanting to serve as one, would be required to contact a non-profit State Surrogacy Board—that is, a very specialized type of *public* adoption agency. If enough volunteers did not surface, the Board could set a fair fee for gestational mothers. The Board would also require evaluation and psychiatric counseling for all parties and would supervise their agreements.[22]

Yet even if supporters of the adoption approach disagree about the wisdom of paying a fair fee to gestational mothers, they all agree that gestational mothers and contracting couples should be offered some sort of "change of heart" period. Current adoption law gives adopting parents an opportunity to change their minds about being parents at any time before or, lately, even after the adoption papers are signed.[23] Similarly, current adoption law gives a biological mother several days, weeks, or even months after the baby's birth to decide whether she really wants to relinquish him or her to the adopting parents.[24] This being the case, there seems to be no good reason for the law to treat contracting couples and gestational mothers differently than it treats adopting couples and biological mothers.

To the objection that giving custodial advantage to the gestational mother is unfair to the contracting couple, supporters of the adoption approach reply that it is no more unfair to the contracting couple than the kind of disappointment adopting parents sometimes sustain. From the very beginning of the adoption negotiations, adopting parents know that if the biological mother decides not to give up her child for adoption after all, they will go home to an empty nursery. Thus, provided that a contracting couple know from the outset that the gestational mother is permitted to change her mind about relinquishing the child, she does them no legal wrong if she decides to keep the baby.

To the further objection that the adoption and gestational motherhood cases are disanalogous because in the case of gestational motherhood the man trying to adopt the child also genetically fathered the child, supporters of the adoption approach argue that genetic linkage is not necessarily the determining criterion for parenthood. Genetic linkage to a child gives a man or a woman a limited right to *establish* a relationship with a child, where "relationship" means any mode of nurturance from the most physical to the most psychological. Thus, the fact that a man's sperm constitute 50 percent of the genetic material necessary for conception does not make him 50 percent *owner* of any resulting child. Likewise, the fact that a woman's egg constitutes 50 percent of the genetic material necessary for conception does not make her 50 percent *owner* of any resulting child. Children are not possessions; rather they are the kind of beings with whom relationships can be forged, and at birth the only *direct* relationship a child has is with the woman who has gestated him/her. Although this gestational relationship is not an interpersonal one, it is one that shows that the gestational mother was committed enough to the fetus to bring it to term.[25]

Feminist Assessments of the Legal
Responses to Gestational Motherhood

Feminists are divided as to the proper legal response to gestational motherhood. In evaluating feminist arguments for and against these remedies, it is useful to refer to what Alison Jaggar has termed the practical goals of feminist ethics. Jaggar claims that feminist ethics has three aims:

> first, to articulate moral critiques of actions and practices that perpetuate women's subordination; second, to prescribe morally justifiable ways of revisiting such actions and practices; and, third, to envision morally desirable alternatives that will promote women's emancipation.[26]

If Jaggar's interpretation of feminist ethics is correct—and I think it is—any feminist position on gestational motherhood needs to be evaluated in terms of its ability to disrupt oppressive patterns of domination and subordination. We must ask, then, which of the proposed legal remedies for gestational motherhood will make women and other oppressed groups as free as they possibly can be in a less than perfectly egalitarian world. More precisely, we must ask which of the proposed legal remedies for gestational motherhood serves the best interests of the most women possible. Does it or does it not liberate poor women? rich women? white women? women of color? young women? old women? fertile women? infertile women? Feminists must address these and other crucial questions of power if they wish to identify the most *ethical* remedy for gestational motherhood.

Assessing the Non-Enforcement of Gestational Motherhood

Although most feminists seconded the New Jersey Supreme Court's concerns about gestational motherhood, its "hands-off" remedy for surrogacy arrangements affirms a *status quo* that few, if any, feminists wish to maintain. To be sure, as soon as they realize that the state will not assist them should their contract fail them, some prospective adopters will eschew surrogacy arrangements. Others, however, will cheerfully go about their business, ignoring history's lessons that high-priced desires lead to high-risk consequences. When the desire is *theirs*, couples too often assume that nothing can go wrong in their particular case.

In the first place, profit-making surrogacy agencies are tempted to employ slipshod or bogus medical evaluations and psychiatric counseling in order to serve their paying clients as quickly as possible. The fact that no one at the Infertility Center of New York bothered to question Mary Beth Whitehead about her ability to relinquish a baby suggests that the center may have been overly eager to supply the well-to-do Sterns with a "compatible surrogate" (the physical resemblance between Elizabeth Stern and Mary Beth Whitehead has not gone unnoticed).[27] Concerned that the Sterns would take their business elsewhere, the center hurried to supply them with whatever or whomever they demanded.

Second, in order to maintain a large supply of gestational mothers, profit-making surrogacy agencies tend to minimize the risks and to exaggerate the benefits of gestational motherhood. In *The Sacred Bond: The Legacy of Baby M*, author Phyliss Chesler reports that most surrogacy agencies fail to well prepare gestational mothers for the possibly traumatic experience of relinquishing a baby. What is more, they frequently put gestational mothers in "support groups" the overall purpose of which is to enable them to repress their feelings.[28]

Finally, the logic of greed directs profit-making surrogacy agencies to charge contracting couples as much as possible and to pay gestational mothers as little as possible. Although some agencies refuse to enroll indigent women into their programs,[29] others prefer such women. Indeed, John Stehura, president of the Bionetics Foundation, Inc., believes that a gestational mother can never be poor enough. Since the going rate for gestational mothers is high even by middle-class American standards, he has urged surrogacy agencies to move either to poverty-stricken areas of the United States, where a gestational mother can be contracted for one-half the standard fee of $10,000 or, better, to the Third World, where a gestational mother can be contracted for one-tenth the standard fee.[30]

Clearly, we have reason to think that women's (and children's) best interests suffer from the state's refusal to regulate at least *commercial* surrogacy. Not only do profit-making surrogacy agencies routinely violate the spirit, if not the letter, of informed consent requirements, but courts also frequently award custody to the contracting couple for the wrong reasons. Just because one parent is wealthier than another parent does not mean that s/he qualifies as the better parent. Nevertheless, courts often give custody to the parent who can provide his/her child with a higher material standard of living. Thus, the fact that a gestational mother is typically poorer than the contracting couple works to her disadvantage in a custody hearing.[31] So, too, is the fact that she signed the contract in the first place. Indeed, in the Whitehead/Stern dispute over Baby M, Judge Sorkow observed that when she signed on the dotted line, Mary Beth Whitehead *proved* her "unfitness" as a mother.[32] In any event, custody disputes, especially if they terminate in a unwieldy set of visitation rights, are not likely to be in the child's best interests if her/his parents are unwilling to collaborate peacefully and joyfully as s/he grows towards adulthood.

Assessing the Criminalization of Commercial Gestational Motherhood

Some feminists—particularly Marxist and radical feminists—believe that criminalization is the appropriate legal remedy for gestational motherhood arrangements, especially the commercial versions. Their arguments against gestational motherhood differ in some respects from more traditional arguments against it, however. The authors of the United Kingdom's Surrogacy Arrangements Act explicitly argued that surrogacy arrangements are not necessarily *harmful*, but that they are always immoral:

> . . . [e]ven in compelling medical circumstances the dangers of exploitation of one human being by another appears to the majority of us far to outweigh the potential benefits, in almost every case. That people would treat others as a means to their own ends, however desirable the consequences, must always be liable to moral objection. Such treatment of one person by another becomes positively exploitative when financial interests are involved.[33]

In addition, the authors of the Surrogacy Arrangements Act implicitly argued that there is something morally wrong, or at least morally imperfect, about families that are intentionally based on non-biological foundations or on unusual biological foundations.

Although Marxist and radical feminists agree that commercial gestational motherhood is exploitative, they insist that they do not intend to privilege traditional, nuclear, genetically related families over single or many-parented families of adopted, partially genetically related, or genetically related children. Claiming that they have no desire to praise Leave-It-to-Beaver families and to condemn *La-Cage-aux-folles* ones, Marxist and radical feminists emphasize that their paramount goal is simply to prevent palpable harms to women (and also children).

Marxist feminists believe that it is not difficult to show how surrogacy arrangements harm gestational mothers since gestational motherhood is, in their estimation, a type of prostitution.[34] Much as the prostitute sells her sexual services for a fee, the gestational mother sells her reproductive services for a fee. In neither case, however, is the woman who does the "selling" making a free choice. Unable to secure a job that pays her enough to live in dignity, a woman may be driven to sell her body and/or its functions, the only thing she has that anyone seems to want. A woman "chooses" to do this, says the Marxist feminist, only in the sense that when a woman's sole alternatives are being poor or being exploited, she may opt for exploitation as the lesser of the two evils.

Agreeing with Marxist feminists that, like most prostitutes, most gestational mothers are usually much poorer than those who pay for their services, radical feminists deepen the Marxist feminist analysis of exploitation to include cases of non-economic exploitation. The "choice" of a well-heeled college graduate to work as a high-price call girl, or the "choice" of a wife to satisfy all of her husband's sexual desires even though he cares nothing about satisfying any of hers, is not necessarily more free than the "choice" of a high-school dropout to work as a low-paid streetwalker. Similarly, the "choice" of a woman to serve as a gestational mother for no fee at all is not necessarily more free than the "choice" of a woman who agrees to work as a gestational mother for a mere $10,000 fee so that she can feed, clothe, and shelter her own children, or the "choice" of a woman who agrees to work as a gestational mother but only for an outrageously high fee—say a $1,000,000—so that she never has to work again.

Whereas Marxist feminists emphasize that under capitalism there is always a price high enough to entice even the most resistant person to sell what is most precious to him or her, radical feminists emphasize that, under patriarchy, there is always an appeal strong enough to convince even the most hesitant woman that it is her duty to help an infertile couple have a child. In the estimation of radical feminists, patriarchal society convinces a high percentage of women not only to put the interests of others above their own, but also to measure their "goodness" in terms of how self-sacrificial they are. In other words, patriarchy teaches women that women who do not help others when it is in their power to do so are "bad women"—that is, the kind of woman who would deprive desperately lonely, tragically unfilled infertile couples of the gift of life.[35]

Radical feminists also claim that sometimes the women who join with their husbands in contracting for a mother's gestational services are not nearly as eager to do so as their husbands are. Realizing that her fertile husband wants a child genetically related to him, an infertile wife may consent to a surrogacy arrangement even though she would prefer to adopt, or to forsake having a child altogether. Unless she is secure about her value as a person, the infertile wife may begin to view herself as a *second-rate* woman. Indeed, she may even begin to regard the gestational mother as a rival for her husband's affections.

Finally, radical feminists underscore the fact that gestational motherhood harms not only particular women but women in general by creating or exacerbating certain destructive divisions among them. The first of these pernicious gaps is that between economically privileged women and those who are disadvantaged. Relatively rich women hire relatively poor ones to meet their reproductive needs, adding child*bearing* services to the child*rearing* services which women of few means have traditionally provided to the well-to-do. The second destructive division is the one which feminist Gena Corea envisions as cutting between childbegetters, childbearers, and childrearers. According to Corea, society is segmenting reproduction as if it were simply another form of production. In the future, no one woman will beget, bear, and rear a child. Rather, genetically superior women will beget embryos *in vitro*; strong-bodied women will carry these "test-tube babies" to term; and sweet-tempered women will rear these newborns from infancy to adulthood.[36]

As a result of this undesirable division of labor, Corea fears that the fictional dystopia Margaret Atwood describes in her novel *The Handmaid's Tale* may yet become a reality. What we see in the Republic of Gilead, Atwood's dystopia, are women reduced to their respective functions: there are the Marthas, or domestics; the Wives, or social secretaries and functionaries; the Jezebels, or sex prostitutes; and the Handmaids, or reproductive prostitutes. One of the most degrading Gileadean practices, from a woman's perspective, consists in the Commanders' engaging in ritualistic sexual intercourse with their Wives. The Wife, who is infertile, lies down on a bed with her legs spread open. The Handmaid, one of the few fertile women in Gilead, then puts her head between the spread-out legs of the wife, whereupon the Commander engages in sexual intercourse not with his Wife but with her Handmaid. Should the Handmaid become pregnant, the child she bears will be regarded as that of the Commander and his Wife. Indeed, on the day the Handmaid gives birth to the child, the Wife will simulate labor pains, and all the Wives and Handmaids in Gilead will gather round the fortunate Wife and her blessed Handmaid, experiencing through them an ephemeral moment of female bonding—of women's pride, passion, and power.

After one such birth day, the central character, a woman named Offred, thinks back to better times, and speaks in her mind to her mother, who had been a feminist leader:

> Can you hear me? You wanted a women's culture. Well, now there is one. It isn't what you meant, but it exists. Be thankful for small mercies.[37]

And, of course, they are *very* small mercies, for with the exception of birth days—those rare occasions when a Handmaid manages to produce a child—women have little contact with each other. The Marthas, Wives, Jezebels, and Handmaids are segregated from each other. And what contact women do have—even within their own class—is largely silent, for they are permitted to speak to each other only when absolutely necessary.

In addition to focusing on the ways in which gestational motherhood allegedly harms women, Marxist and radical feminists also speculate about the ways in which it may harm children. Without any possibility of saying "yes" or "no" to their parents' surrogacy arrangements, contracted children might be subject to more psychological harms than are coitally produced children. For example, should a contracted child—say, a little girl—be born impaired, she could face what is probably the greatest harm any child can face: rejection by all her parents, as was the case with Judy Stiver's child. Moreover, even if the child is born healthy and is very much accepted by her parents, she will probably still experience the kind of psychological harm an adopted child sometimes experiences—not understanding, for example, why her genetic parent(s) would not or could not keep her.

Finally, permitting paid contracts for babies comes close, in radical and Marxist feminists' estimation, to permitting a market in babies, thereby "commodifying something—life—which should not be treated as a commodity."[38] Over the years, parents might come to view babies as a special kind of consumer good—one that they can choose to purchase instead of some equally costly good; for example, a luxury car. Under such conditions, parents' love for their children would no longer be unconditional; rather, it would depend on whether or not their children were "good" products.[39] In a worst-case scenario, parents might trade in their defective "models" for the latest "models" science and technology have to offer.

In this connection, philosophers Hilde Lindemann Nelson and James Lindemann Nelson have argued that when parents bring a child into existence, they "create a vulnerability."[40] Having created a person with a set of basic needs, one parent, for example, may not let another parent, however willing, assume full child-rearing responsibilities, because both parents owe a personal debt "*to the child*."[41] It may be okay with mom if dad fails to spend time with junior, but it may not be okay with junior. Similarly, even if the contracting couple is willing to rear by themselves the child they contracted for, it remains the gestational mother's obligation to help rear her child unless she is unable to do so.[42] It makes no difference that the gestational mother *believes* that the contracting couple will meet her child's needs, for the gestational mother "herself is the only person she can bring to *perform* the required services."[43] Parents, no less than children, are not interchangeable. One is not necessarily as good as another, and certainly not the same as the other. Comment Nelson and Nelson:

> To engineer a situation in which the biological father can discharge his responsibility daily, but the mother cannot, is to put her under an obligation to the child that she does not intend to meet. Apart from making deceitful promises to Nazis, there would seem to be few cases where we can legitimately act in such bad faith.[44]

Assessing the Enforcement of Commercial Gestational Motherhood through Contract Law

Not all feminists agree with Marxist and radical feminists that gestational motherhood harms women and children. Nor do they concede that the state should paternalistically (maternalistically) protect women from making mistakes in the event that gestational motherhood is proven, on balance, to be harmful.

In fact, liberal feminists often argue that gestational motherhood is at least as beneficial to the affected parties as are a variety of other parenting arrangements. First, liberal feminists claim that gestational mothers, like male sperm "vendors," are permitted to sell their reproductive wares for a good price, thereby enhancing the material quality of their own lives. Less crassly, gestational mothers also get an opportunity to do something worthwhile. In fact, many such mothers insist that gestational motherhood is a good practice, since "there is no greater gift" to give than the gift of a child.[45] As in the Anthony case, some women are willing to bear children for beloved family members or intimate friends—the ultimate act of love and friendship.

Second, liberal feminists claim that contracting couples also benefit as the result of their being able to purchase and use the services of gestational mothers. Indeed, anyone who has ever known an infertile couple who have tried virtually everything in order to have a child genetically related to at least one of them, can imagine how happy a contracting couple must feel when they finally secure a "child of their own." Although liberal feminists concede that our patriarchal culture has probably overemphasized genetic connection because it is the only kind of connection a *father* can have to his child at birth, they immediately add that most female as well as male parents hope to see some physical and psychological aspects of themselves reflected in their children. Rather than dismissing this desire as "male," liberal feminists simply describe it as a very human one.

Third, liberal feminists claim that contracted children are the primary beneficiaries of surrogacy arrangements. Since everyone went through such trouble to bring them into the world, contracted children are "excruciatingly wanted" children[46]; and wanted children tend to be loved—and therefore happy—children. Whatever "crisis of confidence" such children *may* experience when they discover that they were reproduced non-coitally, that crisis will be at most momentary. It is hard to feel badly about one's biological origins when everything else in one's life is going well.

Liberal feminists also assert that women (and men) should be permitted to use whatever reproduction-controlling or reproduction-aiding technologies they want, provided that they do not harm anyone in the process. Although they concede that society is not required to enforce any and all contracts—say a contract to kill someone, or a contract to sell one's self into slavery, or a contract to sell one's soul to the devil— liberal feminists insist that, given widely accepted interpretations of constitutional law, two or more consenting adults have a right to contract with each other to procreate a child collaboratively. They also insist that two of these collaborators—namely, the sperm and egg contributors—have what amounts to property rights over their co-produced child.

What is clear on this line of reasoning is that William Stern, for example, had as much claim to Baby M as Mary Beth Whitehead initially had. He contributed the sperm; she contributed the egg. Similarly, the genetic "father" who sued for joint custody of his and his ex-wife's frozen embryos had as much right to destroy them as she had to preserve them.[47] Finally, the gestational mother who sued for joint custody of the child she had gestated had no cause to sue, since she was genetically unrelated to the child.[48] What is also clear on this line of reasoning is that surrogacy arrangements do not constitute "baby-selling." When a gestational mother relinquishes her genetic child to a contracting couple for a fee, she is no more "selling" that child than they are "buying" that child. Rather she is simply waiving and transferring her parental authority over that child, while the genetic father is reaffirming his.

Yet even though liberal feminists do not think that gestational motherhood arrangements are wrong in general, they concede that they can be wrong in particular. To the degree that a surrogacy arrangement violates a woman's constitutional rights, says feminist lawyer Lori B. Andrews, it is wrong. According to Andrews, any contract to which a gestational mother is a party must be worded so that she is free during her pregnancy (1) to engage in self-chosen activities; (2) to refuse or accept proposed medical treatments; and (3) to abort or not abort the gestational child. Under no circumstances, says Andrews, should the gestational mother be liable for damages or subject to a court suit in the event that the fetus spontaneously aborts, is delivered stillborn, or is born with defects.[49]

Andrews also believes that no matter how correctly worded a contract is, a gestational mother need not heed it unless she has given her informed consent to it. Physicians and psychologists must clearly outline to would-be gestational mothers all of the physical and psychological risks that attend surrogacy arrangements. But, cautions Andrews, too much information of the wrong kind, as well as too little information of the right kind, can undermine a woman's reproductive freedom. Andrews notes, for example, that several years ago the city of Akron, Ohio, passed an ordinance that required physicians to inform women seeking abortions that the fetus is sentient (able to feel pain) and that the abortion procedure is often dangerous.[50]

Speculative, oftentimes misleading information caused numerous women to change their abortion decision from "yes" to "no." Andrews worries that some physicians and psychologists, fearing liability suits or worse, will exaggerate the risks that attend gestational motherhood arrangements. As a result, the medical establishment will deprive (1) *fertile* women of a new way to profit from their reproductive abilities, and (2) *infertile* women of a new way to secure a deeply desired child.

Not surprisingly, some liberal feminists question the logic behind a ban that focuses solely on *commercial* surrogacy. Why, asks Andrews, is it exploitation to serve as a gestational mother if a woman is paid but *not* if she is not paid? Andrews reasons that if gestational motherhood is not inherently exploitative but becomes so only when women are economically coerced into it, then "our focus should not be on banning payment, but on making sure the surrogates get paid more."[51] Although we can *imagine* situations in which a woman would become a gestational mother in order to avoid destitution or worse, says Andrews, in point of fact most women who become gestational mothers do so not because they have been "tricked into it" or because they need food, clothing, or shelter, but because they want "luxuries" such as children's education, a redecorated house, or a second car.[52]

Liberal feminists also maintain that there is an analogy to be drawn between the feminist debate on pornography and the one on gestational motherhood. Feminist anti-pornographers have found themselves sitting on the same side of the room with some of the most conservative and moralistic segments of society—for example, the Eagle Forum, an organization associated with anti-feminist Phyllis Schlafly. This type of unholy alliance is primarily pragmatic rather than ideological, however. Feminist anti-pornographers object to pornography, which they define as "the graphic explicit subordination of women, whether in pictures or in words,"[53] on the grounds that it harms women in one of three ways: (1) by causing men to harass, rape, and/or batter women; (2) by defaming women; or (3) by leading to policies, actions, and attitudes that discriminate against women. In contrast, conservatives object to pornography, which they define as sexually explicit material, on the ground that it is an immoral and/or offensive display of human flesh calculated to release the polymorphously perverse snakes harbored deep within the human heart. Nevertheless, even if laws were promulgated against pornography and/or gestational motherhood for feminist reasons, liberal feminists suspect that their interpretation as well as enforcement would be controlled by the powers that be—powers that tend to be non-feminist, if not positively anti-feminist. As a result, sexually explicit feminist classics like *Fear of Flying, Our Bodies, Ourselves,* and *Gyn/ecology* could be banned together with the likes of *Deep Throat, Pink Flamingos* and *Chester, the Molester*; and reproduction-controlling technologies such as contraception, sterilization, and abortion could be restricted together with reproduction-aiding technologies such as artificial insemination by donor, in vitro fertilization, and gestational motherhood.

Finally, liberal feminists contend that any premature closure on issues such as pornography and/or gestational motherhood disserves women. Women are only beginning to discuss among themselves which sexual practices actually give them pleasure and which reproductive technologies actually liberate them from roles and responsibilities they would prefer not to shoulder. Until women—all different kinds of women— have had ample time to decide for themselves under what circumstances, if any, pornography and/or gestational motherhood are good/bad for them, no one group of women should make impossible or very difficult the experimentation necessary for such determinations.

Assessing the Adoption Approach for Non-Commercial Gestational Motherhood

Agreeing that it is too early to announce *the* final feminist perspective on gestational motherhood, some feminists, among whose number I find myself, argue that the best possible legal remedy for gestational motherhood *now* is its assimilation into some type of adoption law. To be sure, there may be, as Phyllis Chesler has observed, something conceptually (sic) inappropriate about viewing surrogacy arrangements as just another form of adoption. Traditionally, adoption has been regarded as a *child-centered* practice whereby adults, willing to give children the kind of love they need to thrive, take into their homes and hearts *already*

conceived and/or existing children. In contrast, a surrogacy arrangement is an *adult-centered* practice whereby children are *deliberately* conceived and brought into existence so that infertile adults can have someone to love.[54]

Like infertile people, however, few fertile people decide to start a
family for purely child-centered or altruistic reasons. Some families
procreate in order to add extra hands to their farms; others to do what
most "normal" people do; and still others to give an existing child a
sibling playmate. I procreated because I felt that doing so would add a
dimension of positive meaning to my life and to that of my husband.
For this reason alone, I find it difficult to insist that the only proper
motivation for adoption is a purely child-centered one.

One of the main *feminist* advantages of the assimilation of surrogacy
arrangements into properly modified adoption law—for instance, the
creation of non-profit State Surrogacy Boards—is that this legal remedy
would eliminate profit-making brokers without *requiring* gestational
mothers to endure a pregnancy simply to help an infertile couple. Being
paid for one's gestational services does not necessarily demean those
services, nor does it always signal the fact that one is being treated
merely as a means. Gestational mothers can indeed remain in control of
their pregnancies, especially if they are assured the "change of heart"
period described above and if they are permitted to control the course
of their pregnancies.

The value of a "change of heart" period is very important from a
feminist point of view. First, it acknowledges a parental relationship
whose moral significance traditional philosophy has ignored—namely,
the gestational relationship. Lawyer George Annas argues that there are
at least two moral reasons why a gestational mother should be legally
presumed to have primary parental rights and responsibility to rear
the child. First, because the gestational mother has made such a large
"biological and psychological" investment in the child, she deserves to
maintain her relationship with the child.[55] What makes a person a parent is the degree to which s/he has shown that his/her commitment to
a child is more than a matter of mere intention; and certainly a nine-
month pregnancy connotes more than mere intention. Second, because
the gestational mother "will of necessity be present at birth and immediately thereafter to care for the child," designating her the legal or
"natural mother" of the child is more likely to protect the child's interests than any alternative arrangement.[56]

A second advantage of the "change of heart" period is that it challenges the notion that contracts must be honored no matter what—as if
contracts were more important than people. Virginia Held cautions

against using the contract model as a moral paradigm in the private as well as the public domain. Women's relationships to their helpless infants, aging parents, and ailing siblings—relationships between persons who are not equally rational and powerful—do not fit the contract model. The way in which two bankers negotiate a business deal is not to be compared to the way in which a mother "negotiates" a bedtime for her child. Life is about more than conflict, competition, and controversy—about making sure that one's interests are protected. It is, as mothering persons know, also about cooperation, consensus, and community—about meeting other people's needs. Held speculates that were the relationship between a mothering person and a child, rather than the relationship between two rational contractors, the paradigm for good human relationships, society might look very different.[57] Certainly, there would be little temptation to view children as commodities and gestational mothers as incubators.

Having just argued some of the advantages of stressing the gestational connection and of letting gestational mothers have changes of heart, I think it is only honest to articulate some of the disadvantages of doing so. First, although it is wrong to trivialize the value of the gestational connection, as California's Judge Parslow did when he equated gestating an embryo with providing day-care or "nanny" services for it,[58] it is also wrong to dismiss as entirely irrelevant genetic and/or intentional connections to a child. However primary the gestational relationship is, it is a relationship that is readily supplemented and gradually replaced by other caring acts of parental commitment—the kind of acts that a genetic or adopting father, for example, can perform: feeding, rocking, diapering, and washing the baby. Moreover, one of the primary motivations for having a child is to see one's self live on in him or her. Although this motivation may be criticized as "narcissistic," Mother Nature may have been wise when she found a way for humans to concretely link the past with the future. Children, no less than adults, often derive comfort from the fact that they have mom's eyes or dad's smile.

Second, emphasizing the gestational relationship may as easily harm women as benefit them. Lately, national attention has focused on the ways in which society is increasingly eager to control the course of women's pregnancies in the best interests of the children to whom they intend to give birth. Not only are all women encouraged to take care of themselves during pregnancy so that they can give birth to healthy infants, but some women have also been forced to submit to unwanted cesarean sections or unwanted insulin treatment for gestational diabetes. Others have been sanctioned in a variety of ways for giving birth to cocaine or alcohol "addicted" infants. Given a worrisome social tendency to punish or blame women for "mishandled" pregnancies, it may be politically inadvisable for women to emphasize the degree to which "mothering" begins in the womb.[59]

Third, privileging the interests of gestational mothers over contracting mothers is troubling from a feminist point of view. Consider the Stern-Whitehead case. Under the contract model, Elizabeth Stern emerges happy; under the adoption model, Mary Beth Whitehead emerges happy; and under either of these models, baby Sara/Melissa emerges at least as happy as most wanted children ever do. The question to raise from a feminist perspective, then, is whether it is "right" that one but not the other of these women should experience the joy of rearing her child to adulthood? Do we want to "punish" Elizabeth Stern on account of her many advantages, by trying to compensate for the fact that, on the average, the Mary Beth Whiteheads of this world get the short end of the stick? Or do we want to teach Mary Beth Whitehead a lesson for having gotten herself into a situation a savvy feminist would have avoided? Would women as a class be better off as a result of a policy that systematically favors gestational mothers over contracting mothers, or would they be better off were contracting mothers always given the edge over gestational mothers?

Conclusion

Although I would prefer to live in a world where some sort of invisible hand arranged things so that the most important interests of each and every contracting mother and gestational mother both were honored, I know that no such hand exists. What we need is some sort of criterion, principle, or standard that will enable us to decide whether, as I am proposing, a properly modified adoption model is the best way to honor the most important interests of the most kinds of women possible. In an illuminating article, David Wong has maintained that moral relativism allows for different and conflicting moralities to be "equally true and justifiable."[60] He believes that if we cannot justify to others why our moral beliefs are better than theirs, we should choose a position of noninterference regarding their actions. Each side can continue to engage in debate and to attempt to sway the other to their side. However, neither side should coercively restrict the actions of the other.

The more I ponder the moral arguments for and against gestational motherhood, the more I am convinced that there are indeed *two* approximately equal and certainly reasonable sides to this debate. For this reason, plus the reason that it restricts the freedom of more kinds of women than any other alternative policy, I oppose a ban on gestational motherhood. Although such a ban might have the welcome effect of protecting some gestational and contracting mothers from exploitation, these women (and their children) can be legally protected in less restrictive ways.

What has been harder for me to decide is whether the "contract model" or the "adoption model" is the one that serves the most kinds of women best. The main problem with the contract model is that it may disserve the interests of the *gestational* mother, whereas the main problem with the adoption model is that it may disserve the interests of the *contracting* mother. For me, what breaks the tie between gestational and contracting mothers is that over and beyond their particular interests in having access to their children, both contracting and gestational mothers will benefit if society acknowledges just how important women's *willingness* to bear children is. If women refused to commit themselves to the birth of their children, no children would be born.

In other words, because it underscores the importance of the (maternal) gestational relationship, I believe that the adoption approach is preferable to the contract approach, with its focus on the (paternal) genetic relationship. What is more, the adoption approach provides (1) contracting mothers with a good opportunity to gain access to children they would have *no* chance to gain access to otherwise, and (2) gestational mothers with a modest financial incentive that makes it more reasonable for them to assume the risks and responsibilities of a pregnancy they might not undertake otherwise, altruism not withstanding.

In contrast, the contract model gives gestational mothers no chance to gain access to the children who, were it not for them, would have never been born. Favoring the father over the mother, as the contractual approach does, deepens the schism patriarchal society thrusts between the abstract and particular, reason and emotion, contracts and the persons involved. Preferring the letter of an agreement to the feelings involved reduces people to pawns—especially the mothers and children. Women as a *whole* will benefit from an approach that stresses their right, not their duty, to be mothers (and not simply baby machines). The adoption approach, with its change of heart clause, replaces what strikes me as the *heartless* contract approach. A deal is not always a deal—at least not when one is trading in some of the deepest emotions human beings can ever feel. Any approach that *binds* women to reproductive decisions—as does the contract approach—must be regarded with deep suspicion.

But even though I believe that a modified adoption approach—one that permits the payment of regulated fees to gestational mothers as well as a change-of-heart period—best serves the most important interests of the most kinds of women *now*, I certainly do not think that this legal remedy is the best overall solution to either infertility or the kind of baby-craving that is the result of women thinking that they are of little worth unless they have a child. What would serve the most important interests of the most kinds of women overall is (1) the kind of sexually sensitive health care and environmentally safe work places that prevent the conditions that often contribute to infertility, and (2) the fostering in women of the kind of self-esteem and self-respect that is not dependent on their ability to have children. As long as women continue to see their essential function as reproductive, they will fall prey to those who want to treat them as baby machines. Surrogacy exploits women where men control the rules, the courts, and women's bodies. Feminist ethics demands that women expose, resist, and overcome this and other kinds of patriarchal control. Only then will we be in a position to determine whether gestational motherhood has a future as a truly collaborative mode of reproduction—a process that enhances the freedom and happiness of the women who choose to help each other have a child.[61]

Notes

1. Phyllis Chesler, *Sacred Bond: The Legacy of Baby M* (New York: Times Books, 1988), p. 187.

2. For a full discussion of an arguable distinction between baby-selling and surrogate-parenting contracts, see note, "Developing a Concept of the Modern Family: A Proposed Uniform Surrogate Parenting Act," *Georgetown Law Journal* 73, part 2 (1985), pp. 1289–1295.

3. Chesler, *Sacred Bond*, p. 197.

4. Ronald Munson, *Intervention and Reflection: Basic Issues in Medical Ethics*, 4th ed. (Belmont, California: Wadsworth Inc., 1992), p. 464.

5. Munson, *Intervention and Reflection*, pp. 464–465.

6. John D. Battersby, "South Africa Woman Gives Birth to Three Grandchildren, and History," *New York Times* (Oct. 2, 1987), p. 9a.

7. I once used the term "contracted motherhood," but I now realize that this term is as problematic as the term "surrogate motherhood." After all, what is at stake is whether the contract model *is* the best way to conceive of the network of relationships that is being created.

8. In "The Overdue Death of a Feminist Chameleon: Taking a Stand on Surrogacy Arrangements," *Journal of Social Philosophy* (Fall/Winter 1990), I

argued that commercial surrogacy should be recognized as the selling of relationships and should be banned, whereas non-commercial surrogacy should be recognized and dealt with as a form of adoption. I now disagree with my previous position.

9. Alison Jaggar has argued that the practical goals of feminist ethics "must be sensitive to the ways in which gendered norms are different for different groups of women—or in which the same norms affect different groups differently." See Alison Jaggar, "Feminist Ethics: Projects, Problems, Prospects," *Feminist Ethics*, ed. Claudia Card (Lawrence: University Press of Kansas, 1991), p. 98.

10. "Excerpts From Decision by New Jersey Supreme Court in the Baby M Case," *The New York Times* (February 4, 1988), p. B6.

11. Lori B. Andrews, "The Aftermath of Baby M: Proposed State Laws on Surrogate Motherhood," *Ethical Issues in the New Reproductive Technologies*, ed. Richard T. Hull (Belmont, CA: Wadsworth, 1990).

12. *Report of the Committee of Inquiry into Human Fertilization and Embryology*, Department of Health and Social Security, United Kingdom, London, HMSO (July 1984), p. 47.

13. Surrogacy Arrangements Act, 1985, United Kingdom, Chapter 49, p. 2, (1)(a)(b)(c).

14. Ibid., p. 3, (1)–(5).

15. Andrews, "The Aftermath of Baby M: Proposed State Laws on Surrogate Motherhood," pp. 191–192.

16. Lori B. Andrews, "Alternative Modes of Reproduction," *Reproductive Laws for the 1990s*, eds. Sherrill Cohen and Nadine Taub (Clifton, NJ: Humana Press, 1989), pp. 380–388.

17. Andrews, "The Aftermath of Baby M: Proposed State Laws on Surrogate Motherhood," pp. 193–99.

18. There are two types of gestational mothers: those who gestate an embryo genetically related to them (so-called partial surrogacy) and those who gestate an embryo genetically unrelated to them (so-called full surrogacy). At present most cases of gestational motherhood are cases of partial surrogacy. A woman contracts to be artificially inseminated with the sperm of a man who is not her husband; to carry the subsequent pregnancy to term; and to turn the resulting child over to the man and his wife to rear. Because the child is genetically related to the gestational mother, at the time of transference she must relinquish her parental rights to the child; and because the child is not genetically related to the woman who wishes to rear the child, at the time of transference or some time later this second woman must legally adopt him/her. In the future, an increasing number of cases of gestational motherhood may be cases not of partial but of full surrogacy. Full surrogacy involves an embryo transfer after in vivo or in vitro fertilization. A woman may be able to produce eggs but unable to carry a pregnancy to term. If she and her husband are able to conceive a

genetic child in vivo, physicians can flush the resulting embryo out of her womb into the womb of the woman who has agreed to gestate it. However, if she and her husband are not able to conceive a genetic child in vivo, physicians will first remove one or more eggs from the women's womb, fertilize them outside her womb with her husband's sperm in vitro, and then introduce the resulting embryo into the womb of the woman who has agreed to gestate it. Clearly, full surrogacy is technologically more complex than partial surrogacy, a factor that accounts for its current limited use.

19. Note, "Rumpelstiltskin Revisited: The Unalienable Rights of Surrogate Mothers," *Harvard Law Review* 99 (1986), pp. 1953–1954.

20. Anthony Kronman develops a similar case in "Paternalism and the Law of Contract," *Yale Law Journal* 92 (April 1983), pp. 780–784.

21. Andrews, "Alternative Modes of Reproduction," pp. 365–366.

22. Peter Singer and Deane Wells, *Making Babies: The New Science and Ethics of Conception* (New York: Scribner's, 1985), pp. 173–182.

23. Andrea Sachs, "When the Lullaby Ends," *Time* (June 4, 1990), p. 82.

24. Mary Beth Whitehead, "A Surrogate Mother Describes Her Change of Heart—and Her Fight to Keep the Baby Two Families Love," *People* 26 (October 26, 1986), p. 47.

25. For more reflections on this subject, see Sara Ann Ketchum, "Is There a Right to Procreate?", paper presented at the Pacific Division Meetings of the American Philosophical Association, 1987 (unpublished).

26. Jaggar, "Feminist Ethics: Problems, Projects, Prospects," p. 48.

27. Chesler, *Sacred Bond*, p. 21.

28. Chesler, p. 60.

29. Gena Corea, *The Mother Machine* (New York: Harper & Row, 1985), p. 279.

30. Corea, *The Mother Machine*, p. 214.

31. Kelly Oliver, "Marxism and Surrogacy," *Hypatia* 4, no.3 (Fall, 1989), p. 103.

32. Chesler, *Sacred Bond*, p. 38.

33. Surrogacy Arrangements Act, United Kingdom, Chapter 49, p. 46.

34. Christine Overall, *Ethics and Human Reproduction* (Winchester, MA: Allen & Unwin, 1987), p. 116–119.

35. Patricia A. Avery, " 'Surrogate Mothers': Center of a New Storm," *U.S. News and World Report* (June 6, 1983), p. 76.

36. Corea, *The Mother Machine*, p. 276.

37. Margaret Atwood, *The Handmaid's Tale* (Boston: Houghton Mifflin, 1986), p. 164.

38. J. R. S. Pritchard, "A Market for Babies?" *University of Toronto Law Journal* 34 (1981), p. 352.

39. Nancy Davis, "Reproductive Technologies and Our Attitudes Toward Children," *From the Center* 7, no. 1 (Summer 1988), pp. 1–4.

40. Hilde Lindemann Nelson and James Lindemann Nelson, "Cutting Mother-hood in Two: Some Suspicions Concerning Surrogacy," *Hypatia* 4, no. 3 (Fall 1989), p. 91.

41. Nelson and Nelson, "Cutting Motherhood in Two," p. 93, emphasis in original.

42. Nelson and Nelson, "Cutting Motherhood in Two," p. 93.

43. Nelson and Nelson, p. 93.

44. Nelson and Nelson, p. 93.

45. Howard A. Davidson, "What Will Surrogate Mothering Do to the Fabric of the American Family?" *Public Welfare* (Fall 1983), p. 12.

46. David Gelman and Daniel Shapiro, "Infertility: Babies by Contract," *Newsweek* (Nov. 4, 1985), p. 74.

47. On June 1, 1992, the Tennessee high court ruled in favor of Junior Davis, declaring that "ordinarily, the party wishing to avoid procreation should prevail": therefore, Junior could not be made a father against his will. Ellen Goodman, "A Strange Custody Battle," *Charlotte Observer* (June 7, 1992), p. 3C.

48. Ellen Goodman, "Whose Child?" *Charlotte Observer* (Sunday, October 28, 1990), p. 3c.

49. Andrews, "Alternative Modes of Reproduction," p. 365.

50. Andrews, p. 369.

51. Andrews, p. 371.

52. Andrews, p. 371.

53. Catharine A. MacKinnon, *Feminism Unmodified: Discourses on Life and Law* (Cambridge, MA: Harvard University Press, 1987), p. 146.

54. Chesler, *Sacred Bond*, pp. 109–146.

55. Sherman Elias and George J. Annas, "Noncoital Reproduction," *Journal of the American Medical Association* 225 (January 3, 1986), p. 67.

56. George T. Annas, "Death without Dignity for Commercial Surrogacy: The Case of Baby M," *Hastings Center Report* 18, no. 2 (1988), pp. 23–24.

57. Virginia Held, "Non-Contractual Society," *Science, Morality and Feminist Theory*, eds. Marsha Hanen and Kai Nielsen (Calgary, Alberta: University of Calgary Press, 1987), pp. 127–128.

58. Goodman, "Whose Child," p. 3c.

59. Lawrence J. Nelson and Nancy Milliken, "Compelled Medical Treatment of Pregnant Women: Life, Liberty, and Law in Conflict," in Hull, ed., *Ethical Issues in the New Reproductive Technologies*, pp. 224–240.

60. David Wong, *Moral Relativity* (Berkeley: University of California Press, 1984), p. 190.

61. Portions of this paper have been adapted from Rosemarie Tong, "The Overdue Death of a Feminist Chameleon: Taking a Stand on Surrogacy Arrangements."

Listening to the Voices
of the Infertile

Barbara J. Berg

> Ideas are clean. They soar in the serene supernal. I can
> take them out and look at them, they fit in books, they
> lead me down that narrow way. And in the morning they
> are there.
> Ideas are straight—
> But the world is round, and a messy mortal is my friend.
> Come walk with me in the mud. . . .
>
> —Hugh Prather[1]

There has been much discussion surrounding the new reproductive technologies. Feminists have entered this discussion voicing concern over the pervasive influence of pronatalism in our society, the increasing medicalization of reproduction, the commodification of women and children, the overvaluation of genetic versus social linkages, and the potential exploitation of women. There is much to be concerned about. But much of the feminist discourse on this subject has come from the perspective that these technologies should not be pursued because of their potentially negative effects on women and children. Although many legitimate concerns have been raised, complex issues have sometimes been oversimplified and, most disturbing of all, some feminists do not appear to be taking the role of advocating for infertile women so much as speaking for them. But the infertile have their own voices.

What follows is based upon what I have learned as a feminist psychologist working with the infertile. I will attempt to broaden the boundaries of the feminist analysis to include some of these perspectives. These perspectives can elucidate traditional areas of focus, such as genetic versus social linkages in parenting, while some newer areas of concern will be explored, including limitations in access to treatment, lack of funding for preventive health care, sexist medical terminology, and assumptions about psychogenic infertility.

Biological versus Adoptive Parenthood

The pervasive and tenacious pronatalism of our culture has resulted in the view that motherhood is a woman's *raison d'être*.[2] Although women are employed outside the home in ever-increasing numbers, being a wife and mother is still viewed as a woman's primary and central function.[3] Outside work is acceptable as long as the house is clean and the husband and children are well tended. Pronatalism has promoted the view that a woman without husband and children (whether voluntarily or not) is somehow deficient. Consequently, childless women continue to be perceived in a pejorative light (i.e., as selfish). The pronatalist perspective also views having genetically related children as superior to adopting children. The pronatalist motherhood mandate, then, is that women must bear children for their husbands. Understandably, feminists have rejected this mandate and affirmed the value of women separate from spouses and progeny, as well as the value of social versus genetic ties in parenting.

From an impersonal perspective, it is easy to equate the value of parenting an adoptive and a biological child. Both can involve rearing a child from infancy to adulthood. However, it is undeniable that among the individuals choosing to rear children, most prefer to have a biological child. Adoption is usually considered only when a couple[4] is unable to have a biological child. This nearly universal preference (which is observed among feminists as well as others) reveals not only a value placed on the genetic linkage but on other aspects of the experience of parenting a biological child (e.g., the experience of pregnancy and childbirth). Although it may be equally valid and valuable, the experience of rearing an adopted child is different from that of rearing a biological child, and it is important to examine these differences.

Our society's emphasis on genetic linkages has given feminists pause. When genetic connections are emphasized at the expense of social relationships, the interactions which are truly most meaningful in life have been diminished. Rothman makes a cogent argument for our need to re-examine the importance of our social relationships.[5] She claims that the maternal tie for biological mothers is established by the relationship between the woman and her fetus during gestation. Since the man lacks such a relationship to the growing fetus, the paternal tie is simply reduced to the act of impregnating—a genetic contribution. A societal emphasis upon the genetic tie can deny the importance of the experience of gestation or growing a fetus within one's body, and reduce women to gaining rights to children not as mothers, but essentially as father-equivalents. Thus, the genetic emphasis can be interpreted as the basis for men's control over the children of women. But the desire for biological motherhood is not simply comprised of seeking a genetic tie to a child, it is often comprised of seeking the relational experiences of pregnancy, birth, and nursing as well.[6]

However, interest in the genetic continuity represented by a child

[handwritten margin note: gestational v. genetic ties]

need by no means be confined to the child's biological father. When a child is born there is often an intensive search, by biological parents and those around them, for the characteristics in the child which most resemble each parent (e.g., he has his mother's hair or temperament; she's tall or stubborn or bright just like her father). Overall suggests that "in rearing one's genetically related offspring, very real experiences are involved in discerning and appreciating the similarities between oneself and one's children . . . there is a sense of continuity and history created by the genetic tie."[7] This need not reflect the eugenic notion that these particular biological characteristics are superior to others; these characteristics may simply symbolize to the parents the child's connection to past generations and the ability to extend that lineage forward into the future. The biological parent is enmeshed in the cycle of life that began in the distant past and now is extending through them into the future. Knowledge of one's ancestors can assist in developing one's identity, whether it is specific to one's ethnic or cultural background/traditions or to the types of individuals from whom one is descended. This is not the only way to form one's identity, but it is an important aspect of doing so for many individuals. Biological parents may feel that the knowledge of this "genealogical heritage" is an important contribution to give to their children. Additionally, a biological parent may appreciate being an intimate part of the process which creates a new generation in the family.

We can thus interpret the valuing of genetic lineage negatively as an example of eugenics, narcissism, or a way of achieving immortality; or we can make a more neutral or positive interpretation, such as seeing the value of creating a new generation, giving a child a known genealogical heritage, or simply possessing another bond between parent and child which allows parents to weather the invariable strains associated with parenthood. Attachment to lineage, for whatever reason, may not have much intrinsic value, but its value to potential parents may be sufficient to require that we accord it respect.

Adopting parents do not have this automatic connection or linkage to their child. They must be able to love a child who does not represent an extension of their own bodies and genetic lineages, one who has the potential to be quite different from either parent (not that biological children do not continually surprise parents with their differentness). Adopting parents must also cope with more uncertainty about the child's background, such as unfavorable genetic influences (e.g., inherited illnesses), harmful environmental factors during pregnancy (e.g., drug usage), the potential for the biological parent(s) to change their mind(s) about the adoption, and the possibility that the adopted child will later seek out his or her biological parents.

The difficulties associated with adoption have been widely documented. The increasing numbers of young women choosing abortion or
electing to continue their pregnancies and keep their children has reduced the availability of children for adoption. Most middle–class white
couples seek to adopt white infants (which are the most difficult to obtain) instead of considering non–white infants or children who are older,
disabled, and so on. It may be argued that the strong preference for
white infants is misplaced, and that these couples should be willing to
provide a home for any children who might need one. However, we must
understand that the desire of many of these couples may not be the
simple reflection of prejudice or bias. The childless couple may feel less
able than a couple with parenting experience to face the challenges involved in rearing the child of a different race or an older child (who may
have emotional or physical problems). In the case of adopting a child of
another race, the parent must struggle with the question of how to retain the child's cultural heritage when the parent does not possess
intimate knowledge of the culture or subculture. The childless couples
who take on such challenges are to be admired, but the childless couples
who know they are not ready for these potential complications should
not be criticized. Interestingly, infertile couples can be placed in a
double bind. If they do not adopt children of another race they can be
characterized as selfish or narrow-minded, but if they do, they may be
criticized because they purportedly lack the cultural sensitivity to properly parent a child from a different ethnic heritage.

There is not much support for adoption in our culture. Adopting parents have to make their way through a bewildering array of legal red
tape with little guidance. They do not experience the same anticipation
and preparation for dealing with an infant that is associated with pregnancy.[8] The pregnant woman becomes a social stimulus for advice concerning childrearing and is "showered" with information and items that
can help her adapt to her new role as mother. Adopting parents get much
less of this support and preparation for their new role. Because there is
so much uncertainty built into the adoption process, it is too often
difficult for prospective adopting couples to reach out for support and
for others to provide it. As a result, preparation for this transition and
the transition itself is often made in seclusion and silence.

Biological parenting is a vastly different experience. First, there is the
ability to directly experience pregnancy and childbirth. The process of
watching one's own body undergo transformations during pregnancy,
establishing emotional connections with the fetus by feeling movements
through the abdomen, and giving birth are unique to biological parents.
This ability to share in the creation of a child and to experience the

early stages of fetal development are highly valued by many individuals. Biological parenting may be especially meaningful to many because it allows the woman to participate in a remarkable natural process which is unlike any other. With adoption you enter the world of parents, but with childbirth you enter the fertile world.[9] The fertile world encompasses the sisterhood of women who have experienced pregnancy and childbirth, and it establishes a new basis for interaction with others. The sharing of stories related to one's pregnancy and childbirth experiences is an important bonding experience for many women. Childbirth can represent an important milestone in the development of a woman's ability to face fear, pain, and uncertainty.

Feminists understand the value of fertile women striving for a natural childbirth experience which avoids unnecessary medical interventions. But can we understand the value to the infertile woman striving to attain parenthood in a manner that is "as natural as possible"? With adoption, parents receive their child from a stranger in a process which is regulated by lawyers, adoption agencies, and the courts. An individual's ability to parent is scrutinized by various professionals using questionable criteria, and the individual's *social* linkage to the adopted child does not always take precedence in a system that juggles the simultaneous needs of children, biological, and adopting parents.

Although the assisted reproductive technologies (ART) represent a considerable amount of medically related intrusion, they still afford the best approximation to the *natural* processes of conception, gestation, and childbirth available to the infertile. It is important to view adoptive and biological parenting as equally valuable experiences; but it is also important to recognize the many differences between the two and to realize that some individuals may be better suited to one than to the other. An understanding of these two very different parenting experiences makes it inappropriate to simply reduce them to the competing value of genetic versus social linkages.

Biological Motherhood and Feminism

For all of recorded history, motherhood has often come at a high price— one which has been paid willingly by some, and not so willingly by others. Overall has argued that an infertile woman should not be blamed for her pursuit of infertility treatment because the desire to become a mother is "socially created" in our pronatalist culture.[10] But the social forces that encourage women to bear children cannot entirely explain the desire of some women to become biological mothers and their willingness to pay dearly for this experience. Automatically reducing this desire to an example of effective pronatalist influence is condescending and patronizing toward infertile women as a group and denies the diversity of these women.

In my years of research and clinical experience with the infertile, I have found that most women pursuing medical treatment for infertility are high achievers who have attained remarkable educational and occupational goals. Yet, despite their level of personal accomplishment in these spheres, they also desire to become biological mothers. No matter how much money, prestige, and higher education are touted as signs of personal achievement in our patriarchal society, many women who possess these things still value becoming biological mothers. Even though they have achieved so much in their lives, some still feel that something is missing. To dismiss their desire to experience pregnancy, childbirth, and rearing their own biologically related children is to endorse traditional patriarchal symbols of achievement. Ruth Hubbard seems to suggest that, somehow, a true feminist could not desire motherhood via assisted reproduction: "Some strong, deep feminist consciousness raising might end up being far more therapeutic in the long run than broadening the scope of the technological fix."[11] But using these technologies to achieve biological motherhood does not necessarily reflect that a woman is acting out of mindless socialization. Nor is this incompatible with a feminist consciousness. To claim as much reveals a profound insensitivity to the experience and feelings of infertile women. In fact, the infertile women I have worked with have usually given a great deal of thought to why they want to be biological mothers—often much more thought than fertile women—because they have had to face greater obstacles in order to become biological mothers. As Frost has pointed out, "infertile women sometimes don't hear from the feminist movement that it can be a rational choice to have as well as not to have children."[12]

Let us make sure that when we make a stand against the pronatalist motherhood mandate, we do not oppose mothering. Mothering occurs in many shapes and forms, and we need to embrace this diversity. To dismiss the infertile woman's desire to be a biological mother as simply a pronatalist creation is not even congruent with how we feminists celebrate the wonder of birthing. Feminists have understood childbirth as a way to affirm our uniqueness and power as a gender.[13] Feminists often take inspiration from the tradition of goddess worship, which draws many images of power from the woman giving birth.[14] Since the powerful images of the birth experience can be promoted and affirmed by the feminist community, it hardly seems consistent or reasonable to erect a double standard about the wonders of childbirth when it comes to the infertile.

The Medicalization and Commodification
of Reproduction

Other feminist concerns regarding the new reproductive technologies have focused on the extent to which these technologies medicalize reproduction. We have already witnessed the medicalization of pregnancy and childbirth by the introduction of the disease model, fetal monitoring, uterofetal therapy, and cesarean sections. Although, in certain cases, these interventions can be lifesaving, they have represented an increasing tendency for physicians to control childbirth and to view the fetus as a separate patient, often to the detriment of the pregnant woman. In the world of medicalized childbearing fetal rights have become primary; control of the natural processes of pregnancy and birth have shifted from pregnant women to physicians.

Medicalized reproduction carries this tendency one step further. With increasing medical intervention in conception, physicians become viewed as the co-creators of children.[15] The focus of who is responsible for a pregnancy has shifted from the women to the physicians, who can be congratulated on "getting her pregnant." Since the majority of physicians are still men, this can represent men taking control over the final vestige of power which formerly remained within the female sphere.

When a physician exerts control over the process of hormonal fluctuations, ovulation, transfer of gametes or embryo to the fallopian tube or uterus, placement of sperm and ova in close proximity, and selection of embryos for implantation, this clearly medicalizes conception. For fertile women, these interventions constitute a loss of control over a normal reproductive process, much as a woman undergoing a cesarean section has lost control over her labor. However, for an infertile woman who cannot conceive "naturally," these interventions can represent her only chance at exerting *any* control in reproduction. Further, some of these technologies, such as artificial insemination, expand the reproductive options available to lesbian and single heterosexual women. It is important to realize that many feminists have embraced technology in certain areas of reproduction, such as contraception and abortion, that assist women in avoiding unwanted conception or in terminating an unwanted pregnancy. Although we accept medical interventions in reproduction when they help us resist the pronatalist agenda, some feel less comfortable with medical interventions when they are used to enable procreation. But we must be aware that the acceptance of medical interventions to maximize the choices available to infertile women is not the same as uncritically accepting the medicalization of reproduction.

Related to concerns about the medicalization of reproduction are concerns about the commodification of reproduction and children, which are also raised by feminists.[16] In general, body parts have become increasingly viewed as "products" which can be assigned monetary value and exchanged for financial reimbursement. In human reproductive medicine, sperm has been a purchasable commodity in artificial insemination for decades. Although the amount of money paid for sperm is nominal (e.g., $35), the selling and buying of sperm symbolizes the commodification of life-giving potential. Similarly, reproductive technologies have evolved to the point where one woman can "donate" eggs to another or can have an embryo implanted in her uterus in order to gestate a fetus for herself or someone else. In the latter case, a woman effectively "rents" her womb in serving as a contract mother who is expected to surrender the child at birth. Although oocytes can be given without the expectation of financial compensation (especially if the donor knows the recipient or is already undergoing IVF), in the United States, compensation is typically given for anonymous oocyte donation, with payment ranging between $900 and $1200 per cycle.[17] Contract motherhood arrangements can involve payments in the $10,000 range.[18]

The processes of donating sperm, donating an egg, and using one's womb to gestate a fetus are all quite distinct.[19] For a man to donate sperm, masturbation into a container is all that is required. While this may not be a psychologically comfortable process, it does not involve any physical injury or risk to a man's health. On the other hand, a woman making an egg donation assumes a degree of physical risk. Egg or oocyte donation involves taking injections of powerful hormones for a period of time to promote the simultaneous maturing of several oocytes (egg cells) and then undergoing a surgical procedure where oocytes are aspirated from the ovary through a puncture in the vagina. Finally, a woman who agrees to become a "surrogate" or contract mother may also undergo some hormonal manipulations, will experience an embryo transfer or artificial insemination procedure, may take hormones to maintain the pregnancy, and, of course, is exposed to all the attendant risks of pregnancy and childbirth.[20]

The issue of whether financial reimbursement is ethical and appropriate requires careful consideration. First, there is the question: For what is a prospective "donor" or provider being remunerated? Does the money represent payment for the process of "donation" (e.g., time, effort, pain) or for the gamete/baby? In oocyte donation, donors receive reimbursement for undergoing the process of donation, regardless of whether viable oocytes are obtained.[21] However, in sperm donation, the donors are required to meet specific sperm parameters necessary for the freezing process, and compensation is not provided for this initial screening of the sperm sample.[22] If the donor continues to meet the criteria, then compensation is provided for subsequent sperm samples. Therefore, compensation appears to be provided more for the sperm itself, rather than for the process of providing the sperm. Similarly, compensation in contract motherhood arrangements, which is ostensibly for the services of gestation and childbirth, is not provided if the child is not turned over to the infertile couple. Therefore, the payment appears to be for the child and not for the process of gestation. Only oocyte donation appears to circumvent the symbolic purchase of a child or of life-giving potential.

The effects of reimbursement in gamete donation needs further exploration. Financial reimbursement can contribute to the commodification of gametes and of reproduction more generally, as well as potentially lead to exploitation of the economically disadvantaged. Moreover, payment for the "donation" can change the process of giving. The financial payment can alter the meaning of the "donation" for the donor, the recipient, and the child born from such an arrangement. An adult born from artificial insemination by donor (AID) echoes this sentiment when she stated, "No one considers how the child feels when she finds that her natural father was a $25 cup of sperm."[23] At the same time, however, payment makes anonymous donation more viable and circumvents difficulties involved with obtaining known donors. Additionally, if financial incentives are eliminated, those who donate primarily for eugenic reasons may predominate in the remaining pool of donors—a possibility many find repugnant.

If anonymous gamete donors are not used, pressure may be exerted upon infertile individuals to provide friends or family members to assist them in their quest for pregnancy. Friends and family may sympathize with the infertile couple and feel subtle or not-so-subtle pressure to donate. "Known donation" potentially involves all the physical risks detailed previously, but there may be particular long-term psychological risks as well. A harmonious friendship or sibling relationship may be jeopardized at a later point when the donor feels uncomfortable about his or her donation, how the child is being reared, decisions made regarding secrecy versus openness, and so forth. However, when a donor is known to the recipient, greater background information is available (including the medical history, which may be important). Some may argue that family medical history is not always clearly known, even when children are reared with their biological parents. But circumstances may make this information indispensable, and it needs to be available to be gathered whenever possible. Even with anonymous "donors," a great deal of non-identifying information can be obtained and provided to the recipients. For example, the overwhelming majority of sperm donors in a U.S. sample were willing to complete a detailed 12-page questionnaire covering in-depth medical and psychosocial information on themselves which could be made available to the recipient(s) and any resulting children.[24] In Australia, donors can be contacted through a registry when the child reaches 18 years,[25] and 60 percent of a U.S. sample of sperm donors also expressed a willingness to meet the child at age 18.[26] A great deal of information can be obtained from a "donor" while protecting his or her identity. But we do need to remain cognizant that financial incentives might influence the level of a potential "donor's" honesty in responding to queries about his or her background.

Psych. effects

Given the paucity of research in this area, it is difficult to ascertain the relative risks and benefits of financial compensation and of using gamete donors known to those seeking pregnancy. We do not understand what it means to be a gamete donor—whether it is similar to donating blood or a kidney, or is more like giving a child up for adoption; and we particularly do not understand whether gender differences exist in the psychology of donation.[27] Further, we know little about the impact that these processes have upon the recipients and the children born as a result of these new technologies. It is inexcusable that we continue experimenting with reproduction with so little attention to the psychological ramifications. Our ignorance is particularly alarming in the case of AID, which has been practiced for over 100 years. The shroud of secrecy veiling the practice of AID needs to be lifted. This is not to say that AID couples should never have the option to maintain privacy regarding their particular method of family-building, but we as a society cannot rely on their silence any longer to avoid what may be an uncomfortable examination of what this process entails for all involved. Furthermore, since other countries, like Australia, appear to have successfully adopted a policy of not allowing payment for sperm donations and since the process of sperm donation does not involve an overwhelming investment of time, physical effort or physical risk, and since, moreover, financial motives might distort testimony on medical history and negatively influence resulting children's perception of themselves, it would be beneficial to explore the feasibility of eliminating payment for sperm donation in this country.

Although there are concerns about the process of gamete donation, they pale in comparison to the psychological, physical, and moral concerns involved with contract motherhood. This practice is the most potentially problematic of all the new technologies. Although such an arrangement may be well-intentioned by all the parties involved, the contract mother is in a perilous legal, physical, and most importantly, moral/psychological position. Contract motherhood will be discussed in greater depth elsewhere in this collection, but it deserves some attention here as well.[28]

Use of terms like *uterine environments* or *incubators* sums up the public status of the contract mother. This derogatory language of dismemberment encourages us to consider the womb instead of the whole woman and to view the woman as somehow loaning the use of her womb for nine months, as if pregnancy only involved the womb. Such language encourages the woman to devalue herself and her social and physical relationship to the fetus. The notion that the contract mother is simply "renting" her womb has been challenged by Rothman, who points out that you can't rent a body part without renting the entire woman, and that "women experience pregnancy with our whole bodies—from the changes in our hair to our swollen ankles—with all of our bodies and perhaps with our souls as well."[29] This process of dissociation is different from what is involved in abortion. In electing abortion, a woman is psychologically refusing to enter into a relationship with a fetus,[30] whereas with contract motherhood a woman is beginning a relationship and severing it at a later point (i.e., birth). As a psychologist, I try to listen non-judgmentally to the voices of the infertile: but the pain expressed by women who have placed children for adoption haunts me. How can we expect women to voluntarily subject themselves to this kind of turmoil? And if a woman does not feel any pain as a contract mother, have we succeeded in having the woman dismember and dissociate herself to the point where she is no longer whole? It is hard enough for most women to place an unwanted child up for adoption; how can we encourage women to voluntarily undergo such a treacherous path? The notion that a woman can predict her level of attachment to her fetus and should be held to a previously signed contract is unacceptable. That a woman should be able to respond with emotional distance to the movements of her fetus, to the changes in her body, and to the birth experience, and, somehow, to deny that this child is hers, is not what we as a society should promote. Further, since many contract mothers already have children, how can we expect these children to cope with the fact that their mother has sold their half-sibling at birth?[31] Surely this can cause anxiety in the children regarding the severing of their relationship to the half-sibling and the stability of their own position in the family. In addition, because contract motherhood arrangements serve to enhance the power of white, fertile, middle- to upper-class men at the expense of lower-class women, there are serious concerns about this practice being classist, sexist, and racist.[32] The potential dangers involved with contract motherhood are so great that it is difficult to see how the potential benefits of this procreative option could outweigh its potential risks and negative implications for the women and children involved.

Exploitation of Women

Now men are far beyond the stage at which they expressed their envy of woman's procreative power through couvade, transvestism, subincision. They are beyond merely giving spiritual birth in their baptismal-font wombs, beyond giving physical birth with their electronic fetal monitors, their forceps, their knives. Now they have laboratories.[33]

The potential for women to be exploited with these new technologies is great. Especially since the majority of researchers and clinicians are male, procedures that are unpleasant or risky for women may be approached without sufficient caution. Science for the sake of science tends to take on a life of its own, despite the existence of potential risks or negative side effects. Corea has detailed some of the early experimental efforts in the field of reproductive medicine which illustrate researchers' greater concerns for their own status than for the need to proceed cautiously in order to ensure that the risks to women and future children were minimized.[34] The demands for thorough testing with animal models before procedures were applied to humans were ignored in the scramble to achieve personal scientific status (e.g., to achieve the first IVF birth). It is not difficult to imagine that in the future, the welfare of women may continue to be secondary to the pursuit of medical knowledge about reproduction and furthering the careers of scientific pioneers.

The specter of the new reproductive technologies has also raised much futuristic speculation. The frightening brave new world imagined by Aldous Huxley lurks in the back of our minds.[35] Corea's chilling description of embryo manipulation in the cattle industry leaves one wondering what the future might hold for women submitting to this technology.[36] Concerns have been raised that reproductive technologies can lead to "the objectification of children, impoverishment of meaning in the experience of reproduction, damage to notions of kinship, and the perpetuation of degrading views of women."[37] Indeed, all technological advances have within them the potential for abuse. Just as genetic testing and abortion can result in the selective abortion of female fetuses resulting from the general preference for male children, the new reproductive technologies can be used to harm and exploit women, as in the case of contract motherhood. But for the most part, the new technologies involve minimal "known"[38] risks and can provide important options to individuals and couples experiencing infertility.[39] Feminists have taken a pro-choice stance in the abortion debate. It should be equally important to develop and maintain options for those who are limited in their ability to have biological children. The ability to choose if and when to have children is as important for the infertile woman as it is for the woman with an unwanted pregnancy.

Risk Factors for Infertility

The forces that contribute to infertility make a pro-choice position even more essential. Epidemiologically, there are three primary risk factors for infertility: being black, being a woman with a lower education level, or being a woman of advanced age.[40] It is thought that the higher rates of sexually transmitted diseases (STDs) in the black population place blacks at increased risk to experience reduced fecundity. Since the best contraceptive protection against STDs remains the male-controlled condom, women are at a distinct disadvantage in protecting themselves and their fertility. More research needs to be done into what factors— e.g., STDs, IUD use, occupational/environmental hazards, and complications following childbirth or abortion—contribute to the higher incidence of infertility among blacks and women with less education and how infertility, particularly in these populations, can be prevented.

Comparatively, more is known about the risk of infertility in middle-aged women. A woman becomes less fertile with age, and there is a greater possibility of various processes interfering with reproduction (e.g., diseases like endometriosis). Increasingly, however, if a woman is to establish an independent economic position she must pursue educational and occupational goals early in life, even though this coincides with her most fertile biological period. For such a woman, it is at the point when she is established in her career and motherhood will not jeopardize her economic position (e.g., she is able to negotiate maternity leave or afford child care) that she is subject to a much higher probability of infertility.

On the other hand, pregnancy during the most fertile time of a woman's life can have the unfortunate effect of trapping women into lower income levels because there is so little governmental, educational, and occupational support for young mothers. As Rothman argues,[41] if we want to decrease infertility by having women concentrate childbearing in their younger years, we have to make that possible economically. The relationship between pregnancy in young women and the cycle of poverty is well established. As a society, we need to understand how economic forces may serve to create reproductive problems. Unfortunately, as part of the backlash against feminism, conservative forces have attempted to interpret the infertility rates among middle-aged career women as the justifiable punishment for trying to have it all—careers *and* motherhood.[42] But we must be cognizant of the political and economic forces which have contributed to these women's "choice" to delay childbearing.[43]

Disagree ✱

It has been estimated that as much as 39 percent of infertility is either solely or partially due to iatrogenic factors,[44] which can include pelvic inflammatory disease from IUDs or obstetrical surgery, side effects from drugs like diethylstilbestrol (DES), the aftereffects of cervical conization and cesarean sections, and inadequately treated sexually transmitted diseases.[45] Other factors, such as chemical toxins and nuclear radiation, can also contribute to infertility. As Menning stated over two decades ago, "I think the reproductive organs are the miner's canary of the human species. When our miscarriage rate approaches 40 percent in some areas near illegal chemical waste dumps and nuclear reactors; when our children are born defective, not in the 5 percent range, but in the range of 25 percent where Agent Orange has been sprayed; when our infertility rate approaches 20 percent, as it will be in the 1980s—then I think we as a species are in deep trouble."[46] The infertile have paid a high price for the technologies that we have, and technology may at the very least owe them the children they desire to have. We need to look closer at the ways we can prevent that infertility which is preventable. But for those who are presently infertile, primary prevention is too late: their interests lie in having tertiary treatment options made available to them.

The Silence of Infertile Women

While the issues of pronatalism, medicalization, commodification, and the exploitation of women represent the concerns most often voiced by feminists, there are many others which feminists should begin to consider. Among these, the most important is the relative silence of infertile women, an issue not addressed because the feminist dialogue largely emanates from the perspective of the fertile. Amid the numerous viewpoints raised from various members of ethics committees and feminist conferences on the subject of the new reproductive technologies, the voice least often heard is that of the infertile. Instead of allowing those most affected by these technologies ample time to present their viewpoint, fertile individuals demonstrate an amazing lack of concern for the perspective of those who experience difficulty having children. For example, the Health, Education, and Welfare Ethics Advisory Board on reproductive technology was comprised primarily of clergy, physicians, and lawyers, with no identified infertile individuals among them.[47] At board hearings, witnesses opposed to IVF were invariably either people who had achieved their families or members of the celibate clergy. B. Menning, an infertile woman, described how "right to lifers" would bear witness at these hearings and preface their comments by telling the number of children they had, as if this were a credential for credibility.[48] But, to the contrary, as she points out, the fact that they had achieved their families makes it unlikely that they understand the pain of childlessness.

Similarly, the feminist literature and proceedings from feminist conferences are replete with academic discourse on potential problems with the new reproductive technologies while scant attention is paid to the perspective of infertile women.[49] Feminist discussion on topics such as the status of African American, Native American, or disabled women would never be conducted in a manner such that the women who have these experiences would be essentially excluded from presenting their viewpoints. Yet, infertile women who seek assisted reproduction are almost always perceived as mindless automatons who have succumbed to the pronatalist agenda and are therefore excluded. Their collective voice, perspective, and varied experiences have somehow been easy to ignore and dismiss.

Reproduction is an area in which nearly everyone feels expert. Infertile individuals are continually assaulted with suggestions to try relaxation, vacationing, alcohol, or adoption to enhance the chances of conception. These suggestions come with great vigor and frequency from fertile individuals who possess no knowledge of the effectiveness of these techniques.[50] The infertile are constantly instructed by others regarding what desires they should have and whether or not they should pursue available reproduction assisting treatments. But the question remains: Who should be making these decisions, fertile individuals or the infertile themselves? Whatever we may learn about the risks and benefits of reproduction-assisting technologies, who is in the better position to make decisions about whether to pursue a particular reproductive technology than infertile women themselves?

The infertile are held to an idealistic standard which is not required of the fertile.[51] Society questions their reasons for having children, their willingness to pursue reproductive technologies, their reluctance to adopt, and their discomfort with adopting "special needs" children. There is a bias against the infertile that is revealed when we picture ourselves questioning the fertile in the same manner. For example, the bias against homosexuals is revealed when we turn typical queries made of them toward heterosexuals (e.g., "When did you first realize you were heterosexual?" or "How do you find each other?"). Similarly, the fertile are not questioned about why they want to have children, or why they don't adopt a child. The desire to have children is rarely challenged unless the individual is having difficulty reproducing. Society doesn't ask fertile parents who are comfortable and confident with parenting to adopt children who need homes. Is it then fair to expect the infertile to live up to an ethical standard which is not applied to the average fertile individual? This double standard based on the vagaries of reproductive ability reveals a form of bias not unlike sexism, racism, ageism, or as I have already suggested, heterosexism (perhaps this should be termed "fertilism"). Interestingly, fertile individuals view adoption as a significantly more acceptable alternative than do infertile individuals.[52] Perhaps attitudes towards adoption are influenced by one's own fertility status and the likelihood of personally pursuing such an alternative.

There have been numerous references to the desperation of the infertile found in everything from scientific journals to the popular media. The depiction of the infertile as desperate can serve the interests of the medical profession, which profits from the provision of infertility treatments.[53] Pfeffer asserts that "the views of the infertile are superfluous; they could in fact prove counterproductive because they may contradict those of their doctor. What is required of the infertile is that they submit in silence to the claim that they are desperate."[54] While desperation among the infertile may help physicians justify their desire to develop reproductive technologies, a denial of such desperation can serve to ease our collective feminist consciousness when we resist the development and use of these technologies. A number of studies have been conducted on the psychological reactions of infertile individuals pursuing infertility treatment. These data do suggest that the infertile are distressed, but not at psychiatric levels.[55] Problems have been noted in the form of depression and interpersonal alienation, with psychological and marital adjustment particularly declining in the advanced stages of treatment.[56] Interestingly, women felt their femininity was compromised by infertility to a greater degree than men did their masculinity, irrespective of which spouse had the infertility problem.[57] The majority of studies investigating the psychological reaction to infertility are conducted on couples pursuing medical treatment.[58] Therefore, we know little about the distress level of the infertile population that does not actively seek out medical alternatives. Nonetheless, a determination of the average overall distress level in this population may be less important than a recognition that infertility is distressing for some, and that if these individuals find it useful to pursue medical alternatives, these options should be preserved.

The Right to Reproduce

In addition to the conspicuous silencing of infertile women, there are other issues which merit some consideration, including the question of the right to reproduce, the myth of infertility as a female problem, the diagnosis of psychogenic infertility, the absence of primary prevention, limitations in treatment access, and sexist medical terminology. Let me take these in turn, beginning with the right to reproduce.

Some feminist authors have argued that while women have the right *not* to reproduce, there is no corresponding right *to* reproduce in the sense of a right of access to reproductive technologies.[59] Overall argues that women are entitled to abortion services but that access to reproductive technologies sets the stage for potential exploitation of children and women's bodies. While concern for infertile women who are unable to have children without technological assistance is appropriate, the dangers to the society of women are viewed by Overall as superseding the personal needs of the infertile. But can the good of women as a group really be emphasized over the rights of individual women? The alarming rate of unnecessary cesarean sections and hysterectomies on women has not led us to call for the abolition of cesarean sections and hysterectomies. In fact, the potential harm to the community of women may be much more difficult to prove in the case of reproductive technologies than it is for current known rates of unnecessary gynecological surgery.

The United Nations Declaration of Human Rights claims that individuals have the right to establish a family; but this does not necessarily mean that services should be promised to the infertile. This right generally refers to fertile persons' ability to exercise their own judgement regarding the number and timing of their children and does not otherwise guarantee procreative options for the infertile. Arguing against the state provision of reproductive technologies, some have claimed that we do not have a right to certain biological capabilities, much as we have no right to a certain IQ or blue eyes.[60] Yet, when individuals suffer from a disfiguring condition that does not threaten their health but can be corrected with surgery, we do not deny them access to the medical technol-

ogy which could alleviate the physical stigma they suffer. The stigma of
infertility might be similarly understood. Infertility is not a life–threat-   Yes
ening medical condition, but it can potentially be remedied through
medical intervention. Treatment which can enable the infertile to bear
children is the restoration of a normal aspect of our biology. This is not
analogous to the individual who aspires to have an ideally shaped nose
or bustline. Infertility treatment is not the augmentation of normal
functioning so that an imagined deficiency can conform to some idealistic standard of beauty; it is the restoration of functioning within
the normal range. Infertile women do not wish to aspire to some above-
average standard of fertility; they simply want to be able to bear a child
just as other women do.

Absence of Primary Prevention and
Limitations in Access

Infertility is a problem for many in our society. But under the current
system, there is little effort made towards primary prevention of infertility from known risk factors. Instead there is a focus on "technological
overcompensation," with tertiary treatment only available to those individuals who can afford it.[61] Ineffectual sex education in schools and the
lack of funding for infertility prevention has put present and future
generations at risk for reduced fecundity. Sexually transmitted diseases
(STDs) account for 20 percent of infertility in the United States
and 80 percent of infertility in developing countries.[62] In addition to
STDs, other factors associated with infertility include IUDs, illegal
abortions, dilation and curettage, frequent douching, occupational/envi-
ronmental hazards, and smoking.[63] Faludi has noted the irony in the recent U.S. Republican administration's promoting the myth of a serious
infertility epidemic while refusing to allocate funds for the prevention
of infertility.[64]

Approximately one-third of all couples experiencing infertility seek
medical treatment.[65] We know very little about the other two-thirds,
since most research concentrates on those seeking treatment.[66] There
are many reasons why someone who is infertile might not pursue medical intervention, including lack of desire to have children; limitations on
finances, time, and access; and so on. The current rate of infertility has
been conservatively estimated at 9 percent of married heterosexual
couples in their reproductive years.[67] Actually, although there has been
much press given to the "infertility epidemic,"[68] the overall rate of infertility has not changed much since 1965.[69] What has changed is the

frequency of certain types of infertility. While the number of couples with primary infertility (i.e., childless) has doubled between 1965 and 1982, this has been offset by the decline in rates of secondary infertility (i.e., couples who have had a child but who are currently unable to have another).[70] This inflation in the rate of primary infertility is thought to be the demographic result of the baby-boom generation reaching their childbearing years. Although the overall rate of infertility has not risen, the demand for infertility services has, which is partially a result of the increase in absolute numbers of couples with primary infertility. The reproductive fundamentalism observed in recent years is centered around the provision of technology in order for white, middle-class heterosexual couples to have babies.[71] However, the mostly white middle- to upper-class couples who pursue infertility treatment are not necessarily the population at greatest risk to develop infertility.[72] As mentioned previously, the infertility rate for African Americans is one and one-half times that of white couples. Our society is not motivated to address preventable infertility caused by STDs among minorities and the poor in our country, or the infertility caused by the mass sterilization of Third World women and the export of toxic chemicals to Third World countries.

The financial barriers to infertility treatment can prevent many infertile couples from having a child. Since infertility treatments are not typically well covered by insurance policies, couples must be able to personally afford these treatments. Advanced medical techniques like IVF are used by only 10 to 15 percent of all infertile couples.[73] But the cost of just one in vitro fertilization cycle can be several thousand dollars. While some forms of infertility treatment are extremely expensive, many could be handled if we had mandatory insurance policies or a socialized health care system. In essence, infertile couples already pay health insurance premiums for the maternity care and sterilization procedures of fertile individuals, but are expected to cover all their own treatment costs as well.[74] It is ironic that the infertile can receive help in paying for the psychological treatment of depression and anxiety which might result from infertility, but not for the infertility treatment itself.[75] In response to such considerations, some states have already begun to introduce legislation to mandate infertility coverage among insurance carriers.

Some have questioned the ability, wisdom, and morality of society's financially assisting infertile couples in their quest to have biologically related children, especially when resources are already limited for existing children. Interestingly, the cost of pursuing infertility treatment is roughly comparable to the cost of adoption.[76] While there are valid concerns about how our economic resources should be allocated, we must not let social and health programs compete against each other for limited dollars while preventing them from competing with other areas of the budget, such as defense spending. As a society, we need to first prevent what infertility we can and then examine the issues of distributive justice. Genuine procreative choice simply does not exist if economic barriers effectively prohibit treatment options for the infertile of limited means.

The Myth of Infertility as a Female Problem

Infertility is often assumed to be the result of a woman's faulty biology. However, male factor infertility occurs at a rate comparable to female factor infertility. Infertility is the result of a solitary female factor for 35 percent of couples, a solitary male factor in another 35 percent, combined male and female factors in 20 percent, and a factor or factors whose source is unknown in the remaining 10 percent.[77] The bias towards looking at problems in women partially results from the tradition of contraceptive research, which has usually focused efforts on learning more about the female reproductive system. Since more is known about the female reproductive system, a disproportionately larger number of diagnostic and treatment procedures exist for infertile women than for infertile men.[78] Therefore, men are subjected to fewer of the direct strains of diagnosis and treatment. Even when male factor infertility is diagnosed, many of the treatments still primarily involve women (e.g., artificial insemination, IVF). In the past, the assumption that the problem always existed with the woman led some women being subjected to extensive medical testing even before a simple semen analysis was ordered.[79]

Some of this bias may have resulted from men's reluctance to take responsibility for conception, and it may be compounded by the difficulty men have in dealing with their feelings about their own infertility. Male infertility has been encased in a shroud of secrecy. Even though artificial insemination has been practiced widely for decades, there has been comparatively little public debate about the advisability of using "donor" semen in couples with male factor infertility. The explosion of public attention has only occurred in relation to female infertility in which assisted reproductive technologies such as IVF and contract motherhood have been used. Given sex-role socialization processes, it is not surprising that infertile women are more comfortable than infertile men in sharing their difficulties with others.[80] In fact, some women have reported that they wished they had the infertility problem instead of their husbands;[81] and some fertile women with infertile partners have even assumed the infertile identity for their husbands.[82] Our society as a whole seems more comfortable discussing female infertility than male infertility. Future research needs to be concentrated on developing treatment alternatives for male factor infertility so that women do not continue to remain at the center of most interventions, where they are subjected to all the attendant risks. The debate about the advisability of pursuing reproduction-assisting technologies also needs to include those which involve male factor infertility. In particular, we need to fully understand how the secrecy which envelops male factor infertility impacts on women, men, "donors," and the children created through assisted reproduction technology, particularly AID.

Psychogenic Infertility

Early attempts to understand the relationship between psychological factors and infertility portrayed psychological factors as the cause of the infertility. This psychogenic infertility model was popularized by Helene Deutsch,[83] who utilized clinical case studies to illustrate how unconscious processes (e.g., unconscious rejection of pregnancy) could lead to infertility. Despite its questionable scientific merit, Deutsch's work helped to establish this approach in the scientific and clinical literature. From there the psychogenic infertility model has found its way into the public psyche, as evidenced in the frequently proffered advice, "Relax and you'll get pregnant."

The psychogenic model has typically been applied when no obvious organic pathology has been identified after an infertility work-up. A few decades ago, this involved approximately 30 to 40 percent of the infertile population.[84] However, advances in diagnostic methods have lowered the estimated percentage of "psychogenic infertility" to 10 percent. The process of diagnosing psychogenic infertility by simply excluding medical factors runs the risk of being limited by the current level of medical knowledge. Case studies used to illustrate psychogenic infertility were typically drawn from an author's psychiatric practice. Since women seek mental health services more frequently than men,[85] women became the focus in the search for unconscious processes that could cause infertility. The precedent for a primary focus on women was thus established. Unfortunately, this conceptual model places the responsibility for infertility squarely upon the psyche of women and can be interpreted as another form of blaming the victim.[86] This is especially troubling because making a diagnosis of psychogenic infertility is fraught with so much ambiguity; conclusive evidence for the mechanisms of psychogenic infertility has remained elusive. Susan Sontag's analysis of illness as metaphor may be particularly pertinent here.[87] She reminds us that "psychological theories of illness are a powerful means of placing blame on the ill."[88] According to Sontag, "theories that diseases are caused by mental states and can be cured by will power are always an index of how much is not understood about the physical terrain of a disease."[89]

It is interesting that the tendency of professionals to blame the infertile for their infertility has been echoed by the conservative movement and by many infertile women themselves. The recent backlash against women has included the view that infertility is the direct and justifiable result of increased sexual and reproductive choice for women.[90] The tendency of others to blame infertile women has been internalized to some extent as well. Roughly one-third of infertile women have been found to interpret their infertility as punishment for some past mistake.[91]

Sexist Medical Terminology

Some of the medical language used to describe various aspects of reproduction is blatantly sexist and pejorative.[92] The use of this language can exacerbate the distress that many women feel in regard to reproductive events and the medical milieu. Infertile women are especially subject to an array of derogatory diagnostic terms. The woman who has experienced multiple miscarriages may be referred to as a *habitual aborter*, while her miscarriage is labeled a *spontaneous abortion*. This use of the term *abortion* departs from the ordinary colloquial use, which is associated with voluntary termination of an unwanted pregnancy. For the woman who has involuntarily lost a much-desired pregnancy, the use of the term *abortion* can be offensive and demeaning. The term *habitual aborter* makes it sound as if the woman has something comparable to a drug habit over which she can, but does not, exert proper control. Miscarriages might be attributed to an *incompetent cervix* or a *blighted ovum*. Yet, when a man's sperm lacks sufficient motility or adequate morphological shape we do not describe him as possessing incompetent or blighted sperm. The diagnosis of a *blighted ovum* is often made even when the embryonic stage has been reached, suggesting that although both sperm and ovum have united to form the conceptus, the fault is clearly with the woman's ovum. Women having trouble conceiving may be diagnosed with *hostile cervical mucus* or an *inadequate luteal phase.*

Meanwhile, the uterus has been identified as a *hostile environment* for the early embryo, while the ovaries are sometimes characterized as *senile*.[93] Descriptive terms like *hostile, inadequate, barren,* and *senile* are not typically applied to male functioning. Rowland further cautions about the inherent dangers of the language of dismemberment, when women are simply reduced to *uterine environments*. There is simply no question that such language devalues women in general and infertile women in particular. It needs to be rejected as unacceptable and eliminated entirely from the professional vocabulary.

Conclusion

A number of feminist authors view reproductive technologies as an aggregated whole. But reproductive technologies are greatly varied, and include practices as different as pergonal treatment, AID, tubal surgery, contract motherhood, and in vitro fertilization. When these are viewed as an aggregate, those approaches which are clearly morally problematic (because, for example, they clearly involve the potential exploitation of women) tend to cast their shadow on the remaining interventions. But each of these interventions needs to be examined separately. Perhaps the reluctance of some analysts to do so reflects an overall discomfort with any treatment that corresponds to the pronatalist agenda. It is important, however, to evaluate the potential value or risk involved in each intervention,[94] much as the different international ethics committees have. In a review of 15 ethics committee statements representing eight different countries, Walters found that the committees uniformly viewed in vitro fertilization to be ethically acceptable, while there was strong opposition to contract motherhood.[95] Even infertile couples, who have more favorable overall attitudes about reproductive interventions than fertile couples do, rate contract motherhood as the least acceptable option.[96] These findings suggest that though attitudes can become much more positive when medical interventions are seen as a "personal necessity," infertile couples still do discriminate among the technological options. Yet, many feminists have been willing to denounce all the reproductive technologies by pointing to problematic practices like contract mother arrangements, even though they have been willing to make distinctions between practices when the technologies are counter to pronatalism. The abuses related to prenatal sex identification and the resulting gynocide of female fetuses in countries such as India and China have not led us to denounce abortion. We are able to distinguish between abortions which allow women to terminate unwanted pregnancies and abortions which are specifically designed to kill an unwanted female fetus. Such distinctions need to be made with the reproduction-assisting technologies as well.

Ultimately, the feminist pro-choice position on reproductive control needs to be extended to the arena of infertility. These new reproductive technologies may require the infertile to make a "Sophie's choice" between two undesirable alternatives (i.e., between remaining infertile or pursuing medical interventions).[97] Similar to the "choice" of amniocentesis, which can make a pregnancy experience more tentative and fraught with anxiety,[98] the technologies change the possibilities and experience of reproduction. Whitbeck notes that "although technologies give us control over certain matters . . . they require that we make explicit decisions where formerly we made none. As a result, they change our responsibilities."[99] Yet, it is the infertile (not the physicians, the fertile, the pro-lifers, or even the feminists) who are in the best position to make the choices involved. And this choice represents part of the continuum of options regarding reproduction. As Rothman has argued, "The treatment of infertility needs to be recognized as an issue of self-determination. It is as important an issue for women as access to contraception and abortion, and freedom from forced sterilization."[100]

The specter of the reproductive technologies contains much to be both hopeful and fearful about. It is important for the community of feminists to express their views and be heard in the debate over how these technologies should be applied. But as feminists we should, as we do in so many other areas, make sure that the voices of those most affected, the infertile women, are not kept silent anymore. Theirs is not an easy path to traverse. It is replete with physical, psychological, and moral peril. Let us not condemn their desire to explore this path merely because it would be more comfortable for the rest of us to avoid the dilemmas involved. Let us reach out to our infertile sisters and make our way with care.

Notes

I want to thank several individuals for their helpful comments and suggestions on earlier drafts of this chapter: Anne Berg, Terry Caffery, Katherine Schwarz, Paul Weingartner, John Wilson, and most important, Joan Callahan.

1. H. Prather, *Notes to Myself: My Struggle to Become a Person* (Toronto: Bantam, 1970).

2. N. F. Russo, "The Motherhood Mandate," *Journal of Social Issues* 32 (1976), pp. 143–153.

3. N. Chodorow, *The Reproduction of Mothering: Psychoanalysis and the Soci-*

ology of Gender (Berkeley: University of California Press, 1978); J. H. Williams, *Psychology of Women: Behavior in a Biosocial Context*, 3rd ed. (New York: W. W. Norton, 1987).

4. Infertility is usually revealed when a heterosexual couple is unable to conceive or experiences repeated pregnancy loss. Regardless of which member(s) of the couple has the infertility, infertility is essentially a couple's problem. Given the infrequency with which single or homosexual individuals have occasion to discover their infertility, this analysis will deal primarily with the heterosexual couple. Although male reactions to infertility have been generally overlooked and there is a need to learn more about them, this paper will primarily concentrate on the female experience of infertility.

5. B. K. Rothman, *Recreating Motherhood: Ideology and Technology in a Patriarchal Society* (New York: W. W. Norton, 1989).

6. Although mothers with adopted children can attempt to nurse the child, it is much more difficult to establish the nursing relationship, and nursing is rarely done.

7. C. Overall, *Ethics and Human Reproduction: A Feminist Analysis* (Boston: Allen & Unwin, 1987).

8. The time it takes to become an adopting parent can be much longer than for a biological parent, yet adopting parents can reach parenthood with less preparation. When pregnancy occurs, biological parents can be reasonably certain that they will become parents at the end of the gestation period. However, a couple wishing to adopt has little assurance, even if they have passed agency screening and are awaiting the birth of a specific child, that they will get to parent a child. A biological mother who is intending to give her child up for adoption has, and should have, the right to change her mind within a certain period of time after the birth. Nonetheless, this places an enormous burden of uncertainty upon an adopting couple and makes it much more difficult for them to prepare for parenthood. Biological parents do not face this kind of uncertainty and tenuousness in establishing their linkage to the child.

9. Although many medical interventions have the potential to assist infertile women in achieving conception, they may not be able to restore fertility per se. Some interventions can restore fertility permanently, while others can do so temporarily or simply circumvent the problem (e.g., IVF for blocked fallopian tubes). Therefore, an infertile woman may still be dependent upon the medical profession if she wants future children. Entering the fertile world refers to the experiential level of knowing pregnancy and childbirth; it does not require that the infertility problem has been permanently corrected.

10. Overall, *Ethics and Human Reproduction*, pp. 137–165.

11. R. Hubbard, "The Case against In Vitro Fertilization," in *The Custom-Made Child? Women-Centered Perspectives*, ed. H. B. Holmes, B. B. Hoskins, and M. Gross (Clifton, NJ: Humana, 1981), pp. 259–262.

12. C. Frost, "Feminism and Infertility," *Resolve, Inc. Newsletter* (December, 1980), p. 5.

13. E. F. Kittay, "Womb Envy: An Explanatory Concept," in *Mothering: Essays in Feminist Theory*, ed. J. Treblicott (Rowman & Allanheld, 1984).

14. J. Campbell, *The Power of Myth*, ed. B. S. Flowers and B. Moyers (NY: Doubleday, 1988).

15. E. H. Baruch, "A Womb of His Own," in *Embryos, Ethics, and Women's Rights: Exploring the New Reproductive Technologies*, ed. E. H. Baruch, A. F. D'Adamo Jr., and J. Seager (New York: Haworth, 1988), pp. 135–139.

16. Rothman, *Recreating Motherhood*, pp. 65–84.

17. L. R. Schover et al., "Psychological Follow-up of Women Evaluated as Oocyte Donors," *Human Reproduction 6* (1991), pp. 1487–1491.

18. Rothman, *Recreating Motherhood*, p. 236.

19. In the United States, donors are typically paid for their gametes, whether the latter are sperm or oocytes. Therefore, the connotations of the word "donation" may not be entirely appropriate to this type of financially based transaction. It is important, however, to note that while "donors" are being paid for their gametes, this may not be the principal reason they donated their gametes. More research needs to be done on the motivations of gamete donors and how financial reimbursement influences the practice.

20. Although the term "surrogate mother" enjoys more common usage, this term implies that this woman is not the *real* mother. Since the woman can be either the gestational and/or genetic mother, the term "contract mother" is a more parsimonious term and will be used throughout the text.

21. Lewis, personal communication (March, 1992).

22. Centola, personal communication (March, 1992).

23. R. Rowland, "Decoding Reprospeak," *Ms. Magazine 1* (1991), pp. 38–41.

24. P. P. Mahlstedt and K. A. Probasco, "Sperm Donors: Their Attitudes toward Providing Medical and Psychosocial Information for Recipient Couples and Donor Offspring," *Fertility and Sterility 56* (1991), pp. 747–753.

25. P. P. Mahlstedt and D. A. Greenfeld, "Assisted Reproductive Technology with Donor Gametes: The Need for Patient Preparation," *Fertility and Sterility 52* (1989), pp. 908–914.

26. Mahlstedt and Probasco, pp. 747–753.

27. Little is known about how the act of "donating" gametes affects the "donor." I am currently conducting a study of male and female gamete providers to investigate their differing motivations and feelings of connectedness to their gametes.

28. See also Overall, *Ethics and Human Reproduction*, pp. 111–136; Rothman, *Recreating Motherhood*, pp. 229–245.

29. Rothman, *Recreating Motherhood*, p. 20.

30. Rothman, *Recreating Motherhood*, pp. 106–124.

31. See the discussion in J. C. Callahan, "The Contract Motherhood Debate," *Journal of Clinical Ethics* 4:1 (1993), pp. 82–91.

32. Callahan, p. 86.

33. G. Corea, *The Mother Machine: Reproductive Technologies from Artificial Insemination to Artificial Wombs* (New York: Harper & Row, 1985).

34. Corea, *The Mother Machine*, pp. 99–186.

35. A. Huxley, *Brave New World* (New York: Harper & Row, 1932).

36. Corea, *The Mother Machine*, pp. 59–98.

37. M. A. Ryan, "The Argument for Unlimited Procreative Liberty: A Feminist Critique," *Hastings Center Report* (July/August, 1990), pp. 6–12.

38. Since the technologies have been developed so recently it is hard to assess what long-term impact they may have.

39. S. A. Salladay, "Ethics and Reproductive Technology," in Holmes, Hoskins, and Gross, ed., *The Custom-Made Child?* pp. 241–248.

40. Office of Technology Assessment, *Infertility: Medical and Social Choices* (OTA-BA-358) (Washington, D.C.: U.S. Government Printing Office, 1988). The term "advanced age" refers to a woman's reproductive years. Although chronologically a woman who is 40 years old is middle-aged, reproductively speaking she is close to menopause and is nearing the end of her reproductive years.

41. Rothman, *Recreating Motherhood*, p. 147.

42. S. Faludi, *Backlash: The Undeclared War against American Women* (New York: Crown, 1991); J. C. Shattuck & K. K. Schwartz, "Walking the Line between Feminism and Infertility: Implications for Nursing, Medicine, and Patient Care," *Health Care for Women International* 12 (1991), pp. 331–339.

43. Rothman, *Recreating Motherhood*, p. 147.

44. Corea, *The Mother Machine*, p. 147.

45. Corea, *The Mother Machine*, p. 147.

46. B. Menning, "In Defense of In Vitro Fertilization," in Holmes, Hoskins, and Gross, eds., *The Custom-Made Child?* pp. 263–267.

47. B. B. Hoskins, "Manipulative Reproductive Technologies Discussion: Part II," in Holmes, Hoskins, and Gross, eds., *The Custom-Made Child?* pp. 275–280.

48. Menning, "In Defense of," pp. 263–267.

49. It is difficult to discern whether particular authors have experienced infertility problems. But the frequency with which authors fail to identify themselves as infertile suggests that they have not experienced these problems and may be counted among the fertile.

50. B. E. Menning, *Infertility: A Guide for the Childless Couple*, 2nd ed. (New York: Prentice-Hall, 1988).

51. I recognize that not all infertile individuals wish to have children. The

infertile I am talking about here are those who *are* unhappy because of their infertility.

52. L. J. Halman, A. Abbey, and R. M. Andrews, "Attitudes about Infertility Interventions among Fertile and Infertile Couples," *American Journal of Public Health 82* (1992), pp. 191–194.

53. Corea, *The Mother Machine*, pp. 172–173; N. Pfeffer, "Artificial Insemination, In-Vitro Fertilization, and the Stigma of Infertility," in *Reproductive Technologies: Gender, Motherhood, and Medicine*, ed. F. M. Stanworth (Minneapolis: University of Minnesota Press, 1987), pp. 81–97.

54. Pfeffer, "Artificial Insemination," p. 91.

55. B. J. Berg & J. F. Wilson, "Psychiatric Morbidity in the Infertile Population: A Reconceptualization," *Fertility and Sterility 53* (1990), pp. 654–661.

56. B. J. Berg & J. F. Wilson, "Psychological Functioning across Stages of Treatment for Infertility," *Journal of Behavioral Medicine 14* (1991), pp. 11–26.

57. B. J. Berg, J. F. Wilson, and P. J. Weingartner, "Psychological Sequelae of Infertility Treatment: The Role of Gender and Sex-Role Identification," *Social Science and Medicine 33* (1991), pp. 1071–1080.

58. B. J. Berg, "Psychological Sequelae to Infertility: A Critical Review of the Literature," unpublished manuscript (1993).

59. Overall, *Ethics and Human Reproduction*, pp. 166–196.

60. Hubbard, "The Case," pp. 259–262.

61. Overall, *Ethics and Human Reproduction*, pp. 137–165.

62. Office of Technology Assessment, *Infertility*, pp. 85–96.

63. Office of Technology Assessment, *Infertility*, pp. 85–96.

64. Faludi, *Backlash*, pp. 27–35.

65. Office of Technology Assessment, *Infertility*, pp. 49–60.

66. Berg, "Psychological Sequelae."

67. Office of Technology Assessment, *Infertility*, pp. 49–60.

68. Faludi, *Backlash*, pp. 27–35.

69. Office of Technology Assessment, *Infertility*, pp. 49–60.

70. Office of Technology Assessment, *Infertility*, pp. 49–60.

71. J. G. Raymond, "International Traffic in Reproduction," *Ms. Magazine 1* (1991), pp. 29–33.

72. Office of Technology Assessment, *Infertility*, pp. 49–60.

73. Office of Technology Assessment, *Infertility*, p. 7.

74. J. S. Fox, "Infertility Insurance Update" (Serono Symposia USA pamphlet, 1991).

75. Overall, *Ethics and Human Reproduction*, p. 147.

76. Office of Technology Assessment, *Infertility*, pp. 49–60.

77. Menning, *Infertility*, p. 5.

78. Office of Technology Assessment, *Infertility*, pp. 49–60.

79. Frost, p. 5.

80. Berg, Wilson, and Weingartner, "Psychological Sequelae," pp. 1071–1080.

81. C. Crowe, " 'Women Want It': In-Vitro Fertilization and Women's Motivations for Participation," *Women's Studies International Forum 8* (1985), pp. 547–552.

82. J. D. Czyba and M. Chevret, "Psychological Reactions of Couples to Artificial Insemination with Donor Sperm," *International Journal of Fertility 24* (1979), pp. 240–245.

83. H. Deutsch, *Psychology of Women: Volume II, Motherhood* (New York: Grune & Stratton, 1945), pp. 106–125.

84. M. D. Mazor, "Barren Couples," *Psychology Today 12* (1979), pp. 101–112.

85. Williams, *Psychology of Women*, pp. 445–463.

86. Frost, p. 5.

87. S. Sontag, *Illness as Metaphor and AIDS and Its Metaphors* (New York: Doubleday, Anchor Books, 1990), pp. 55–57.

88. Sontag, *Illness as metaphor*, p. 57.

89. Sontag, p. 55.

90. Faludi, *Backlash*, pp. 27–35; M. Sandelowski, "Sophie's Choice: A Metaphor for Infertility," *Health Care for Women International 7* (1986), pp. 439–453.

91. Berg, Wilson, and Weingartner, "Psychological Sequelae," pp. 1071–1080.

92. B. J. Berg, "Sexism and Medical Terminology," Letters to the Editor, *Women's Health Issues 2* (in press); Menning, "In Defense of," pp. 263–267.

93. Rowland, pp. 38–41.

94. Ryan, pp. 6–12; Rothman, *Recreating Motherhood*, pp. 140–151.

95. L. Walters, "Ethics and New Reproductive Technologies: An International Review of Committee Statements," *The Hastings Center Report* (1987), pp. 3–22.

96. Halman, Abbey, and Andrews, "Attitudes," pp. 193–194.

97. Sandelowski, "Sophie's Choice," pp. 439–453.

98. B. K. Rothman, *The Tentative Pregnancy: Prenatal Diagnosis and the Future of Motherhood* (New York: Viking, 1986).

99. C. Whitbeck, "Ethical Issues Raised by the New Medical Technologies," in *Women and New Reproductive Technologies: Medical, Psychosocial, Legal, and Ethical Dilemmas*, ed. J. Rodin and A. Collins (Hillsdale, NJ: Lawrence Erlbaum, 1991), pp. 49–64.

100. Rothman, *Recreating Motherhood*, p. 140.

The Metamorphosis
of Motherhood

Patricia Smith

Motherhood, as traditionally understood, is obsolete. It is not yet as obsolete as, say, knighthood, but it is moving just as inevitably in the same
direction. No one wants to admit that, but it is true. Traditionalists are
horrified. Most men are uncertain. Even progressive women are ambiva-
lent. We don't know what it will mean. If the standards we should use
are radically different from the standards we grew up with, women, like
men, do not know what to do, how to act, how to evaluate ourselves.

Basic change is difficult. So we avoid it by means of every tactic and
device that we can find. And some reject change altogether. The "new
right" calls for a return to traditional family values, meaning, as I understand it, that women should stop working for pay, or at least stop
thinking that it is important to work for pay, and return to the traditional relationships of the nuclear family featuring a male breadwinner and a female homemaker who is a full-time wife and mother. Conservative evangelists and politicians proclaim the virtues of traditional
motherhood and chide working women and feminists for supposedly
pursuing their own interests at the expense of the moral development of
their children. Traditional motherhood is the destiny of women as well
as the solution to the moral crisis of postmodern civilization, we are
told. Despite these urgent admonitions, however, there are at least three
world-class revolutionary changes occurring in this century that make
the traditional notion of motherhood obsolete.

I think that it is time that we faced these social facts and the enor-
mity of their implications. The truth is, we cannot go back, any more
than the entrepreneurs of the eighteenth century could go back to the

feudal society that held sway for centuries before the industrial revolution finalized its decline. We must find new solutions to our moral and social problems, because the world has already changed in ways that make a return to the past impossible. We are experiencing a reproductive revolution in this century at least as profound and inevitable as the industrial revolution of two centuries ago.

This, of course, is not to suggest that cultural change progresses at the same rate among all classes or in all parts of the world. Beliefs, attitudes, and living conditions vary widely. Many women of Third World nations live as they have lived for centuries. The cultural revolution that I, in my leisure, am exploring here, has not yet reached them. It is my belief, however, for reasons I will supply shortly, that these changes will inevitably encompass the entire world—not in my lifetime, but eventually. In any case, my remarks obviously do not apply to those who have not yet experienced the twentieth-century changes that I will be discussing here.

Perhaps I should also make clear that I am not suggesting that most women in technologically advanced nations manage to avoid restrictive and discriminatory conditions. A great many women live with poverty, oppression, and prejudice on a daily basis, even in highly developed societies. I would be the last to deny the existence or significance of such conditions; but they are not the point of this essay. My objective in this particular paper is to examine the norm of middle-class motherhood in technologically advanced societies. Unless otherwise stated, what I say here should be understood to refer to that context. The norm of middle-class motherhood, I contend, has changed so drastically during the twentieth century that the traditional notion of motherhood must be viewed as obsolete.

In order to see this, first consider what "traditional motherhood" means. I take that role to have three salient features. First, the primary mission of the traditional woman was to get married and provide reproductive services to her husband. Her pride and destiny consisted in producing and rearing children. That was her purpose in life, and it was a purpose predetermined for all women. It was not a matter of choice. It was not up to individuals. Any woman who deviated simply was not normal. This presumption was pervasive at least through the 1950s in the United States with only slight variations elsewhere, and is still rather widely held. But it is no longer virtually universally believed.[1]

Second, in all but a few truly exceptional cases of exceedingly highborn women, the reproductive role was combined with domestic duty. All women were presumed to be naturally domestic and solely responsible for the home. Either they were responsible to do the work—the cooking, cleaning, marketing, production and care of clothing, and child care—or they were responsible to manage servants who did it. This might be combined with other work they did (if they were poor) either inside or outside the home, but even if they worked outside the home for pay, their primary responsibility was the home. This included service to their husbands, that is, waiting on them as well as deferring to them. Husbands were not responsible for daily household chores. These were considered women's work. If this work was not done, or not done well, it was the woman's fault. This belief that woman is, by nature, properly suited only to the role of domestic duty held true from the beginning of civilization, consistently and almost universally, until about the 1960s. It was never seriously challenged before that time and it is still strongly and widely believed today. But, again, it is no longer virtually universally believed.[2]

Third, a corollary of the idea that women were naturally domestic was the belief that they were not fit to function in the public sphere. Traditional wives were dependent on and answerable to their husbands. Until the nineteenth century they had no legal status of their own. They could not conduct business, execute contracts, or own property. Their wages were owned by their husbands or fathers. They were not independent and they certainly were not equal to men in either the eyes of society or the eyes of the law.

Still hierarchical and patriarchal as an institution, the traditional family today continues to function as a unit that revolves around the male head of household, the husband and father. The wife and mother provides the support system. The success of the family unit depends on the success of the head of household. Thus, it falls to the woman to provide whatever support she can to ensure her husband's success. If she works, her work is subsidiary, a contribution that may never interfere with or compete with her husband's career. Her success and the success of the family unit depend on the success of the breadwinner, and not on any separate work that a wife and mother might do on the side. At least in Europe and the United States, these attitudes may have broken down more than the attitudes captured in the other two defining features of the traditional mother. But they were little challenged before the 1960s, and they still manage to comprise the norm in much thinking about the wife and mother, despite the wailing of traditionalists regarding the disintegration of traditional family values.[3]

To sum up so far, the three salient features of the traditional mother are that her livelihood and self-respect rest in (1) producing children and caring for them, (2) keeping a good house, and (3) providing support for the success of her husband's career, on which depends the success of the family unit. Her primary dedication is to her family. She may do other things "on the side," but they are incidental to her material well-being and to her self-respect. She is answerable to and dependent on her husband, and her success is measured vicariously through the success of her husband and children.[4]

Now, what are the three world-class cultural changes that I claim undermine the viability of the traditional portrait of motherhood? First, and most basically, the mission to populate the planet has been more than accomplished. The goal now is to restrict, not increase, the population. Furthermore, much of the world's population has shifted from an agrarian to an urban economy, making large families financially unfeasible for members of these populations. These two factors, coupled with amazing advances in medicine and birth control, shrank the average family size in industrialized nations from 8.3 children in 1785 to 1.8 in 1985. The world does not need babies any more; at least not many of them. If you don't need babies, you don't need mothers.[5]

Second, technological advances have revolutionized all human life in modern societies, particularly the lives of women. Most significantly, technology has not only given women control over their childbearing role, it has streamlined their housekeeping role, restructuring the daily duties that once comprised the bulk of the homemaking occupation of mothers. And it has revolutionized the workplace, making physical strength largely irrelevant, increasing clerical and administrative jobs, and pulling women into the workforce. Now mom and dad both spend their days at work and housekeeping has become a part-time, after-hours job. The result is that the "natural domesticity" of women doesn't look so natural any more.

Third, despite many setbacks and disappointments, social changes and political victories have liberated women more during the twentieth century than during all of the history of civilization before it. It is commonly held that once people have tasted freedom they will never again be satisfied without it, and there is no reason to think that does not apply to women. This means that many women who were once dependent on and answerable to their husbands now consider themselves to be equals. That attitude is incompatible with hierarchical family relationships, and it cannot be eradicated once it is acquired. Traditional motherhood was a subordinate role; but many women today do not and cannot consider themselves subordinate to men as such, and those women are living counterexamples to the received wisdom necessary to support traditional patriarchal family structures.

There you have it. Every major feature of traditional motherhood (full-time child-bearing, dependence, and domesticity by nature) is undermined by significant cultural changes that have occurred largely during this century. Taken together, these changes constitute a revolution. The changes are permanent. They cannot be undone. And it is foolish to think that no consequences will follow from them. In fact, as a result of these revolutionary changes, the lives and the thinking of women, at least in modern industrialized countries, are so drastically different from the life and thought of women just eighty years ago, that it is unrealistic—indeed, it is delusionary—to think that women could live the way they used to live, even if they wanted to (as many of them seem to think they do).

We do not realize this impossibility because of an interesting feature of cultural revolutions, namely, that they are basically invisible to their participants. I am not saying that people who are going through a period of great change do not know it. Most of us have a vague sense now that these are anxious, unsettled times when roles and relations and responsibilities are uncertain and in flux. But since cultural revolutions actually evolve over time and progress unevenly, we, who are part of them, do not tend to characterize our own part as revolutionary. That gets done later, by historians, who can look back over a period of time and identify certain centuries as revolutionary because the changes that took place during those times were so fundamental that human thought and human life could never again be quite the same. That, I submit to you, is the kind of time in which we now live, even if it is hard to perceive it clearly. If we can take a step back to examine the cultural changes I have mentioned, and compare the lives of our grandmothers with the lives we live today, we will see that fundamental and irreversible steps have already been taken that eliminate the possibility of a societal return to the traditional family. In the remainder of this paper I want to show why the changes I have cited inevitably lead to the total eclipse of traditional motherhood.

The Reproductive Revolution

Let's consider my first claim: The world does not need babies any more, at least not very many of them. This ought to be obvious to all of us. It isn't, of course, but it should be. Given the population explosion of the twentieth century, the whole world (not just China) would be better off if we could manage to limit our reproduction to one or two children per family. There is no question about this. Any minimally well-educated person should know that it is true.[6]

In 1987 the world population reached five billion, and with eighty million children born every year, our population will redouble every three to four decades. With our present population, we are depleting our resources, using up our farmlands, diminishing our forests, destroying our atmosphere, and polluting ourselves off the planet. If that is what it is like with five billion people, what will it be like with fifteen billion? Keep in mind that, given our current growth rate, that day is only 60 to 80 years off. We may not be in a catastrophic condition now, but it is not hard to see it coming quickly up the road.[7]

Given our great human capacity for avoidance and denial (and despite the best efforts of early observers, such as Malthus), we have managed more or less to ignore our population problem for over a hundred years. But it is getting more difficult to ignore it as the years go by and the evidence mounts. Assuming that one of the most useful human traits is still our adaptability, it is only a matter of time until recognition of a human condition of this sort (that is, a species-threatening condition) gradually works its way into societal attitudes and becomes manifested in our moral codes. Religious and social attitudes toward family size have already begun to change. Not more than 80 years ago, it was considered virtuous for a woman to have many children. This is no longer the case. Birth rates have fallen dramatically, not only throughout Europe and the United States, but in a number of so-called Third World nations where governments have pressed for lower birth rates.

But falling birth rates need not be attributed to moral concern about global overpopulation. There are also practical economic explanations. Given changes in many modern societies from agrarian to industrial and service economies which prohibit or greatly restrict child labor, most families cannot afford more than one or two children. That is, parents know that the quality of their own lives and their children's lives will be diminished by the birth of more children.

Children were once practical assets, or at least not serious expenses. They helped to run the farm or the family business. They earned their own way quite early on, and provided a needed work force with minimal preparation. Much food and clothing was produced, or at least processed and maintained in the home, which eliminated much expense and employed many children, even if informally. Even four- and five-year-olds regularly helped out with family chores, did farm work, and, unfortunately, also worked in factories until the 1930s, when it became illegal for them to do so. Children earned their own keep. Children were also the primary source of old-age security for their parents until fairly recent times, even in most highly developed countries of the world. All this was still generally true in the first quarter of the twentieth century.

But these economic arrangements have changed dramatically in much of the world. Today, children commonly represent a significant economic investment for at least 15 to 25 years before they will be merely self-sufficient. Children in contemporary developed countries do not earn their own keep. And they are no longer the main source (or the first choice) of economic security for parents in old age. The state and individual businesses have now taken over that function through insurance, pension plans, and socialized medicine. And the cost of providing for and raising a child today has quadrupled in 50 years, even adjusting for inflation. Economically speaking, children are neither working assets nor individual investments for the future. As far as middle-class parents are concerned, children are luxuries, and costly luxuries at that.[8]

So, less than one hundred years ago it was not only considered virtuous, but practical and responsible as well, to have many children. Children were not only blessings, but assets and investments for individuals. Today, unless one is wealthy, having many children is not only not virtuous, it is impractical and irresponsible. Thus, morality, utility, and self-interest (both egoistic and enlightened) are all united in lowering birth rates.

The other factor that decisively affects the restriction of family size is the technological advancement that now enables women to exercise birth control at a level of reliability and safety that was unheard of before the 1960s. It would be difficult to overstate the significance of this technological development. Women's lives in much of the world were transformed literally within a decade by the availability of reliable birth control. All other major advances and freedoms for women followed that one. Mary O'Brien puts it this way:

> . . . In 1975, I and many others could see that this development [of reliable birth control] was enormously significant, that it was what Hegel called a "world-historical event," a happening which would transform not only ancient institutions but which would bring about transformations in our consciousness of ourselves, our bodies, our historical and social being.[9]

What does all this mean? What does it amount to in practical terms for ordinary people in daily life? It means that as people are beginning to believe that it is not a virtue to produce a great many children, they are finding themselves in a position to do something about the size of their families. The size of the typical family in Europe or the United States no longer includes twelve children, or even six, but rather one or two. Manhood is no longer commonly gauged by the production of numerous offspring; a woman who prefers a career to raising children is no longer universally considered deranged; and couples with no children at all are now fairly acceptable, when they were once considered tragic. In other words, it is becoming clear to increasing numbers of people that the "mission" to populate the earth has been fulfilled, and moral attitudes about the virtue of having large families are changing or have changed accordingly.

All this makes a huge difference in the lives of everyone, but just think of what it means for women. My two grandmothers were married in 1910 and 1920 and each had her first baby within a year. One was unable to have any more children. The other had ten. It was not unusual to have ten children at that time; in fact, the average then was about seven. Imagine what that must have been like. My grandmother was pregnant or nursing or both from the time she was 18 until she was 40. Now, *that* is full-time motherhood! Although my other grandmother was not able to have any more children, that was her burden to bear. And she lived exactly the same way that she would have if she had had ten children. She lived as a full-time mother, because that is what all women were supposed to do. Reproducing was the sign of a virtuous woman, as it always had been. The reproductive role which was central to the lives and identity of women did not change significantly throughout all history until the twentieth century. But after that it changed so profoundly that women today cannot even conceive of what womanhood meant a century ago. We have lost our past identity collectively and individually, and with it the traditional understanding of motherhood. Let me illustrate with another example.

Mary Clap was a fairly typical virtuous woman, who could have been plucked from any century until the twentieth. Mary had six children, four of whom died. This is close to the average 50 percent infant mortality rate which held fairly constant until this century. Mary died in childbirth at age 24. She was a refined and well-educated woman for her time, the wife of Thomas Clap, the president of Yale College. But it did not matter then how much education you had, how well born you were, to whom you were married, or how much money you possessed. All women (unlike autonomous men) were fundamentally fated, destined to be childbearers, and all were susceptible to die for that mission. In his elegy for Mary, President Clap recalled her attitude toward her lot in life, the attitude of a virtuous woman:

> She always went through the difficulties of childbearing with re-markable steadiness, faith, patience and decency. She had calm and humble resignation to the divine will. Indeed, she would some-times say to me that bearing, tending, and burying children was hard work, and that she had done a great deal of it for one of her age. Yet, she would say it was the work she was made for, and what God in his providence had called her to.[10]

Not all women died in childbirth. For every one like Mary there were four who survived their childbearing years. Yet the risk she faced and the attitude she expressed was the risk and view of virtually all women for all time until this century. Childbearing was their destiny and the centerpiece of their lives. But that destiny became fully and finally obsolete with the advent of modern medicine and birth control in this century, at least for women of moderate means. And the change that represents is so profound that the basic psychology and even the identity of women are changed. Women were *fundamentally* childbearers, all of them, and now they are not.

Let me indulge in a personal comparison. Exceeding the average in the 1960s, I gave birth to five children in six years. At the end of that time I was financially impoverished, physically and emotionally run down, and frustrated with birth control measures that did not seem to work. I was living in a time when doctors, in their infinite moral wisdom, still refused to sterilize a woman like me (that is, a young woman in minimally good health). Elective abortion was illegal, and the pill was just becoming available (the fact that changed the rest of my life). I have an inkling of what it must have been like to feel fated—to feel destined to be a childbearer forever. I feared that somehow I would be pregnant for the rest of my life, and that nothing would be able to prevent it. That is the closest that I can come to imagining what it was like for women in earlier times. But the analogy is not really apt. In my case, that feeling was irrational. Doctors had told me that they would sterilize me after my sixth pregnancy if necessary. So, in fact, my greatest risk was one more pregnancy. Furthermore, my friends and relatives did not think that it was my destiny or duty to continue having children until I could not have any more. Nor did I. And finally, although I was tired, I was never in fear for my life. It never crossed my mind that I could die in childbirth. I knew full well that the odds were greater that I would die in a car accident on the way to the hospital than that I would die once I got there.

So, although Mary Clap had six children before she was 25 years old and, 200 years later, I had five children by the same age, I know that it wasn't the same. I know that I still cannot understand what life was like for her, or even for my grandmothers. I do not know what it means to be fated. I do not know any woman who died in childbirth. I know in the abstract that it still happens, and more than occasionally to impoverished Third World women; but that is different. Those women die because measures that are known and available to others are not available to them. Most of their deaths (and unwanted pregnancies) could be prevented. They could be put in charge of their lives. But the destiny of Mary Clap was faced by all women until recently and there was nothing anyone could do about it. Mary Clap knew each year that she was pregnant that she might die that year carrying out her maternal mission, just as had many of her friends and relatives. And she knew that nothing could change that, no matter who you were.

I cannot imagine what that would be like, much less imagine accepting it. And I think that if I cannot imagine it, then the average middle-class woman of the late twentieth century—the woman who gives birth to one or two children as relatively safe and isolated events in an otherwise long and varied life—that is to say, the vast majority of women in all industrialized nations today cannot even begin to imagine what it was like to be a woman less than a century ago. This single remarkable fact about reproduction changes the life and thought—indeed, the very identity—of women so profoundly that we are practically a different species. Women were childbearers. Now we are not. That was our identity. Now it is not. That was our destiny. Now, like men, we are responsible for our own destiny.

The reproductive revolution alone is necessary and sufficient to make traditional motherhood obsolete because it has changed the very identity of women. Everything else is supplementary and it was always supplementary. The only intrinsic feature of motherhood is childbearing. That function now requires, on the average, a few months out of most women's lives. Nevertheless, all the supplementary matters are crucially significant in their own right, so I will turn to them now.

The Feminization of Freedom

Accompanying the reproductive revolution is a social revolution which, within two hundred years, has led to the legal, educational, moral, and economic emancipation of women. This revolution (like the other two) is very uneven and incomplete, and varies greatly with the development of a particular country or region. And the cultural phenomenon is so complex that all I can do here is offer the barest sketch of an account, basically a list of reminders of well-known historical developments. The point of this section is to note that, while women today are autonomous legal persons, before the nineteenth century women were not only not free, they were the property of men—their fathers and husbands. Revolutionary changes in the attitudes that allowed women to be held as property were already beginning in the nineteenth century; but the changes were not yet comprehensive enough to undermine the pervasive system of subordinating mechanisms until late in the present century. Thus, until this century motherhood continued to be a subordinate role. Wives were dependent on and answerable to their husbands. This was based on the general presumption that men and women are fundamentally different and that a basic feature of that difference is that women, unlike men, are dependent and domestic by nature. This presumption was actually enforced rigidly by an elaborate system of coercive mechanisms, and it is precisely this system of coercion that has begun to crumble measurably in the present century. Let me mention a few examples.

First, role models and the process of socialization were clear at the beginning of this century and very unclear by the end of it. As Catharine MacKinnon has put it, patriarchy is the most effective ideology ever invented.[11] Thus it was generally thought that women, being intrinsically dependent, were unable to engage in business, politics, or the professions. And just to ensure that the truth of that fundamental presumption remained unchallenged, women were banned from these occupations. Of course, poor women always went out to work. That, however, was not considered an opportunity but a misfortune that befell them because they or their husbands were failures. The common wisdom was that successful women did not work. Middle-class emulation of aristocratic ladies of leisure, observed and described at the turn of the century by Veblen, was still deeply entrenched through the 1950s in the United States and Western Europe.[12]

Successful career women even during the first half of the twentieth century were aberrations, abnormalities. And this was hardly surprising. Men and women were socialized to believe that independent women were abnormal and immoral, since they were ignoring or rejecting their feminine nature. In fact, as late as the 1950s the "rejection of femininity" was a widely recognized theory of abnormal behavior for women.[13] The popular view has been that women are naturally demure, deferential, passive, and dependent. That is what femininity has meant. Socialization into this stereotype was clear and uniform, ensured by all the powerful structures and devices available for conditioning human behavior at the beginning of this century. But as we approach the end of the century, role models have become unclear and even contradictory, and our socialization processes are no longer uniform.

Secondly, women were poorly educated before the twentieth century, and what education of women was available was commonly focused on producing good mothers. Into the 1900s, for example, it was argued by educational experts that advanced education for women would produce dire consequences, including (but not limited to) withering of the breasts and uterus, menstrual and reproductive problems, sleeplessness, hair loss, immorality, and even insanity.[14]

In addition to the warnings of experts, women were formally banned or informally discouraged from advanced education.[15] At the beginning of this century most women received very little education, and little or no professional training. Thus, education (or the lack of it) reinforced the socialization of women to be dependent on and answerable to men—usually their husbands. But educational practices have changed dramatically during this century, and most women are now educated in more or less the same way that men are.

Until we think about it we do not realize how much educational opportunities for women have changed in our time. At the turn of the century, most colleges were not open to women, only about 3000 women in the entire United States were enrolled in undergraduate programs, and the number of women educated for the professions was too small to measure. Today, American and European women comprise roughly half of the undergraduate student population, earn 30–40 percent of the legal and medical degrees, and are readily admitted to most professional schools (although informal discrimination is still strong, especially in certain areas). The point is that U.S. and European women are now commonly well educated; and while breasts and uteruses have not withered away, the old educational experts were in fact right about one thing. Advanced education is not compatible with subservience. Educated people are less likely to defer uncritically to the opinions of others. And many women find it unacceptable to spend years acquiring a professional education, only to give up their professional careers after a short time. Furthermore, the achievement of modern women (despite the continued discrimination against them) belies the old view that women are essentially dependent and unfit for public or professional pursuits. So, education today undermines the subordination of women, instead of reinforcing it as it did just 80 years ago.[16]

Thirdly, not much more than a century ago women could not legally own property, run businesses, or even work in most areas of the public sphere, and certainly not the professions. Even poor women who were allowed to work in mills and sweat shops or as domestic servants or field hands were legally obliged to turn their wages over to their husbands or fathers. Married women had no separate legal existence. Like children and idiots, they were not legally competent to contract debts or legally responsible for them.[17] They were first the property and then the responsibility of their fathers and husbands. Women simply were not free; nor were they given equal treatment or legal standing with men. At the turn of the century, many trades and professions (ranging from bartending to practicing law) still banned women outright, denying them licenses to practice.[18] Thus, women had no choice but to be dependent until the present century.

Even in the twentieth century, when legal restrictions eased and educational opportunities increased, social pressure remained strong and employment discrimination remained common. In the depression years of the 1930s, women were condemned as immoral for working, and ordinarily they were not hired if any unemployed man were available to fill a job. This held true whether a woman was single or married, head of household or not. In the late 1940s women who were recruited to manufacturing for the war effort were summarily fired to give jobs to returning servicemen. And even as late as the 1960s, many women who worked when they were young were automatically fired when they married, and if not when they married, then certainly when they became pregnant. Thus, women had little choice about staying home with the children, and few viable options for economic independence earlier in this century.[19] Today, practices like those mentioned would violate federal law. The legal restrictions on women are almost entirely gone in many countries; and while informal discrimination continues, discrimination does not have the overt institutional support that it had just a few years ago. Today, economic independence may still be difficult for many women, but it is entirely possible and not uncommonly actual.

Finally, the legal institution of marriage has changed drastically during this century. Until late in this century, a marriage changed the status of the man and woman who entered into it permanently and hierarchically. Women vowed to obey their husbands and men to protect their wives. Yet, while a man was bound to protect his wife from strangers, he was the ruler of his home—the family was a private domain into which the state should not and would not intrude. A man was entitled to define wifely duty more or less as he saw fit. It certainly included sexual as well as housekeeping services, and he had the right of "reasonable chastisement" to ensure obedience. Wife beating was not assault; it was discipline—the punishment of an inferior by a superior. And even when wife beating was legally demoted from its official status as justifiable discipline, overriding male authority was still widely recognized as appropriate in the family.[20]

Today many women are equal partners in their marriages, sharing decisions and responsibilities with their husbands. And even though women still tend to earn less than men, the economic and legal subordination of women to men is no longer comprehensive. Many women are actually economically independent, thus providing living counterexamples to the old view that women must be taken care of because they simply cannot function on their own. The traditional model of the innately dependent woman has broken down.

The Decline of Domesticity

Not only was the traditional woman inescapably dependent and maternal, she was also intrinsically domestic. Since the beginning of civilization women have always been the keepers of the hearth, the primary caregivers, the homemakers. The reason for this, it was always assumed, is that women (unlike men) are domestic by nature. Nowadays it has become hard to figure out exactly what that was supposed to have meant. It could refer to behavior that is inevitable: cows eat grass; cats chase mice; women keep house. They can't help themselves. It's just their nature. There seem to be too many counterexamples for that interpretation to remain plausible today. Or it could refer to preferences. Cows like eating grass. Cats like eating meat. Women like puttering around the house. That's just what they all prefer to do. It is their source of fulfillment. Again, counterexamples abound. It could refer to the scope or limit of capabilities. Cows are not good predators. Cats are not suited to farming. Women can't function well outside the home. Once more, counterexamples.

Presumably, "being domestic" was open to all the above interpretations, and none of them works well today. It is still suggested that somehow women care more about the home than men do. Women are more nurturing, more patient, more tidy than men, we are told. And that must be what it means to "be" domestic these days. Yet, there can be no doubt that the norm of domesticity has fallen on hard times. Socialization is scanty and sporadic. Role models are in short supply. Young girls are more likely to emulate Madonna (unfortunately) or Hilary Clinton (fortunately) than—who? Homemakers as public figures are hard to find these days, and most girls' mothers work outside the home.

Corresponding to the upsurge of women participating in the public sphere is a decline in the norm of domesticity. Just as fewer women identify themselves as mothers, essentially, fewer also identify themselves as homemakers, essentially. For better or worse, working women particularly in the professions, tend to identify themselves with their jobs. Or, more intellectually, women may identify themselves as autonomous individuals who are defined, if at all, in terms of their own choices throughout life. Expectations have been altered; presumptions about women's identity have been challenged, and with them the bases of responsibility and self respect. Women may still do housework, but they are no longer considered homemakers by nature.

The sources of this transformation are diverse and cannot be discussed comprehensively here. Among them are the industrial revolution itself. It is no news that the industrial revolution has radically transformed human life in every nation that it has reached. So it should be no surprise that it reorganized the home and family as well. I believe that the industrial revolution has had at least a triple impact on the home and homemaking role, one that has contributed greatly to our current unstable circumstances. For one thing, industrialization has restructured the character of the family itself and reorganized the relations within it. Secondly, it has revised many basic values that were taken as given before it occurred. What people think about home, homemaking, and family roles and relationships has been radically restructured in ways that have undermined the traditional family, but have not yet replaced it with an adequate substitute. Finally, on the simplest level, it has changed the nature of the work that homemakers do. Since all these phenomena cannot be discussed here, I will at least attempt to illustrate the profundity of the transformation of homelife that they constitute by showing the depth of change represented in even the simplest level—the nature of the work of homemaking.[21]

Technological advances have changed the structure of daily living that once comprised the bulk of the housekeeping occupation for mothers. Domestic duties of cooking and cleaning that once accompanied full-time childcare have changed remarkably in recent years. Commercial and managerial expertise are now the greatest requirements of homemakers. That is, one must know which products to buy and how to use them; but with modern conveniences, cooking and cleaning have been so streamlined and mechanized that the kind of time and expertise that were once required for producing and preserving one's own food, preparing it from scratch, and for keeping one's home and clothing clean and repaired are no longer necessary. You can grow your own peaches and preserve them if you like; but it is not the case that if you do not, you will not have peaches. You can bake your own bread and make your own clothing, but not because you have to.

Furthermore, it is not clear that your end product will be cheaper or even better than what you could buy; and it is very unlikely that producing it will be the most efficient use of your time. That is, you can work for pay, buy very good peaches, or clothing, or bread, and probably have both time and money left over. Domestic duties (such as preserving food, making clothing, and seeing to various household needs) that were once crucial, are now hobbies. The character of housekeeping has changed fundamentally.

Before 1800 life throughout the world was completely different; primarily agrarian, it placed the home at the center of growing, processing, preserving, and preparing food. The home was also the manufacturing center for clothing and other necessities. Enormous amounts of time and energy went into carding fiber, spinning thread, weaving cloth, and sewing, as well as providing fuel, food, and household necessities. These, and not cleaning, were the primary occupation of women worldwide.[22]

But home manufacturing was basically gone by 1855. Although the United States was still predominantly agricultural, the typical housewife in the 1890s bought soap, underwear, and cloth, sent her child out to school, preserved food in an icebox, and had linoleum on her kitchen floor. She had no spinning wheel and no loom and more time than her mother had, even though she had much higher standards of cleanliness to meet—unless she was poor. If she was a member of the working class, she simply moved the location of her labor from the home to the factory or mill—unfortunately, with a considerable decrease in the quality of her life. And her children did too, at least until the 1930s, when child labor was banned. But if she was part of the rising middle class, she became more educated, had more time, and did more shopping. By 1929, most people had electricity, running water and indoor plumbing. The enormous amount of time and effort saved by these three basic conveniences alone is hard to estimate. By 1930 the United States (as well as Europe) was predominantly urban and 80 percent of family needs were satisfied by the purchases (rather than the products) of women.[23]

So we can see that by 1855 the industrial revolution had revolutionized not only the U.S. and European markets, but U.S. and European homes, as well. By 1955 the character of housekeeping had been so drastically transformed as to be completely unimaginable to the people of the previous century. And by 1985 we had moved beyond a mechanical to an electronic age filled with computers, TV sets, microwave ovens, and characterized by swift transportation, mass communication, universal markets, high-tech industry, slick advertising, and shopping malls. Housekeeping is no longer a skilled craft requiring years of apprenticeship and producing crucial household needs. Today, housekeeping primarily consists of shopping and cleaning, which together do not comprise a full-time occupation.

That is not to say, however, that there is no housekeeping job left. That is what women discover when they take full-time positions outside the home. Unless you have a preschool child to care for (which can certainly be a full-time job for a few years), housekeeping is only about half of a job if you stay home. But it is a job and a half if you go to work. That puts all homemakers at a disadvantage in competing with those who are not homemakers. It also pushes them toward taking part-time jobs, or less demanding (and less lucrative) positions that will be more compatible with their homemaking responsibilities.

The important point that needs to be recognized and increasingly is recognized about this aspect of the traditional motherhood role is that it has nothing whatever to do with motherhood, intrinsically. Combining childbearing, child care, and housekeeping may have once been a convenient and practical division of labor. Of course, other explanations have been suggested for the traditional division of labor between men and women;[24] but whatever their relative merits, it is also easy to see that the traditional motherhood/homemaker role, at one time at least, could have been construed plausibly as a part of a practical division of labor, and that it no longer can be. Given changes in populations, economies, and technologies, there is no longer any valid ground for maintaining the traditional division of labor and the traditional housekeeping role of motherhood. To suggest that women instinctively shop and clean house is not only intuitively implausible; it is not borne out by history, since women did little of either before the nineteenth century. These time-fillers are twentieth-century inventions that have failed to provide full-time occupations for women since childbearing and home manufacturing have declined. Nor are they, at this point in time, viewed as occupations or as crucial components of a broader role that expresses the domestic nature of women. Shopping and cleaning are extras, after-hour chores to be done after the primary occupation of the day is over. Women still do these jobs most of the time, largely out of inertia, and because some-one has to, but not because they assume that it is inevitable or preferable that women be responsible for domestic chores, and least of all because they believe women are intrinsically domestic.

Conclusion

If we put these various factors together—the legal, social, educational, economic, and moral structures—we see a clear picture of a new world. The difference in the degree and consistency of oppression has made the difference between the virtual impossibility and the reasonable possibility of freedom for women. The patriarchal picture is now so full of cracks that everyone can see it is just a picture. It is not the only way the world could be. Both the conditions and the conditioning have changed.

These changes have transformed the very identity of women and with it, the institutions of marriage and motherhood. The psychological changes are as profound as the material changes of reproductive life and correspond to them. I can see this in my own family. My grandmother really cannot understand what it means to be free. Even today when she is, in fact, economically independent, she cannot after all the years of subordination deal with independence. It is foreign to her entire life's experience. My daughters, on the other hand, cannot really understand what it means not to be free. This is not to say that they cannot understand being oppressed, but that they cannot understand accepting it as just the way things are, as a neutral description of the world as it must be, or as an expression of innate differences between men and women, rather than as domination or injustice. They can understand being subordinated, but they cannot imagine *being* subordinate in some essential way.

The great difference between my grandmother's generation and my daughters' is that almost all women of my grandmother's generation, like Mary Clap before them, accepted their destiny—and with good reason. The odds against escaping it were astronomical. Their acceptance was entirely reasonable and understandable, and yet it sealed their doom, because freedom depends on how one thinks. Frederick Douglass and his mother before him lived under the yoke of slavery, but no one was able to enslave their minds. Legal, social, and economic structures will make it more or less difficult to realize your freedom in practice; but what *really* makes you free is knowing that you are. Women, like my grandmother, understood that they were subordinate, unequal, and so they were. They understood that they were not free; and so they were not. That was the great difference between men and women.

But many women of my daughters' generation understand that they are responsible for their own choices and their own futures. They know that they are free; and so they are. But if they are free as women, then they are not subordinate, as women, to men. That undermines the sexual hierarchy intrinsic to traditional marriage and motherhood.

I don't think I have said anything here that most people do not already know. I am just reviewing well-known historical developments and drawing a conclusion that too often seems to go unrecognized. A reproductive revolution has occurred in this century, although the roots of the revolution reach back into the last century and the fruits will be more fully harvested in the next. This revolution is substantially complete and irreversible, and it has profound implications for the traditional role of motherhood. Traditionally, women were essentially childbearers and domestic servants, the property and responsibility of their fathers or husbands. Women were breeders, very valuable, but certainly not persons in the male sense of the term. During the twentieth century women's lives have been transformed. Women have become persons who, among other things, occasionally (or, if they choose, never) give birth to children. In the 1990s they are not necessarily subordinate or domestic. They are frequently well educated, often economically independent, not uncommonly professionals, often have goals of their own, usually work for wages outside the home, and not infrequently consider themselves free and equal to men, and entitled to justice and equal rights. In the 1890s none of those things were true. Now they are all true.

We do not generally notice all this because, as I noted earlier, cultural revolutions tend to be invisible to their participants. But it means that the fundamental revolution has already occurred. It's over. What that means for the future of motherhood is an open question. What is not open is going back.

So, when traditionalists select a model of the ideal family from the 1950s, a decade not particularly distinguished by anything but the cold war, it should be recognized that the family arrangements prevalent at that time were themselves transitional. They were just a phase in the transformation that was taking place between the old world of the eighteenth century and the new world of the twenty-first. There is no good reason to select the 1950s as having captured the ideal family to be emulated. Indeed, since that decade was characterized by widespread injustice, prejudice, and repression, it cannot stand generally as a model of virtue or morality. And since the lives of women and the role of mother have been in a continuous state of transition during the entire twentieth century, there is no reason to select the 1950s or any other decade as particularly expressive of the essential nature of women or the true role of motherhood. We just do not know whether there are any such things, much less that they are accurately represented by June Cleaver—or for that matter by Murphy Brown.

We know only one thing about women as a class at this point in time. We know that until this century women were profoundly affected by their reproductive destiny. During this century that destiny was dissolved. Many find that frightening, especially traditionalists. They want to know what, then, replaces the old picture of woman and motherhood. But we cannot say. We cannot, ever again, define motherhood for all women, because the dissolution of destiny is freedom.

Notes

1. Cultural change, of course, progresses unevenly, with variations resulting from national, regional, and class-based biases or customs. Working-class attitudes, for example, have always differed from those of the upper classes. Subcultures differ from dominant cultures, as well as from one another. The point is simply that despite the many variations in detail, the general belief that a woman's destiny is motherhood was virtually universal until the late twentieth century. The only honorable exception was the convent.

2. Again, it should go without saying that there are significant cross-cultural

and subcultural variations, and certainly there are huge differences in the technological development of individual countries. Despite these differences, the belief that women are responsible for the home and domestic by nature continues to be widespread and was held almost universally until the quite recent past.

3. Unlike the first two factors, which cut across class lines, there is a significant deviation from this norm for the wife/mother which is based directly on class. A more accurate statement of the norm, then, is that women are to be wives and mothers, and middle- and upper-class women have been dependent on and answerable to their husbands until recently. At the same time, poor women commonly have been breadwinners or otherwise not economically dependent, but until recently were legally answerable and are still physically susceptible to the superior strength of their husbands with little protection available to them from the state. The interesting point is that the lives and status of poor women have always been completely ignored in the understanding of so-called normal behavior for women, even when the norm was formulated in terms of the essential nature of women. Thus, poor women would have been counterexamples if they had counted. In the nineteenth century, for example, American courts declared that women were too frail and unfit to be allowed to practice law; yet the same courts considered poor women sufficiently fit to work in factories and sweatshops without state interference. Thus, despite significant numbers of poor working women, the norm has always been that women are, in virtue of their very nature, wives and mothers, who are dependent and properly answerable to their husbands.

4. This, it may be noted, contrasts directly with the traditional role of men, which is primarily that of breadwinner and/or public participant (e.g., statesman, scholar, scientist, soldier, craftsman) and only secondarily husband and father, except in the context of procreation. Traditionally, it has been considered a sign of manhood to produce children (especially sons), but not to spend time raising them. This is an oversimplification. Until two or three centuries ago, formal education was reserved for the aristocratic elite, who hired (male) tutors for the job. The children of the masses were informally trained by example, girls following their mothers and boys their fathers. But the point still holds. The traditional standard of accomplishment for men is determined by material success or public contribution, not by childrearing. Man is the breadwinner. Woman is the homemaker and caretaker. Those are the traditional complementary roles.

5. The general statistics on birth rates and infant mortality rates are widely quoted, especially for the drop in both during the nineteenth and twentieth centuries. See, e.g., C. Scholten, *Childbearing in American Society, 1650–1850* (New York: New York University Press, 1985), pp. 9–13, 29, 110.

6. I wish I could say that this point is uncontroversial. Unfortunately, there are actually some who deny it. I will not, however, address those views here, since my own view is that the problem is not with those few who deny our overpopulation problem, but with the many who simply ignore it.

7. For statistics on world population and projections of growth see (among others) J. W. Knight and J. C. Callahan, *Preventing Birth: Contemporary Methods and Related Moral Controversies* (Salt Lake City: University of Utah Press, 1989), ch. 2. The figures I use are conservative.

8. To say that children are not investments for individuals is not to deny that they are social investments in the sense that the future of human society is in their hands. But even socially, given changes in technology, the focus is not on producing masses for armies and workforces, but on producing rather well educated individuals who can contribute to future advancement.

9. M. O'Brien, *Reproducing the World*, (Boulder, CO: Westview, 1989), p. 23.

10. Cited in Scholten, p. 13.

11. See, e.g., C. A. MacKinnon, *Toward a Feminist Theory of the State* (Cambridge, MA: Harvard University Press, 1989).

12. See T. Veblen, *The Theory of the Leisure Class* (New York: New American Library, 1958).

13. See, e.g., T. Benedek, "Infertility as a Psychosomatic Disease," in *Fertility and Sterility* 3 (1952): 527ff.

14. See, e.g., B. Ehrenreich and D. English, *For Her Own Good* (New York: Anchor/Doubleday, 1978), pp. 125ff.

15. See, e.g., Deborah Rhode, *Justice and Gender* (Cambridge: Harvard University Press, 1989), pp. 288ff.

16. See, e.g., Rhode; Ehrenreich and English, chs. 3 and 4; D. Kaufman, "Professional Women: How Real Are the Recent Gains?" in *Feminist Philosophies* (Englewood Cliffs, NJ: Prentice Hall, 1992), J. Kourany, J. Sterba, and R. Tong, (eds.), pp. 149–160, noting that in 1920 women comprised 5% of the doctors and 1.4% of the lawyers in the United States, and even in 1960 only 6.8% were doctors and 3.5% were lawyers. But by 1987, 36.5% of U.S. medical degrees and 38.5% of U.S. legal degrees went to women. Kaufman's argument is that these gains are illusory in certain respects, and they are; but they are nonetheless revolutionary.

17. See, e.g., Rhode for a comprehensive treatment.

18. See, e.g., Rhode.

19. Job discrimination in the 1930s, 1940s, and even 1960s is amply documented. See, e.g., Rhode, or A. Kessler-Harris, *Out To Work* (New York: Oxford University Press, 1982). Job discrimination in western Europe during this century has also been documented, although not as thoroughly as in the United States. This does not mean that there was little or no discrimination, but only that it has not been studied as much. Furthermore, women's work patterns began to vary quite a bit during the twentieth century, perhaps the most interesting case being the divergence of patterns within the former Communist bloc. Here sexist discrimination was rather different (but not less prevalent) than in the West. Because of differences in ideology, women of Eastern bloc countries were afforded greater educational and employment opportunities earlier in this century than were

Western women. But these opportunities did not have the same effect that they tend to have in free countries. For instance, they did not make women free, because almost no one was free. They did not put women into positions of (equal or comparable) power, thereby contributing to equality between the sexes, because the sources of power shifted and narrowed to party politics from which women were largely excluded, at least at higher levels. Finally, although women moved into positions of professional equality, there was no corresponding shift toward sharing the burdens of childcare and housekeeping. Eastern European women were afforded the dubious opportunity of juggling conflicting roles several decades before the phenomenon hit Western women hard in the 1980s. But notice that all this occurred during the twentieth century, and is completely compatible with the thesis that the twentieth century is a time of revolutionary change for women, the conclusion of which we cannot yet foretell. The example of women in the Eastern bloc simply shows us that the form and progress of the revolution varies from place to place.

20. "Reasonable chastisement" was a long-standing right of husbands over wives in common law (see, e.g., Rhode, pp. 237ff). Despite its legal demise, chastisement, now in the form of wife battering, continues to be a problem of epidemic proportions that has been outrageously ignored in otherwise civilized societies.

21. I do discuss these issues, as well as others raised in this paper, much more fully in a forthcoming book tentatively titled *The Reproductive Revolution*. Accordingly, the thoughts I offer here should be viewed as a summary and preliminary draft of a larger work in progress.

22. See, e.g., B. Ehrenreich and D. English, *For Her Own Good* (New York: Anchor/Doubleday, 1978), pp. 142–146. It goes without saying, of course, that aristocratic women engaged in neither manufacturing nor cleaning. But they have always constituted a tiny minority.

23. Ehrenreich and English, pp. 142–146, 186, 213.

24. For example, some feminists have argued that the division of labor is due to the desire to keep women at home as a protection of paternity (see, e.g., O'Brien) or to keep them out of competition in labor markets with men (see, e.g., H. Hartmann, "The Unhappy Marriage of Marxism and Feminism," in L. Sargent [ed.], *Women and Revolution*, [Boston: South End Press, 1981], pp. 10ff). Some Marxists have argued that the division of labor provides capitalists with the services of both husband and wife for the price of the man alone, and also that women provide a reserve work force, called in only when needed and dismissed when not (see, e.g., Hartmann).

PART II:
PRENATAL AND
POSTNATAL AUTHORITY

Introduction

Joan C. Callahan

The skills and technologies that have emerged with the development and the use of artificial insemination, oocyte retrieval, in vitro fertilization, embryo transfer, embryo cryopreservation, and various forms of abortion have allowed for the manipulation of gametes, embryos, and fetuses both within and outside of women's bodies, raising a battery of extremely difficult questions regarding the morality and wisdom of developing these manipulations. They have been developed, however, and because they are now available for deployment, they give rise to a set of further questions regarding who should be recognized as having the authority to decide on the disposition of gametes, embryos, and fetuses that are physically detached from women. Closely associated with these questions are others pertaining to born children. For example, when an infant is born to a woman who is not prepared to raise it and she and the genetic father disagree on the custody of their genetic offspring, who should have authority to decide on such custody?

The papers in this section focus on four aspects of these issues, namely, authority to choose a child's sex, authority in the disposition of cryopreserved embryos, authority in the disposition of aborted fetuses, and authority over child custody in nonmarital cases where a woman elects not to retain parental rights and custody of her child.

Sex Selection

Sex selection can be attempted or accomplished in various ways. As Helen Bequaert Holmes points out, the single foolproof way to avoid the birth of a child of the undesired sex is to elect abortion. Using abortion as a sex selection technique, of course, raises all the standard questions about the morality of abortion, some of which will be taken up in part III. But sex selection by abortion raises other questions as well. For example, abortion is usually chosen either because an anomaly is detected in a fetus, or because a woman's health is threatened by a pregnancy, or because a woman chooses not to become a biological parent. In some cases, abortion on the basis of sex is elected because of the possibility of a so-called sex-linked disease, making these cases significantly (if not completely) like those where abortion is elected because of a genetic anomaly in the fetus. But when abortion is elected simply on the basis of the sex of a fetus, none of the ordinary reasons for choosing abortion obtain—there is no anomaly or threat of malady to a fetus; there is no extraordinary threat to a woman's health (at least in most contemporary societies[1]); and the woman would become a parent but for the sex of the fetus. Those who might have no moral reservations about abortion in the "standard" cases are usually much less supportive of abortion purely for the purpose of ensuring that a child will be of a desired sex.

As in the cases of other technologies related to reproduction, the moral and legal questions here are complicated and it is important to answer them separately. That is, it is one thing to hold that abortion simply to fulfill the desire for a child of a certain sex is morally unacceptable; but it is quite another thing to hold that this conclusion should be captured in liberty-limiting legislation. As Holmes points out, feminists have divided on both of these questions; but there is general agreement even among the most strident feminist opponents of sex selection that the practice should not be prohibited by law, whether the selection is attempted or accomplished preconceptually or prenatally through abortion. The two chief reasons feminists have given for this view are that such a prohibition would be unenforceable and, even more important, that permitting prohibition of abortion for this reason opens the door to too much potential interference with women. Perhaps Tabitha Powledge put this point as well as it can be put when, over a decade ago, she said that

> [t]o forbid women to use prenatal diagnostic techniques as a way of picking the sexes of their babies is to begin to delineate acceptable and unacceptable reasons to have an abortion. . . . To make it illegal to use prenatal diagnostic techniques for sex preselection is to nibble away at our hard-won reproductive control. . . . I hate these technologies, but I do not want to see them legally regulated because, quite simply, I do not want to provide an opening wedge for legal regulation of reproduction in general.[2]

Sex selection can also be attempted through manipulation of gametes prior to fertilization. Here, questions regarding the morality of abortion do not arise, but other questions do, chief among them questions pertaining to the interests of women and children when sex selection is practiced. For example, and as Holmes emphasizes, given existing preferences, if sex selection were widely practiced, it is likely that we would see significant changes in the ratio of female to male births, with boys being chosen much more frequently than girls.[3] The possible implications for society generally and for women in particular have been well discussed by numerous commentators, and many of them are extremely troubling, to say the least.[4]

Yet another set of questions has to do with whether meaningful reproductive choice includes being able to choose the sex of one's child and, if it does, whether public monies should be expended on the development of sex selection technologies and whether these technologies, as a matter of justice, need to be made available to all women, not just those wealthy enough to purchase their use. The consensus among feminists seems to be that even though sex selection (via abortion or some other method) should not be prohibited, meaningful reproductive choice does not include an entitlement to choose the sex of one's child and that research on these techniques should be discontinued. In particular, a number of feminists have argued that public funding should not be made available for sex-selection research. Holmes's paper, however, raises an interesting problem for those with this view, namely, that much of the research on methods for discovering genetic anomalies in fetuses—particularly for minimally invasive methods, such as detecting anomalies through a pregnant woman's blood—is dependent first on a method's being able to give unequivocal information on a relatively clear and unambiguous feature, namely, the genetic sex of the fetus. Thus, advances in research on minimally invasive procedures for detecting fetal anomalies are, at this point, directly dependent on research on prenatal sex detection. If funding for this research is discontinued, that would amount to significantly impairing the research progress on better and earlier methods of identifying genetic problems in a fetus.

Perhaps the most interesting question regarding sex selection is whether employing a sex selection technique for reasons other than preventing the birth of a child with an X-linked disease is inherently sexist. Interestingly enough, the late Michael Bayles, whom Christine Overall classifies as a nonfeminist (but not an antifeminist),[5] holds that preferences for a child of a certain sex are inherently sexist, a position embraced by feminists like Powledge. Overall disagrees with this. At the same time, however, she draws a careful distinction between preferences and practices. That is, she argues that an individual's preference for experiencing sexual similarity or sexual complementarity with one's off-spring need not be sexist at all, but that widespread practice of sex se-lection would nonetheless contribute to sexism in societies.[6] Thus, in Overall's view, the *practice* of sex selection should not be condoned, even though preferences for sexual similarity and complementarity need not be morally stained by sexism.

Perhaps the most difficult questions raised by the issue of sex prese-lection have to do with the interests of children. One set of troubling issues here pertains to the expectations that underpin a preference for a child of a certain sex. If (say) one prefers a girl, expecting that she will be a feminist companion, how is a parent likely to feel if that daughter turns out differently? Or if one prefers a son, expecting that he will be "manly" or, to use Overall's distinction in discussing mothers, just significantly unlike oneself, what if he turns out not to be so?

I recently spoke with a woman who was expecting her first grand-child. Her daughter-in-law had had amniocentesis, and they'd learned the child would be a boy. The woman had no discernible preference for a boy grandchild over a girl grandchild, but she was delighted to know that her grandchild would be a boy because, she said, she could now "begin getting ready for him." When asked what that meant, she saw immediately that it meant certain colors for blankets and sweaters, cer-tain sorts of toys and room decorations. Long before he was even born, this child would be started on a "boy track," surrounded by blues and trains, never pinks and dolls. One cannot help but wonder how much of a disappointment he will be if he turns out to prefer pinks and dolls and what the costs of that disappointment might be for him.[7]

The "boy track"/"girl track" dichotomy in our society is genuinely astonishing in its pervasiveness. We need only to spend a few minutes in the local K-Mart to see how we steep our children in what they should be—little-girl bikes are pink and white, often bearing the Little Mermaid or a reasonable facsimile; little-boy bikes have names like "Predator." One of the most popular bike seats for boys these days is boldly stamped "Dominator."[8] And when the children come in from riding their bikes, they play games such as "Old Maid," which effec-tively helps to teach children that women who are not married to men are to be detested and scorned, and which typically offers up the most offensive gender stereotyping for our children's consumption. One ver-sion of Old Maid currently in circulation includes fourteen roles for males (doctor, postman, parachutist, pirate, conductor, farmer, pilot, taxi driver, mountain climber, cameraman, chef, magician, disk jockey, artist) and four roles for females (ballerina, singer, witch, and, of course, the old maid). The numbers of roles alone are sufficient to com-municate the marginalization of girls and women. And, as might be guessed, none of the female roles and only one of the male roles (disk jockey) portray persons of color.[9] Our assumptions about who counts and our expectations are all around our children, long before they even begin their social lives as infants. They are relentlessly schooled in an interlocking system of sex and gender dualisms, male dominance and female subordination, and a host of racial, ethnic, classist, heterosexist, and ageist biases from the beginning. When this is the way the world is, selecting for sex seems a terribly bad idea.

On the other hand, despite Overall's contention that to practice sex selection, particularly selection for male children, is to collude with the patriarchy, there are, in plain, terrible fact, situations in which it is predictable that a female child will have an extremely difficult life. In situations of profound scarcity, for example, where sons continue to be more highly valued than daughters, mothers may face a "Sophie's Choice," needing to decide which of their children will flourish. It is all well and good for us to realize that opting for sons in such circumstances supports patriarchy. Perhaps many of the women in these societies who elect to birth or sustain only boys realize this, as well. But until their political, social, and economic situations change, it is not at all clear that these women haven't a moral obligation to avoid raising daughters in order to do the best that they can for their children.[10] That, however, shifts the burden of responsibility to those of us in more open and privileged societies to do whatever we can to see that the political, social, and economic conditions of women in cultures other than our own do not force those women into such terrible choices. As in so many other issues related to reproduction, and women's health more generally, the issue of sex selection presses us to realize that we are an international community and that the community as a whole will not flourish unless those of us who are relevantly better placed attend to the conditions of other women's lives.

Cryopreserved Embryos

Like artificial insemination by a donor (AID), gamete intrafallopian transfer (GIFT), and most cases of contract motherhood, the deployment of in vitro fertilization (IVF) and cryopreservation of embryos (CE) for future implantation are technologies most frequently used to accomplish the reproduction of a child genetically related to one or two individuals, and the technology therefore raises again all the questions associated with the emphasis on genetic connections that was much of the focus in part I.

Like sex preselection, IVF and CE can also raise the standard problems associated with abortion. That is, the moral center of the anti-choice position is that personhood commences with fertilization. Thus, even though IVF and CE as such do not involve pregnancy, they do, from the anti-choice perspective, involve very early-stage persons. Thus questions regarding the disposition of embryos produced by IVF and the disposition of cryopreserved embryos include the question of the moral status of embryos and fetuses which is at the heart of the abortion debate. Again, we shall take up some of the main questions in the abortion debate in some detail in part III, but some attention needs to be given to them in discussions of CE. For one thing, the legal status of embryos detached from the bodies of women is not as clear as it is in cases of pregnancy, where women, in the United States, at least, are guaranteed the right to seek abortion for any reason through the end of the second trimester of pregnancy. Much of the reasoning in *Roe v. Wade* which yielded that decision in 1973 was based on the dangers to a woman's health as pregnancy proceeds.[11] When embryos are cryopreserved and stored outside a woman's body, the arguments from a woman's health forwarded in *Roe* are not available to settle the question of who should have authority to decide what will happen to them.

Christine Overall's paper in this section focuses on CE, and most particularly on the question of who should have authority in the disposition of cryopreserved embryos when there is disagreement about that disposition between the embryos' progenitors. Overall concentrates her analysis on *Davis v. Davis v. King*, a landmark 1989 Tennessee court case involving the disposition of seven cryopreserved embryos.[12] The two crucial questions for the case, and for this issue more generally, pertain to the legal status of embryos detached from women and to authority to decide what will happen with and to those embryos.

Overall's detailed analysis of the case uncovers a plethora of philosophical assumptions and leaps in reasoning on the part of the court in *Davis*, as well as a number of questions of special interest to feminists. Among the assumptions is the crucial one, made without argument, that both moral and legal personhood commences with fertilization, leading the court in *Davis* to a custody model for resolution. Among the arguments of particular interest to feminists is Junior Davis's claim that his ex-wife should not be permitted to implant the embryos because this would force him to be a parent against his will.

Overall devotes considerable attention to this claim that Mary Sue Davis's successful gestation of one or more of the embryos would violate Junior Davis's right to not reproduce, and she argues that the relevant reproductive right of a man is limited to deciding at the time the sperm leaves his body and is "conveyed to another location." Thus, she says, men "who want to control their sperm should be careful where they put it." According to Overall, there is no plausible argument for extending men's reproductive authority beyond this point and, in particular, no argument for affording men *any* authority whatever once their sperm has been combined with a woman's gamete to produce an embryo.

The matter is quite different, however, when it comes to the question of women's authority. Overall argues not only that Mary Sue Davis should have been granted full authority over the disposition of the embryos, but that in every case where such questions arise, women should be recognized as having full dispositional authority unless they have passed authority over the embryos to another woman or some other agent. Interestingly, part of Overall's reasoning turns on the position that there is something wrong-headed in thinking that embryos' being located "in a petri dish or freezer [makes] them independent of a woman's body" (a point that anticipates Mary B. Mahowald's immediately succeeding discussion of fetal tissue use). Although Overall emphasizes that at least one woman is involved with every embryo, namely the woman who undergoes the procedures to provide the egg and/or the woman into whose uterus the embryo will be implanted, she rests her argument for women's authority in the disposition of cryopreserved embryos not on the "sweat equity" of such involvement, but on future-oriented considerations—most important, on reducing the likelihood that a woman will need to repeat undergoing the burdens of IVF if she will want to gestate and birth a child genetically related to her in the future. Other future-oriented considerations include avoiding contract motherhood arrangements if cryopreserved embryos are placed under the authority of a male progenitor, arrangements which, as was mentioned in the introduction to part I, Overall holds should be discouraged.

Perhaps the most interesting feature of Overall's position is its avoidance of the two most common models for these cases, namely, a joint property model, which would dictate an "equitable distribution" standard for such cases, and a custody model, which would dictate a "best interest of the child" standard, which the *Davis* court adopted. This feature of Overall's view is both conceptually and morally attractive insofar as one thinks that human embryos are neither mere property nor children, a position taken by Joan Mahoney in part I.

Fetal Tissue Use

Although the moratorium on use of public funds for fetal tissue use was lifted by President Clinton shortly after his inauguration, the debate on the moral acceptability of this practice was not (and could not be) quelled by executive order. Mary B. Mahowald's paper takes up both the question of the moral acceptability of fetal tissue use and the question of authority to decide on the disposition of fetal tissue.

A number of the objections to fetal tissue transplantation are also tied to the issue of abortion. It has been suggested that limiting retrieval of fetal tissue for transplantation from fetuses spontaneously aborted does not fall prey to this objection. However, as Mahowald points out, fetuses spontaneously aborted generally are anomalous, and using their tissue might endanger, rather than help, recipients. What is more, it has been objected that even if retrieval and transplantation of fetal tissue were initially limited to spontaneously aborted fetuses, that use would commence entry onto a slippery slope, and we would soon see the movement to using tissue from healthy fetuses intentionally aborted for various reasons followed by using tissue from healthy fetuses intentionally aborted (and perhaps intentionally conceived) for the purpose of retrieving their tissue.

This sort of wedge argument, of course, rests on empirical assumptions that require independent justification. The mere fact that we *could* see these movements does not entail that we would see them or even that it is likely that they would occur. Further, the assumption that it is not morally acceptable to utilize tissue from intentionally aborted fetuses or fetuses intentionally conceived and/or aborted for the purpose of tissue transplantation itself requires independent justification for the slippery slope argument to have any force.

Another objection is that even if intentional abortion (e.g., for the sake of a woman's health or simply because a woman chooses not to become a mother at a given time) can be morally justified, abortion is always a tragic choice or the election of an evil and a clear sense of this should not be lost by utilizing fetal tissue. That is, deploying fetal tissue should not be used to redeem the evil of abortion. One finds this kind of objection to the use of certain medical information, in particular, to the use of information that was gained by Nazi physicians. But if one accepts the premise here, the reply is that a clear sense of the tragic (or, in the case of Nazi experimentation, a clear sense of moral outrage) can be sustained, and might even be enhanced, by attempting to bring about whatever good one can through the use of whatever is available to one. And, of course, one need not accept the claim that abortion is always a tragic choice. Although, as Mahowald points out, feminists have generally held that abortion is chosen by women as the lesser of two evils, it has sometimes been argued that abortion is a positive good insofar as it is necessary to women's well-being.[13]

Closely related to this last objection is the claim that using fetal tissue from intentionally aborted fetuses not only redeems the evil of abortion, it condones abortion as well. But Mahowald objects that approval of abortion is no more entailed for one who deploys fetal tissue from an aborted fetus than approval of drunken driving is entailed for a transplant surgeon who retrieves organs from the brain-dead victim of a drunk-driving accident. Indeed, Mahowald argues that a genuinely pro-life position requires doing all that one can to further life by the deployment of fetal tissue when an abortion decision has been made by another.[14]

Although she deals with such objections, Mahowald's real concern in this paper is to emphasize that previous discussions of fetal tissue use (like discussions of gestational motherhood, abortion, and other issues in human reproduction) have been importantly wrongheaded insofar as they continually focus on fetuses and/or babies rather than the women who bear those fetuses and birth those babies. She explores three ethical frameworks discussed by a Minnesota research group, two of which treat fetuses as being separate from women, while the third treats fetal tissue as the woman's tissue.[15] Mahowald endorses this last framework because it emphasizes the essential tie between fetuses and the women who bear them. Further, this model is helpful in resolving conflicts in contract motherhood cases. Whether a fetus is genetically connected to a gestational mother or not, this model treats fetuses as essentially related to the women who bear them in a way that ensures the authority of the gestational mother regarding questions of both fetal tissue use and parental authority in contract motherhood cases. Mahowald notes that one of the morally attractive features of this model is that it serves as a check on the possibilities for exploitation of women.

It is interesting that both Overall and Mahowald affirm women's authority over the so-called products of conception; yet they do so in what seem to be mutually incompatible ways. For Overall, it is not the previous connection to a woman that justifies a woman's authority in the kinds of embryo cases she discusses. It is, rather, future-oriented considerations (a woman not having to undergo egg retrieval again, the avoidance of future gestational motherhood arrangements, and so on) that ground women's prenatal and postnatal authority. For Mahowald, on the other hand, it is the very nature of a woman's connection to a fetus which grounds her authority over what will be done with a fetus or embryo after its removal from her body. But both of these arguments create problems for cases dealt with by the other theorist. For example, Overall's argument from future-oriented considerations pertaining to risks and exploitation of women, though cogent for the issue of deciding authority in the case of "spare" embryos, seems not to have force in the case of fetal tissue use, since those cases (ordinarily, at least) are not likely to include the concerns about future events that Overall sees for the "spare" embryos cases. On the other hand, Mahowald's argument from an essential connection between a *pregnant* woman and a fetus has no implications for cases such as the Davis case, where Mrs. Davis was not pregnant with one or more of the embryos in question. If Mahowald will argue from connectedness for these cases, it seems that the relevant connectedness between woman and embryo will have to be the genetic one. But that opens the door to the claim that genetic fathers should be recognized as having the same right to parental authority as genetic mothers in cases such as the Davis case.

It might be argued, however, that different kinds of cases require different kinds of resolutions, and that there is no reason to hold that the manner of dealing with questions regarding the disposition of frozen embryos needs to be the same as the manner of dealing with questions regarding authority over fetuses borne by women and the disposition of tissue from fetuses borne by women. Further, it can be argued that those two kinds of cases are importantly different from cases involving the custody of born children, and that yet another approach might be taken to these custodial questions. In the paper that concludes this section, Mary Shanley takes up the question of unwed fathers' rights to claim custody of children they have sired, taking an approach to the question that departs significantly from the approaches of both Overall and Mahowald to the questions they address.

Unwed Fathers' Rights

In the summer of 1993, the case of *Baby Girl Clausen* received massive coverage in the popular media. Baby Girl Clausen, more widely known as "Baby Jessica," had been born on February 8, 1991, to 28-year-old Cara Clausen of Blairstown, Iowa. Cara Clausen deliberately misreported her current boyfriend, Scott Seefeldt, as Jessica's genetic father, and two days after the birth she and Seefeldt gave "irrevocable" consent to Jessica's adoption by Jan and Roberta DeBoer of Ann Arbor, Michigan. Within two weeks, however, Clausen changed her mind about the adoption, and told her ex-boyfriend, Dan Schmidt, that he was Jessica's genetic father. On March 6, 1991, Clausen filed a motion to get Jessica back, and Schmidt filed a comparable motion within a week. Six months later, testing on Schmidt indicated that he was, indeed, Jessica's genetic father. Schmidt argued that since he had not signed away his parental rights, the adoption of Jessica by the DeBoers was void. An Iowa court agreed on December 27, 1991. But the DeBoers decided to fight the decision. A legal stay permitted them to retain custody of Jessica through their appeal to the Iowa Supreme Court. As the appeal dragged on, Dan Schmidt and Cara Clausen married. The Iowa Supreme Court finally upheld the lower court ruling; but the the DeBoers were still not prepared to submit. They attempted to move the case to the Michigan courts; and in February of 1993, the Michigan Circuit Court ruled that the best interests of the child dictated that she stay with the only parents she had ever known—the DeBoers. The Schmidts, however, refused to concede, and they appealed to Michigan's Supreme Court. In July of 1993, Michigan's highest court ruled that Michigan had no jurisdiction in the case and that Jessica was to be handed over to the Schmidts, as had been decided by the Iowa courts, within a month. Still determined not to give up, the DeBoers appealed to the U.S. Supreme Court. On Friday, July 30, 1993, the Court declined to hear the case and instructed the DeBoers to surrender custody of Jessica to the Schmidts on Monday, August 2, 1993. And so, it was done. At two and one-half years of age, Jessica was handed over to her genetic progenitors by the couple who had raised her since her infancy.[16]

Shanley correctly points out that the case, as it unfolded, obscures a central question, namely, whether an unwed father's interest in his genetic offspring should be allowed to justify a veto of an adoption decision made by an unwed mother. This question, Shanley observes, was obscured in this case because Cara Clausen came to regret her decision and Dan Schmidt undertook his attempt to claim the child with her full support. What needs to be noticed is that even though Clausen and Schmidt eventually married, the Iowa courts upheld Dan Schmidt's parental right as an unwed father. Specifically, the Iowa courts upheld the right of an unwed father to claim custody of his genetic offspring when adoption to someone other than the genetic father is willed by a child's genetic and gestational mother. It is this right that Shanley examines.

Shanley lays out four alternatives for settling these cases: (1) adoption of a rule of maternal preference for all cases; (2) a best-interest-of-the-child standard; (3) adoption of a rule affording all interested genetic fathers custody when a genetic/gestational mother relinquishes parental rights, including those cases in which a woman does not want the genetic father to have custody; and (4) a parental responsibility model.

Shanley is concerned to avoid a solution that gives preference to women or men on the basis of sex alone. A pure maternal preference solution would privilege women in a way that Shanley holds will not bear scrutiny. That is, even though it might often be assumed that genetic/gestational mothers will make good judgments for their children, Shanley suggests that it cannot be assumed that genetic fathers will make poorer judgments for theirs. That assumption, according to Shanley, both takes for granted and helps to perpetuate stereotypes regarding men that exclude them from nurturing infants and young children, and it ignores the de facto commitment that a number of individual men have to assuming responsibility for the children they have sired.

Shanley finds the best-interest-of-the-child standard highly questionable, since it may automatically disadvantage a genetic father who is not able to offer a child a two-parent home. In addition, it invites abuse by stacking the deck in favor of potential adopting parents who are economically better off than a genetic father, a complaint raised by some contract motherhood cases.[17]

Shanley rejects the third alternative (affording custody to all interested genetic fathers despite the will of genetic/gestational mothers) on the grounds that a general rule privileging a genetic father's will to take custody over a mother's willing his not taking custody violates sexual equality every bit as much as a maternal preference rule does; that such a rule privileges genetic connections in a troubling way by letting a genetic tie alone establish a right to custody; and that such a rule fails to recognize that context always matters in these cases. Thus, Shanley argues that not only may it not be assumed that a woman who elects to relinquish her child to adoptive parents is not interested in the child; it must be assumed that she may have very good reasons for not wanting the child to be placed in the custody of its genetic father. Serious attention, then, must be given to a woman's reasons for not wanting her child's genetic father to take custody. This leads to the fourth alternative, which Shanley adopts.

The model Shanley suggests is a parental responsibility model, which takes into central account a genetic father's attempt to do all that he can to express paternal concern prior to a child's birth. At the very least, says Shanley, this would include a man's attempting to ascertain whether a woman with whom he has had sexual relations has gotten pregnant and a public registering (on, say, a "father's registry") prior to the child's birth of his desire to assume custody of the child. Other requirements would (again) involve careful consideration of any reasons a woman might have for not wanting the genetic father to take custody of the child.

Although such a policy is far more complicated to administer than a clean rule of maternal preference or paternal custody in these cases, Shanley's hope is that such a policy will attend to genetic ties, while not overemphasizing them, and will foster meaningful equality between men and women, while doing all that reasonably can be done to ensure that all children will be nurtured by committed parents. With this suggestion, Shanley rejects parental *authority* as a fundamental moral category, making that authority instead an implication of the assumption of parental *responsibility*. In this way, her paper is strongly reminiscent of Joan Mahoney's paper in part I, which argues that the ties that should bind by law are those of commitment and nurturance.

Notes

1. But see Holmes' discussion of the risks to Indian women who fail to bear sons and the examples from other cultures offered in Gena Corea, *The Mother Machine: Reproductive Technologies from Artificial Insemination to Artificial Wombs* (New York: Harper & Row, 1985), Ch. 10.

2. Tabitha Powledge, "On Choosing Children's Sex," in Helen Bequaert Holmes, Betty B. Hoskins, and Michael Gross, eds., *The Custom-Made Child: Women-Centered Perspectives* (Clifton, NJ: Humana Press, 1981), pp. 193–199. Other examples are Roberta Steinbacher, "Sex Preselection: From Here to Fraternity," in Carol C. Gould, ed., *Beyond Dominion: New Perspectives on Women and Philosophy* (Totowa, NJ: Rowman and Allenheld, 1984), pp. 274–282; Dorothy C. Wertz and John C. Fletcher, "Sex Selection Through Prenatal Diagnosis: A Feminist Critique," in Helen Bequaert Holmes and Laura M. Purdy, eds., *Feminist Perspectives in Medical Ethics* (Bloomington: Indiana University Press, 1992), pp. 240–253.

3. For another current discussion of the worldwide preference for male children, see Robyn Rowland, *Living Laboratories: Women and Reproductive Technologies* (Bloomington: Indiana University Press, 1992), ch. 2.

4. See, e.g., L. Fidell, D. Hoffman, and P. Keith-Spiegel, "Some Implications of Sex-Choice Technology," *Psychology of Women Quarterly* 4/1 (1979): 32–42; S. F. Hartley and L. Pietraczk, "Preselecting the Sex of Offspring: Technologies, Attitudes, and Implications," *Social Biology* 20 (1979): 232–46; Roberta Steinbacher, "Preselection of Sex: The Social Consequences of Choice," *The Sciences* 20/4 (1980): 6–9, 28; several papers in Holmes, Hoskins, and Gross, eds., *The Custom-Made Child*; several papers in N. Bennett, ed., *Sex Selection of Children* (New York: Academic Press, 1983); Steinbacher, "Sex Preselection: From Here to Fraternity"; Corea, *The Mother Machine*; Mary Anne Warren, *Gendercide: The Implications of Sex Selection* (Totowa, NJ: Rowman and Allanheld, 1985); several papers in Gena Corea et al., *Man-Made Women: How New Reproductive Technologies Affect Women* (Bloomington: Indiana University Press, 1987); Rowland, *Living Laboratories*.

5. Christine Overall, *Ethics and Human Reproduction: A Feminist Analysis*

(Boston: Allen and Unwin, 1987). See Michael D. Bayles, *Reproductive Ethics* (Englewood Cliffs, NJ: Prentice Hall, 1984), p. 33.

6. Overall, *Ethics and Human Reproduction*, Ch. 2.

7. The costs are all too often deadly. Gender stereotypes are intimately tied to heterosexism, which remains one of the most oppressive features of patriarchy. It is well known that in recent years hate crimes, many of them violent, against gay men and lesbians are being reported with increasing frequency, and that jurisdictions throughout the United States are, with greater and greater frequency, attempting to ensure that the civil rights of gay men and lesbians are not expressly protected by the law. What is not as well known is that heterosexism and the internalized homophobia it brings with it may be a chief cause of suicide among teenagers. Currently, it is thought that as many as 30 percent of gay male and lesbian teens have attempted suicide, with their sexual orientation a significant causal factor. See, e.g., Chris Bull, "Suicidal Tendencies: Is Anguish over Sexual Orientation Causing Gay and Lesbian Teens to Kill Themselves?" *The Advocate* 652 (5 April 1994): 34–42.

8. Susan Bordo makes the same point with a similar example, carrying it into mapping sexuality for teenagers:

> Consider a K-mart advertisement for boy's and girl's bicycles. The ad describes three levels of bikes: one for toddlers (three-wheelers), one for pre-teeners, and one for teenagers. Each model has a boy's version and a girl's version, each with its own name. The toddler's models are named "Lion" and "Little Angel"; the pre-teener's, "Pursuit" and "St. Helen." But while the duality of male activity and female passivity is thus strikingly mapped onto pre-adolescence, once sexual maturity is reached, other dualities emerge: the teenager's models are named "Granite Pass" and "White Heat"!

The quote is from Susan R. Bordo, *Unbearable Weight: Feminism, Western Culture, and the Body* (Berkeley: University of California Press, 1993), p. 14.

9. *Old Maid*, a Benny Card Game, made in China, distributed by East-West Distributing Company, Deerfield, IL 60015.

10. The point was first brought home to me by one of my graduate students, Beth Rosdatter.

11. *Roe v. Wade*, 410 U.S. 113 (1973). See the introduction to part IV for an articulation of the argument from women's health in *Roe*.

12. *Davis v. Davis v. King*, E-14496 (5th Jud. Ct. Tennessee, 1989).

13. See Joan C. Callahan, "Ensuring a Stillborn: The Ethics of Lethal Injection in Late Abortion," this volume, n. 9.

14. For further development of such characterizations of a genuinely pro-life position, see Mary Briody Mahowald, *Women and Children in Health Care: An Unequal Majority* (New York: Oxford, 1993).

15. Dorothy E. Vawter et al., *The Use of Human Fetal Tissue: Scientific, Ethical and Policy Concerns* (Minneapolis: University of Minnesota Press, 1990).

16. See, e.g., Nancy Gibbs, "In Whose Interest?" *Time*, 19 July 1993, 45–50; and Maryanne George, "DeBoers Give Up Fight," *Detroit Free Press*, Wednesday, 28 July 1993, A1, A2.

17. An example of this bias is baldly expressed by George P. Smith III in "The Case of Baby M: Love's Labor Lost," in Larry Gostin, ed., *Surrogate Motherhood: Politics and Privacy* (Bloomington: Indiana University Press, 1990), pp. 233–242. Says Smith (p. 235):

> Parents with good educations, attractive jobs, and financial security should—in the normal course of affairs—be able to afford a child better care and better opportunities for growth than would a less advantaged family. It is really that simple.

But, of course, it isn't that simple. For a discussion of the middle-class biases against Mary Beth Whitehead in the Baby M case, see Bonnie Steinbock, "Surrogate Motherhood as Prenatal Adoption," in Gostin, ed., pp. 123–135.

Choosing Children's Sex: Challenges to Feminist Ethics

Helen Bequaert Holmes

> If the person is from a month old up to five years old,
> your valuation shall be for a male five shekels of silver,
> and for a female your valuation shall be three shekels of
> silver.
>
> —Leviticus 27:6.

> WHEN THE STORK
> DELIVERS A BOY
> OUR WHOLE
> DARN FACTORY
> JUMPS FOR JOY
> BURMA SHAVE
>
> —1963 Burma-Shave roadside rhyme.

> IT'S A BOY!
> —Great Moments 1992 Michelob Beer television commercial.

From prehistory through the twentieth century, the preference has been for males—as tiny newborns, as teenage athletes, as senators, whatever. Females may be preferred for one or another specific purpose, such as gestating fetuses or changing diapers or caring for the senile, but not in general. Those who *simply* prefer females or who genuinely have no preference are in the minority.

Choosing the sex of a future child, or choosing *not* to choose, is no longer a hypothetical issue. Wherever "Western" medicine is practiced, pregnant upper- and middle-class women receive ultrasound scans of their fetuses and are told the sex unless they assertively preempt the message by begging nurse, doctor, or technician to keep the secret. For unplanned pregnancies—and for some planned ones—the idea must flit through each woman's head: shall sex influence my choice to abort?

Unless targeted killing of female fetuses occurs, the normal secondary sex ratio—the ratio at birth—in human populations is 50 females to 53 males.[1] Unless female infanticide or neglect occurs, this reaches 50:50 in the early teens: boys are more vulnerable to childhood diseases and accidents. In the United States, by the age of marriage this ratio has

148

skewed to 52 females for every 50 males; as people age, the ratio becomes more skewed—for example, to 50:20 at age 85.[2] In an extensive study of human sex ratios, Guttentag and Secord found that throughout history in various geographical locations, sex ratios have been highly skewed—from losses in war, mass migrations of men, or such cultural practices as child neglect and infanticide. Their review of the effects of various ratios on peoples' lives shows that, in general—although there are many exceptions—women seem to benefit most when sex ratios are close to 50:50. When their proportion is lower, women may be confined to traditional gender roles and excluded from high-status positions; when their proportion is higher, misogyny increases, and women are likely to be exploited in sexual relationships and have difficulty in finding committed male partners.[3] Although I have deliberately oversimplified here to argue *for* the 50:50 society, a biased sex ratio might indeed *benefit* women, given certain power relationships between the sexes in a given society. Mary Anne Warren, author of the first major book on sex selection, presents a thorough and thoughtful analysis of the nuanced implications of Guttentag and Secord's discussion.[4]

In what follows, I plan to show how the case of choosing a child's sex raises perplexing questions about legitimate use of autonomy and can get us into hot water as we attempt to apply feminist theory and feminist ethics to reproductive medicine. First, I shall select and examine some arguments supporting sex selection and then some arguments opposing it. My aim here is not to be comprehensive nor to survey the considerable literature on the ethical issues, but merely to introduce themes for in-depth analysis later.[5] For further background, I'll summarize the state of the art—what is technically possible now in sex detection and sex determination. Then I shall describe how certain aspects of the technology foster commercialization of sex selection by "hoaxers, incompetents, madmen, and cranks, as well as scientists."[6] After discussing the special case of sex-linked diseases and the feminist issues they raise, I turn to four challenges to feminist ethics for which sex selection is an ideal exemplar. I conclude by outlining difficulties that hinder the formulation of effective and just policies on sex selection, policies that can foster feminist goals.

Sex selection has been called a "paradigm, a type case, for policy decisions about genetic engineering in general."[7] Further, it is perhaps the best type case for applying feminist ethics to *all* reproductive technologies, not just to genetic engineering. One commonly used type case, infertility "treatment" (artificial insemination, in vitro fertilization [IVF], etc.) applies to only one-tenth of the population; another, prenatal diagnosis of genetic anomalies, is relevant in even fewer pregnancies. However, since *every* fetus is "at risk" for sex, every pregnancy is at risk for sex selection. Furthermore, sex selection is no pipe dream: some techniques—not, of course, the hoaxes—are now completely effective.

In my arguments I make no moral distinction between preconception and postconception sex selection. If a couple wishes to choose the sex of their child but does not do so because it involves abortion, the *desire*, in my view, is the moral issue. Potential consumers of sex selection technologies, however, are likely to make a strong distinction between preconception and postconception methods. The reasons someone does not abort a fetus of the "wrong" sex may be practical, political, social, or moral: for example, cost, refusal of a doctor to cooperate, fear of objections from friends or relatives, religious dictum, bonding already with that fetus, a state law, a belief that elective abortion is immoral. Commercial methods that purport to select sex are more likely to succeed in attracting the public when they use *preconception* sex selection methods and preempt the variety of reasons people have for not selecting sex via abortion.

Arguments for Sex Selection

Several reasons have been advanced for letting people choose their children's sex. First, of course, is freedom of choice—we should have the right to do anything we wish as long as it doesn't harm other people. This includes using the advances of technology to exercise our freedom—for example, taking the Concorde to Paris to visit the Louvre or selecting the sex composition of our family. According to Bill Allen, a prospective father interviewed on the 1981 *Hard Choices* "Boy or Girl?" TV program, "Why shouldn't we have the right . . . to do that sort of [family] planning?"[8]

Of course, such a person would not select sex unless he or she believed that it would increase happiness—for one or both parents and for the selected child. Warren considers in depth the happiness aspect of the free choice argument, pointing out the dangers inherent in unrealistic expectations of one's child. Yet she concludes, "Getting what one wants is not a guarantee of happiness, but it is usually a good deal more conducive to happiness than *not* getting what one wants."[9]

Acquiring a "balanced family" is yet another facet of the happiness and free choice argument. One nonsexist justification for trying to achieve such a family is that children would grow up without sex bias, that girls would learn to get along with boys and vice versa. Balance (for whatever reason) is very important to upper- and middle-class parents in North America. In her analysis of 2505 letters written by couples wishing to have sperm separation for sex selection, Nan Chico found that 86 percent of the writers gave balance (not necessarily using that term) as an important reason for applying.[10] (And how many of us have said when visiting a new baby, "How nice to have one of each!") The search for balance is a key reason why parents can be victims of unproved sex selection schemes and the motivation for most sex selection case studies in textbooks: "Mr. and Mrs. X have three daughters; Mrs. X discovers that she is pregnant. . . . "

Christine Overall, whose book is a feminist analysis of reproductive technologies, argues persuasively for another nonsexist and morally acceptable reason to prefer a child of a certain sex. Putting a strong emphasis on experience, she claims that sex preferences in "the lived experience of close human relationships" are not necessarily sexist.

> [F]undamental differences between the experiences of the sexes are not just the result of socialization, but they are not just biological either, since they are constituted by our *awareness* of the capacities unique to our sex.
>
> If one's sex is central to one's own identity, then . . the sex of other persons will be significant in . . . relationships involving strong friendship, love and/or sexual intimacy . . . [11]

According to Overall, a lesbian's preference for intimate relations with another women is not sexist. She continues, "One would be seeking a child of a specific sex because of the anticipated rewards and pleasures to be gained through a parenting relationship with a younger human being who is either like oneself or different from oneself in . . . sexual identity." Yet she then questions whether this reason is "*sufficient* to justify the practice of sex preselection."[12]

A step beyond *permitting* sex selection is *advocating* it. For example, some physicians favor its use to avoid sex-linked diseases.[13] Even those authors who generally denounce sex selection may sanction it for families at risk of any such disease.[14] Prima facie, this seems to be a straightforward argument for sex selection because sex-linked diseases are relatively common, usually afflict only males, and are often devastating or lethal in their effects. Yet a feminist ethics sees a nuanced mesh of complications in what seems to be a clear argument—so important that I discuss the mesh separately below.

Population control is yet another reason proposed for choosing sex, that is, for choosing males. John Postgate claimed in 1973 that overpopulation is "the only really important problem facing humanity today."[15] The argument that selecting males can ameliorate overpopulation is mathematically sound: equations used in population ecology show clearly that rates of population growth decrease when the proportion of females in a population drops. The population control movement has long advocated male selection: Ehrlich in his 1968 *Population Bomb*; Postgate, who in 1973 urged stopping "multiplication in . . . unenlightened communities"; Luce, who in 1978 proposed "the manchild pill"; and, recently and cautiously, Kuhse and Singer.[16]

Feminists might claim that if sex choice were practiced universally, then all girls who exist would be wanted as girls. Many women suffer because they've been unwanted—in a family, in a job, in a classroom— simply because of their sex. So why not spare the next generation this pain? We have no way to measure how much or how little suffering would be prevented by knowing that one was wanted only for one's sex (and hence to play some sex role), wanted to be a little sister for a first-born male, or wanted to balance a family. And, as a perceptive Spelman College student once pointed out to me, what her father expected of a boy would have made life very difficult for his son, and she thus was better off as an obviously unwanted girl.

However, wantedness or unwantedness in an affluent American family is trivial compared to the neglect, abuse, and even death suffered by girls in such countries as India, China, and Korea.[17] Therefore logic might dictate that feminists concerned about women worldwide should aggressively advocate the development of cheap, safe, and effective means of male sex selection—a much stronger stance than simply considering the process morally permissible. This blends into another feminist argument for sex selection—mere survival of adult women. Mothers who have only daughters in India and China, for example, undergo ostracism, are at risk for suicide, and often face beatings, divorce, or fatal "accidents."[18]

An assertively feminist reason for selecting children's sex is to use it as a strategy for resistance to patriarchy. Warren argues that some feminists might choose to have sons to raise them to be nonsexist; others might raise daughters in order not to contribute to the ruling sex class or to establish all-female communities. Although, in her view, these uses of sex selection are ways in which women may resist male domination, sex selection in itself will not be sufficient to overthrow that domination. Warren argues that these tactics are not "a substitute for any of the substantive goals of feminism," and "to the extent that these goals are met, interest in selecting sex will decline."[19]

Arguments against Sex Selection

Few doubt that if sex selection were cheap and effective, many more males than females would be born. From this Amitai Etzioni postulated dire consequences: more crime, less culture and churchgoing, "the rougher features of a frontier town."[20] If fewer men can marry, this is likely to have a negative impact on their health and longevity.[21]

Sex selection literature often emphasizes the desire of most prospective parents for a firstborn male. Are girls handicapped if they are not firstborns? Most authors who take an anti-selection stance argue that they are. However, after surveying the literature, Warren adopts the opposite view. Strongly influenced by the conclusions of Ernst and Angst, who in 1983 reviewed the results of some 1500 studies, Warren states, "Nearly all of the reports of birth-order effects are due to errors in the design of the studies and the analysis of the data. . . . [I]t would seem that virtually any outcome can be 'explained' in terms of birth order, but that no particular outcome can ever be predicted."[22]

Another argument counteracts the population control advocates: use of sex selection for such a purpose is not only morally suspect, but might have the opposite effect—it might actually *increase* population. First on the moral question here, Warren and I have each pointed out the pernicious misogyny, racism, and classism of eliminating females to control populations.[23] If a cheap chemical to put in drinking water, a pill, or an injection were developed, its use might be required for under-developed countries, say, to get World Bank loans or to become "most favored nation" trading partner of the United States. Second, there is the mathematical argument that selecting males might lead to higher population because a shortage of women is likely to change other numbers in the population equation as well. For example, the fact that women were few might cause governments to decree (or might cause customs to arise among the people for) an earlier age for first childbearing, shorter intervals between children, or prohibition of the lesbian lifestyle—all of which would tend to increase population.

Many feminists and their sympathizers argue vehemently that any sex selection is sexist: "one of the most stupendously sexist acts in which it is possible to engage"[24]; that it moves us into the "realm of previctimization . . . women being destroyed and sacrificed before even being born;"[25] that "a preference for one sex over the other, for its own sake, is simply sexism. . . . [M]any of the most common instrumental reasons [for desiring a child of a particular sex] probably mask an irrational sexism"[26]; or "[A]ny argument for sex selection cannot overcome the unfair and sexist bias of a choice to select the sex of a child."[27]

A variant of the sexism allegation is that exercising sex selection, even if one has nonsexist reasons, reinforces sexism. Consider Overall's response to Warren's arguments that selecting a boy "may be motivated by an unselfish desire to ensure that the child will have the best possible life" and that "poor people have the right to seek to better their economic status by having sons rather than daughters."[28] Warren concludes that these actions and desires may be a result of sexism in society, but are not inherently sexist. Overall, however, holds that such reasons represent "complicity with the patriarchal system," and that choosing sons for these reasons is "still a way of saying yes . . . to patriarchal power and the oppression of women."[29]

Many authors believe that sex selection is nothing more than eugenics and base their strongest objections on this. Sex selection clearly fits the definition, "the striving to increase wanted traits in the population."[30] According to Ruth Hubbard, "Eugenics died down in the 1930s . . . partly because it didn't work. . . . We now have a whole series of techniques that *will* do the job. Sex preselection is one of them."[31] Another facet to the discussion is a slippery slope variant: if sex has nothing to do with disease, will we set precedents for attempts to select other nondisease characteristics that many people already include in visualizing their perfect children?[32] Still another consideration is that sex selection may be the entrée into a game of *personal* eugenics. Previously, we worried about evil dictators imposing eugenics on large populations; now parents may impose it on their children.[33]

Before we ferret out the feminist dilemmas sparked by these arguments and discuss some perplexing questions of public policy, let's take a close look at what currently is technically feasible.

The State of the Art

Fetal Sex Detection in the Uterus. With access to modern medical technology, prospective parents almost invariably learn the sex of their fetus. Routine ultrasound in the second trimester can identify sex correctly about 90 percent of the time.[34] Visualization is difficult in obese women and in breech presentations; accuracy depends on the skill of the sonogram readers and the quality of the equipment. Recent improvements in ultrasonography include putting the transducer up the vagina instead of on the abdomen, which has increased the accuracy of ascertainment to about 95 percent.[35] Therefore, except for the possibility of false results (and sonographers usually honestly report any uncertainty about the sex), all couples in Western Europe, North America, and Australasia can, at least in theory, act on a sex preference by requesting abortion.

Two other prenatal diagnostic technologies—chorionic villus sampling (CVS) and amniocentesis—are routinely prescribed to screen for defective fetuses in women over 35. Sex detection is usually incidental in these cases—but the accuracy here is essentially 100 percent (except when vials get mixed or mislabelled).[36] Results from CVS can be reported during the first trimester, and a few centers also do "early amnio," which can give results early in the second trimester before quickening.[37] If one plans to abort for sex, such early data can minimize emotional problems (which often occur after quickening or when the pregnancy shows) or political problems (in locations where second-trimester abortion is not permitted).

To be done properly, ultrasound, amniocentesis, and CVS require costly equipment and skilled technicians; they are done with the pregnant women's knowledge; all three are inconvenient; the latter two are unpleasant and worrisome.[38] Therefore, a 1989 breakthrough in finding fetal cells circulating in women's blood is significant. Because very few fetal blood cells cross the placenta, sophisticated technologies are required to find them, to concentrate them, and then to determine whether they really come from the fetus.[39] These techniques, which have been hailed as potential noninvasive methods of detecting fetal abnormalities, are still quite crude. However, once they get refined, fetal sex might be detected without a woman's knowledge after a mere needle stick; furthermore, in the current poor state of the art, sex is the trait experimenters must use in working out each technique. (And they must take care not to be fooled by male cells still circulating in the blood from a previous pregnancy!) Every pregnant woman's fetus has a sex; so any pregnant woman could be recruited for *any* experiment involving sifting through blood for those elusive cells.

Sex Detection in the Test Tube Embryo. Called "preimplantation diagnosis" or "embryo biopsy," analysis of the chromosomes in a cell removed from an early "test tube" embryo has been touted as a marvelous way to prevent the birth of defective infants *without* using abortion.[40] Some mothers of children with cystic fibrosis (CF) would like this method to be perfected so that, by using IVF, they could have an embryo implanted that is free of CF. This would let them avoid the message that abortion of a CF fetus otherwise would give to their living CF child.[41] The techniques take considerable skill, and many bugs must still be worked out. For example, the covering of the early embryo—the zona—must be dissected away for a cell to be removed. The removed cell, of course, is destroyed in the testing, but the remaining cells should be able to form a complete baby with no missing parts.[42] Another caution, however, is the poor success of IVF. Only 16 to 18 percent of transferred embryos result in a "take-home baby,"[43] although with *fertile* couples the percentage might be higher.

But here again, as in the technologies already mentioned, the easiest trait to detect is sex and so the early experiments on preimplantation diagnosis are in sex detection. Most researchers do recruit experimental subjects who are indeed at risk for offspring with sex-linked diseases, and many such women are very eager to participate.[44] Yet, confidence in this method is so low that usually the sex of each implanted fetus is checked later by CVS and by repeated ultrasonography.[45]

Sex Determination before Conception. A logical way to specify sex would be to separate sperm in a semen sample so that either those with X-chromosomes or those with Y-chromosomes are the only ones contacting an egg.[46] A clinic's laboratory might separate the sperm, or an at-home method might use a device or take advantage of some aspect of the female reproductive cycle. Since the 1960s many have played with both at-home and laboratory methods and produced theories for separating or favoring one or another sperm type—imaginative and ingenious theories. But none works. Any proposed theory gets nourished by the fact that the actual 52:50 ratio is really quite good as gambling odds go.

a) *At-home methods.* Folk methods from previous centuries have reappeared disguised in twentieth century medical language. One involves specifying the prospective mother's diet: in modern lingo, minerals in her diet might affect the cervical mucus, the inner surface of the fallopian tubes, or the egg surface and thus allow only one kind of sperm to pass through the cervix, travel up the fallopian tube, or penetrate the egg, as the case may be.[47] But only the diet theorists themselves publish the data to "prove" their theories; there are no independent confirmations. One critic has pointed out that the high calcium in the "girl diet" puts women at risk of kidney problems or excessive nervousness, while the "boy diet" with high salt and very low calcium is especially risky, since it may lead to edema and hypertension.[48]

Other hardy perennials are douches (alkaline for boy; acidic for girl), positions for intercourse (from the rear for boy; missionary for girl); female orgasm (before male orgasm for boy; not at all for girl); frequency of coitus (more for boys).[49] Not all folk methods agree with each other—they are notably discrepant about when, in a woman's cycle, to time intercourse (a really hardy perennial).

Let us scrutinize two conflicting timing theories. According to the Shettles theory, which has been presented to the U.S. public in popular magazines and in three editions of a book written by Landrum Shettles with David Rorvik (1970, 1984, 1989), the Y-bearing sperm are smaller, travel faster up the fallopian tube, and reach the ovary before the X-sperm. If a Y-bearing sperm reaches an egg just as it poofs out of the ovary, it will fertilize the egg and determine a boy; if the Y-sperm have to wait, the somewhat tougher X-sperm will arrive on the scene. For data, Shettles claims to have observed microscopically two different sizes of sperm, with the smaller ones moving more quickly. He also claims that couples who use his method do indeed have boys if they time intercourse close to the moment of ovulation, and girls if intercourse occurs two or three days before ovulation.[50] However, independent researchers have not corroborated these results; in fact, studies designed to test his results and other studies in which time of fertilization can be correlated with sex of a baby at birth seem to *refute* rather than support Shettles's hypothesis.[51]

In 1977, Elizabeth Whelan proposed a competing theory in her book *Boy or Girl?* She advocated intercourse close to ovulation to obtain a girl and based her theory on reports in the medical literature by Guerrero and by Harlap.[52] Those two researchers' results are suspect, however, because Guerrero's clients were ones who failed at the rhythm method of contraception and Harlap asked mothers to recollect the time of intercourse nine months later, that is, after each baby was born.[53]

In the 1970s and 1980s, disciples who believed in a timing theory used thermal and mucus methods to time ovulation; now, with the advent of ovulation test kits, ovulation can be timed better—but that can't correct a faulty theory.

If any timing theory really worked, selecting sex could be done without telling friends, family, or professionals, and would avoid the intricacies of abortion. Although a partner's cooperation would be useful, it could be controlled by the woman without his knowing by feigning "headaches" or lust, or by appropriate use of the diaphragm. It would be cheap: one could copy instructions from a library book and use the cervical mucus test (free), a basal body temperature thermometer ($6–$10), or an ovulation detection kit ($15–20).

b) *Laboratory sperm separation.* Separation techniques that have survived into the '90s are the sephadex method, which allegedly concentrates X-bearing sperm, and the albumin swim-up, which allegedly concentrates Y-bearing sperm. Ronald Ericsson has several patents on the latter, known as the "Ericsson Method." In each technique, the treated sperm sample is then used in artificial insemination. Advocates of each method claim up to 85 percent success.[54] Several challengers, however, have used one or another technique to detect Y chromosomes in sperm from the separated semen and demonstrated that the methods do not work—that is, they do not enrich above 50 percent.[55]

Although advocates argue that the proof is in the babies, no independent investigators have assessed the sex of those babies. According to Renee Martin, a physician skilled in detecting Y chromosomes, "Some studies . . . have relied on clients to inform the clinic of the baby's sex. This practice could easily bias the results as couples who had a child of the desired sex . . . might be more likely to report their success."[56] Furthermore, clients using any sex-selective methods are required to sign a consent form that states that they know the method is not foolproof and agree to accept (not abort) the fetus whatever its sex. This means that clients who have ultrasound or amniocentesis (routinely or for the purpose of learning sex) and find out that the technique did not work must sneak off somewhere else for an abortion if they decide to renounce the consent form. They certainly will not report the sex of their conceptus, and clinic directors are unlikely to chase down such clients because they know that artificial insemination, even with nonmanipulated semen samples, often fails.

c) *Hormone stimulation.* When prescribing fertility drugs to subfertile women became standard medical practice in the late 1970s and early 1980s, practitioners began to notice a slight preponderance of female offspring.[57] Clomiphene citrate (Clomid), especially, seems to have this effect. Paul Zarutskie and his colleagues, after reviewing the published reports in this area, conclude that statistically the percentage of females does indeed increase, but so little that the use of these drugs is of little practical importance for an individual couple.[58]

Physicians, thus, have played with a variety of methods which seem to change the secondary sex ratio a little when used by their proponents. This nebulous situation has stimulated several reputable physicians to try the shotgun approach. Sharon Jaffe and her colleagues at the Columbia University College of Physicians and Surgeons and Mark Geier and his colleagues in Bethesda, Maryland, use intrauterine insemination with husband's sperm after sperm separation, timing in the cycle, *and* Clomid. The Columbia team tries for both males and females, using the Ericsson method; for female selection, they use Clomid and a sperm fraction allegedly *not* enriched for Y-sperm. For boy babies, their results are no better than chance alone; for girls, they report 78.6 percent success.[59] Geier's team separates with sephadex and tries only for females, reporting 80 percent success.[60] The latter report so far has prompted two criticisms: one challenges their statistics; the other suggests that they may not have included all births, and that Clomid or intrauterine insemination, but not the sephadex technique, might have been responsible.[61]

Sex Selection Entrepreneurs

In 1968, Etzioni predicted, "If a simple and safe method of sex control were available, there would probably be no difficulty in finding the investors to promote it because there is a mass-market potential."[62] He did not say "effective." Now we have simple, safe, ineffective methods and we find that his "promotion" prediction has come true. Two factors should nourish the business in sex selection in the United States: (1) Most couples want a "balanced" family; (2) any method tried, even an ineffective one, has a 52:50 success chance—excellent odds. In fact, because of those odds, and because couples who "fail" rarely tell, some entrepreneurs fool even themselves—that is, they honestly believe in what they are doing.

Colorado entrepreneur Robert Marsik, after personal "success" in using Shettles's method to get a daughter to balance the son he already had, founded a company to capitalize on that method. In 1986 his Pro-Care Industries Ltd started selling Gender Choice, in pink and blue kits, for $49.95. Each kit contained a douche powder, several disposable thermometers to detect the moment of ovulation, and instructions. Later in 1986, however, the Food and Drug Administration told Pro-Care to halt distribution of Gender Choice until documents on its efficacy were submitted. Arguing that the kit was not a medical device, Pro-Care removed the douche powder, modified the instructions to say that not all members of the scientific community agreed with the theory, and offered a money-back guarantee. Although Pro-Care's 1986 sales were $1.1 million, sales dropped in 1987 when the FDA labelled the product a "gross deception on the consumer." Product returns in 1987 and 1988 were greater than sales, so Pro-Care filed for bankruptcy in 1988.[63]

Another entrepreneurship was developed by Ronald Ericsson in the 1970s when he franchised the albumin swim-up method of enriching for Y-sperm described above. His Gametrics Limited sells the method to clinics, which charge customers various rates, usually about $500 per insemination attempt. Since almost any manipulation of semen lowers sperm count, and since artificial insemination has a poor success rate even with a good count, the method takes many inseminations (not a very pleasant experience) and thus can be quite expensive. In 1987 Gametrics Limited reported a success rate of 86 percent boys.[64] Ever since 1975, the "Ericsson Method" has inspired some researchers in the gynecology community to test sperm samples "enriched" via albumin gradients; as described above, all studies outside the Gametrics Limited circle find no enrichment of Y-sperm. Nevertheless, the franchise continues to open clinics, including, recently, one in London.[65]

The situation with physician John Stephens is quite different—first, because his method *is* effective, and second, because it involves selective abortion. In 1984 Stephens incorporated his California Prenatal Diagnosis institute to do ultrasound for identifying fetal sex and named it Koala Labs with the "Service Mark" FASA (Fetal Anatomic Sex Assignment). He promises accurate sex assignment of females at 14 weeks and males at 12 weeks.[66] Although he advertised widely, especially in San Francisco periodicals aimed at South Asians, critics objected to the obvious sex selection, and by 1988 his business was not going well. Presumably, also, some potential customers were getting routine ultrasound covered by their health insurance. In 1990, Stephens set up another Koala Labs in northern Washington; in 1991 he was granted United States Patent #4,986,274 on FASA. He now advertises this $500 service across the border in Canada via direct-mail flyers in the Punjabi language and in *The Link*, an Indo-Canadian community newspaper in Vancouver. "Indo-Canadian women have taken up the fight against Stephens; we are still waiting for other groups of women to take up this fight with us."[67]

Sex-Linked Disease as a Feminist Issue

The problem of how to alleviate, to "cure," or to prevent sex-linked disease ought to be of concern to feminists. Each sex-linked disease is caused by a defective gene or an aberration on an X-chromosome, but not on a Y-chromosome because that tiny entity carries only a very few of the X-chromosome genes. It is therefore more accurate to call such diseases "X-linked." In females, usually the corresponding "good" gene on one X-chromosome can cover up (be dominant to) any defective gene on the other X, but males (with only one X) have no such protection. Since these deleterious genes are rare in the population, the chance that a female will be affected (have two of them) is very low; thus, these diseases appear mostly in males. Abortion of male fetuses would thus eliminate all full-blown cases of these diseases, but not the disease genes, since these would persist in the carrier females.

Some 400 X-linked diseases have been described. Some are so mild as to be hardly considered diseases: colorblindness is one example. Hemophilia is the most well known; nowadays men with that disease usually survive to reproduce. Fragile-X mental retardation, Duchenne muscular dystrophy, and Lesch-Nyhan syndrome are the most common serious X-linked diseases.[68]

If he is able to reproduce, a male with an X-linked disease can never pass such a gene to his sons because he gives his sons only his Y-chromosome; yet, *all* his daughters will become (usually symptomless) carriers of the bad gene. A female carrying such a gene will give it to *half* her sons, who will then have the disease, and to half her daughters, who will then become carriers. Thus, any male child with such a disease received it from his mother, not his father.

X-linked diseases raise serious questions for feminists. The first, of course, is unjustified blame and guilt, because all boys with the disease get it from their mothers. If the family understands the genetics, a woman with one or more such sons may be blamed by others or burden herself with self-blame. Even if she aborts all males and has only daughters, she may feel guilt for having given a carrier daughter the same problems she has faced. Because the inheritance pattern is complicated, many families do not understand it, even when it is clearly and carefully explained. Despite the common belief that knowledge is power and, therefore, that obtaining knowledge is empowering, in the case of X-linked disease knowledge may well *disempower* women.

The burden of caring for children with these diseases is extreme. For hemophilia, parents need to give blood factor VII injections.[69] In Lesch-Nyhan disease, the baby boy first shows uncontrollable writhing; then spasms of the limbs prevent walking; a few years later bizarre self-mutilation and aggressive behavior start and get progressively worse until the child dies, usually in his teens.[70] In Duchenne-type muscular dystrophy, the boy's muscles progressively degenerate—every year it gets worse until he dies, again usually as a teenager.[71]

Fragile-X syndrome—the most common cause of severe mental retardation in boys—is especially pernicious in its implications for women. It occurs in one in every 2,500 live births. Its gene was just located in 1991 and found to be a "repeated sequence" of three DNA bases. Everyone has from 6 to 2000 repeats. The more repeats, the more serious the retardation. Children with mild cases may be symptomless or show slight to severe learning disabilities; children at the other extreme are profoundly retarded. Furthermore, this X-linked disease is atypical in that girls can also be affected (also in varying degrees). But the repeated sequence behaves peculiarly through the generations. In male testes the number of repetitions usually decreases, but in female ovaries it increases. Therefore, men usually beget daughters with less retardation, whereas women—if they pass on that particular X-chromosome—are likely to produce both sons and daughters with greater retardation.[72]

Let's consider the view that sex selection is in principle unacceptable yet nonetheless acceptable (and even recommended) for preventing the birth of a male who might have an X-linked disease. First, note that half the males aborted will *not* have the disease; next note that all girls born from a carrier mother have a 50:50 chance of being carriers. In solving a problem of health expenses in the present, one creates girls who must in the future endure the psychological problems of being carriers. Of course, many researchers are confident that reasonably soon we shall be able to detect each X-linked gene itself; *then* we can select both healthy boys and noncarrier girls. But note that the "Sophie's Choice" for women, already bad, becomes worse as each such gene is found. A carrier would then be forced to choose whether to abort (or not to have implanted) a daughter *genetically like herself*. (I use the term "choose" loosely here—in all likelihood the clinic would automatically make the appointment for abortion, but she might well carry guilt for years believing that she had complied too easily.) The Sophie's Choice is even more painful in women who carry fragile-X, because the degree of retardation in both boys and girls cannot be predicted. This lose-lose situation well illustrates Tabitha Powledge's claim that sex selection may be a paradigm for policy decisions about genetic engineering in general,[73] a very cogent example of the problems that can arise for women as a result of increasing genetic knowledge. As potential mothers, we are at risk of living not only as Sophies, but also as Cassandras.

Sex Selection and Four Type Cases for Feminist Ethics

As I discuss these issues, I may seem sometimes to favor one position over another. Instead, I mean to illuminate the richness of the feminist debate. All women cited here are sincerely concerned about alleviating women's oppression; all have valid, helpful contributions to make. To reach any solution, diverse views must be taken into account—not by a masculine practice of compromise, but by a synthesis in which the whole is better than its parts, a synthesis that combines and reinforces women-enhancing strategies.

Compensatory Justice. Should women be given preferential treatment because it is owed to them due to past discriminatory practices? Or would such treatment be instead "reverse discrimination" or "turning the tables" and mean that the "girls" then simply play by the rules that the "boys" used previously? I shall not cite any of the voluminous literature on this topic, but shall instead apply this dilemma to sex selection.

The issue is this: if a cheap and effective method of sex preselection were available, general preferences in the population mean that it would usually be used to select boys in general and boys to be first-born. Is the appropriate feminist response then to use the technology selectively to choose *girls*, in order to compensate for its use by others? This tactic might reflect a deliberate plan to raise strong feminists. Or is the appropriate feminist response to beget boys in order to bring them up to be nurturing, nonviolent persons necessary for human survival on our planet?[74]

This issue stirred up lively discussion in 1979 at the first feminist workshop on reproductive technologies even though, ironically, essentially everyone—of whatever view—was against the development of sex selection technologies. Tabitha Powledge sparked the issue by stating that she "would *of course* object to the use of this technology selectively against males. . . . The work of the past ten years . . . will have gone for nothing if all we want to do is take revenge and reverse the oppression."[75] Janice Raymond responded that any turning-the-tables argument is "utterly ahistorical" and "shifts the focus off the fact that anti-feminism and woman-hating is all around us."[76] Diana Axelsen countered with the question, "[G]iven a social context that encourages both men and women to prefer male children, . . . is the right answer really women wanting daughters rather than both parents deciding . . . [to] educate their girl and boy children to have a feminist, humane outlook?"[77]

Supporting Axelsen and Powledge, Betty Hoskins raised the discussion to another level. In a "world and social context with women-generated values," she would hope to stop "that patriarchal, hierarchal 'I'm better than, because I'm this kind or that kind.' " She argued that we should not "continue to participate in a male model of rank ordering, better-worse dichotomies."[78] The metaquestion here for feminists, then, is whether we should utilize *any* patriarchal tactics in struggling for a world free of oppression. And in particular, should we refrain from ordering, prioritizing, and using either-or dualisms? Should we not strive for win-win solutions, rather than win-lose (or as so often happens in medical ethics casebook crises, lose-lose) solutions?

Autonomy and Rights. Sex selection is a perplexing autonomy issue. Should not each woman have the right to control her body and to have no interference with any aspect of reproduction, including choosing the sex of her children? Women have fought long and hard for reproductive rights, and all segments of North American society have adopted rights language. A major "principle" of mainstream medical ethics is autonomy. Genetic counselors are trained in their lessons in nondirective counseling to respect clients' autonomy. A study in 1988 showed that, when asked their response to a hypothetical ethical dilemma in which a couple with four daughters wanted amniocentesis to make sure that their next child would be a son, 62 percent of medical geneticists in the United States (35 percent women) would "either perform prenatal diagnosis for this couple . . . or would refer them to someone who would."[79] Women geneticists were twice as likely as men to comply with the request. A study in 1991, in which 199 master's-degree genetic counselors (93.5 percent women) responded to that same dilemma, found that 82 percent of them would perform or refer for sex selection. Many counselors "reasoned that the patient has a right to choose and felt it their duty to respect patient autonomy."[80] These responses illustrate women's strong belief that reproductive autonomy is sacrosanct. Another illustration is the issue of surrogate motherhood: many women think that any woman should have the right to *be* a surrogate and to hire a surrogate.

Many feminist scholars, however, have raised concerns about emphasizing rights. Some point out that the concept of "rights" is masculinist and patriarchal. For example,

> [I]n our assertion of rights we play a masculinist game. . . . "Rights" language seems to assume that society is a collection of atomic particles in which any given individual's happiness or utility is viewed as mutually disinterested from another's, that communities or love relationships are not ethically relevant in deciding what action ought to be taken. Rights language is fundamentally adversarial and negative. . . . Humans come into being related to one another, not as disinterested egoists, and thus duties and responsibilities are more fundamental notions than rights.[81]

Furthermore, rights discourse can be nonproductive and indeterminate:

> [Rights language] fails to resolve moral disputes conclusively. . . . When a dilemma is stated as a conflict between rights, a hierarchical judgment is required to decide whose rights ought to prevail.[82]

Alison Jaggar describes this feminist concern with the

> core intuition of autonomy . . . [of] the self as the ultimate authority in matters of morality or truth. . . . On the one hand, [contemporary feminists] . . . have insisted that women are as autonomous in the moral and intellectual senses as men . . . and they have also demanded political, social and economic autonomy of women. . . . On the other hand, however, some feminists have questioned traditional interpretations of autonomy as masculine fantasies. For instance, they have explored some of the ways in which "choice" is socialized and "consent" manipulated. In addition, they have . . . suggested that freeing ourselves from particular attachments might [not result in] a truly moral response.[83]

Moreover, feminist ethics ought to focus on reducing oppression.[84] We can argue that any practice that increases the oppression of women is wrong and reason then that other factors, such as autonomy and reproductive rights, which are important to women, lose their prerogative if they increase oppression. Powledge claims that "we can ignore" reproductive freedom "when it works against" the ultimate goal of social justice. "Therefore we should embargo sex choice in any form because it abrogates the principle that people (in this case the sexes) should be regarded as equally valuable."[85]

Individual Survival vs. the Status of Women. Around the world women are expected to do most of the "shitwork," the basics necessary to keep people clean, healthy, fed, and clothed. Collectively, women are absolutely necessary for patriarchal society; individually, one or more devoted, sacrificing woman is almost always behind any "successful" man. Despite this (because of this?), women are devalued. Despite this (because of this?), men "prefer" sons.

A woman's valuation is lowered if she produces daughters and raised if she produces sons. Of course, the amount of value change is heavily culture-dependent. In the United States, her value changes little; in fact, her production of a daughter to balance a family might increase her value. In India, daughter production lowers a woman's value so much that she becomes expendable—her in-laws may demand more dowry from her parents, force a divorce, even kill her. Sex selection, therefore, can be life-saving. If such women can select sons, they "make correct moral choices, using flawless utilitarian reasoning, [for] they maximize their own and their family's happiness and minimize the suffering of little girls."[86]

However, the process is circular. Each act of son-preference, while increasing the value of a particular mother, further devalues women as a class. It ingrains sex selection into the society's mores, making it more necessary in the future. In northwest India, the part of India with the strongest son-preference and the largest sex ratio imbalance, entrepreneurs introduced amniocentesis for sex selection in the mid-1970s. It became very popular.[87] This use of amniocentesis in northwest India caused the practice to spread to other areas of India and to ethnic groups which had had much less son-preference.

The feminist dilemma is now to balance the survival—the very life—of individual women against the increasing societal devaluation of women caused by those women's individual "choices." Or how can we make a lose-lose situation into a win-win one?

The Strange Bedfellows Problem. Strong stances taken by feminists against reproductive technologies often find us advocating the same policies as those proposed by conservative religious groups. If we are against surrogate motherhood, the marketing of infertility "treatments," and abortion for sex selection, we find that the Vatican agrees with us. However, we reach these conclusions by a path of concern for relationships and for alleviating the oppression of women, a path of giving women full status as persons, a path that does not define women solely as reproductive vessels, whereas the Vatican follows the different path of concern for the fetus as an innocent with the fully human right to life.[88] But the "bedfellow" might say to us, "If you won't abort an innocent fetus because of its sex, how can you approve aborting a fetus because it comes from rape or incest or will be the fifth child in an impoverished family?"

Still another aspect of this problem is the banning of research. Some right-wing groups impose bans against the funding of politically charged areas of research, such as fetal tissue transplants or simple methods of abortion . . . and sex detection. Yet, the ethos of science and "enlightened" thought contends that it is wrong to set any restrictions to the search for truth. The feminist analysis of science, however, has regularly pointed out that the *choice of what to study*, that is, what piece of "truth" one searches for, is not disinterested, but politically and socially determined.[89] Thus, for entirely different political and social reasons, right-wing groups and feminists may both happen to say "nay" to certain lines of research. For example, feminist Tabitha Powledge is against funding any research on sex detection techniques.[90] If humans are not wise enough to make proper use of results from certain lines of research, perhaps that research ought not be done. Sex detection may well fall into that category. I believe that we must face up squarely to any bedfellow problems in four ways. First, and most important, should be the emphasis on our *values* and the reasoning from those values. Second, the policies for action we propose must be different: some of those are discussed below. Third, it is possible that good-hearted, well-intentioned people from entirely different mindsets may reach the same conclusion because each taps into a common moral force or transcendent virtue without being aware of it. Fourth, we should make use of any commonalities to raise a bedfellow's consciousness: to achieve a humane, feminist world, such conservatives must be converted, and we have an opening here with a joint concern. At bioethics conferences I have sometimes complimented speakers on their remarks and then continued by showing that their views can be reframed to include concern about the oppression of women.

Public Policy for Sex Selection

Regulation. Most authors who contend that selecting children's sex is morally wrong maintain just as strongly that legal prohibition of it would also be wrong.[91] Sex selective abortion is, however, illegal in Great Britain under the 1967 British Abortion Act[92] and in Pennsylvania under the part of that state's 1989 antiabortion law that was not brought to the Supreme Court.[93] Despite her strong anti-selection views quoted above, Powledge uses slippery slope arguments to claim that prohibition would "begin to delineate acceptable and unacceptable reasons to have an abortion" and would "provide an opening wedge for legal regulation of reproduction in general."[94] Wertz and Fletcher maintain that any such laws would be "a step backward" and "pose real dangers to civil liberties."[95]

Further, according to Wertz and Fletcher, prohibition would not work. "[F]ew would-be murderers tell gun-shop owners than they intend to shoot people and few prospective parents tell doctors that their real reason for having prenatal diagnosis is to discover fetal sex."[96] Certainly the experience in Maharastra state in India shows the difficulties of enforcement. Passed on May 10, 1988, the Regulation of Use of Prenatal Diagnostic Techniques Act banned the use of medical technologies for prenatal sex determination in Maharastra. The Act forbids advertising, spells out procedures for complaints, and specifies punishments. But it has not been implemented, and the government would not take action in a test case against a clinic that advertised its sex selection services.[97]

According to Warren, not only will it be impossible to prohibit sex selection, but prohibition might "aggravate the very ills which it was designed to prevent." She classifies sex selection (if indeed it is wrong) as a "victimless crime," along with several other "crimes," such as gambling, prostitution, and production of pornography. For these, Warren and others believe prohibition would have far worse consequences than "legal toleration with regulation."[98] Among the extremely bad consequences are lucrative markets for crime syndicates, encouragement of police and judicial corruption, and the creation of systems of informers.

I agree with Warren about the importance of avoiding these consequences, but doubt they are likely to follow from prohibition of sex selection because the financial incentives are far below those, say, in prostitution and pornography. But I firmly disagree in calling sex selection "victimless." Indeed, I believe that prostitution and pornography are called victimless only because society fails to recognize exploitation of women and children as victimization. Similarly, society does not recognize that lowering the status of all women—not just those directly involved—is a form of victimization. The victims of sex selection are many: selected children, their siblings, unselected children, and finally all women in society. Stereotypes about the sexes become more firmly ingrained with each complicit action taken.

As for legal toleration with regulation, I am uncertain whether "regulation" would be a lesser burden on women or more enforceable than outright prohibition. (Presumably the United States Food and Drug Administration already has regulation meant to protect us against ineffective or unproven selection schemes, as discussed above in the Gender-

Choice case.) Powledge suggests that we ought not to include "any form of sex choice in the . . . medical procedures supported out of tax funds" and we ought to "tax it, perhaps heavily."[99] Some pro-selection authors have concocted extremely cumbersome, to say the least, schemes for regulation should sex-ratio imbalances arise (their only concern). For example, Singer and Wells suggest that sex selection be done only by registered practitioners who would have waiting lists for couples who want a child of the sex being chosen too frequently.[100] Or regulation could be positive, according to suggestions such as Bayles's that "incentives, such as extra tax deductions, . . . be offered for having children of a particular sex, or for having them first."[101]

Withholding Information about Sex. Wertz and Fletcher have suggested that information about sex is nonmedical and usually clinically irrelevant: legally, medical practitioners are not required to give it out. These authors are quick to point out that imbalance in information is a power issue for feminists, but they suggest that information about sex could "reside in the laboratory" so that her doctor knows no more than a pregnant woman. However, a direct request for information about sex would be honored.[102] Lynda Birke and her colleagues argue that withholding information about the sex of a fetus is dangerous and paternalistic, but then come to essentially the Wertz/Fletcher position when they "favour better counselling of women" before women choose to have prenatal diagnosis "to help them decide . . . precisely what information about the results they wish to be given."[103] They argue for "informed refusal," a concept Barbara Katz Rothman also advocates. The women whom Rothman interviewed, however, found it extremely difficult to tell a genetic counselor that they did *not* wish to be told certain information.[104]

Wait and See. A good many feminists and nonfeminists see nothing problematic about sex selection. They suggest waiting to find out whether there are problems and then turn to regulation—to them, problems would be imbalances to the human sex ratio that turn out to have deleterious consequences. In 1983 Fletcher's view was, "Prior to having evidence that [social harm from effects of sex choice] exists, however, there is no reason to prevent an extension of freedom and fairness to the first decisions about sex choice. . . . The mills of a democratic society . . . are probably sufficient to grind and resolve the problems."[105]

Warren's wait-and-see policy suggests research on and monitoring of the consequences of using sex selection throughout the world. "If evidence that it *is* detrimental [to women] emerges, we will need to publicize this fact. . . . [W]e will have to argue for self-regulatory practices by those providing sex-selection services."[106]

Some male scholars have predicted that, if a girl shortage should occur, this would affect parents strongly, first leading to an excess of girls, but the oscillations would eventually damp out, with an eventual return to a balanced sex ratio. One such scholar, Keyfitz, says that selection technology therefore "could be a major force for sex equality. . . . [Women] will become more desirable in marriage."[107] Rothman and Holmes have each pointed out the absurdity of both the damping off and the sex equality claims. Rothman asks, "In a real woman shortage, would nonsexual and nonreproducing women be tolerated?"[108]

Moral Exhortation. To Powledge, one acceptable method of trying to stop sex selection is moral exhortation. "We must say over and over again to friends and neighbors, in the pages of magazines and newspapers, . . . that this technology, even if available, should simply not be used."[109]

Although Warren recommends regulation (if necessary), most of her policy recommendations fit under the moral exhortation category, that is, persuading prospective parents not to use sex-selection services and urging providers to self-regulate. Wertz and Fletcher also suggest that state medical societies—because they control licensure—should discourage private doctors from using prenatal diagnosis merely for sex selection.[110]

But in the long run, the only way to stop sex selection, should cheap and easy methods become available, is to eliminate sexism. According to Warren, to "eliminate the cultural and economic bases of son-preference . . . will require nothing less than the elimination of patriarchy itself."[111] An extremely difficult task, especially with the current conservative backlash against feminism! Warren proffers numerous recommendations on how to snip away at patriarchy: each may seem insignificant, but each is clearly morally right in itself—and what other course have we to follow? Among her suggestions are the repeal of laws that property be inherited through the male line, equal education for females, the elimination of sexist discrimination in hiring and promotion, and improving women's wages.

In a humane, feminist utopia, no one would wish to select children's sex. Suppose they gave a sex selection clinic and nobody came?

Notes

1. Barry Bean, "Pregenitive Sex Ratio among Functioning Sperm Cells," *American Journal of Human Genetics*, 47 (1990):351. The standard way to express sex ratio is to put the male figure *first* per 100 females. I deliberately reverse the convention, putting females first, and also cut 100 in half to jibe with the more common expression "50:50." In putting females first,

I become a "militant feminist," according to Ronald Wells. See his *Human Sex Determination* (Tharwa, Australia: Riverlea, 1990), 25.

2. *A Profile of Older Americans—1986*, American Association of Retired Persons, Washington, D.C.

3. Marcia Guttentag and Paul F. Secord, *Too Many Women? The Sex Ratio Question* (Beverly Hills: Sage, 1983), 190.

4. Mary Anne Warren, *Gendercide: The Implications of Sex Selection* (Totowa, NJ: Rowman and Allanheld, 1985), 132–138.

5. For additional ethical arguments, some supporting, some opposing, sex selection, and a competent, detailed analysis, see Warren, *Gendercide*, chs. 4–8. See also ch. 2 in Christine Overall, *Ethics and Human Reproduction: A Feminist Analysis* (Boston: Allen & Unwin, 1987), 17–39, and two essays in *Biomedical Ethics Reviews—1985*: Helen Bequaert Holmes, "Sex Preselection: Eugenics for Everyone," 39–71; and Mary Anne Warren, "The Ethics of Sex Preselection," 73–89. Other issues are raised in three interdisciplinary collections: Janice Raymond, section ed., "Sex Preselection," in Helen Bequaert Holmes, Betty B. Hoskins, and Michael Gross, eds., *The Custom-Made Child? Women-Centered Perspectives* (Clifton, NJ: Humana, 1981), 177–224; Neil G. Bennett, ed., *Sex Selection of Children* (New York: Academic Press, 1983); and Gena Corea et al., eds., *Man-Made Women: How New Reproductive Technologies Affect Women* (Bloomington: Indiana University Press, 1987).

6. William H. James, "Timing of Fertilization and the Sex Ratio of Offspring," in Bennett, *Sex Selection*, 73. James has published over 20 papers analyzing the timing of intercourse.

7. Tabitha M. Powledge, "Toward a Moral Policy for Sex Choice," in Bennett, *Sex Selection*, 208.

8. PBS, "Boy or Girl? Should the Choice Be Ours?" *Hard Choices* (1981 TV series).

9. Warren, *Gendercide*, 173.

10. Nan Paulsen Chico, "Confronting the Dilemmas of Reproductive Choice: The Process of Sex Preselection" (Ph.D. diss., University of California at San Francisco, 1989).

11. Overall, *Ethics and Human Reproduction*, 26.

12. Overall, *Ethics and Human Reproduction*, 27, 28.

13. See, for example, Landrum B. Shettles and David M. Rorvik, *How to Choose the Sex of Your Baby* (New York: Doubleday, 1989), 21; John C. Hobbins, "Determination of Fetal Sex in Early Pregnancy," *New England Journal of Medicine* 309 (1983):979–980.

14. See, for example, Michael D. Bayles, *Reproductive Ethics* (Englewood Cliffs, NJ: Prentice-Hall, 1984), 351; Dorothy C. Wertz and John C. Fletcher, "Sex Selection Through Prenatal Diagnosis: A Feminist Critique," in Helen Bequaert Holmes and Laura M. Purdy, eds., *Feminist Per-*

spectives in Medical Ethics (Bloomington: Indiana University Press, 1992), 251n.

15. John Postgate, "Bat's Chance in Hell," *New Scientist* 5 Apr. 1973:12–16. See also Peter Singer and Deane Wells, *Making Babies: The New Science and Ethics of Conception* (New York: Scribner's, 1985), 153.

16. Paul Ehrlich, *The Population Bomb* (New York: Ballantine, 1968); Postgate, "Bat's Chance," 14; Clare Boothe Luce, "Next: Pills to Make Most Babies Male," *Washington Star* 9 July 1978:C1, C4; Singer and Wells, *Making Babies*, 154; Helga Kuhse and Peter Singer, "From the Editors," *Bioethics* 7(4) (1993), iv.

17. Warren, *Gendercide*, 15–16, 36, 175–176; Elizabeth Moen, "Sex Selective Abortion: Prospects in China and India," *Issues in Reproductive and Genetic Engineering: Journal of International Feminist Analysis* 4(3) (1991):231–249; Irene Sege, "The Grim Mystery of World's Missing Women," *Boston Globe*, 3 Feb. 1992:23, 25; S. H. Venkatramani, "Female Infanticide: Born to Die," *India Today* 15 June 1986:10–17; Madhu Kishwar, "The Continuing Deficit of Women in India and the Impact of Amniocentesis," in Corea et al., *Man-Made Women*, 30–37; Kusum, "The Use of Pre-Natal Diagnostic Techniques for Sex Selection: The Indian Scene," *Bioethics* 7(2/3) (1993):150–152, 163.

18. Venkatramani, "Born to Die," 16–17; Kishwar, "Continuing Deficit," 30.

19. Warren, *Gendercide*, 176.

20. Amitai Etzioni, "Sex Control, Science, and Society," *Science* 161 (1968):1107; Powledge, "Moral Policy," 204–205; Warren, *Gendercide*, 109. In ch. 5 of *Gendercide*, Warren discusses detailed evidence from the biology of hormones and from anthropological studies of gentle and violent cultures and questions the hypothesis that a higher proportion of males will result in more aggression.

21. Jessie Bernard, *The Future of Marriage* (London: Souvenir Press, 1973), 19, 24.

22. Warren, *Gendercide*, 141. See Cécile Ernst and Jules Angst, *Birth Order: Its Influence on Personality* (New York: Springer-Verlag, 1983).

23. Warren, *Gendercide*, 163ff; Holmes, "Eugenics," 57–59.

24. Powledge, "Moral Policy," 196.

25. Janice G. Raymond, "Introduction," in Holmes et al., *The Custom-Made Child?* 177.

26. Bayles, *Reproductive Ethics*, 34–35.

27. John C. Fletcher, "Is Sex Selection Ethical?" *Research Ethics: Progress in Clinical and Biological Research* 128 (1983):347.

28. Warren, *Gendercide*, 83, 86.

29. Overall, *Ethics and Human Reproduction*, 22.

30. K. M. Ludmerer, "Eugenics: History," *Encyclopedia of Bioethics* (New York: Macmillan, 1978), 457–461.

31. Ruth Hubbard in Emily Culpepper, moderator, "Sex Preselection Discussion," in Holmes et al., *The Custom-Made Child?* 224.

32. Wertz and Fletcher, "Feminist Critique," 245; also cited in Matt Ridley, "A Boy or a Girl: Is It Possible to Load the Dice?" *Smithsonian* June 1993:122.

33. Holmes, "Eugenics," 39; Powledge, "Moral Policy," 211. Anne Waldschmidt calls this "grassroots eugenics" in her "Against Selection of Human Life—People with Disabilities Oppose Genetic Counselling," *Issues in Reproductive and Genetic Engineering* 5(2) (1992):164–166.

34. William J. Watson, "Early-Second-Trimester Fetal Sex Determination with Ultrasound," *Journal of Reproductive Medicine* 35 (1990):247–249; B. R. Elajalde et al., "Visualization of the Fetal Genitalia," *Journal of Ultrasound in Medicine* 4 (1985):633–639.

35. M. Bronshtein et al., "Early Determination of Fetal Sex Using Transvaginal Sonography," *Journal of Clinical Ultrasound* 18 (1990):302–326; I. E. Timor-Tritsch, D. Farine, and M. G. Rosen, "A Close Look at Early Embryonic Development with the High-Frequency Transvaginal Transducer," *American Journal of Obstetrics and Gynecology* 159 (1988): 676–681; Karen M. Ferroni and Avis Vincensi, "Ultrasound Frontiers: Transvaginal and Doppler Sonography," *Genetic Resource* 6(1) (1991):12–14.

36. David H. Ledbetter et al., "Cytogenetic Results of Chorionic Villus Sampling: High Success Rate and Diagnostic Accuracy in the United States Collaborative Study," *American Journal of Obstetrics and Gynecology* 162 (1990):495–501.

37. Wayne A. Miller and Barbara Thayer, "Early Amniocentesis," *Genetic Resource* 6(1) (1991):10–11; D. E. Rooney et al., "Early Amniocentesis: A Cytogenetic Evaluation," *British Medical Journal* 299 (1989):25; C. A. Penso and F. D. Frigoletto, "Early Amniocentesis," *Seminars in Perinatology*, 14 (1990):465–470.

38. Barbara Katz Rothman, *The Tentative Pregnancy* (New York: Viking Penguin, 1986), 87–92; Powledge, "Moral Policy," 201.

39. Diana W. Bianchi et al., "Isolation of Fetal DNA from Nucleated Erythrocytes in Maternal Blood," *Proceedings of the National Academy of Sciences, USA* 87 (1990):3279–3283; Frank Lesser and Ian Anderson, " 'Safe' Test May Spot Fetal Abnormalities," *New Scientist* 11 August 1990:32; U. W. Mueller et al., "Isolation of Fetal Trophoblast Cells from Peripheral Blood of Pregnant Women," *Lancet* 336 (1990):197–200; Y-M. D. Lo et al., "Prenatal Sex Determination by DNA Amplification from Maternal Peripheral Blood," *Lancet* 9 Dec. 1989:1363–1365. For a discussion of related social and ethical issues, see Rothman, *Tentative Pregnancy*, 79–82.

40. A. Dokras et al., "Trophectoderm Biopsy in Human Blastocysts," *Human Reproduction* 5(7) (1990):821–825; John D. West et al., "Sexing Whole Human Pre-Embryos by In-situ Hybridization with a Y-Chromosome Specific DNA Probe," *Human Reproduction*, 3(8) (1988):1010–1019; A. H.

Handyside et al., "Biopsy of Human Preimplantation Embryos and Sexing by DNA Amplification," *Lancet* 18 Feb. 1989:347–349; A. H. Handyside et al., "Pregnancies from Biopsied Human Preimplantation Embryos Sexed by Y-Specific DNA Amplification," *Nature* 344 (1990):768–770; Gail Vines, "Early Embryo Sex Test Forewarns of Disease," *New Scientist*, 25 Feb. 1989:25.

41. Dorothy C. Wertz, "How Parents of Affected Children View Selective Abortion," in Helen Bequaert Holmes, ed., *Issues in Reproductive Technology I: An Anthology* (New York: Garland, 1992), 182.

42. K. Hardy et al., "Human Implantation Development *in vitro* Is Not Adversely Affected by Biopsy at the 8-cell stage," *Human Reproduction*, 5 (1990):708–714.

43. Medical Research International, "In Vitro Fertilization-Embryo Transfer (IVF-ET) in the United States: 1990 Results from the National IVF-ET Registry," *Fertility and Sterility* 57(1) (1992):17.

44. Judy Berlfein, "The Earliest Warning," *Discover* Feb. 1992:14.

45. Handyside, "Pregnancies from," 770.

46. In humans, sex is determined when the sperm merges with the egg. Each human egg contains 23 chromosomes, one of these an X-chromosome. Each human sperm also contains 23 chromosomes, but one of these is either an X or a Y. In normal fertilization, the chromosome count is brought to 46 and either a female (XX) or a male (XY) progeny is conceived.

47. Sally Langendoen and William Proctor, *The Preconception Gender Diet* (New York: M. Evans, 1982); J. Stolkowski and J. Lorrain, "Preconceptional Selection of Fetal Sex," *International Journal of Gynaecology and Obstetrics* 18 (1980):440–443; Sandra Ann Carson, "Sex Selection: The Ultimate in Family Planning," *Fertility and Sterility* 50 (1988):16.

48. Shettles and Rorvik, *How to Choose*, 105–107; Jonathan Hewitt, "Preconceptional Sex Selection," *British Journal of Hospital Medicine* 37 (1987):154.

49. See, for example, Carson, "Sex Selection," 17; Ridley, "A Boy or a Girl," 113–114, 118–119; Wells, *Human Sex Determination*, ch. 11. For explanations in medical lingo, see Ridley, 118–119, and Wells, 171.

50. Shettles and Rorvik, *How to Choose*, 64, 72–74; Landrum B. Shettles, letter to the editor, *Fertility and Sterility* 29 (1978):386.

51. For tests of Shettles's theory, see John T. France et al., "A Prospective Study of the Preselection of the Sex of Offspring by Timing Intercourse Relative to Ovulation," *Fertility and Sterility* 41 (1984):894–900, and B. W. Simcock, "Sons and Daughters—A Sex Preselection Study," *Medical Journal of Australia* 142 (1985):541–542. For evaluation of such studies, see Paul W. Zarutskie et al., "The Clinical Relevance of Sex Selection Techniques," *Fertility and Sterility* 52 (1989):891–905, especially table 3, p. 896. For discussion of various timing theories, especially before 1970, see James, "Timing of Fertilization," 74–80, 91–92, and William H. James,

"Timing of Fertilization and Sex Ratio of Offspring—A Review," *Annals of Human Biology* 3 (1976):549–556.

52. Elizabeth M. Whelan, *Boy or Girl? The Sex Selection Technique That Makes All Others Obsolete* (New York: Bobbs-Merrill, 1977); Rodrigo Guerrero, "Association of the Type and Time of Insemination within the Menstrual Cycle with the Human Sex Ratio at Birth," *New Engand Journal of Medicine* 291 (1974):1056–1059; Susan Harlap, "Gender of Infants Conceived on Different Days of the Menstrual Cycle," *New England Journal of Medicine* 300 (1979):1445–1448.

53. James, "Timing of Fertilization," in Bennett, 78–79.

54. For both methods, see W. L. G. Quinlivan et al., "Separation Of Human X and Y Spermatozoa by Albumin Gradients and Sephadex Chromatography," *Fertility and Sterility* 37 (1982):104; for the Sephadex method, see Stephen L. Corson et al., "Sex Selection by Sperm Separation and Insemination," *Fertility and Sterility* 42 (1984):756; for the albumin method, see Ferdinand J. Beernink and Ronald J. Ericsson, "Male Sex Preselection through Sperm Isolation," *Fertility and Sterility* 38(4) (1982):493–495.

55. For example, see Brigitte F. Brandriff et al., "Sex Chromosome Ratios Determined by Karyotypic Analysis in Albumin-Isolated Human Sperm," *Fertility and Sterility* 46 (1986):678–685; Sharon B. Jaffe et al., "A Controlled Study for Gender Selection," *Fertility and Sterility* 56(2) (1991):254–258; and Teresa A. Beckett, Renee H. Martin, and David I. Hoar, "Assessment of the Sephadex Technique for Selection of X-bearing Human Sperm by Analysis of Sperm Chromosomes, Deoxyribonucleic Acid and Y-Bodies," *Fertility and Sterility* 52 (1989):829–835; Gail Vines, "Old Wives' Tales 'as Good as Sperm Sorting'," *New Scientist* 30 January 1993:4.

56. Renee H. Martin, "Reply of the Author," letter, *Fertility and Sterility* 53(6) (1990):1112. See also Carson, "Sex Selection," 17–18.

57. For example, see E. Caspi et al., "The Outcome of Pregnancy after Gonadotropin Therapy," *British Journal of Obstetrics and Gynaecology* 83 (1976):976; William H. James, "Gonadotropin and the Human Secondary Sex Ratio," *British Medical Journal* 281 (1980):711; and William H. James, "The Sex Ratio of Infants Born after Hormonal Induction of Ovulation," *British Journal of Obstetrics and Gynaecology* 92 (1985):299.

58. Zarutskie et al., "Clinical Relevance," table 5, p. 898 and discussion, pp. 894–895.

59. Jaffe et al., "A Controlled Study" 251–256.

60. Mark R. Geier, John L. Young, and Dagmar Kessler, "Too Much or Too Little Science in Sex Selection Techniques," letter, *Fertility and Sterility* 53(6) (1990): 1112.

61. Paul G. McDonough, "Editorial Comment," *Fertility and Sterility*, 53(6) (1990):1113; Martin, "Reply," 1112–1113.

62. Etzioni, "Sex Control," 1108.

63. Christine Russell, "Boy or Girl? FDA Says the Outcome Isn't as Simple as Home Kit Implies," *Washington Post* 28 Jan. 1986; "Deception Charged on Choosing Sex of Babies," *New York Times* 1 Feb. 1987:26; L. Wayne Hicks, "Gender Choice Saga Ends with Liquidation of Assets," *Denver Business Journal* 26 March 1990:1, 23.

64. Gametrics Limited Memorandum #3 (in-house publication), Alzada, Montana, October 1987.

65. Vines, "Old Wives' Tales," 4; Kuhse and Singer, "From the Editors," iii.

66. John D. Stephens, "Morality of Induced Abortion and Freedom of Choice," *American Journal of Obstetrics and Gynecology* 159 (1988):218; John D. Stephens, "Fetal Anatomic Sex Assignment by Ultrasonography during Early Pregnancy," patent no. 4,986,274, 22 Jan. 1991; "It's a Girl!" advertisement in *India Currents* June 1988.

67. Sunera Thobani, "More Than Sexist . . . ," *Healthsharing*, Spring 1991:10, 13.

68. Arthur P. Mange and Elaine Johansen Mange, *Genetics: Human Aspects*, 2nd ed. (Sunderland, MA: Sinauer, 1990), 18–21, 36, 322, 514–515.

69. Mange and Mange, *Genetics: Human Aspects*, 514–515.

70. Mange and Mange, *Genetics: Human Aspects*, 322; W. N. Kelley and J. B. Wyngaarden, "Clinical Syndromes Associated with Hypoxanthine-Guanine Phosphoribosyltransferase Deficiency," in J. B. Stanbury et al., eds., *Metabolic Basis of Inherited Disease* (New York: McGraw-Hill, 1983), 1115–1143.

71. Mange and Mange, *Genetics: Human Aspects*, 36; A. E. H. Emery, *Duchenne Muscular Dystrophy*, Oxford Monographs in Medical Genetics 15 (New York: Oxford University Press, 1987).

72. "Retardation Gene Found; Prenatal Test Now Expected," *Washington Post* 16 June 1991:17; G. R. Sutherland et al., "Hereditary Unstable DNA: A New Explanation for Some Old Genetic Questions?" *Lancet* 338 (1991):289.

73. Powledge, "Moral Policy," 208.

74. Warren, *Gendercide*, 175–176.

75. Tabitha M. Powledge, "Unnatural Selection: On Choosing Children's Sex," in Holmes et al., *Custom-Made Child?*, 199.

76. Janice G. Raymond, "Sex Preselection: A Response," in Holmes et al., *Custom-Made Child?*, 210.

77. Culpepper, "Discussion," 221.

78. Culpepper, "Discussion," 220.

79. Wertz and Fletcher, "Feminist Critique," 250n; Dorothy C. Wertz and John C. Fletcher, "Fatal Knowledge? Prenatal Diagnosis and Sex Selection," *Hastings Center Report* 19(3) (1989):21.

80. Deborah F. Pencarinha et al., "Ethical Issues in Genetic Counseling: A

Comparison of an M. S. Genetic Counselor and a Medical Geneticist Perspective," *Journal of Genetic Counseling* 1(1) (1992):24.

81. Helen Bequaert Holmes and Susan Rae Peterson, "Rights Over One's Own Body: A Woman-Affirming Health Care Policy," *Human Rights Quarterly* 3(2) (1981):73. See also Susan Sherwin, "A Feminist Approach to Ethics," *Resources for Feminist Research RFR/DRF* 16(3) (1987):25–26.

82. Holmes and Peterson, "Rights Over Body," 74.

83. Alison M. Jaggar, "Feminist Ethics: Some Issues for the Nineties," *Journal of Social Philosophy* 20 (1990):100.

84. Susan Sherwin, *No Longer Patient: Feminist Ethics and Health Care* (Philadelphia: Temple University Press, 1992), 54–57, 75.

85. Powledge, "Moral Policy," 206.

86. Holmes, "Eugenics," 60; see also Kusum, "Indian Scene," 163–164.

87. Kusum, "Indian Scene," 152–153.

88. For personal experiences with the strange bedfellows phenomenon and an excellent analysis of the paths, values, and goals involved, see Barbara Katz Rothman, *Recreating Motherhood: Ideology and Technology in a Patriarchal Society* (New York: W. W. Norton, 1989), 240–245.

89. See, for example, Sue V. Rosser, "Re-visioning Clinical Research: Gender and the Ethics of Experimental Design," in Helen Bequaert Holmes and Laura M. Purdy, eds., *Feminist Perspectives in Medical Ethics* (Bloomington: Indiana University Press), 128–129; also in *Hypatia* 4(2) (1989):126–127; see also the reference lists in these.

90. Powledge, "Moral Policy," 209.

91. Helen Bequaert Holmes, review of *Gendercide*, by Mary Anne Warren, *Bioethics* 1(1) (1987):109; Powledge, "Moral Policy," 207; Powledge, "Unnatural Selection," 197; Wertz and Fletcher, "Feminist Critique," 248; Wertz and Fletcher, "Fatal Knowledge," 26.

92. Lynda Birke, Susan Himmelweit, and Gail Vines, *Tomorrow's Child: Reproductive Technologies in the 90s* (London: Virago, 1990), 248.

93. Charlotte Allen, "Boys Only," *New Republic* 9 March 1992:16.

94. Powledge, "Unnatural Selection," 197.

95. Wertz and Fletcher, "Feminist Critique," 248; see also Wertz and Fletcher, "Fatal Knowledge," 26.

96. Wertz and Fletcher, "Feminist Critique," 248.

97. Radhakrishna Rao, "Sex Selection Continues in Maharastra," *Nature* 343 (1990):497; see also Kusum, "Indian Scene," 153–154, 159–162.

98. Warren, *Gendercide*, 186.

99. Powledge, "Moral Policy," 210–211. The Canadian Royal Commission on New Reproductive Technologies does indeed recommend that no tax monies be used to support any sex choice in clinics or research into methods (ch. 28 in *Proceed with Care* [Ottawa: Canada Communications

Group, 1993]). Elsewhere Owen Jones proposes a countercycle earmarked
excise tax (CEET) in which sex selecting procedures or products would be
taxed and the taxes used to fund advertising programs that combat sex
sterotyping or publicize adverse consequences of sex selection. Owen D.
Jones, "Sex Selection: Regulating Technology Enabling the Predetermina-
tion of a Child's Gender," *Harvard Journal of Law and Technology* 6
(1992):1–62.

100. Singer and Wells, *Making Babies*, 154; also quoted in Warren, *Gendercide*,
    168.

101. Bayles, *Reproductive Ethics*, 37.

102. Wertz and Fletcher, "Feminist Critique," 248–249; Wertz and Fletcher,
    "Fatal Knowledge," 27.

103. Birke at al., *Tomorrow's Child*, 292.

104. Rothman, *Tentative Pregnancy*, 255–256.

105. John C. Fletcher, "Ethics and Public Policy: Should Sex Choice Be Dis-
    couraged?" in Bennett, *Sex Selection*, 248.

106. Warren, *Gendercide*, 194. Teresa Marteau of Guy's Hospital in London
    also recommends monitoring. See Gail Vines, "The Hidden Cost of Sex
    Selection," *New Scientist* 1 May 1993:13.

107. Nathan Keyfitz, "Foreword," in Bennett, *Sex Selection*, xii; see also
    Charles F. Westoff and Ronald R. Rindfuss, "Sex Preselection in the
    United States: Some Implications," *Science* 184 (1974):636. Both are
    cited in Holmes, "Eugenics," 52.

108. Rothman, *Tentative Pregnancy*, 136; Holmes, "Eugenics," 52. See also
    Gail Vines, "Killing Girls and Aborting Female Fetuses," *New Scientist* 1
    May 1993:13.

109. Powledge, "Unnatural Selection," 198.

110. Wertz and Fletcher, "Feminist Critique," 248; Wertz and Fletcher, "Fatal
    Knowledge," 26.

111. Warren, *Gendercide*, 195.

Frozen Embryos and "Fathers' Rights": Parenthood and Decision-Making in the Cryopreservation of Embryos

Christine Overall

In this chapter I examine some aspects of the current practice of cryopreservation of "spare" human embryos that are "left over" after in vitro fertilization (IVF).[1] This practice raises a number of significant issues in applied ethics, many of them relating to the general justifiability of cryopreservation. On the one hand, claims about low success rates and possible damage to the embryo with resulting disability in any viable offspring have been used to argue against cryopreservation.[2] On the other hand, claims about the reduction of the likelihood of multiple pregnancy resulting from transfer of all embryos generated through IVF, minimization of the stress and cost of repeated egg removals, and possible use of embryos for research purposes have been used to justify cryopreservation.[3] While the claims on both sides deserve further examination, especially in light of serious feminist criticisms of in vitro fertilization (on which embryo cryopreservation depends) and of contract motherhood (a possible way of using frozen embryos), this paper will not attempt to assess the general justification of cryopreservation, nor of all the issues related to this practice.

Instead, this paper will analyze and assess what the current practice of cryopreservation in North America assumes and implies about prevailing social and moral concepts of parenthood, especially fatherhood, and will suggest some tentative conclusions about parental decision-making with respect to frozen embryos. The possibility of long-term "banking" of embryos, and recent cases of parental unavailability or disagreement about the disposition of fertilized eggs, raise questions about the nature of relationships to embryos, and about who is entitled

178

to decide what happens to them. Decisions about frozen embryos require the contemplation of a variety of possible alternative outcomes, including prolonged cryopreservation (which only serves to postpone some moral questions, and even raises others having to do with posthumous implantation and intergenerational transfer), transfer ("donation") of embryos to the uterus of an unrelated woman, destruction of extra embryos, and use of embryos for further research. While these alternatives are all deserving of evaluation, my discussion, again, will be devoted not to the assessment of *what* is done to embryos, but rather to the analysis of *who* gets to decide, and what that suggests about concepts of parenthood and authority over reproduction.

Davis v. Davis: Some Preliminary Concerns

One obvious place to begin discussion of embryo cryopreservation is the Davis case, a landmark example of controversy about frozen embryos. In 1988, nine ova were removed from the ovaries of Mary Sue Davis. They were fertilized with the sperm of her then-husband, Junior Davis. Two of the resulting embryos were placed in Mary Sue Davis's uterus, but no pregnancy resulted. The seven remaining embryos were cryopreserved for possible future attempts at pregnancy. Some months later, however, the couple were divorced. A legal dispute arose about the disposition of the seven embryos. Mary Sue Davis sought entitlement to have the embryos implanted in her uterus; Junior Davis opposed both her plan to have them implanted and anonymous donation to any other woman.

In a Tennessee Circuit Court decision, Judge W. Dale Young opined that the seven embryos were not property, that human life begins at the point of conception, and that "Mr. and Mrs. Davis [had] produced human beings, in vitro, to be known as their child or children." The best interests of these "children," he concluded, were served by permitting Mrs. Davis, their "Mother" (with a capital M), "to bring them to term through implantation." He vested temporary custody of the embryos in Mary Sue Davis, for the purpose of implantation.[4]

This decision is rife with both apparent errors of fact and philosophical confusions, some of which can be described only briefly. First, in his assessment of the status of embryos, Judge Young draws extensively upon the testimony of Jerome Lejeune, described as a world-recognized expert in human genetics. No claim is made that Lejeune possesses any special ethical expertise, yet Young explicitly relies not only on Lejeune's scientific authority but also on his philosophical reasoning.

According to Young, Lejeune testified that "at the moment of conception" a human being with a "unique personal constitution" has its beginning.[5] Such a claim ignores the extensive body of scientific evidence that shows that conception is not a momentary event, but rather a process that takes place over a period of about twenty-four hours.[6] More significantly, however, both Lejeune and Young assume, without argument, that because the embryos in question are indisputably human, they are also human beings. This latter status, in Young's view, endows them with the same moral status as that possessed by children; the embryos are not property.[7]

But these broad ethical/metaphysical leaps from "human" to "human being" and then to "child" are in no way sanctioned by scientific evidence about fertilization. Young's use of the term "human" involves an unaware equivocation: He assumes that to say that a living entity is human, a species classification, is equivalent to saying that it is a person, a moral classification. But while the humanness of the embryos is not in question (they are not canine, bovine, equine, etc.), the terms "human being" and "child" imply a much wider range of moral entitlements, the sorts of rights attributed to persons.[8] And that status must be argued for, not assumed on the basis of simple genetic constitution. The humanness of a four-celled embryo does not suffice to make it equal in moral standing to, say, a four-year-old child.

Second, there are conceptual ambiguities in talk about the embryo that are either deliberately conflated or accidentally ignored in Young's decision. For example, the judge appears to have rejected the claim made by most of the expert witnesses that the individual cells of the embryo are undifferentiated on the grounds of the quite different claim that a particular embryo can be uniquely differentiated from other embryos on the basis of DNA manipulation.[9] He concludes that "[f]rom fertilization, the cells of a human embryo are differentiated, unique and specialized to the highest degree of distinction,"[10] thus confusing the genuine uniqueness of the embryo as a whole with a false claim about the distinctness of the embryo's parts. In fact, up to the eight-cell stage, each single embryonic cell is distinct and totipotent; that is, each one has the capacity to become, separately, an independent individual.[11] In addition, part of the dispute between Mary Sue Davis and Junior Davis concerned whether or not the embryos were "alive," or were "life." While Junior Davis and three of the expert witnesses claimed that the embryos were not life but had the potential for life,[12] Mary Sue Davis argued that "in order to die [allowing the embryos to die was one solution offered to the Court] one must first live"; if the embryos could suffer a "passive death," then they must constitute life."[13]

It seems likely that the two disputing parties disagree not (or not only) about a matter of fact, but rather about a conceptual question concerning the meaning of the terms "alive" and "life." While Mary Sue Davis seems to interpret "alive" to mean merely "not dead," Junior Davis takes "alive" to have a more complex meaning having to do with ongoing functioning and development. As David T. Ozar suggests, in a paper predating the Davis case:

> "life" . . . means not only that the organism is not dying, but also that it is able to continue to perform life functions (with or without mechanical assistance) outside of a womb. On this interpretation, the frozen embryo is not viable. For while capable in their frozen state of not dying, these embryos cannot continue to perform life functions, even simple cell divisions, independent of the nutritive and protective environment of a woman's womb.[14]

Young, however, ignored both the ambiguity in the term "life" and the questionable appropriateness of referring to cryopreserved embryos as "alive" and ruled that the embryos were simply "life" from the time of conception.

Assessing the Case's Preconceptions

The problems just described are of obvious philosophical interest. But other aspects of the case must be of particular concern to feminists. Junior Davis testified that he opposed Mary Sue Davis's use of the embryos because he did not want to be "raped of [his] reproductive rights."[15] Her use of the embryos without his consent would force parenthood on him, he stated, and after Young's decision he complained to the press, "they are going to force me to become a father against my wishes."[16] Junior Davis's subsequent appeal of the Young decision claimed that the earlier decision "was tantamount to the court's deciding that Junior may be required to become a parent against his will, thus denying him the right to control reproduction."[17] His lawyer stated to the press, "If we are ever to make men truly equal partners, you can't just say that because she is female, she has greater rights."[18]

What is astonishing about these comments is their explicit and incendiary appeal to the language and values of two standard feminist political issues: the struggle against nonconsensual sexual activity and the demand for reproductive freedom and rights. Whereas what feminists seek for women is bodily autonomy, the choice of whether or not to be pregnant, and freedom from enforced maternity, what Junior Davis was seeking was to control the destiny of his sperm. His complaints must be heard within the context of a long cultural history in which men have expressed fears about women "tricking" them by becoming pregnant. There is nothing new about men's worries about women's use of their sperm; what is new is the expression of that worry within a coopted system of feminist language and values.

Do Junior Davis's concerns about the use of the frozen embryos have any moral legitimacy? In an early book on reproductive ethics, philosopher Michael D. Bayles enunciated the principle that "No one should involuntarily have parental responsibilities," and he added that the principle "prohibits completely involuntary parenthood."[19] Bayles applies this principle to the defense of a man whose wife becomes pregnant through alternative insemination without his consent; Bayles argues that a man's consent to his wife's insemination is an ethical prerequisite for his having parental responsibilities.

However, as I have argued elsewhere, such a claim unjustifiably disregards the well-being of offspring, rendering them vulnerable by exonerating male partners from parental responsibility whenever they have not explicitly consented to taking it on.[20] It would create the possibility of a man's having to assume parental responsibility for only some but not all of the offspring born to his female partner during the partnership itself, so that the interests of some of the children within a family would be better protected than those of others, and it would exacerbate the already exaggerated cultural isolation of mothers.

Moreover, it cannot be assumed that reproductive freedom for men—the absence of which might mean loss of control over donated or commercially supplied sperm—is comparable to women's reproductive freedom—the absence of which means forced reproductive labor and the loss of bodily integrity. Once their sperm has been used to fertilize a woman's ovum, men do not have a right to determine whether a child will be born. Men who want to control their sperm should be careful where they put it, and should pause to think before they provide their sperm for insemination or for in vitro fertilization—even with women who are their partners.

Men are therefore entitled to exercise reproductive choice at the time that sperm leaves their body and is conveyed to another location—whether a woman's vagina or a test tube; there are no grounds for extending male reproductive freedom beyond this point. Hence, failure to assign a veto to men like Junior Davis over the use of cryopreserved embryos generated using their sperm is not a violation of their "reproductive rights," or, more specifically, their right not to reproduce. In application to men, the acknowledgement of a right not to reproduce requires that sexual behavior be genuinely autonomous, and that sperm donation and sales be genuinely voluntary. It does not require the extension of indefinite control over what is done with sperm, after it has been freely provided.

Unfortunately, in the appeal, Judge Franks cites both a right to procreate and a right to prevent procreation, and affirms that Junior Davis has a "constitutionally protected right not to beget a child where no pregnancy has taken place."[21] While Franks's decision in fact created no new problems for Mary Sue Davis, who had remarried since the earlier decision and no longer wanted to implant the embryos,[22] and while his views have been lauded by at least one progressive commentator as being both "sensibl[e]" and "reasonable,"[23] the implications of the decision may be neither sensible nor reasonable.

The decision's reasoning seems to imply an entitlement of donors and vendors of both sperm and eggs to retain ongoing control over their gametes, even after the gametes have, by the donors' or vendors' choice, been removed from their bodies.[24] Similarly, a recent report on ethical issues relating to new reproductive technologies advocates that a woman "should have control over what happens to her eggs since they are her eggs."[25] The suggestion is that donors and vendors of either sex should be able to determine whether their donated gametes are used for research, to produce a pregnancy in recipients, or for both. But the question is whether one's gametes remain one's own after one has donated or sold them for use by another person, and particularly after they have been combined with another's gametes to form new embryos.

John A. Robertson, a professor of law who testified as an expert witness at the original *Davis v. Davis* hearing, claims,

> Just as one 'owns' their own body and its parts vis-a-vis other persons, so gametes are owned by the parties providing them or their transferees. It follows that the embryo resulting from the fusion of gametes from two persons is owned by the persons providing the gametes. The gamete providers' wishes should control over the wishes of other parties, at least until they transfer that authority to other persons.[26]

But when should the transfer of authority be considered to have occurred? I suggest that gametes that have been donated or sold are no longer "one's own" in terms of any entitlement to determine their disposition, and that embryos resulting from the combination of one's own gametes with those of another are not simply "one's own" in the same way the original gametes were. While it may be important to ensure prospective donors the initial choice whether their gametes are used for inducing pregnancy (via alternative insemination or in vitro fertilization) or for research, there is no justification for further rights of disposal such as, for example, the entitlement to determine whether one's gametes go to a person of the same race or sexual orientation as the donor or that the gametes not be used at all if a recipient of a donor's preferred sort is not available. The fact that sperm or eggs once originated from a particular individual does not give that individual an entitlement to impose his or her agenda or prejudices on the disposition of the gametes once they have been provided to an individual or institution for further use, and particularly once they have been combined with the gametes of another person.

Franks's assertion of a "right not to beget a child where no pregnancy has taken place" could have additional undesirable implications for donors' control over embryos produced from their gametes. It might, for example, imply a right to withdraw embryos after a couple had donated them to another woman. Thus in a 1987 paper, Robertson argued that "A person's interest in having or avoiding biologic heirs also supports the gamete providers' authority over embryos formed from their gametes."[27] According to Robertson, this authority should extend even past one's own life: he seeks to recognize the "procreative rights of the gamete providers to reproduce after death."[28] But once a body part or product has, by one's own choice, left one's body, there are morally justifiable limits on the degree of control one may have over it. Before the donation, the recipient is not, of course, entitled to the embryos, but after the donation she has acquired an entitlement to them, which ought not to be withdrawable by the original donors.

In the appeal, Judge Franks reasoned that just as it would be "repugnant and offensive" to order Mary Sue Davis to be implanted with the embryos if she chose not to be, so also "it would be equally repugnant to order Junior to bear the psychological, if not the legal, consequences of paternity against his will."[29] But this judgment betrays an erroneous assumption about analogies between reproduction in women and reproduction in men. If the embryos were successfully implanted in Mary Sue Davis against the will of her former husband, Junior Davis would have become a parent only in the minimal genetic sense of being biologically related to the resulting offspring. Bayles's reason for prohibiting "involuntary parenthood" is that "parental responsibilities and rights are significant burdens and privileges which can greatly affect people's lives."[30] While this is true in most cases, and is certainly true for all women who actually gestate and bear children, it need not have applied to Junior Davis, since Mary Sue Davis was quite willing to raise the child alone, without his support or involvement. She did not seek to impose on her former spouse any legal, economic, or social responsibilities for any children that might result from implantation. So Junior Davis would have had a choice not to be a "social parent" to any children Mary Sue Davis might bear as a result of implantation of the embryos.

Hence, a concern for Junior Davis in the event of his former wife's successful pregnancy would have to be founded upon a concern for the significance of genetic parenthood, and biological, not emotional or social, attachment to one's offspring. Robertson recognizes that

> Whether an unwanted but unidentified biological link is sufficient to ground a right will depend upon the social and psychological significance which individuals and society place on the existence of lineal descendants when anonymity and no rearing obligations exist.[31]

Predictably, however, he hypostatizes "the reproductive and personal significance of potential biologic offspring for the gamete source," and argues that "a person's interest in avoiding biologic heirs, even if they do not rear them, is significant and deserves respect."[32] The argument is that there is an important value simply in avoiding what Janice Raymond has called "ejaculatory fatherhood"[33]:

> The very concept of fatherhood is being extended to include sperm donors, as if by virtue of ejaculation alone a man becomes a father. . . . What we see in repeated litigation involving new reproductive technologies is another version of what Mary O'Brien has termed "ejaculatory politics." Ejaculation doth a father make. Ejaculation confers father-right. This is not mere metaphor but grossly material if you will.[34]

But of course it cannot merely be assumed, without argument, that avoiding a simple genetic connection with offspring has any moral significance at all, let alone a significance so great as to justify refusing to release embryos to the woman who underwent extensive medical interventions in order for them to be generated.

The only evidence of such a significance that is provided in the proceedings of the hearing—and the only evidence that is ever provided in debates where biological ties are taken to be significant—consists of statements about feelings concerning the value of a biological tie. In the Davis case, we have to estimate the significance of the feelings Junior Davis would experience from merely knowing that a child or children existed who were genetically related to him. These feelings are described by Robertson, in the initial hearings, as "the traumatic psychological burdens of being forced to be a parent against his will."[35] But again, the only sense in which Junior Davis would be forced to be a parent would not be in terms of social parenting and a relationship to children, but rather in terms of being the genetic father of the children. The burdens here are not the burdens that would result if children were born whom Junior Davis came to know, and from whom he was then forcibly separated. Junior Davis is not complaining of the potential pain of separation from his children; he is complaining of the potential pain of being biologically related to children whom, if he so chooses, he need never know or even see. So the situation here is not in any way analogous to that of a woman who gestates a fetus, subsequently surrenders or is forced to surrender the infant for adoption, and then regrets having done so.

Nevertheless, this fact was not, apparently, any comfort to Junior Davis, who testified that he did not want "a child produced [through implantation of the embryos in Mary Sue Davis's uterus] to live in a single-parent situation." His argument was that he himself had suffered because of the divorce of his parents; he grew up in a boys' home and experienced "despair because there was no natural bond with his parents":

> He strongly and sincerely insists that because of his poor relationship with his own parents he strenuously objects to bringing a child into the world who would suffer the same or a similar experience without any opportunity on his part to bond with his child.[36]

Given that Mary Sue Davis was committed to a permanent relationship with her child, Junior Davis was assuming that his own absence from the life of his offspring would be a major impediment to its wellbeing. So on the one hand, he was trying to prevent the existence of his genetic children; on the other hand, he was also worrying about their possible suffering without his presence in their lives. Since of course Junior Davis's life could have been just as miserable if his birth family had been intact, he seemed to be committed to a belief in an almost-mystical power of genetic fathers, or of himself in particular as a genetic father, to prevent children from exiencing despair.

Junior Davis further testified that if a child were born to Mary Sue Davis as a result of the implantation of the embryos, he would try to develop a relationship with it; he would actively seek both to support and to gain custody of the child. Hence, it must be assumed that Junior Davis sees some potential value in supporting and caring for his potential future children. This value is difficult to reconcile with the notion of "traumatic psychological burdens."

In his testimony for the Davis case, Robertson claims that in the "balancing of the equities," Junior Davis would be more injured by being made to become a (genetic) parent than Mary Sue would be injured by being prevented from implanting the embryos.[37] How is this assessment of harms arrived at? In his earlier paper, Robertson states, without argument, that what he regards as the interest of "persons" (sex unspecified) "in avoiding biologic heirs, even if they do not rear them, is significant and deserves respect."[38] Moreover, since achieving pregnancy is uncertain with the use of frozen embryos, Robertson assesses the destruction of embryos as at most a "purely psychological" loss for the individuals who provided the gametes for them,[39] and only because the individuals have "an important procreative interest at stake." The value of the loss should, in his view, be estimated simply on the basis of the "cost of creating the embryo."[40] This loss, then, is said to be more than compensated for by Junior Davis's interest in avoiding biologic heirs.

Robertson does not specify what the "cost of creating the embryo" includes. But, given his blithe assumption in the Davis case that Mary Sue Davis can "apparently successfully participate in the IVF program with another partner in the future,"[41] he is likely not including the often-hidden costs involved in the creation of embryos. In the Davis case these costs would include what Judge Young himself, on the basis of Mary Sue Davis's testimony, called "the painful, physically trying, emotionally and mentally taxing ordeals she endured to participate in the [IVF] program."[42] After an earlier history of five tubal pregnancies, resulting in the rupture of one fallopian tube and the tying of the other,[43] Mary Sue Davis underwent extensive hormonal priming on many occasions (the number is unspecified) to prod her body into producing multiple ova. She was subjected to twenty-one aspirations of eggs, and the transfer of fourteen embryos during six attempts, at a cost between \$4,000 and \$6,000 for each attempt.[44] The "costs" for Mary Sue Davis's loss of the embryos should also include the further physical and psychological pain, medical risks, and economic expenses associated with additional attempts to generate and remove ova, fertilize and implant them. Her physician, Ray King, testified that there were no guarantees that Mary Sue Davis could ever produce another usable egg, although he optimistically estimated her chance of pregnancy using the existing embryos at 52%.[45] Finally, in assessing the "balance of equities" between Mary Sue Davis and Junior Davis, the likelihood of difficulties and lack of success in the generation of new embryos in future IVF attempts must also be factored in.

So, whatever the perceived psychological "burdens" to Junior Davis of becoming merely a genetic parent, it is impossible to accept Robertson's claim that they would have been greater than the very real material burdens to Mary Sue Davis if she were to lose the embryos she was seeking.

Parenthood and Children

The value of the Davis case for a feminist assessment of the cryopreservation of "spare" human embryos lies in the opportunity it provides to raise more general questions—questions about the status of embryos themselves and their relationship to the persons whose gametes engender them. Do embryos have a moral status that is independent of their location or of their connection to persons? This question has, of course, been subjected to extensive exploration in connection with the abortion controversy. Feminists have argued that in instances of unwanted pregnancy, the embryo or fetus cannot be treated in moral isolation, but must be viewed within the context of its corporeal location in a woman's body. But the importance of context might seem less plausible when embryos exist outside of a woman's body. Thus Ozar writes that in abortion decisions,

> the state's interest in protecting [embryos'] potential life could not outweigh the fundamental constitutional right of a woman to control her own body. But in the case of frozen embryos, no woman is involved, and thus no woman's right to control her body.[46]

So, according to Ozar, obligations to cryopreserved embryos can be considered independently of concern for women. With this assumption about the radical independence of fertilized eggs, cryopreserved embryos are often seen as possessions, objects, instruments, or even "unclaimed luggage."[47] Robertson is most enthusiastic about this approach, regarding embryos as potential investments and bankable capital:

> Cryopreservation of embryos will . . . facilitate such novel means of family formation as egg and embryo donation and gestational surrogacy. . . . Couples not ready to form a family might bank embryos as insurance against future sterility or age-related birth defects.[48]

He adds, "Widespread embryo banking with shipment to distant points will increase the choice of prospective recipients."[49] In this cooptation of the feminist concept of reproductive freedom, procreative choice becomes consumer choice, facilitated by market forces that make available and regulate the buying and selling of cryopreserved embryos.

The apparent obverse of this reification and commodification of embryos as purchasable instruments for furthering individual goals is the growing fetishization of fertilized eggs. The *Merriam-Webster Dictionary* defines "fetish" in part as "an object . . . believed to have magical powers (as in curing disease); an object of unreasoning devotion or concern." The transformation of the embryo into a fetish in this sense is evidenced in a practice reported by Andrea Bonnicksen:

> Patients may develop attachments to their embryos during regular IVF, as indicated by their naming the embryos, asking for the petri dishes in which the embryos were fertilized as mementoes, acting and feeling pregnant after the embryos are transfered to their uteruses, and mourning the embryos' loss if they do not implant.[50]

Indeed, Mary Sue Davis testified at the first hearing that she regarded herself as the mother of the embryos, that she felt an attachment to them, and viewed them as children.[51] While concern for and attention to these women's experience is of course essential to any feminist analysis of embryo cryopreservation and IVF, their perceptions of the embryos must also be assessed critically in terms of both the pronatalist environment preserved and generated by infertility treatments and the promotion of embryos as child-substitutes. For example, some clinics apparently cater to this fetishization of embryos by providing death rituals for the disposal of the embryos;[52] and Robertson notes that donating embryos for research may provide "meaning" for couples.[53] Through these processes, the embryo appears to become a child, or a child substitute, in the eyes of the gamete providers. Bonnicksen adds:

> To clients, the embryo symbolizes hope and potential parenthood. It affirms the wife's femininity, the husband's masculinity, and the couple's potency. It is a powerful symbol with which clients establish emotional connections. It may be the closest thing to parenthood the wife and husband experience.[54]

Within the lived relationships of gamete providers to their embryos, Judge Young's decision that the seven embryos are children in need of judicious care appears to acquire its experiential validation. Young saw his role as the exercise of *parens patriae*, seeking the best interests of the children whose well-being he believed was in question,[55] and he cited

Lejeune's view that his decision was comparable to Solomon's biblical assessment of the true claimant to motherhood in a dispute over a baby.[56]

But the cryopreserved embryo is a frail vessel indeed for bearing this degree of emotional, social, and moral weight. What does it say about adult/child relationships in North American culture when for some adults, yearning over an embryo in a dish is an instantiation of parenthood? What does it say about the status of children within North American culture when care and love are lavished on a four-celled fertilized egg, and four-year-olds go hungry? Certainly, embryos have the advantage of being, in some ways, both easier to handle and less demanding than children; though it is not cheap to maintain an embryo in a cryopreserved state, it is probably less expensive and certainly less demanding on the "parents" than feeding, clothing, and educating a toddler. And while commentators ranging from Judge Young to George Annas may reject the notion that embryos can be owned, still it is easier to give away, sell, or destroy an unwanted embryo than to dispose of an unwanted child. Thus, the more that embryos are regarded as being physically and morally independent of women's bodies, the more they come to be regarded as purchasable and undemanding child-substitutes for the "parents" that generate them.

Decision-Making About Embryos

Do "ejaculatory fathers" (i.e., sperm providers) have any moral rights to control over embryos? How should competing claims from women and men about reproductive rights with respect to embryos be handled?

Ideally, of course, gamete contributors would agree about the disposition of resulting embryos, and would make prior arrangements concerning the treatment of the embryos and the role and authority of the storage facility in the event of the death of one or both, divorce or separation in the case of married couples, or a decision not to undergo future implantations. Their decisions should include assessment of the various alternatives of discarding, donating for research, or giving the embryos to another women—without being entitled to specify which woman, or type of woman, is entitled to have the embryos. But in the absence of such agreements, a decision like that of the appeals court in the Davis case to give joint control of the embryos to the disputing parties simply assigns a de facto veto to men like Junior Davis who seek to prevent their ex-partners from gestating the embryos.

Should their location make a difference to our assessment of who should make decisions about embryos? In questions of abortion, the location of the embryo or fetus in a woman's body is crucially significant to her entitlement to decide whether to continue the pregnancy. In the case of cryopreserved embryos, the fact that the embryos are outside of a woman's body does not necessarily make her interest in decision-making about them less than it is when she is pregnant. For the location of the embryos, in a petri dish or freezer, does not make them independent of a woman's body. Ozar's claim that with laboratory-produced embryos, "no woman is involved," is false. These insouciant words betray the error, egregiously shared by the embryo-fetishists, of regarding the embryo as a sort of technological *ding-an-sich*, a being existing independently of any woman's body. For at least one woman is crucially involved: that is, the woman who provides the eggs from which the embryos are produced, and into whose uterus the embryos may be implanted. The involvement of this woman gives her the entitlement to decide what happens to the embryos.

But it is important to be clear just why her involvement confers this entitlement. Janice Raymond straightforwardly appeals to the woman's "greater contribution to the embryos, . . . her repeated attempts at implantation and gestation, and considerable bodily investment."[57] Robertson, by contrast, rejects what he calls the " 'sweat equity' position that always favors the woman's decision because she has put more effort into production of the embryo, having undergone ovarian stimulation and surgical retrieval of eggs." The reason, he says, is that

> Great differences in physical burdens do not require that divorcing mothers always receive custody of children. Moreover, the difference in bodily burdens between the man and woman in IVF is not so great . . . that it should automatically determine decisional authority over resulting embryos.[58]

But Robertson's belief that embryos are property is inconsistent with his assumption that custody decisions about children are relevant to decision-making about embryos. As an advocate of the view that embryos are not persons, and not comparable to children, Robertson is the last person who should appeal to legal decisions about the custody of children.

Moreover, the argument that the difference in "bodily burdens" between women and men in IVF is insufficiently great to justify assigning decision-making to the woman fails because of the implausibility of its premise. There is, presumably, little burden involved in masturbating to produce sperm, but the physical and psychological burdens of hormonal treatments, aspiration of eggs, and implantation can be almost over-whelming.[59] Judge Young claimed that Junior Davis

> spent many anxious hours, early in the morning and late at night, waiting at the hospital while Mrs. Davis underwent the aspiration and implant procedures and . . . he spent many anxious hours, as a prospective Father, awaiting word as to whether he would be a Father.[60]

But if the man's anxiety and uncertainty over the possible outcome of IVF are evidence of his "burdens," they hardly compare to the physical and emotional stress on the person whose body is the site of the interventions, and who experiences even greater stress about their consequences.

Nevertheless, the argument for assigning decisional authority for embryos to the woman should rest not on an appeal to the woman's "investment," a claim that too readily buys into the view of embryos as capital. And it should not, or not only, rest on the woman's clearly greater prior burdens. Nor should it involve, as Janice Raymond tentatively suggests, an appeal to the woman's "right to what issues from her body,"[61] since in the process of in vitro fertilization, ova, not embryos, are what issue from her body, and the sperm provider can equally argue that the sperm that fertilized the ova issued from his body. Instead, *the argument should be future-oriented.* What the Davis case shows is that the justification for assigning decisional authority over embryos to the woman in cases of dispute is to reduce the likelihood that the woman will have to undertake the burdens of IVF in the future. Giving the embryos to the woman for implantation means that she may be able to avoid being subjected to further massive amounts of hormones and the removal of more ova.

The justification of giving the embryos to the woman can also be demonstrated by imagining the consequences if the intentions of the disputing parties in the Davis case had been reversed. Suppose, that is, that the sperm provider wanted the embryos, and his ex-wife, the woman who supplied the ova, wanted them to be destroyed. What are the implications if the woman's decision is not determinative? It seems that the embryos would be given to the man. But since he cannot gestate them, and since, as even Judge Young recognizes, it would be wrong to *force* the woman to gestate them against her will, it would seem to be necessary for the man to find another woman who is willing, for payment or other reasons, to gestate them. In other words, the claim that it is appropriate to "give the embryos to the sperm provider," against the will of the woman who provided the eggs, requires in its practical implications that some form of contract motherhood, whether commercial or "altruistic," be endorsed.

There is not space here to review the arguments against this practice. But the complex and serious problems relating to the recruitment and possible exploitation of women in contract motherhood, and to later custody of any resulting children, militate against its endorsement.[62] While commercial "surrogacy" raises obvious problems with respect to the misuse of women's bodies and the sale of infants, so-called altruistic "surrogacy" is also of questionable moral value, since it is not clear to what degree the "surrogates" participate willingly, and their infants, while not purchased, are handed over like objects to new recipients, without concern for the infants' own interests. To provide embryos to men in situations like that of Junior Davis would constitute a tacit de facto state approval for some forms of contract motherhood. In view of the very strong reasons against state endorsement of this practice, the embryos ought not to be provided to the man—who, in most cases, is still fertile and capable of future procreation through heterosexual intercourse or donor insemination.

Suppose, however, that Junior Davis had become infertile shortly after the end of his marriage. If Mary Sue Davis did not want the embryos implanted in her uterus, should they not then be given to Junior, even against Mary Sue's will?[63] Such a proposal assumes without argument that the significance to Junior of having his own genetically related children is greater than the significance to his future female partner of having her own genetically-related offspring. For if his female partner gestates the embryos of Mary Sue and Junior Davis, any resulting child will, of course, not be genetically related to her. And although the woman's chances of a successful pregnancy and birth, with few medical interventions, would be much higher if she were to be inseminated with donor sperm, giving the embryos to Junior assumes the willingness of his future female partner to choose the much riskier reproductive path of embryo implantation. Moreover, it also *endorses* that path: that is, providing the embryos to Junior implicitly says that it is preferable for his future female partner to attempt gestation of unrelated embryos, with all the attendant risks of such a pregnancy, than to go through a low-risk pregnancy initiated through alternative insemination.

Nevertheless, it is imaginable that Junior's future female partner might, herself, have certain problems with infertility; she might have, for example, blocked fallopian tubes, the classic indication for IVF. In this circumstance, it might be argued, Junior should be given the embryos for precisely the sort of reason I outlined earlier for giving them to Mary Sue Davis: to reduce the likelihood that his female partner will have to undergo a future course of hormonal priming and egg withdrawal. Notice, however, that once again, this proposal assumes, without evidence, that the female partner will choose gestation of unrelated embryos over gestation of her own: that is, it assumes her consent to a procedure designed to guarantee Junior's genetic connection to the offspring, but not her own. Indeed, it assumes, without evidence, her willingness to be a mother in any way. But, aside from begging the question of the female partner's choice with respect to her reproductive activities, and perhaps even putting pressure on her to engage in such activities, giving the embryos to Junior Davis implies that the physical and emotional pain and medical risks suffered by Mary Sue Davis should be used to benefit another woman, even against Mary Sue's will. While it would perhaps be good of Mary Sue Davis to surrender the embryos—providing that Junior Davis's future female partner wants to gestate them—it is unfair to compel her to do so. Giving the embryos to Junior Davis, against Mary Sue's will, is disrespectful of her suffering, and inappropriately treats Mary Sue's IVF ordeal as a means to another woman's procreative end.

I conclude, therefore, that giving the embryos to Junior Davis, against Mary Sue Davis's will, has one or more of the following consequences: endorsing contract motherhood, presuming upon the procreative choices of and placing pronatalist pressure on Junior Davis's future female partner, affirming the value of embryo implantation over donor insemination, or using one woman's medical treatment as a means to another woman's reproductive goals. Since all of these consequences are undesirable and undeserving of state endorsement, the embryos should not be given to Junior Davis, against Mary Sue's will, even when Mary Sue does not intend to have them implanted in her own uterus.

Thus, in cases of disagreement about the disposition of cryopreserved embryos, joint decision-making gives an effective veto to the man, while giving the embryos to the man entails the de facto endorsement of several morally questionable assumptions and practices. Moreover, under these conditions, the woman faces the burden of undergoing IVF once again. Therefore, decision-making about cryopreserved embryos should, in cases of disagreement, be assigned to the woman, who is entitled to choose whether or not they will be implanted in her uterus.

Some Final Comments

The current terms of much of the debate about the disposition of embryos, a debate that often replicates right-wing views about "maternal feelings" and women's proper reproductive role, lends some credence to the radical-feminist speculation that control of reproduction is central to the preservation of patriarchy.[64] "[New reproductive] technologies focus medical, legal, and media attention on the status and rights of fetuses and men while rendering the status and rights of women at best incidental and at worst invisible."[65] The apparent dispute over a four-celled organism is at least as much a debate about reproductive control of women. The message of Junior Davis, of his lawyers, supporters, and approving commentators, and of the appeals court judge, is that even after a woman undergoes the arduous and usually unrewarding processes of IVF, she can and should be prevented from deciding her reproductive future. The subtext appears to be fear—fear of the specter of sperm theft, and fear that a man's loss of control over his sperm is the loss of control over his life. The Davis case illustrates not only the ongoing fetishization of embryos, but also the fetishization of sperm, and an uncritical yet morally problematic equation of ejaculation with fatherhood, and embryos with babies.

Notes

I wish to thank Joan Callahan for her challenging and provocative comments on an earlier draft of this paper, and Jennifer Parks, whose work on the issue of "respect" for embryos helped me to think through some of the problems discussed here.

1. I use the term "embryo" throughout this paper to refer generally to entities produced through the combination of a human ovum with a human sperm, from fertilization to approximately two months' development. The embryos discussed in this paper have usually developed only for a few days, although in another sense they can be much "older," by virtue of having been cryopreserved, in a very early stage of development, and maintained for months and even years in that state. I chose not to use the term "pre-embryo," which is advocated by some writers as appropriate for the post-conception entity up to fourteen days of development, when the primitive streak first appears. (The best example of use of this term is the anthology, *Embryo Experimentation*, edited by Peter Singer et al. [New York: Cambridge University Press, 1990].) In my view, the arguments for making a terminological distinction of this sort are not convincing.

2. Hans O. Tiefel, "Human In Vitro Fertilization: A Conservative View," in *Ethical Issues in the New Reproductive Technologies*, ed. Richard T. Hull (Belmont, CA: Wadsworth, 1990), p. 129.

3. American Fertility Society Ethics Committee, "Ethical Considerations of the New Reproductive Technologies," *Fertility and Sterility* 42, 3 Supplement 1 (September, 1986): 53S.

4. *Davis v. Davis v. King* E-14496 (Fifth Jud. Ct. Tennessee), Young, Judge (1989), pp. 1–2. To be consistent with his own decision, Judge Young should have added that, since grand multiple pregnancies are more dangerous for fetuses, the embryos should be implanted in stages, and gestated during several pregnancies, in order to provide them a greater chance of surviving to birth.

5. *Davis v. Davis v. King*, p. 28.

6. Karen Dawson, "Fertilization and Moral Status: A Scientific Perspective," in *Embryo Experimentation*, p. 43.

7. *Davis v. Davis v. King*, p. 10.

8. Mary Anne Warren, "On the Moral and Legal Status of Abortion," in *The Problem of Abortion*, ed. Joel Feinberg (Belmont, CA: Wadsworth, 1984), p. 110.

9. *Davis v. Davis v. King*, p. 9.

10. *Davis v. Davis v. King*, p. 1.

11. Helga Kuhse and Peter Singer, "Individuals, Humans and Persons: The Issue of Moral Status," in *Embryo Experimentation*, p. 67.

12. *Davis v. Davis v. King*, pp. 5 and 10.

13. *Davis v. Davis v. King*, pp. 9 and 27.

14. David T. Ozar, "The Case Against Thawing Unused Frozen Embryos," *Hastings Center Report* 15, 4 (1985): 8.

15. *Davis v. Davis v. King*, p. 21.

16. Ronald Smothers, "Woman Given Custody in Embryo Case," *New York Times* (22 September 1989).

17. *Davis v. Davis* WL 130807 (Tenn. App.), Franks, Judge (1990): 2.

18. Quoted in Janice Raymond, "Of Ice and Men: The Big Chill over Women's Reproductive Rights," *Issues in Reproductive and Genetic Engineering: Journal of International Feminist Analysis* 3, 1 (1990): 49.

19. Michael D. Bayles, *Reproductive Ethics* (Englewood Cliffs, NJ: Prentice-Hall, 1984), p. 16.

20. Christine Overall, *Ethics and Human Reproduction: A Feminist Analysis* (Boston: Allen & Unwin, 1987), p. 183.

21. *Davis v. Davis*, p. 2.

22. *Davis v. Davis*, p. 4.

23. George J. Annas, "Crazy Making: Embryos and Gestational Mothers," *Hastings Center Report* 21, 1 (1991): 35 and 36.

24. The word "donors" is usually used misleadingly to refer not only to men who donate sperm but also to those who sell it. For the latter, the term "vendor" is more appropriate. Unfortunately, there is not room here to present the arguments against the merchandising of reproductive products and services; its undesirability is assumed in this paper.

25. Combined Ethics Committee of the Canadian Fertility and Andrology

Society and the Society of Obstetricians and Gynaecologists of Canada, *Ethical Considerations of the New Reproductive Technologies* (Toronto, 1990), p. 40.

26. John A. Robertson, "Embryos, Families, and Procreative Liberty: The Legal Structure of the New Reproduction," *Southern California Law Review* 59, 5 (1986): 976.

27. John A. Robertson, "Ethical and Legal Issues in Cryopreservation of Human Embryos," *Fertility and Sterility* 47, 3 (1987): 373.

28. Robertson, "Ethical and Legal Issues," p. 374. By contrast, the American Fertility Society Ethics Committee recommends that "Storage should be continued only as long as the normal reproductive span of the egg donor or only as long as the original objective of the storage procedure is in force" (p. 55).

29. *Davis v. Davis*, p. 3.

30. Bayles, p. 16.

31. Robertson, "Embryos, Families, and Procreative Liberty," p. 979.

32. Robertson, "Ethical and Legal Issues," p. 376.

33. Raymond, p. 47.

34. Raymond, pp. 46 and 48.

35. *Davis v. Davis v. King*, p. 22.

36. *Davis v. Davis v. King*, p. 21.

37. *Davis v. Davis v. King*, pp. 22–23.

38. Robertson, "Ethical and Legal Issues," p. 376.

39. Robertson, "Ethical and Legal Issues," p. 379.

40. Robertson, "Ethical and Legal Issues," p. 380.

41. *Davis v. Davis v. King*, p. 23.

42. *Davis v. Davis v. King*, p. 27.

43. Raymond, p. 46.

44. *Davis v. Davis v. King*, pp. 24 and 27.

45. *Davis v. Davis v. King*, p. 24.

46. Ozar, p. 8.

47. George J. Annas, "Redefining Parenthood and Protecting Embryos: Why We Need New Laws," *Hastings Center Report* 14, 5 (1984): 51.

48. Robertson, "Ethical and Legal Issues," p. 371.

49. Robertson, "Ethical and Legal Issues," p. 376.

50. Andrea L. Bonnicksen, "Embryo Freezing: Ethical Issues in the Clinical Setting," *Hastings Center Report* 18, 6 (1988): 27.

51. *Davis v. Davis v. King*, p. 27.

52. Bonnicksen, p. 29.

53. Robertson, "Ethical and Legal Issues," p. 378.

54. Bonnicksen, p. 29.

55. *Davis v. Davis v. King*, p. 11.

56. *Davis v. Davis v. King*, p. 31.

57. Raymond, p. 46.

58. John A. Robertson, "Resolving Disputes Over Frozen Embryos," *Hastings Center Report* 19, 6 (1989): 7.

59. Linda S. Williams, "No Relief until the End: The Physical and Emotional Costs of In Vitro Fertilization," in *The Future of Human Reproduction*, ed. Christine Overall (Toronto: Women's Press, 1989).

60. *Davis v. Davis v. King*, p. 3.

61. Raymond, p. 46.

62. Christine Overall, "The Case Against the Legalization of Contract Motherhood," in *Debating Canada's Future: Views From the Left*, ed. Simon Rosenblum and Peter Findlay (Toronto: James Lorimer, 1991).

63. I am grateful to Joan Callahan for suggesting this scenario and the next one.

64. Jalna Hanmer, "Transforming Consciousness: Women and the New Reproductive Technologies," in *Man-Made Women: How New Reproductive Technologies Affect Women*, ed. Gena Corea et al. (Bloomington: Indiana University Press, 1987).

65. Raymond, p. 45.

As If There Were Fetuses without Women: A Remedial Essay

Mary B. Mahowald

As with abortion, most of the moral controversy regarding fetal tissue transplantation focuses on fetuses rather than pregnant women. In both of these related issues, that focus needs to be corrected so as to avoid the fallacy of abstraction, that is, consideration of an object as if it exists without a context. For example, "pro-life" arguments are generally based on the claim that the fetus is a person, and "pro-choice" arguments are generally based on the claim that the fetus is not a person.[1] Assuming the validity of arguments on both sides, the truth status of their conclusions depends on whether the criteria for personhood have been met by the fetus. Despite the fact that fetuses do not exist apart from women, who are inevitably affected by decisions about fetuses, women are ignored by either side so long as fetuses are the pivotal focus of the argument.

With regard to fetal tissue transplantation, women are ignored to the extent that arguments supporting and opposing it are linked with abortion as the means through which the tissue is made available. Women are also ignored where the focus is solely on commercialization of fetal tissue, the experimental status of the technique, or the needs of possible recipients. Interestingly, the important parallel between this issue and others that principally and undeniably affect women (such as contract motherhood, egg provision, and prostitution) is that women have been neglected, and in some cases, flatly ignored.

In this chapter, I want to redress the omission that prevails by reviewing the issue of fetal tissue transplantation with a focus that explicitly includes women as necessary participants in the process. In doing so, I

199

will compare and contrast this with other issues that particularly affect women, and examine different frameworks for ethical assessment of fetal tissue transplantation. First, however, I want to say why it is wrong to focus on fetuses apart from their relationship to women.

Fetuses as Such

The term "fetus" is defined as "the unborn young of an animal while still within the uterus."[2] Fortunately or unfortunately, medical technology has not yet produced an artificial uterus, and it may be biologically impossible to do so. To speak of the uterus without acknowledgment that it is within a woman is thus another example of prescinding from necessary context. According to *Stedman's Medical Dictionary*, the human fetus "represents the product of conception from the end of the eighth week to the moment of birth."[3] Human birth is understood to mean the emergence of a fetus from a woman's body. Stedman's defines the human embryo as "the developing organism from conception until approximately the end of the second month."[4] Since the advent of in vitro fertilization techniques, development of an embryo can be initiated and sustained for several days apart from a woman's body. By definition, nonviable fetuses cannot be so sustained. No matter how early the gestation, a viable fetus removed from a woman's body is no longer a fetus but a newborn. If a nonviable fetus is removed from a woman's body, it is an abortus. In other words, no fetus as such exists apart from a woman's body.

Two major (overlapping) feminist criticisms of traditional ethics are exemplified in our insistence that fetuses not be considered as if they were not present in women. First is the objection that traditional ethics calls for a deductive process through which universal principles are applied to cases.[5] Starting from different principles, whether these are a priori or a posteriori in their derivation, the process (if conducted correctly) leads inexorably to answers about what should be done in specific situations. Feminists argue that this type of deductive analysis cannot adequately attend to the complexity and uniqueness of real cases and issues. To rectify the inadequacy, attention to context is essential.[6]

Second is the objection that much of traditional ethics emphasizes the rights of individuals, neglecting the realm of relationships.[7] In fact, through its assumption that impartiality is a requirement of ethically justifiable judgments, traditional ethics eschews considerations based on particular relationships such as occur between pregnant women and their fetuses. Many of the arguments in which abortion is supported or opposed solely on grounds of the moral status of the fetus exemplify this. In contrast, feminists insist on the moral relevance of relationships, whether these are based on choice, chance, genetics, or affection.[8] The ethics of care elaborated by Carol Gilligan, Nel Noddings, and Sara Ruddick provide frameworks for understanding the essential role that relationships play in moral decision making.[9]

When it is consistently recognized that fetuses exist only in relationship to women who are inevitably affected by decisions regarding them, the above concerns are addressed. Inattention to this ongoing relationship is unscientific because it neglects an element of analysis that affects the validity of scientific interpretation. It is unethical because it ignores the interests and preferences of pregnant women, which may be at odds with the interests of the fetus.

Use of Fetal Tissue in Transplantation

An accurate understanding of reality can only be attained through analysis of the complexity of context. With regard to fetal tissue transplantation, the analysis involves at least the following variables: (1) the empirical status of fetuses or abortuses used for grafts, (2) different purposes and sites of tissue retrieval or implantation, (3) therapeutic potential for the recipient, (4) the means through which fetuses are made available for transplantation, and (5) possible motives, "donors," and recipients of fetal tissue.[10]

Regarding (1), human fetuses or abortuses used for tissue grafts may be living or dead. Living fetuses or abortuses may be viable, nonviable, or possibly viable, and they may be sentient, nonsentient, or possibly sentient, depending in part on the duration of gestation.[11] Viability is particularly relevant because it implies that others in addition to the pregnant woman can maintain the fetus ex utero if it is to be delivered or aborted. Sentience is relevant because the prima facie obligation to avoid inflicting pain on others applies to fetuses regardless of whether they are persons. While that obligation does not imply that killing is always wrong, it does imply that pain relief or prevention should be attempted for all sentient, or even possibly sentient, individuals.

Regarding (2), the procedure may be undertaken solely for research purposes, as experimental treatment, or (if and when the procedure becomes standard therapy) solely as therapy for recipients. Ordinarily, therapeutic reasons are more compelling than research reasons for medical procedures. Thus governmental and institutional regulations are more strict for research protocols than for therapeutic protocols.[12] Tissue may be retrieved from the brain or from other parts of a fetus, and implanted directly into a recipient's brain or into other regions of the recipient's body. Brain grafts are generally more problematic than nonbrain grafts because the brain is usually seen as, and may in fact be, the source of a person's identity as well as cognitive function. Nonetheless, the small amount and immaturity of tissue used in transplants serve to minimize this concern.

Regarding (3), non-neural fetal tissue has been transplanted for many years to treat diseases such as DeGeorge's syndrome and diabetes mellitus, without creating public controversy.[13] The prospects that have evoked public debate involve use of neural tissue for treatment of severe and previously incurable neurological disorders. Among the neurological conditions that are potentially treatable are Alzheimer's disease, Parkinson's disease, amyotrophic lateral sclerosis (Lou Gehrig's disease), Huntington's disease, multiple sclerosis, spinal-cord injury, epilepsy, and stroke.[14] The research is most advanced in treatment of Parkinson's disease, but this treatment is still experimental. Comparatively few Parkinson patients have thus far been treated.[15] One case of apparent success in treatment of Hurler's syndrome (through fetus-to-fetus transplant) has also been reported.[16] While preliminary results are promising, there are too little data as yet to generalize about the treatment's effectiveness.

Regarding (4), abortion is the means through which human fetal tissue becomes available for transplantation. Abortions may be spontaneous or induced, and induced abortions may be performed for medical or non-medical reasons. Medical reasons for induced abortion include those based on the pregnant woman's health, those based on fetal anomaly, or both. While use of tissue obtained from spontaneous abortions may be less ethically controversial than use of tissue obtained from induced abortions, the tissue from spontaneously aborted fetuses is unlikely to be normal or suitable for transplantation.[17] Because of that likelihood, it may be argued that use of tissue from spontaneously aborted fetuses constitutes undue risk to the recipient. Nonetheless, the first reported human use of fetal neural tissue for treatment of Parkinson's patients involved tissue retrieved from a spontaneously aborted fetus. This work evoked criticism from researchers involved in neurografting.[18]

Regarding (5), fetal tissue may be "donated" for altruistic reasons, self-interested reasons, or both. Ordinarily, the recipient is unrelated and unknown to the pregnant woman. Anonymity has been proposed by at least two panels reviewing the issue as a requirement for donor status.[19] However, an ethic that emphasizes relationships supports a decision to donate the tissue on the part of someone such as a friend or spouse who is both known and related to the recipient. A care ethic may also support a decision to become pregnant in order to provide the tissue to someone with whom one has a special relationship.

Further, a pregnant woman might herself be the recipient, and could deliberately become pregnant in order to provide the fetal tissue that might lead to her own cure. There is one published report of a woman with severe aplastic anemia who was transplanted with the liver of her own fetus after an elective abortion.[20] Although the details of the case are sketchy, the pregnancy was probably not initiated with the intention of providing the fetal tissue for two reasons. First, pregnancy is a serious risk to women with this disease, and second, the fetus would not necessarily be an appropriate tissue match for the woman. Nonetheless, a woman's right to self-preservation supports such an attempt to provide the tissue for her own treatment.

From a feminist perspective, all of the above variables are morally relevant to determination of whether fetal tissue transplantation is justified in specific cases. Particularly important is the means through which fetal tissue is obtained, namely, abortion. In order to insure respect for women's autonomy, decisions to terminate pregnancies must be separable from decisions to provide fetal tissue for transplantation. (Note that I have used the word "separable" rather than "separate.") As we will see in the next section, however, the possibility of separating the two has been disputed.

Fetal Tissue Transplantation and Abortion

Although the connection between grafts of human fetal tissue and abortion might have triggered public controversy decades ago, this did not occur until reports circulated early in 1987 about the prospect of using the tissue for treatment of neurological disorders.[21] Apparent reasons for the shift include the fact that abortion was not the volatile issue that it is today when fetal tissue was first used for research or therapeutic purposes. Another reason is that the type of diseases that the tissue may potentially be used to treat afflict literally millions of people who are severely debilitated with otherwise incurable diseases. There seems to be little doubt that political interests were at work in establishing the moratorium on government funding in the United States for research projects involving use of fetal tissue obtained from abortions. Before the

Clinton administration lifted the moratorium in 1993, researchers could only find support for use of electively aborted fetal tissue through private sources. Although the moratorium slowed progress in the United States, researchers in Colorado and Connecticut, states that permit research with electively aborted fetal tissue, pursued their projects through private funding.[22]

The problematic connection between fetal tissue transplantation and abortion was first noted by a group who met in Cleveland in 1986. In collaboration with neuroscientist Jerry Silver, I had organized the meeting to review the issue in order to facilitate informed public debate. In March 1987, a consensus statement of the group appeared in *Science*.[23] We maintained that the procedure held "the promise of great benefit to victims of serious neurological disorders." Despite the legality of abortion, fetal tissue transplantation "was acknowledged to be ethically controversial because of its association with abortion." In light of that controversy, we proposed "separation between decisions related to the acquisition of tissue and decisions regarding the transplantation of tissue into a recipient." Two years later, a panel of experts convened by the National Institutes of Health (NIH), several of whom had signed the earlier consensus statement, offered a similar recommendation.[24]

Feminist support for distinguishing between decisions about abortion and decisions about fetal tissue transplantation is mainly based on concerns about possibilities for exploiting women or pressuring them to undergo abortions, or to delay or modify abortion procedures in order to provide fetal tissue to prospective recipients. As yet, it has not been necessary to delay or modify abortion procedures in treatment by means of fetal tissue grafts. Preliminary data suggest that the gestational age optimal for successful transplants into Parkinson's patients is as early as seven weeks, using tissue obtained from abortions performed by standard clinical methods.[25]

While feminists generally support the right of women to terminate pregnancies, most see abortion as a "forced" and tragic option.[26] It is regrettable that a woman must choose between continuation and termination of her pregnancy because both alternatives involve burdens or harms. Accordingly, we would not like to see the option of providing fetal tissue for transplantation precipitate an increase in abortions. Ironically, this concern coincides with one of the concerns mentioned in minority reports of the NIH Human Fetal Tissue Transplantation Research panel (hereafter, NIH panel). Several members of the NIH panel argued against government support for the procedure on grounds that it would constitute an inducement to abortion, at least for pregnant women who had not yet decided whether to terminate their pregnancies.[27] There are no data supporting this claim.

A further concern of a minority of the NIH panel was that participation in fetal tissue transplantation constitutes complicity in, and legitimation of, abortion. According to James Bopp and James Burtchaell,

> Whatever the researcher's intentions may be, by entering into an institutionalized partnership with the abortion industry as a supplier of preference, he or she becomes complicit, though after the fact, with the abortions that have expropriated the tissue for his or her purposes.[28]

They thus maintain that those who use fetal tissue from elective abortions ally themselves with the "evil" that abortion represents.

Bopp and Burtchaell further claim that legitimation occurs when pregnant women considering abortion construe the possibility of benefiting someone by donating fetal tissue as a positive endorsement of abortion. The abortion is then seen as a less tragic choice than it would otherwise be, and in some circumstances it might even be seen as virtuous. Legitimation would occur on a social level if the good of successful treatment through fetal tissue transplantation became so compelling that the means of achieving the success were never critically assessed. The end would then have justified the means, at least as perceived by those who pursue the end without scrutinizing the end in its own right.

The legitimation argument illustrates more general concerns about slippery slope reasoning. Questions such as the following are then raised: if we now approve use of fetal tissue for transplants under restrictive conditions, are we not likely in time to relax the conditions if the therapy proves highly successful or if the restrictive conditions limit its usefulness? Most people agree that some restrictions are necessary to avoid abuses that could accompany use of the technology; they disagree about where to place wedges along the slippery slope.[29]

Some have proposed less restrictive guidelines than those recommended by the NIH panel, particularly with regard to commercialization. For example, Lori Andrews argues that a woman should be allowed to sell the tissue of a fetus she has agreed to abort. Feminists, she maintains, are inconsistent with their commitment to promote women's right to control their own bodies if they oppose commercial surrogacy.[30] Most feminists, however, oppose both contract motherhood and commerce in fetal tissue because of the possibility they present for exploiting women. Unlike Andrews, we thus place greater emphasis on social equality than on individual liberty. Social equality is seen as a necessary condition for authentic choice. Until and unless gender equality prevails, the liberty of individual women is inevitably curtailed.

Different views regarding abortion also give rise to different views regarding the consent necessary for fetal tissue transplantation. Those who are morally opposed to elective abortion generally deny that women who choose abortion have a right to donate fetal tissue.[31] Such women, they allege, have forfeited that right even as parents may forfeit their right to consent for their child if they abuse or abandon the child. On the other side of the issue are those who stress the importance of the pregnant woman's consent to use of fetal tissue because she has the right to abortion and because the tissue belongs to her.[32] Among those who consider abortion a separable issue from fetal tissue transplantation, some insist that the pregnant woman's consent is necessary because the timing and procedure for abortion may be altered in order to maximize the chance for a successful graft.[33] In other words, if the pregnant woman may herself be affected, her consent to use fetal tissue is morally indispensable.

On therapeutic grounds alone, a comparison of the potential advantages of using fetal tissue from electively aborted fetuses with the potential and actual disadvantages of treatment through other means provides a strong case for use of fetal tissue from elective abortions. Many of the diseases that are potentially curable with fetal tissue grafts are curable by no other known means. However, therapeutic efficacy alone doesn't constitute moral justification. This returns us, then, to the problem of whether the question of induced abortion is morally separable from the question of fetal tissue transplantation. The issue calls for reexamination of the traditional moral dilemma involving the relationship between means and ends. Does the end justify the means in transplantation of fetal tissue for cure of otherwise incurable disorders?

A simplistic version of utilitarianism supports an affirmative answer to the question. In other words, the tremendous good that might be accomplished through the new technique outweighs the harm that might be done through elective abortion. However, if endorsement of the procedure led to widespread increase in elective abortions and to exploitation of women, such undesirable consequences might outweigh the potential benefit of the technique. So, even if ends can justify means, it is not clear that the end justifies the means in this case. Whether or not the overall consequences of treating debilitating disorders through fetal tissue transplantation will generally constitute a preponderance of harms over benefits is an empirical issue for which more data is needed to support a credible utilitarian position.

From a deontological point of view, the end does not justify means that are otherwise morally unacceptable, but this does not imply that fetal tissue transplantation is morally unjustified. The individual who knowingly and freely pursues a specific end, also knowingly and freely chooses the means to its fulfillment. Intention is thus crucial to the moral relevance of the relationship. If a woman were to deliberately become pregnant, choose abortion, or persuade another to become pregnant or choose abortion, solely for the sake of fetal tissue transplantation, she would then be responsible for both means and end because she would be intending both. As we already noted, the motive of the decision may be altruistic, self-interested, or both. Although worthy motives are morally relevant, they do not alter the fact that the intention in such cases applies to both ends and means.

In other situations involving fetal tissue transplantation, the individual who intends to use the tissue need not even be aware of the abortion through which the tissue becomes available. Presumably, she does intend the retrieval procedure. However, just as a transplant surgeon may retrieve essential organs from the brain-dead victim of a drunk-driving accident, without any implication that she thus endorses the behavior that led to the availability of the organs, so may a neurosurgeon who is totally opposed to abortion transplant neural tissue from an electively aborted fetus into a severely impaired patient, without thereby compromising her moral convictions. In fact, one may argue that a truly pro-life position favors the saving or prolonging of life that the transplantation intends, while acknowledging the negation of life that abortion implies. When the abortion decision has already been made by others, a decision not to transplant seems less in keeping with a position that is genuinely pro-life than its opposite. One opponent of abortion even found support for fetal tissue transplants in the biblical account of creation. Barbara Culliton attributed the following statement to the Baptist father whose infant had prenatally been treated with cells obtained from an aborted fetus: "God formed one human being from the tissue of another. Not only does God approve of this [transplantation], he himself performed the first one."[34]

Fetal Tissue Transplants and Use of Women's Bodies

If abortion and fetal tissue transplants are not separable issues, then the latter is parallel in important respects to at least three other practices which can only be undertaken through use of women's bodies. Contract motherhood, egg provision, and prostitution are comparable practices because they all involve both benefit to a third party and material remuneration to the woman who provides the benefit through use of her body. The rationale by which most feminists oppose these practices is also applicable to the apparent tie between abortion and fetal tissue grafts. However, this opposition does not extend to fetal tissue grafts considered as an issue distinct from abortion. From a feminist standpoint, it is possible to support a woman's right to abortion while opposing the practice of fetal tissue transplantation.

Contract motherhood necessarily involves the commodification of a woman's body: she "rents" or lends her womb, and may have contributed an egg to the embryo that develops within her. In commercial contracts, the woman accepts payment from an infertile couple for her "services." According to the final ruling in the Mary Beth Whitehead case, payment for such "services" is equivalent to baby selling.[35] This is an interesting designation because it totally ignores what pregnancy and birth meant to the woman, focusing exclusively on the baby to whom she gives birth. Adoption is the better analogue for the act through which infertile women or couples thus become parents. The woman has agreed to rent her womb and donate or sell her egg, and a child has been produced through the services rendered. Whether or not she is genetically related to the fetus, the surrogate is biologically related to it through gestation.

If contract motherhood is equivalent to baby selling, payment to pregnant women for use of their aborted fetuses may also be equivalent to baby selling.[36] In both cases, it is the use of the woman's body *before* abortion or delivery that is remunerated by someone to whom the fetus is valued. Neither case *necessarily* involves financial remuneration because both *may* be undertaken for altruistic reasons. Contract motherhood and use of fetal tissue may also be undertaken by mutual agreement prior to the establishment of pregnancy. In neither case is there an intent to keep the product of conception. In one case, however, a living infant is provided for a third party; in the other, the tissue of a dead fetus is obtained in order to provide for the health of a third party. In both situations, the intention of the pregnant women may be both self-interested and altruistic, regardless of whether payment is involved.

Egg donation may be compared with sperm "donation" because both involve the provision of gametes, usually for financial compensation. But unlike the provision of sperm, providing eggs involves considerable discomfort and risk. When the procedure was first reported in Cleveland in 1987, it required administration of superovulatory drugs and laparoscopic retrieval of ova under general anaesthesia.[37] In most centers, retrieval is now undertaken through transvaginal aspiration with a local anaesthetic. As with sperm, the term "donation" is misleading because individuals who agree to provide ova generally do so for the money. As a student who volunteered for the world's first egg donor program put it: "I would never go through this if I were not a poor student."[38] The compensation provided to egg donors in the program in which she enrolled was $900-$1200. In 1992, compensation ranged from $1500 to $3000, depending on the clinic.[39]

The practice of egg donation is comparable to fetal tissue provision insofar as the woman in each case contributes genetic material and may receive compensation. Occasionally, the ova retrieved may simply be the product of a normal menstrual cycle, without requiring administration of superovulatory medication. When this occurs, the retrieval is comparable to retrieval of fetal tissue from women who undergo abortions to terminate unwanted pregnancies. Unlike fetuses, ova are regularly disposed of through menstruation. They may even be retrieved as a byproduct of surgery undertaken for treatment purposes. In such circumstances, providing eggs for another is more like providing tissue from spontaneously aborted fetuses than providing tissue obtained from elective abortions.

As with contract motherhood and sperm donation, egg donation is oriented to the development of a new human life. Fetal tissue becomes available for transplantation only after the death of the embryo or fetus, which occurs in the context of either spontaneous or elective abortion. The tissue that thus becomes available constitutes the possibility of extending another human life. In all of these cases, therefore, another life is affirmed through birth or healing.

Prostitution is different from the other issues discussed because it does not involve a comparable goal. To some people, the very suggestion of a parallel between prostitution and egg provision or contract motherhood is offensive because the former practice is clearly illegal and immoral, while the latter two practices are not.[40] Another difference is that prostitution does not involve medical technology. Although contract motherhood through artificial insemination may be undertaken without the help of a medical expert, this is probably a rare event, and arrangements in which gestational and genetic roles are separate require *in vitro* fertilization.[41] Despite these differences, the parallel between prostitution and the other issues is valid insofar as all of them involve the use of women's bodies to satisfy the desires of another. So does fetal tissue transplantation.

By definition, prostitution is practiced for material remuneration, usually money, and not for altruistic reasons intended to benefit those who employ prostitutes.[42] In some cases, however, women sell the intimacy of their bodies in order to support their children; for many women, prostitution is a means of survival, and in some cases it is perceived as (and may in fact be) the only available means of survival.[43] From a moral point of view, prostitution to obtain funds necessary for one's own or others' survival is surely defensible. What is immoral in such a situation is the social situation that presents so tragic a limitation of alternatives to women.[44]

Because prostitution is always practiced for material gain for the prostitute, it is only comparable to fetal tissue transplantation when the latter procedure also procures material gain for the woman who provides the fetal tissue. As with prostitution, however, the material gain that is accessible through fetal tissue grafts may be sought indirectly, and the motive for providing the tissue may be altruistic rather than self-interested. It is possible, for example, for a woman to initiate and terminate a pregnancy to produce fetal tissue for someone from whom she hopes to inherit wealth because of that decision. It is also possible to sell fetal tissue that she develops through a pregnancy that is deliberately undertaken to obtain funds necessary for her own or others' sustenance. A woman could even sell a fetus conceived through intercourse as a prostitute. While there are long-standing social, moral, and religious objections to prostitution, the grounds for these objections are not substantively different from objections that may be raised to contract motherhood, at least when the woman who gives birth is not genetically related to the offspring. Both involve the use of a woman's intimate body parts for payment, and in both cases the woman is generally of considerably lower socioeconomic status than the payor.

If prostitution is practiced to promote one's own survival, it parallels the situation of a pregnant woman who wishes her fetal tissue to be used for treatment of her own devastating disease, that is, to insure her own survival. If a pregnant woman sells her fetus to obtain funds to support others, her act is comparable to that of the woman who prostitutes herself to support her children. Fetal tissue transplantation is more morally problematic than prostitution because it involves not only the use of women's bodies but also the use of human fetuses. The same argument can be made with regard to a comparison between prostitution and egg provision or contract motherhood. The latter practices may be viewed as more problematic because they involve the use of gametes and fetuses or newborns as well as the use of women's bodies for remuneration.

Paradigms and Frameworks for Assessing
Fetal Tissue Transplantation

Different paradigms and frameworks have been invoked to defend or oppose fetal tissue transplantation. The paradigms include transplantation from living donors, as in kidney transplants; transplantation from cadaver donors, as in heart transplants; and "surrogate motherhood."[45] The first two are familiar and generally accepted means of obtaining organs or tissue, so long as consent is obtained from the donor or proxy and the retrieval does not constitute a major threat to the donor's health. Use of tissue from living fetuses has generally been rejected, but it is sometimes difficult to determine whether a fetus is dead. Traditional means of assessing brain death are not applicable to early fetuses or abortuses. Although "surrogacy" is a more controversial paradigm for fetal tissue transplantation, it captures, as the other two paradigms do not, the unique possibilities for exploitation of women that fetal tissue transplantation represents. As I have already suggested, these possibilities are also present in egg provision and prostitution, which are also comparable to fetal tissue transplantation.

Dorothy Vawter and her colleagues at the University of Minnesota have proposed three "competing frameworks" that may be related to the above paradigms.[46] The first is based on the premise that the fetus from which tissue may be retrieved should be regarded as a human research subject. On this view, either of two rationales may prevail, depending on whether the aborted fetus is construed as living or dead. If the former, use of fetal tissue "should satisfy the federal regulations for research involving living fetuses, and be reviewed and approved by an institutional review board." If the aborted fetus is regarded as a cadaver, a proxy decision-maker should be required "to base a decision regarding participation either on the basis of what the dead fetus would have wanted or on some view of what is in the dead fetus' best interests." Not surprisingly, neither of these standards is explained, and the authors acknowledge that it is "extremely difficult to see how a proxy decision-maker could base a decision on [them]."[47]

The second ethical framework proposed by the Minnesota group is a view of the dead fetus as a cadaveric organ donor. This generally means following the standards of the Uniform Anatomical Gift Act, which is applicable in all 50 states in the United States. This Act allows either parent to provide the necessary consent for use of fetal tissue so long as the other parent does not object. Moreover, because the dead fetus can hardly be accredited with wishes or interests, parents may base their decision on their own needs, concerns, and interests. The consensus statement of the 1986 forum in Cleveland utilized this framework. According to the authors,

retrieval of tissue from fetal remains is analogous to the transplantation of organs or tissue obtained from adult human cadavers. Similarities include the fact that the donor is dead, and the expectation that there will be significant benefits for the recipient. These similarities suggest the appropriateness of using the same ethical and legal criteria now followed for cadaver transplantation.[48]

The beginning point of the published reports from both the Cleveland group and the NIH panel is that fetal tissue should only be retrieved from *dead* fetuses. Only then does the analogy with retrieval of tissue from "adult human cadavers" work. Even so, the differences between transplantation from human fetal cadavers rather than mature human cadavers are to be addressed through added requirements, such as the exclusion of familial donors and the observance of anonymity between donors and recipients. Obviously, this excludes the possibility of a woman initiating or terminating pregnancy in order to provide tissue for herself or for another with whom she has a special relationship.

The third framework proposed by Vawter and her colleagues is one in which the dead fetus or abortus is equated with discarded tissue. In that context,

> fetal remains, whether the result of elective abortion, ectopic pregnancy, or spontaneous abortion, are treated as any other bodily tissue and fluid removed during a diagnostic or surgical procedure.[49]

Aborted tissue is thus construed as a tissue specimen of the woman from whose body it was removed. Permission from those whose discarded tissue may be examined for educative, research, or future treatment purposes is routinely obtained in the clinical setting. Typically, the consent forms include "boilerplate" language requesting blanket permission for use of any biological "waste materials" or "tissue specimens" removed during surgical procedures. Similar boilerplate language could be incorporated into the consent form for abortion procedures.

Whereas the first two frameworks proposed by the Minnesota Center focus on the fetus as a separate being from the pregnant woman, the third focuses on the fact that fetal tissue is in fact the woman's tissue, and ought to be treated as such even when aborted. It is appropriate, therefore, to ask the pregnant woman for consent to use of her fetal tissue prior to the abortion, and her consent alone is morally adequate. Some might argue that consent of the man who impregnated the woman should also be required for use of fetal tissue, but this suggests an unusual concept of "discarded tissue," and a departure from the usual manner of dealing with discarded tissue. Moreover, since abortion is a decision legally made by women and not by their male partners, men cannot effectively challenge pregnant women's decisions regarding disposition of their fetuses.

Like the "surrogacy" model, the discarded tissue framework emphasizes the essential tie between fetus and pregnant woman. The latter model is a means of avoiding the abuses that we have seen associated with contract motherhood. Because the discarded tissue model gives priority to the pregnant woman's autonomy, it serves as a check on the possibilities for exploitation of women that transplantation of fetal tissue allows. Thus there are both conceptual and moral reasons for preferring this framework to the others: it takes account of the unique relationship between fetus and pregnant woman, and the practice it engenders is consistent with respect for patient autonomy in comparable situations.

Conclusion

Like abortion, and probably because of its association with abortion, the issue of fetal tissue transplantation is a volatile one. Ironically, both feminists and those opposed to elective abortion are concerned about its association with abortion because for the former it represents possible pressures on women to initiate or terminate pregnancies, and for the latter it expresses complicity in, and legitimation of, abortion. From a feminist standpoint, there is strong support for keeping the two issues separable, but not necessarily separate. "Separable" allows for the possibility that individual women may choose to connect their abortions with the provision of fetal tissue. If the issues are "separate," that connection is precluded.

Because fetuses do not exist apart from women, fetal tissue transplantation raises concerns that may be seen in other troublesome issues that centrally affect women: contract motherhood, egg provision, and prostitution. Examination of the similarities and dissimilarities among these issues facilitates a better grasp of problematic aspects of the involvement of women in fetal tissue transplantation. If abortion decisions are separable from decisions about use of fetal tissue, the problematic aspects are reduced.

Of the frameworks that have been proposed for moral assessment of fetal tissue transplantation, the use of fetal remains from abortions is more like use of discarded tissue than use of tissue from research subjects or from cadaver donors. Whether the abortion through which fetal tissue becomes available is spontaneous or induced, the tissue used for grafts is discarded from the body of the pregnant woman. However, even the analogy with use of discarded tissue misses the uniqueness and complexity of the relationship between pregnant women and fetuses. The uniqueness and complexity of that relationship call for explicit attention to the fact that fetuses do not exist without women.

Notes

1. My use of the terms "pro-life" and "pro-choice" accords with popular usage. In another article I have noted that this usage is not fully affirmative of life and choice, respectively. See my "Abortion and Equality," in Sidney Callahan and Daniel Callahan, eds., *Abortion* (New York: Plenum Press, 1984), 179–180. One notable exception to the tendency to base "pro-choice" arguments on the status of the fetus is Judith Jarvis Thomson's "A Defense of Abortion," in *Philosophy and Public Affairs* 1, 1 (1971), 47–66. Thomson defends a woman's right to abortion *even if* the fetus is a person.

2. E.g., see *Webster's New World Dictionary*, 2nd college ed. (New York: Simon and Schuster, 1982), 517; cf. *Churchill's Medical Dictionary* (New York: Churchill Livingston Inc., 1989), 693.

3. *Stedman's Medical Dictionary*, 25th ed. (Baltimore: Williams and Wilkins, 1990), 573. This calculation of the duration of gestation is based on the first day of the last menstrual period rather than fertilization. If duration of gestation is calculated from fertilization, the fetal stage of development commences at six weeks. See James Knight and Joan Callahan, *Preventing Birth* (Salt Lake City: University of Utah Press, 1989), 205.

4. *Stedman's*, 501. However, Knight and Callahan note that the term "embryo" refers to the developing human organism between weeks 2 and 6 of gestation (205). Implantation in the uterus occurs about two weeks after fertilization. Between fertilization and implantation, the conceptus may be referred to as a "pre-implantation embryo." The term "pre-embryo" is sometimes used by in vitro fertilization specialists to refer to the conceptus before implantation. In popular usage, however, the term "embryo" is often used to characterize the conceptus from fertilization until fetal stage.

5. Susan Sherwin develops this criticism on the part of medical ethics as well as feminist ethics. See her "Feminist and Medical Ethics: Two Different Approaches to Contextual Ethics," *Hypatia* 4, 2 (Summer 1989): 57–72.

6. Marilyn Friedman, "Care and Context in Moral Reasoning," *Women and Moral Theory*, ed. by Eva F. Kittay and Diana T. Meyers (Totowa, New Jersey: Rowman and Littlefield, 1987), 190–204.

7. See Friedman; see also Christina Sommers, "Filial Morality," in Kittay and Meyers, 69–84.

8. Some feminists argue that the genetic tie is hardly relevant in defining parental relationships. See, e.g., Barbara Katz Rothman, *Recreating Motherhood* (New York: W. W. Norton 1989), 37–40. In some cases, however, the

law insists on the significance of the genetic tie. For example, known (genetic) fathers are legally responsible for support of their children. It is well known that statutes requiring such support are only occasionally enforced.

9. Carol Gilligan, *In a Different Voice* (Cambridge: Harvard University Press, 1982); Nel Noddings, *Caring* (Berkeley: University of California Press, 1984); Sara Ruddick *Maternal Thinking* (New York: Ballantine Books 1989). While developing a model of maternal thinking that is applicable to men as well as women, Ruddick refers to the work of mothering as "caring labor" (46). See also Mary Jean Larrabee, ed., *An Ethic of Care* (New York: Routledge, 1993); Joan Tronto, *Moral Boundaries* (New York: Routledge, 1993); Rita C. Manning, *Speaking from the Heart* (Lanham, MD: Rowman and Littlefield, 1992).

10. I have discussed these variables at greater length in "Neural Fetal Tissue Transplantation—Should We Do What We Can Do?" *Neurologic Clinics* 7, 4 (November 1989): 745–753.

11. Technically, a viable or even a nonviable (living) "abortus" is a newborn. What is relevant here, however, is not that technical difference but the moral significance of viability and sentience for any developing organism.

12. Although research with human subjects, including fetuses, must be reviewed by an institutional review board, no such review is necessary for established therapies.

13. Dorothy E. Vawter, Warren Kearney, Karen G. Gervais et al., *The Use of Human Fetal Tissue: Scientific, Ethical and Policy Concerns* (Minneapolis: University of Minnesota Press, January 1990), 45–67, 2128–2129.

14. Cf. U.S. Congress, Office of Technology Assessment, *Neural Grafting: Repairing the Brain and Spinal Cord*, OTA-BA-462 (Washington, D.C.: U.S. Government Printing Office, September 1990), 93–107.

15. Stanley Fahn, "Fetal-Tissue Transplants in Parkinson's Disease," *New England Journal of Medicine* 327, 22 (Nov. 26, 1992): 1550.

16. Barbara J. Culliton, "Needed: Fetal Tissue Research," *Nature* 355 (January 23, 1992): 295.

17. Vawter et al., 136–138.

18. Vawter et al., 109, 138.

19. These were the *Forum on Transplantation of Neural Tissue from Fetuses*, convened by the Case Western Reserve University School of Medicine, Cleveland, December 4–5, 1986, and the National Institutes of Health's *Human Fetal Tissue Transplantation Research Panel*, which met in Washington, D.C. late in 1988.

20. Cited in Vawter et al., 42, from E. Kelemen, "Recovery from Chronic Idiopathic Bone Marrow Aplasia of a Young Mother after Intravenous Injection of Unprocessed Cells from the Liver (and Yolk Sac) of Her 22 m. CR-length Embryo. A Preliminary Report." *Scandinavian Journal of Haemotology* 10 (1973): 305–308.

21. The first of these was a letter in *Science* signed by Mary B. Mahowald,

Judith Areen, Barry J. Hoffer, Albert R. Jonsen, Patricia King, Jerry Silver, John R. Sladek, Jr., and LeRoy Walters, "Transplantation of Neural Tissue from Fetuses," *Science* 235 (Mar. 13, 1987): 1307–1308.

22. Cf. Curt R. Freed, Robert E. Breeze, Neil L. Rosenberg et al., "Survival of Implanted Fetal Dopamine Cells and Neurologic Improvement 12 to 46 Months after Transplantation for Parkinson's Disease," *New England Journal of Medicine* 327, 22 (Nov. 26, 1992): 1549–1555; Dennis D. Spencer, Richard J. Robbins, Frederick Naftolin et al., "Unilateral Transplantation of Human Fetal Mesencephalic Tissue into the Caudate Nucleus of Patients with Parkinson's Disease," *New England Journal of Medicine* 327, 22 (Nov. 26, 1992): 1541–1548.

23. Mahowald et al., *Science*, 1308–1309.

24. Consultants to the Advisory Committee to the Director, National Institutes of Health, *Report of the Human Fetal Tissue Transplantation Research Panel* (hereafter NIH Report), vol. 2 (December 1988), A2.

25. Freed, Breeze, Rosenberg et al., 1550.

26. It is "forced" in the sense that William James delineates one of the marks of a genuine option. In other words, choice is unavoidable. See "The Will to Believe," in William James, *Essays on Faith and Morals* (Cleveland: Meridian Books, 1962), 34.

27. In addition to its three chairs, the NIH panel consisted of 18 members, three of whom disagreed with the majority view.

28. *Report of the Human Fetal Tissue Transplantation Research Panel* (NIH Report), vol. 1 (December 1988), 70.

29. Cf. my "Placing Wedges along the Slippery Slope," *Clinical Research* 36, 3 (1988): 220–222.

30. Cf. NIH Report 1, 56 and Lori B. Andrews, "Feminism Revisited: Fallacies and Policies in the Surrogacy Debate," *Logos* 9 (1988): 81–96.

31. Cf. NIH Report 1, 47–50.

32. Cf. Lori Andrews, "My Body, My Property," *Hastings Center Report* 16, 5 (October 1986): 28–38, and John Robertson, "Rights, Symbolism, and Public Policy in Fetal Tissue Transplants," *Hastings Center Report* 18, 6 (December 1988): 9–10. A key point here is whether externalization of the fetus through birth or abortion terminates or reduces the woman's claims to ownership of the tissue. Mary Ann Warren distinguishes the rights of fetuses and infants, arguing that even late-term fetuses cannot have "the full and equal rights" to which newborns may be entitled. See her "The Moral Significance of Birth," *Hypatia* 4, 3 (Fall 1989), 63.

33. Cf. Mary B. Mahowald, Jerry Silver, and Robert A. Ratcheson, "The Ethical Options in Fetal Transplants," *Hastings Center Report* 17, 1 (February 1987): 13.

34. Culliton, 295. This statement was attributed to the Baptist father of a baby who had prenatally received grafted cells from an aborted fetus for treat-

ment of Hurler's syndrome. Two older children had already died of the disease. Both parents were strongly opposed to abortion and remain so.

35. *In re Baby M*, New Jersey Lexis 1, 79 (New Jersey Supreme Court No. A-39), Feb. 1988.

36. Admittedly, "baby selling" is different from sale of aborted fetuses insofar as "baby selling" involves living infants.

37. "Clinic in Ohio Starts Egg Donor Plan," *New York Times* (July 15, 1987), A16.

38. This was my student in a course on "Moral Problems in Medicine" at Case Western Reserve University in 1987.

39. Paula Monarez, "Halfway There," *Chicago Tribune* (Feb. 2, 1992), sect. 6, 4.

40. Although commercial surrogacy is illegal in some states (e.g., New Jersey), most states have no legislation regarding the practice. The morality of contract motherhood remains a matter of public debate.

41. The practice of self-insemination is not new, but there is no reliable documentation of its incidence, in part because the insemination occurs in private, and through private arrangement with a semen provider. While the desire of some women to become parents without the involvement of men may increase the practice, concerns about the status of semen (especially its HIV status) now prompt women to seek technical assistance to test semen used for insemination. For a description of self-insemination, see Mary Barton, Kenneth Walker, and B. P. Wiesner, "Artificial Insemination," *British Medical Journal* 1 (1945), pp. 40–43; Frederick E. Lane, "Artificial Insemination at Home," *Fertility and Sterility* 5 (1954), 372–373; and *Self Insemination* (London: The Feminist Self-Insemination Group, Sept. 1980). Infants born as a result of self-insemination without medical assistance have sometimes been referred to as "turkey baster babies." The technique allows lesbian couples to obtain sperm, and have one inseminate the other. Lori B. Andrews describes a case of surrogate gestation in which a friend of the infertile couple inseminated herself with the sperm of the husband. See her *New Conceptions* (New York: St. Martin's Press, 1984), 202.

42. E.g., *Webster's New World Dictionary*, 2nd college ed., thus defines "prostitute": "to sell the services of (oneself or another) for purposes of sexual intercourse" (New York: Simon and Schuster, 1982), 1140.

43. Marriage has been compared with prostitution because it similarly involves the use of women's bodies for material remuneration. According to Esther Vilar,

> By the age of twelve at the latest, most women have decided to become prostitutes. Or, to put it another way, they have planned a future for themselves which consists of choosing a man and letting him do all the work. In return for his support, they are prepared to let him make use of their vagina at certain given moments.

See Vilar, "What Is Woman?" in Mary Briody Mahowald, ed., *Philosophy of Woman: Classical to Current Concepts*, revised ed. (Indianapolis, IN: Hackett, 1983), 30.

44. Cf. Alison M. Jaggar, *Feminist Politics and Human Nature* (Totowa, NJ: Rowman and Allanheld, 1983), 263–264. Also, cf. Laurie Shrage, "Should Feminists Oppose Prostitution?" *Ethics* 99, 2 (January 1989): 347–361.

45. Mahowald et al., *Hastings Center Report*, 11–12. Although I here use the term "surrogate motherhood," I agree with Rosemarie Tong's criticism of the term because it implies that the woman who gives birth is not the child's mother. Tong initially preferred the term "contract motherhood," which more accurately reflects the arrangement through which a woman agrees to become a biological mother so that another person may become a social parent. See Tong, "The Overdue Death of a Feminist Chameleon: Taking a Stand on Surrogacy Arrangements," *Journal of Social Philosophy* XXI, 2 (Fall/Winter 1990), 40–56. [Tong now suggests the term "gestational motherhood," since it better captures non-commercial arrangements and it leaves OUT the notion of contract. See her paper in Part I of this volume. —Ed.]

46. Vawter et al., 211–231.

47. Vawter et al., 212–213.

48. Mahowald et al., *Science*, 235, 1308.

49. Vawter et al., 211.

Fathers' Rights, Mothers' Wrongs? Reflections on Unwed Fathers' Rights, Patriarchy, and Sex Equality

Mary L. Shanley

The recent case of *Baby Girl Clausen*, involving a custody dispute between the biological parents, Cara Clausen and Daniel Schmidt of Iowa,
and the adoptive parents, Roberta and Jan DeBoer of Michigan, over
who should be recognized as the legal parents of baby Jessica, focused
national attention on the issue of the rights biological unwed fathers
may have to custody of their infant offspring. When Cara Clausen, at
the time unmarried, gave birth to a baby girl, she gave her irrevocable
consent to the child's adoption two days after its birth, as did the man
she named as the child's father on the birth certificate. Within weeks,
however, Clausen regretted her decision and informed Daniel Schmidt
that he was the baby's father. Schmidt responded by filing a petition to
establish paternity and by initiating legal action to block the adoption.
Schmidt contended that a biological father has a right to custody of his
child unless it is shown that he is "unfit" to be a parent. After some two
years of litigation, Michigan declared it did not have jurisdiction in the
matter. Iowa proceeded to enforce its decree that Schmidt's parental
rights had never properly been terminated and that the child had to be
returned to his physical custody.[1]

Many of those who commented on the case asked whether Daniel
Schmidt's alleged rights should be enforced in the face of the trauma
Jessica, now a toddler, would suffer in being removed from the only
family she had known. While this matter merits serious attention, I
want to focus on a different issue raised by the case, namely the basis
and nature of an unwed biological father's right to veto an adoption decision of an unwed mother. This question was obscured in the case of

Baby Girl Clausen because Daniel Schmidt initiated his action with the full cooperation of Cara Clausen, who had come to regret her decision. But it was *his* rights that the Iowa courts upheld, holding that an unwed biological father had a right to preclude an adoption initiated by the biological mother or the state.

There have been a significant number of cases in which an unwed biological father has sought to reverse the biological mother's decision to allow a child to be adopted, and legal thinking on the matter is quite unsettled. Many courts continue to apply the traditional rule that they must consider the "best interest" of the child in making any decision about custody. Supporters of biological fathers' rights, by contrast, argue that when the biological mother does not wish to retain custody, the biological father's claim automatically takes precedence over that of some "stranger" or potential adoptive parent.[2] Interestingly, some advocates of women's rights have also criticized the best-interest standard as too subject to the biases of individual judges, but have argued that women's unique role in human gestation and childbirth, as well as various aspects of their social and economic vulnerability, dictate that an unwed biological mother must be able to make the decision to have her child adopted without interference by the father or the state.[3] According to this view, neither the biological mother nor the state has an obligation to seek the biological father's consent to the adoption decision, or even to inform him of his paternity. From such a perspective, statutes requiring that biological mothers, but not biological fathers, consent to the adoption of their newborn infant do not deny men equal protection. The debate between advocates of these two perspectives takes us to the difficult issue of what, indeed, should be the grounding of anyone's claim to parental rights.

From my perspective, neither the "fathers' rights" nor the "maternal autonomy" position provides a fully satisfactory basis of thinking about the custodial claims of unwed biological parents. I am persuaded by considerations advanced by advocates in both camps that the best interest standard is unsuitable for cases involving newborns surrendered by their mothers for adoption. But almost all arguments for unwed fathers' rights are based on a notion of gender neutrality that is misleading, not only because of women's biological experience of pregnancy but also because of the inequality inherent in the social structures in which sexual and reproductive activity currently take place. Many arguments in favor of a mother's right to decide on the custody of her child, by contrast, expose the ways in which purportedly gender-neutral rules applied to situations of inequality simply reintroduce patriarchal inequality and run the risk of reinforcing the gender stereotype that women, not men, are the natural and proper nurturers of children.[4]

The theoretical question of who should have parental rights, and on what grounds, is complicated by the practical consideration of what will prove to be the best means of moving toward both greater sexual equality and acceptance of diverse family forms. (I am, for example, concerned that any principles I develop here be compatible with enabling lesbian life-partners to parent a child free from threats by a known sperm donor to seek parental rights after agreeing prior to conception not to do so.[5]) It is possible that the best way to counter the patriarchal tendencies of so much public policy and law dealing with families would be to give women complete or at least preponderant decision-making authority about all reproductive matters, at least until present social and economic inequalities based on sex diminish. I am tempted by such a position, but fear that along with empowering women in the short run it would reinforce traditional gender roles in the long run. I am also influenced by my belief in the desirability of sexual equality in both the public and private spheres, which requires not only free access to jobs and public activity for women, but also the assumption of concrete, day-to-day, "hands on" responsibility for child rearing by men.[6] Law and social policy in the area of parental rights must walk a very fine line between adopting false gender neutrality by treating men and women identically, on the one hand, and reinforcing gender stereotypes on the other.[7]

I argue here that a liberal polity interested in protecting the possibility for intimate association and family life for all its members should articulate norms that ground parental claims in a mixture of genetic relationship, assumption of responsibility, and provision of care to the child (including gestation). In the case of a newborn, this means that the biological father must take concrete steps to demonstrate his commitment to the child prior to the biological mother's relinquishment of the child for adoption, and courts must have the authority to judge both his efforts and the mother's objections to his claim. Only some such standard, I believe, recognizes the complexity of the sexual, genetic, biological, economic, and social relationships between adults and among adults and children that are involved in human reproductive activity.

Beyond the legal issues raised by unwed biological fathers' claims to custody, considering the rights of unwed biological parents also raises issues about individual rights in situations dealing with family relationships. By looking behind abstract assertions of individual rights to examine the dependency, reciprocity, and responsibility involved in family relationships, I suggest that the traditional liberal understanding of autonomous individuals must be revised to take account of the fact that persons are not fundamentally isolated and discrete but constructed in and by their relationships to others.[8]

Unwed Parents' Custody Rights in Common Law and Constitutional Law

The Patriarchal Construction of the Common Law Regarding Custody

Arguing that an unwed biological father has a right to be informed of the birth of his child under any circumstances, John Hamilton complains that "Until a few years ago, unwed fathers were ignored or received virtually no protection from either the United States Constitution or the statutes of most states. Indeed, courts and legislatures traditionally have been openly hostile to the recognition of parental rights of unwed fathers."[9] Elizabeth Stanton argues that "[c]ustody was vested in the mother because the law presumed that she was better suited to raise children," a presumption she regards as both unwarranted and hurtful to men.[10] The notion that laws placing custody of nonmarital children in their biological mothers' hands reflected hostility to biological fathers displays a profound misunderstanding not only of the patriarchal roots of family law, but of the social and economic consequences of unwed motherhood for women.

The common law, which largely regulated legal aspects of family relationships in America well into the nineteenth century, was profoundly patriarchal; legal definitions of who is a father and the extent of paternal responsibilities governed not only a man's relationships with his children but also with women both inside and outside his family. Under the common law a man had complete custodial authority over any children born of his wife, and no legal relationship at all to children he sired out of wedlock. The child of his wife took his surname, the nonmarital child did not. The marital child had a right to financial support from him, the nonmarital child did not. The marital child had the right to inherit from him if he died without a will, the nonmarital child did not.[11]

The husband's authority over the marital child was an extension of his authority over his wife. Under the common law doctrine of coverture, a wife's legal personality was subsumed in that of her husband during marriage. A wife could not enter into contracts, sue or be sued, or engage in other legal transactions without being joined by her husband. He owned outright her moveable property, and had control of (although he could not alienate) her real estate. Torts she committed in his presence were chargeable to him, not to her. A married woman also had no right to refuse her husband sexual access—marital rape was not recognized as an offense. So complete was the husband's custodial authority that during his lifetime he had the power to convey his parental rights to a third person without the mother's consent, and could name someone other than the mother to be the child's guardian after his death.[12]

Thus, under the common law, a man's legal relationship to his offspring was governed by his relationship to their mother. If the woman was his wife, a child was "his," so much so that he exercised exclusive custodial authority. If the mother was not his wife, however, the child was *filius nullius*, the child of no one. Obviously, these rules affected both lineage and property. They allowed a man to lay claim to legitimate heirs (for without marriage, who would know for certain who the father of a child might be?) and to avoid squandering his estate by supporting other children. While the father was shielded from financial responsibility for his "spurious" offspring, a woman who bore children outside of marriage was "ruined." Unmarried mothers' desperate attempts at suicide and infanticide dot the pages of social histories and nineteenth-century novels. Although the nonmarital child could inherit from no one, Poor Laws assigned mothers financial responsibility for their offspring and gave them custodial rights as long as they kept their children off public support. A woman's responsibility for her nonmarital children punished her for sex outside of marriage and increased women's incentives to join themselves to men through marriage.

It is no wonder that women's rights advocates from the mid-nineteenth century on protested against the patriarchal assumptions and the sexual double standard implicit in this configuration of rules governing marital and nonmarital procreation. During the nineteenth century, in part due to women's rights advocacy, legislatures began to replace common law rules with statutes that granted wives equal custodial rights with their husbands. By the early twentieth century, when parents divorced, judges began to prefer mothers as custodians of marital children of "tender years" (usually under seven or ten years of age).[13] Eventually the standard of the "best interest of the child"—which did not automatically prefer either spouse and which purported to recognize the needs of the child as paramount—replaced any presumption explicitly favoring the custodial claim of either married parent when they divorced.

With respect to the custody of nonmarital children the law changed more slowly, and the impetus came mainly from children's rights advocates who wanted to get rid of the legal disabilities of "illegitimacy," such as the inability to collect survivors' benefits, receive child support, and inherit from the father.[14] Thus the common-law protections of fathers against the claims of nonmarital children and their mothers have been largely dissolved and paternal responsibility established for out-of-wedlock children. But the common-law history provides no basis for paternal *rights* to such children. Some advocates of unwed biological fathers' rights have argued, however, that the ability to raise one's biological child is a fundamental interest protected by the United States Constitution, and that under the Constitution men and women must have equal rights to claim custody of their nonmarital offspring.

The Emergence of Unwed Fathers' Constitutional Rights

Over the past twenty years, five decisions of the Supreme Court—*Stanley v. Illinois, Quilloin v. Wolcott, Caban v. Mohammed, Lehr v. Robertson,* and *Michael H. v. Gerald D.*—have laid down some guidelines for thinking about unwed fathers' rights. Although they do not by any means resolve all the dilemmas surrounding the custody of infants born to unmarried biological parents, they provide a useful starting point for thinking about those issues.

The Court first considered the custodial rights of unmarried biological fathers in 1972 in *Stanley v. Illinois* (405 U.S. 645 [1972]). Mr. Stanley had lived with his three biological children and their mother, to whom he was not married, intermittently for eighteen years. When the mother died, the state of Illinois declared the children wards of the state and placed them with court-appointed guardians. This was done without a hearing as to Stanley's fitness as a parent. Stanley protested, arguing that Illinois law denied him equal protection of the laws since neither unwed mothers nor married fathers or mothers could be deprived of custody of their children unless they were shown to be unfit. The state argued that Stanley's fitness or unfitness was irrelevant, because an unwed father was not a "parent" whose existing relationship with his children must be considered; an unwed father was presumed unfit because he had not married the mother. The Supreme Court rejected Illinois' argument, stating that "[t]he private interest here, that of a man in the children he has sired and raised, undeniably warrants deference and, absent a powerful countervailing interest, protection."[15] Failure to provide a hearing on parental fitness for an unwed father, the

Court held, violated both the due process and the equal protection clauses of the Fourteenth Amendment.

In cases after *Stanley* the Court drew distinctions between biological fathers who, like Stanley, had been involved in raising their biological children, and those who had not assumed day-to-day practical responsibility for them. In *Quilloin v. Walcott* (434 U.S. 246 [1978]), Leon Quilloin sought to prevent the adoption of his 11-year-old biological child by the child's stepfather, Mr. Wolcott. The Court upheld a Georgia statute that stipulated that a biological mother alone could consent to the adoption of her child; the consent of the unwed biological father was required only if he had legitimated the child. The Court said that no due process violation occurred when contact between the biological father and child had been only sporadic.

The next year, hearkening back to *Stanley*, the Court said in *Caban v. Mohammed* (441 U.S. 380 [1979]) that a New York statute that required unwed biological mothers, but not biological fathers, to consent to the adoption of their children was unconstitutional when a unwed biological father's relationship to his child was "fully comparable" to that of the mother. The case arose when the mother's new husband sought to adopt her children. Mr. Caban, who had previously lived with the children and their mother for several years, argued that the law which required only the biological mother's consent violated the equal protection clause. Caban also claimed that biological fathers had a due process right or liberty interest "to maintain a parental relationship with their children absent a finding they are unfit as parents."[16] New York argued that the distinction between biological mother and biological father was justified because of the fundamental difference between maternal and paternal relationships with their children. The Supreme Court agreed with Caban, holding that "maternal and paternal roles are not invariably different in importance," but explicitly reserved any opinion about whether a distinction such as New York had made would be valid with regard to newborn adoptions.[17]

Lehr v. Robertson (463 U.S. 248 [1983]) also concerned a biological father's effort to block the adoption of his child by her stepfather, but unlike Mr. Stanley and Mr. Caban, and like Mr. Quilloin, Jonathan Lehr had had almost no contact with his biological daughter, Jessica. Lehr claimed, however, that he had a liberty interest in an actual *or potential* relationship with Jessica, and that the State's failure to provide him notice of her pending adoption violated due process. He also asserted that the New York statute violated equal protection because it required the consent of the biological mother, but not the biological father, for an adoption. The case was complicated by the fact that the majority and minority disagreed over whether Lehr had ignored the child until recently, or, as he claimed, had repeatedly attempted to establish contact with her but was thwarted by her mother. The majority held that Lehr had not made sufficient contact to establish a parental right, declaring that a biological father's constitutional rights are a function of the tangible and affirmative responsibilities he accepts towards his offspring. The biological connection alone, the Court held, is not sufficient to *guarantee* an unwed father a voice in the adoption decision, although it affords him an *opportunity* to be heard: The "biological connection . . . offers the natural father an opportunity that no other male possesses to develop a relationship with his offspring. If he grasps that opportunity and accepts some measure of responsibility for the child's future, he may enjoy the blessings of the parent-child relationship." But if he fails to grasp the opportunity, "the Equal Protection Clause does not prevent a State from according the two parents different legal rights."[18] In a dissent, Justice White, joined by Justices Marshall and Blackmun, disagreed not only about the factual question of whether Lehr had attempted to contact Jessica, but also with the framework used by the majority to determine the existence of the unwed biological father's liberty interest. Justice White asserted that "[t]he 'biological connection' is itself a relationship that creates a protected interest."[19] In Justice White's view, the majority decision is more demanding than the Constitution requires and fails to recognize that the biological tie gives a biological father a constitutionally protected interest that warrants, in this case, an opportunity to a hearing to establish legal paternity and be heard with regard to Jessica's adoption.

The most recent Supreme Court case dealing with an unwed biological father's rights, *Michael H. v. Gerald D.* (491 U.S. 110 [1989]), carved out an exception to the rule of thumb that the Court seemed to be developing in these cases, namely, that an unwed biological father who had established a substantial relationship with his child had a constitutionally protected interest in maintaining that relationship. In *Michael H.* the Court found that a California statute creating an irrebuttable presumption that a woman's husband was the father of a child she bore was constitutional. A biological father, Michael H., who had lived intermittently with and provided care to his biological daughter and her mother even though the mother was married to and intermittently lived with her husband as well, argued that he had a right to a hearing to establish his paternity when the husband and wife sought to cut off his contact with the child.

The case produced no fewer than five opinions from a deeply fractured Court. The plurality decision, written by Justice Scalia and joined only by Chief Justice Rehnquist, rejected Michael's claim. Justice Scalia contended both that the state had an interest in preserving the "unitary family," and that neither Michael nor his genetic daughter had a constitutionally protected liberty interest in maintaining their relationship. Justices O'Connor and Kennedy agreed with Justice Scalia's conclusion but not his reasoning, as did Justice Stevens in a separate concurring opinion.[20] Two dissenting opinions supported Michael's right to a hearing, but used quite different grounds to do so. Justice White, joined by Justice Brennan, reiterated the view he expressed in *Lehr* that biology itself creates a presumptive parental right. Justice Brennan, joined by Justices Marshall and Blackmun, argued that the *combination* of biology and nurture establishes the liberty interest Michael claimed.

It is interesting to note that despite the fact that they arrived at opposite conclusions, both Justice Scalia's and Justice White's opinions adopted male-centered models of the basis of parental rights. Justice Scalia looked to the law to protect the paternal rights of married men by basing those rights on a man's legal relationship with the child's mother. Justice White grounded paternal rights in a biological tie established by blood tests, regardless of a man's legal ties to the mother. Both opinions made it unnecessary for the law to ascertain the mother's wishes or intentions with respect to paternal claims to her child. By contrast, and although they too reached opposite conclusions, both Justice Stevens and Justice Brennan considered the interests and actions of the mother to be relevant to establishing paternal claims. For Justice Stevens, the inherent biological and sociological differences between care of the fetus by woman and man justified different treatment of parental rights at the time of birth. Justice Brennan suggested that once a relationship between father and child exists, the mother cannot then exclude an otherwise fit father from being heard with respect to his paternal rights. Justice Brennan's opinion left open the question of to what extent Mchael's situation was like or unlike that of an unwed biological father of a child born to an unmarried woman.

These decisions do not tell us whether under the Constitution an unwed biological father has a right to veto the adoption of a newborn even if he has had no opportunity to establish the kind of relationship and provide the kind of care that the Court has declared protects parental rights.[21] Must the law provide an unmarried biological father an opportunity to demonstrate his commitment if the biological mother does not allow him access to the child? Advocates of fathers' rights insist that unwed biological fathers do have such a constitutional right, and that when the biological mother has decided to relinquish her parental rights, a biological father, unless shown to be "unfit," is entitled to assume custody of his offspring without a hearing on the best interest of the child.

Fit Fathers and Competent Mothers: When Biological Parents Disagree

An Unwed Father's Right to "Grasp the Opportunity" to Become a Parent: The Pursuit of Abstract Equality

In recent years some biological fathers have claimed that, because of the mother's lack of cooperation, they have not found any way to meet the Court's demand, articulated in *Lehr*, that a biological father who wants to retain his parental rights and "enjoy the blessings of the parent-child relationship" must act to "grasp the opportunity" to develop a relationship with his offspring by assuming some "responsibility for the child's future."[22] Should a biological father have that opportunity? Should adoption proceedings be precluded until the father has been heard? What considerations should guide us as we try to evaluate such issues? To answer these questions we need to think about both the basis of claims for custodial rights and the relative claims of biological mothers and fathers outside of marriage.

The argument that the biological father must be given custody when the biological mother chooses not to raise the child is grounded first of all in the conviction that parenthood is a significant good in the lives of men as well as women. Fathers might wish to raise their children for the same reasons mothers do—sharing intimacy and love, nurturing a child to adulthood, seeing one's genetic inheritance survive into the next generation, and passing on ethnic and religious traditions. A commitment to gender neutrality has led most states to abandon an automatic maternal preference if mother and father, married or unmarried, each sought custody, and the principle that the law should treat similarly situated persons similarly would suggest that the law presume that the father is fit and require the consent of both parents before the child can be adopted.

A variety of commentators support an unwed father's right to veto the adoption of his child. Claudia Serviss says all parents have "a constitutionally-protected opportunity interest in developing a parent-child relationship."[23] John Hamilton argues that all unwed fathers have a right to be notified by the state of the existence of their offspring and be heard before any adoption can proceed, and that the state may therefore require the biological mother to identify the biological father; Daniel Zinman insists that the state must allow a biological father to take custody of his child when the biological mother has relinquished her rights, unless he is shown to be unfit.[24] In a recent California case, *In the Matter of Kelsey S.*, the California Supreme Court appeared to agree that a gender-neutral standard should prevail. It held unconstitutional a statute that gave unwed mothers and legally recognized or "presumed" fathers a greater say in pre-adoption proceedings to terminate parental rights than it gave to unwed biological fathers. The Court declared that the statute rested on a "sex-based distinction" that bore no relationship to any legitimate state interest once the child was outside the mother's body and she had decided to relinquish custody.[25]

The presumption of fitness for biological parents also avoids the dangers of subjective judgment and cultural prejudice that seem unavoidable in attempts to determine the child's best interest.[26] One supporter of an unwed father's right to custody argues that a best interest determination "is subject to abuse and may lead to paternalistic infringement on the parent-child relationship in the name of the child's welfare. Given the long waiting list of adoptive parents that exists today and the traditional preference for rearing a child in a two-parent home, a best interest test is a no-win situation for the unwed father of a newborn with whom he has not yet had the opportunity to develop an emotional tie."[27] In 1987, the Georgia Supreme Court explicitly rejected the best interest test in favor of a fitness standard on the grounds that it was presumptively unfair to compare the putative father with adoptive parents with whom the child had never lived. It held that "If [the father] has not abandoned his opportunity interest, the standard which must be used to determine his rights to legitimate the child is his fitness as a parent to have custody of the child. If he is fit he must prevail."[28]

Use of the best interest test in cases of an infant who has lived with no adult caregiver for any appreciable period of time should be changed not only in the interests of sex equality but of family diversity as well. The best interest standard invites the court to make judgments about the relative merit of a whole array of "lifestyle" issues that are not subject to scrutiny when an unwed biological father does not contest a biological mother's wish to retain custody of her child. One may prefer that a child be raised in a two-parent household rather than by a single male, or predict that middle-class professionals will give a child more "advantages" than the child would receive in a working-class home, but if no action (or failure to act) by the biological father shows that he should not be entrusted with custody, these are not appropriate considerations to enter into deciding who should take custody of his biological offspring at or soon after birth.

To argue that the courts should abandon the best interest standard when an unwed biological father wishes to raise an infant does not, however, imply that the only relevant consideration is the biological father's "fitness." The question of whether an unwed biological father shall have a right to custody of his newborn infant is not about paternal rights *tout court*, but also or alternatively about an unmarried woman's authority to decide who shall take custody of her newborn child. For the biological father to assume custody, the biological mother's expressed wishes concerning the child's placement will of necessity be overridden. Arguments that a biological father should be able to veto the adoption decision of the biological mother and assume custody unless proven to be unfit run up against counter-arguments that the courts should defer to an unwed biological mother with respect to placement of her child. It is to these considerations that I now turn.

An Unwed Mother's Claim to Decisional Autonomy:
Taking Context Seriously

Arguments in favor of the "fitness" standard for unwed biological fathers falsely assume that once a biological mother has surrendered the child for adoption she has no further relevant wishes with respect to custody. Defenders of an unwed biological father's right to veto an adoption often contrast what they portray as his laudable desire to assume custody and to care for the child with the biological mother's uncaring decision not to raise the child herself. The image of the "bad mother," and the assumption that if the mother chooses not to raise the child, she must be indifferent to its fate, hover just beneath the surface of such depictions. The notion that once a mother decides to relinquish her child for adoption she can have no further relevant concerns, distorts and denigrates both her experience of pregnancy and the nature of her decision.[29] But relinquishment of the newborn for adoption may reflect any of a wide array of circumstances: lack of money or job prospects; youth or immaturity; feelings of inadequacy or isolation. While some women may be indifferent to the placement of their children, in most cases relinquishment is not a sign that the biological mother does not care for the child; in most cases women agonize over the adoption decision and try to make certain to do what is best for their offspring.[30]

A woman's decision to place her biological child for adoption also does not mean that she is indifferent about the question of who raises the child. The argument that an unwed biological father should be preferred to adoptive parents because they are "strangers" to the child inappropriately ignores the biological mother's preference that the child be adopted through an agency or private placement rather than placed with a guardian or in the father's custody. If the mother has had very little contact with the father beyond the act of intercourse that led to her pregnancy, the father may be as much a *social* "stranger" to her and the child as the adoptive parents, and his claim rests on genetics alone. Contrasting the biological father's rights to those of strangers obscures the fact that the fundamental or precipitating disagreement about custody is not between the adoptive parents and the biological father, but between the two biological parents. And if the mother has known the father over a considerable period of time, her unwillingness to make him the custodial parent needs to be examined to see why she feels as she does, just as it would be if the parents were married.

Are there any reasons to weigh the biological mother's wishes about who shall (or shall not) take custody of the child more heavily than those of the biological father? At the time of birth the relationship of biological father and mother to the child is neither biologically nor socially symmetrical. She has borne the child for nine months, an activity for which there is no precise male analog; indeed, no one else can perform functions analogous to those of gestation.[31] The biological mother's "expectant" state has affected both her own physiological experience and the ways in which others view and interact with her.[32] The Supreme Court has recognized the significance of this asymmetry between mother and father during pregnancy by holding that a wife is not required to notify her husband or obtain his consent before getting an abortion.[33] To what extent should asymmetry of biological function during gestation affect the right to make custodial decisions concerning a newborn?

According to sociologist Barbara Katz Rothman, parenting is a social relationship and parental rights are established by caregiving. In her view, the biological difference between mother and father is crucial and conclusive in establishing their respective claims for custody of newborns: "Infants belong to their mothers at birth because of the unique nurturant relationship that has existed between them up to that moment. That is, birth mothers have full parental rights, including rights of custody, of the babies they bore."[34] By the same token, other persons with a genetic tie to the child do not have such rights: "we will not recognize genetic claims to parenthood, neither as traditional 'paternity' claims nor as genetic maternity in cases of ovum donation."[35] Rothman would have the gestational mother's absolute claim last for six weeks after giving birth, and so the adoption decision would rest solely in the mother's hands during that period. After six weeks, "custody would go to the nurturing parent in case of dispute."[36] Rothman emphasizes that her preference for the gestational mother rests on her understanding of pregnancy as "a social as well as a physical relationship," and that "*any* mother is engaged in a social interaction with her fetus as the pregnancy progresses."[37] Neither the physical interdependence nor the social relationship between mother and fetus can be fully shared by any other adult, no matter how attentive. Actual caregiving, not genetic connection, creates familial bonds and, in this case, Rothman argues, custodial rights.

Others also have argued that parental rights usually are not symmetrical and that the social or biological bonds (or both) between mothers and children should give mothers the authority to decide who should have custody of their offspring. Nancy Erickson argues that the liberty interest that a parent has "to control the care, custody, and upbringing of the child" pertains only to the mother (not the father) of a newborn. At birth the mother is "not only the 'primary caretaker parent,' she is the only caretaker parent" because of her role during pregnancy.[38] Thinking about custody of older children of parents who divorce, Mary Becker argues that mothers are so frequently the primary caregivers of their children that it makes sense to adopt an automatic "maternal deference" standard rather than hold a hearing to try to determine what arrangement would be in the child's best interest: "When the parents cannot agree on a custody outcome, the judge should defer to the mother's decision on custody provided that she is fit, using the 'fitness' standard applicable when the state is arguing for temporary or permanent separation of parents and children in intact families."[39] Becker is not terribly worried that giving primacy to the mother's wishes might in some instances permit a woman to deprive a caring father of custody: "A maternal deference standard would recognize that mothers, as a group, have greater competence and standing to decide what is best for their children . . . than judges, fathers, or adversarial experts. . . . Mothers will sometimes make wrong decisions, but in the aggregate they are likely to make better decisions than the other possible decision makers."[40] Becker's reasoning applied to custodial decisions affecting newborns suggests that courts should defer to a biological mother, both because the woman has provided direct nurture to the fetus during pregnancy, and because, on average, biological mothers' decisions are likely to be as good as or better than those of anyone else.

Martha Fineman, similarly very critical of the best interest standard, would replace it with a "primary caregiver" standard.[41] Fineman argues that the best-interest-of-the-child standard frequently disadvantages mothers by looking to the likely future financial resources of father and mother. It would be more appropriate (both in terms of fairness to the parents and of the child's emotional well-being), Fineman asserts, to look instead at who has actually given the child physical and emotional care up to the present. In most, but not all, instances, this will be the mother. Although Fineman does not discuss custody of newborns, if courts were to apply the primary caregiver standard to the kinds of disputes I am discussing, it would suggest that the mother who has borne and given birth should make the custody decision concerning the infant.

Many arguments for giving an unwed biological father custody of an infant child whom a biological mother wishes to have adopted not only ignore the physical and social experiences of parenthood that biological mother and father may have had during the months of gestation, but invite no inquiry at all into the conditions under which the woman became pregnant. Fully consensual sexual relations between people who feel themselves to have unequal social and economic resources is difficult to achieve.[42] If the pregnancy resulted from force (perhaps a "date rape" that the woman did not prosecute) or deception (perhaps the man said he was single but was in fact married), or if the girl was under the age of consent, his biological tie and his actions after conception should not decide the issue.

The annihilation of context in the argument that commitment to sexual equality dictates that an unwed biological father must be awarded custody of his offspring if the mother has relinquished her custodial rights, reintroduces patriarchal notions of male ownership of children under the guise of gender-neutral principles. In the face of the assumptions of male right not only to their genetic offspring but to women's bodies that are implicit in such an argument, upholding the unwed biological mother's right to decide that her offspring should be adopted free from interference from the biological father insists upon the relevance of her preference for adoption and the nature of her relationship with the biological father before and during pregnancy.

Rebutting the patriarchal premises of many fathers'-rights arguments by promoting women's reproductive autonomy, however, runs the risk of treating some men unjustly and of locking both women and men into traditional gender roles. If parental claims are properly grounded in the first instance in a combination of biological ties and nurturance, then while a father's genetic link *per se* does not give him parental rights, it becomes a reason *to look to see* if he has attempted to assume responsibility for the child, and has done so without interfering with the mother's well-being. If, and only if, he has acted accordingly, should a court recognize his claim to custody.

Rethinking the Bases of Parental Rights: Responsibility, Relationship, and Care

If unwed biological fathers should have some custodial claim to their children but not the extreme claim qualified only by "fitness," what standards should define the extent of their rights? The law needs to adopt stringent criteria for assessing the biological father's intention to take responsibility for and act as a parent to his child even prior to birth. Such criteria will require us to shift our thinking and mode of argumentation away from an emphasis on parents as owners to parents as stewards, from parental rights to parental responsibilities, and from parents viewed as individuals to parents as persons-in-relationship with a child.[43]

Many discussions of the "rights" of biological mothers and fathers reveal the inherent tension in liberal theory and legal practice between protecting individuals and their freedoms and protecting and fostering those relationships which in fundamental ways constitute every individual.[44] The language of parental rights emphasizes the parent's status as an autonomous rights-bearer, and invoking individual rights has proved useful in minimizing the role of the state in people's procreative and child-rearing decisions. For example, begetting, bearing, and raising children are for many people part of the good or fulfilling life that the liberal state is obligated to protect. No one seriously proposes that children should simply be assigned at birth to the best possible or next available parents without regard to who begot and bore them. Courts have recognized the importance of intergenerational ties for many people and protected the liberty to procreate and parent a child not only in custody cases like *Stanley* and *Caban* but in decisions prohibiting forced sterilization, such as *Skinner v. Oklahoma* (316 U.S. 535 [1942].)[45] And since biological parents have a variety of incentives to care for their children to the best of their abilities, assigning custody to them simultaneously protects children's rights as well as those of adults, and sets important bounds to the exercise of state power.[46]

Yet in other contexts, use of the language of parental rights inappropriately focuses on the individual parent rather than on the relationships that are inherent in being a "parent." Katharine Bartlett has advocated recasting many legal disputes that involve parents and children in such a way that the language used does not pit one "right" against another, but emphasizes the view that parenthood implies deep and sustained human connection and must be grounded in adult responsibility for children: "the law should force parents to state their claims . . . not from the competing, individual perspectives of either parent or even of the child, but from the perspective of each parent-child relationship. And in evaluating (and thereby giving meaning to) that relationship, the law should focus on parental responsibility rather than reciprocal 'rights.' . . . " Bartlett suggests that language based more explicitly on open-ended responsibility toward children would capture the nature of the parent-child relationship better than discussions framed in terms of parental rights.[47]

When someone is considered in the role of parent, he or she cannot be viewed apart from the child that makes him or her a parent; an "autonomous" (in the sense of unfettered or atomistic) individual is precisely what a parent is *not*. A "parental right" should not be viewed as pertaining to an individual per se, but only to an individual-in-relationship with a dependent child. It is therefore entirely appropriate for the law to require that efforts be made to establish a relationship before a parental right can be recognized.

Asking a court to determine whether a man has made efforts to establish a parental relationship with a newborn is, however, fraught with difficulties that involve pregnancy and the different physical relationship of biological father and mother to the fetus, the social relationships between biological father and mother, and the need to minimize both intrusiveness by the courts and subjectivity in their judgments. Indeed, part of the attraction of both the paternal fitness test and the maternal deference standard is that each of these provides a fixed criterion for determining an unwed biological father's custodial claim. Unfortunately, however, the efficiency and clarity of each of these criteria are purchased at the cost of reducing legal discourse about family relationships to an assertion of either fathers' or mothers' rights.

My proposal that an unwed biological father have an opportunity to establish his intention to parent his offspring through his behavior tries to minimize the legal effects of biological asymmetry without ignoring altogether the relevance of sexual difference. I assume that an unwed biological mother has demonstrated a parental relationship with her newborn by virtue of having carried the fetus to term, while an unwed biological father may be required to show actual involvement with prenatal life if he wishes to have custody of the child. The model or norm of "parent" in this case, therefore, is established not by the male who awaits the appearance of the child after birth, but by the pregnant woman.[48]

Some people might object that assuming maternal care simply by the face of pregnancy is invalid, especially in cases where the mother has taken drugs or engaged in other behavior that might have a harmful effect on the fetus.[49] In some cases of fetal damage, however, it is often difficult to distinguish whether the harm resulted from drugs taken by the mother or from other factors such as drugs taken by the father, environmental pollutants (particularly high in poor neighborhoods), and malnutrition.[50] Even if in a particular case it could be ascertained that fetal damage was uniquely caused by drugs the mother took, it does not follow that she was so indifferent to the well-being of her child that she should not be heard with respect to placing the child for adoption. To see the pregnant drug-addict as a child abuser rather than a person who is herself in need of medical treatment is to ignore the inseparability of mother and fetus during pregnancy.[51] The mother's decision to place the child for adoption will often be made in an effort to protect the child from harm once it can be cared for outside her body.

The different biological roles of men and women in human reproduction make it imperative that law and public policy "recognize that a father and mother must be permitted to demonstrate commitment to their child in different ways."[52] How might the law do this? What actions might it accept as indications that an unwed biological father had made every effort to act as a parent to the child? Recent court decisions in New York show that this question is not easily answered. In 1990, in *In re Raquel Marie X.*, the New York Court of Appeals struck down a statute that stipulated that only a father who had established a home with the mother for six months prior to her relinquishment of the child for adoption could veto the mother's adoption decision.[53] The court held that the provision imposed "an absolute condition . . . only tangentially related to the parental relationship" and allowed a woman who would not live with a man the power unilaterally to cut off his constitutionally protected interest in parenting his child.[54] It instructed the legislature to find some other way to gauge a father's commitment to his unborn child's welfare. In the meantime, courts were to follow certain standards when judging an unwed father's parental commitment. According to the Court of Appeals, "[T]he father must be willing to assume full custody, not merely attempt to prevent the adoption, and he must promptly manifest parental responsibility both before and after the child's birth."[55] In assessing the father's demonstration of responsibility, judges should look at

such matters as "public acknowledgment of paternity, payment of pregnancy and birth expenses, steps taken to establish legal responsibility
for the child, and other factors evincing a commitment to the child."[56]
Three recent bills introduced to the legislature (two in the Assembly,
one in the Senate) have differed strikingly in their underlying approaches to unwed fathers' rights, and reflect a widely shared uncertainty over what considerations are relevant in determining the nature
and extent of an unwed biological father's custodial rights.

The weakest requirements for an unwed biological father to establish
his right to consent to his offspring's adoption are contained in a bill,
A. 8028, introduced in the Assembly during the 1993 and 1994 legislative sessions. This bill listed a number of actions an unwed biological
father of an infant under six months might take to establish his right to
consent to the adoption. The bill would make his consent necessary if
he openly lived with the child or the child's mother prior to the placement of the child for adoption; *or* held himself out to be the father of
such child during such period; *or* paid or offered to pay a reasonable
sum, consistent with his means, for the medical expenses of pregnancy
and childbirth; *or* initiated judicial proceedings to obtain custody of the
child; *or* married the child's mother.[57] Since the bill requires the unwed
biological father to have taken only one of these actions, he might obtain
the right to consent to the adoption simply by initiating legal proceedings *after* the child was born.

By contrast with these minimal stipulations, S. 3776, introduced in
the Senate during the 1991 and 1992 legislative sessions, requires that
an unwed biological father have demonstrated his commitment to his
offspring in a number of ways, and have done so both prior to and after
the birth of the child.[58] It does so by replacing most "or"s in A. 8028
with the conjunctive "and," thus insisting that a biological father have
supported the mother or baby financially, *and* held himself out as the
father, *and* taken steps to initiate legal proceedings to assume custody
of the child.

Even stronger provisions are contained in a second Assembly bill, A.
8319, introduced in the 1993 and 1994 legislative sessions. A. 8319
stipulates that the father must have paid or offered to pay a reasonable
part of the medical expenses of pregnancy and childbirth and the
child's living expenses, and that he must have initiated judicial proceedings to establish paternity and to obtain sole custody of the child within
clearly specified time limits. The bill further states that " 'ability to
assume sole custody' shall mean ability to assume guardianship and custody of the child and become the primary caretaker of the child for the

foreseeable future."[59] This bill clearly means to grant the right to consent to an adoption only to unwed fathers who demonstrate that they have been and will be actively engaged in the care and upbringing of their offspring; the stipulations rest on an image of father as caretaker and nurturer, not simply as progenitor.

Although A. 8319 reflects in some respects the spirit of the principles set forth in this chapter, it might preclude legitimate custodial claims of a man without the economic resources to pay medical expenses or support for a child when he is not living with the mother. It might also disadvantage men not familiar with the workings of the legal system and who do not know of the existence of a putative fathers' registry. A satisfactory bill would need to minimize the effects of class on someone's ability to put forward a parental claim. It is also not clear what the requirement that the father become the "primary caretaker of the child" would mean in practice. Insofar as it would prevent a man from turning over full care of his child to someone else (usually a female relative), this provision rightly stresses the importance of direct parental involvement to establishing parental rights. Yet it should not be interpreted to isolate an unwed biological father from family and community relationships that might sustain his childrearing.

A. 8319 goes a long way to enact the spirit of the principles set forth in this essay, but a fully adequate statute would need to go further in protecting an unwed mother's right to be heard concerning her child. The mother's relinquishment of the child for adoption should be viewed as the last in a series of actions meant to provide care for the child, not as an act of abandonment that gives her no interest in the child's placement. Because the disputes between biological mother and father involve their relationship to one another and to the child, it is not sufficient that a court know that the mother has consented to adoption and that the father has acted promptly to assume parental responsibility; it must consider the *reasons* the biological mother opposes placing the child in the biological father's custody. Because parental rights must be grounded in the provision of care and the assumption of responsibility, any biological father seeking custody would have to show that the pregnancy was not a result of force, coercion, deception, or intercourse with a girl under the age of consent. He would have to demonstrate further that he had not harassed the mother, prevented her exercise of the right to abortion, abused her or the child, or performed any other act which would demonstrate lack of care for her or the child. Any such act would be grounds for declaring the father "unfit." This still might not meet the possibility that a man who desired children might impregnate a woman whom he knew would neither abort nor raise a child, provide care and financial support throughout the pregnancy, and petition for paternity and custody—a kind of inexpensive "surrogacy." I am convinced that such intentional instrumental use of any woman's body is morally abhorrent, but I am not certain how to insure that such a man could not assume custody of the offspring.

Finally, a pregnant woman who wishes to make plans for her child should be able to ascertain early in the pregnancy whether or not the genetic father will step forward later to oppose the adoption. The law should provide that she be able to notify him in writing of the pregnancy and preclude him from a veto if he fails to act soon after receipt of such notification. Similarly, if a genetic father is found to be entitled to veto an adoption, a mother should be able to negate her consent to the child's adoption and be put back in the same position she was in prior to her consent, that is, as one of two unwed parents each of whom seeks custody.[60]

For a court to ascertain whether an unwed genetic father has taken the necessary steps to provide care, take responsibility, and establish his intention to assume custody of a newborn will obviously require a hearing. A hearing will, of course, take more time than assigning custody based on a rule that any "fit" biological father prevail or that a mother be able to make the decision to place her child for adoption unimpeded by the biological father. But a hearing to ascertain whether an unwed biological father has grasped the opportunity to parent his offspring should not cause more delay than a best interest hearing. Such a hearing would be to ascertain facts about the unwed father's behavior and the mother's considered opinion concerning custody, not to try to project what custodial arrangement might be in the child's best interest. Moreover, if the biological father is required to enter his name in a putative father's registry prior to the child's birth, the court and the mother will be on notice that a hearing will likely be required. This provision not only signals the man's desire to be recognized as the legal father, but facilitates meeting the need of the infant to be placed in a permanent home as soon as possible after birth.

These considerations leave unresolved the thorny issue of how the law should deal with cases in which a biological mother lies to the biological father about his paternity or otherwise hides her pregnancy, making it impossible for him to take any action to signal his willingness to take care of his offspring. In 1992 the New York Court of Appeals addressed the question of what effect a lack of knowledge of a woman's pregnancy should have on a biological father's right to seek custody after learning of the child's existence. In *Matter of Robert O. v. Russell K.*, an unwed biological father sought to overturn the adoption of his son on the grounds that either the mother or the State had a duty to ensure that he knew of the child's birth, and that their failure to inform him denied him his constitutional rights. The New York Court acknowledged that "the unwed father of an infant placed for adoption immediately at birth faces a unique dilemma should he desire to establish his parental rights." His opportunity to "shoulder the responsibility of parenthood may disappear before he has a chance to grasp it." But although the biological father, Robert O., acted as soon as he knew of the child's existence, the adoption had been finalized ten months previously. "Promptness," said the Court, "is measured in terms of the child's life, not by the onset of the father's awareness." Robert O., having failed to determine in a timely fashion whether the woman with whom he had lived was pregnant, lost the right he would have had to an opportunity to manifest his "willingness to be a parent."[61] The responsibility to know of a child's existence should fall on the man who would assume responsibility for raising the child. By contrast, one defender of unwed fathers' rights proposes a jail sentence of up to two years for a woman who refuses to name the father of her child when surrendering the infant for adoption![62] A biological father aware of a woman's pregnancy should be required to act prior to birth and soon after he suspects his paternity; a biological father who is actively kept ignorant might be allowed to step forward for some specified period after birth (probably not less than six weeks nor longer than six months), but thereafter the importance of establishing a firm parent-child relationship would preclude his advancing a parental claim.

While these reflections suggest various reforms in the laws governing the custody of nonmarital children, they do not answer the question of whether the case of *Baby Girl Clausen* was decided correctly. I find that very hard to do because neither side grounded its position in the kinds of principles I have put forward here. The Iowa statute which Daniel Schmidt invoked to claim that the adoption could not be finalized required the biological father's consent, but no showing that he demonstrate his commitment to the child prior to (or even subsequent to) birth. The father's mere opposition to the adoption was a sufficient basis upon which to grant him custody. The DeBoers, for their part, based their claim that they should be allowed to adopt Jessica on the best interest standard. Placing the child with the Schmidts reinforced the notion that a biological tie between man and child automatically creates a custodial claim, while a decision favoring the DeBoers would not only have reinforced the best interest standard but might have been viewed as rewarding them for prolonging legal proceedings after Schmidt raised his claim. The outcome consonant with the principles advanced here would have granted a hearing to Schmidt, recognizing that while his biological tie alone did not guarantee him custodial rights, the fact that he acted immediately after learning that he was Jessica's biological father and within four weeks after her birth provided grounds for a hearing. That hearing would not have attempted to determine whether the child's best interest would be better served by granting custody to Schmidt or the DeBoers, but whether Schmidt's actions established a claim to custody.

The main lesson to be drawn from the case of *Baby Girl Clausen* is that it is imperative that states formulate adoption laws that will reflect the principle that parental rights are established in the first instance by a combination of biology and the provision of care, a principle already articulated by the Supreme Court. Another lesson may be that in certain instances it would make sense to allow some form of legal recognition to the fact that a child may have multiple "parents": genetic parents (sperm and egg donors), a gestational mother, step-parents, adoptive parents, social parents (that is, those that actually provide care), and legal guardians.[63] The possibility of some such recognition might avoid some cases in which unwed biological fathers seek to block the adoption of their offspring. Some of these cases seem motivated not so much by the man's desire to raise the child as by his fear of losing all opportunity to know the child he has sired. There may be ways of dealing with this fear short of blocking the adoption. Adoption registries that allow adopted children and birth parents to contact one another by mutual consent when the child has reached his or her majority seem to have been helpful to biological parents, adoptive parents, and children alike. They allow for the simultaneous recognition of the importance of both biological and social parenting, and in doing so undercut the suggestion that something about adoption is shameful and is best kept hidden. Such registries also take into account the perspective of children who want to know their biological forebears, without weakening either the legal rights and responsibilities of the social (adopting) parents or the primacy of the emotional bonds between adopting parents and children. Beyond these legal changes, the *Baby Girl Clausen* case should also lead us to try to understand the circumstances that might lead an unwed mother to lie about or conceal the paternity of her child, such as fear of violence or harassment, or shame over an unwanted sexual relationship. Working toward justice in family relationships requires struggling to eliminate the social conditions that give rise to such fear and shame, and also requires making sure that all citizens have access to the resources that allow family relationships to survive and flourish, so that no biological parent will be forced by economic factors to relinquish custody of children they would prefer to raise themselves had they the resources to do so.

Conclusion

This analysis of disputes over paternal custody of nonmarital newborns makes it abundantly clear that the language of individual rights, so central to liberal political theory and to the due process and equal protection guarantees of the U.S. Constitution, is not well suited to dealing with complex issues of parent-child relationships. While notions of maternal or paternal rights are not useless (for example, they allow us to think about limits to state intervention), they tend to focus attention on an adult *individual*, whereas parental issues involve at least two adults and a child, and the relationships among them.[64] Legal and social discourse alike must put the lived relationship between parents and between parent and child, not the rights of individuals alone, at the center of the analysis of parental claims. In particular the language of a father's "right" to custody of his infant child based on his genetic tie obscures the complexity of the relationships involved in human reproductive activity.

Because parenting involves being in a relationship with another dependent person, a parental "right" cannot properly be conceived of as something independent of the relationship. An individual can exercise a parental right, but the existence or the nature of the right cannot be explained by reference to that individual alone. Only by taking account of the interpersonal dependency, reciprocity, and responsibility involved in family relationships will we be able to approach a world dedicated to achieving both lived equality between men and women and committed parents for every child.

Notes

I wish to thank Julie Bartkowiak, Joan Callahan, Ann Congleton, Stephen Ellmann, Nancy Erickson, Leslie Goldstein, Mona Harrington, Alice Hearst, Wolfgang Hirczy, Martha Minow, Uma Narayan, Susan Okin, and Joan Posner for helping me to think about the issues raised in this chapter. I began work on this chapter while a Fellow at the Center for Human Values at Princeton University, for whose support I am very grateful.

This chapter developed from a paper presented at the Conference on Feminist Ethics and Social Policy, University of Pittsburgh, November 5–7, 1993, and appears in a somewhat different form in *Hypatia: A Journal of Feminist Philosophy* 10/1 (1995). An expanded version was presented at the Feminism and Legal Theory Workshop on "Parents and Children: Evolving Issues in Reproductive Rights," Columbia University School of Law, March 25–26, 1994, and appears under the title "Unwed Fathers'

Rights, Adoption, and Sex Equality: Gender-Neutrality and the Perpetuation of Patriarchy," *Columbia Law Review* 95/1 (1995).

1. *In the Interest of B.G.C.*, Supreme Court of Iowa, No. 207/91–476, 92–49, September 23, 1992, and *In the Matter of Baby Girl Clausen*, Michigan Court of Appeals, No. 161102, March 29, 1993.

2. Jeffrey S. Boyd, "The Unwed Father's Custody Claim in California: When Does the Parental Preference Doctrine Apply?" *Pepperdine Law Review* 17 (1990), pp. 969–1010; Elizabeth Buchanan, "The Constitutional Rights of Unwed Fathers Before and After *Lehr v. Robertson*," *Ohio State Law Journal* 45 (1984), pp. 311–382; Laurel J. Eveleigh, "Certainly Not Child's Play: A Serious Game of Hide and Seek with the Rights of Unwed Fathers," *Syracuse Law Review* 40 (1989), pp. 1055–1088; John R. Hamilton, "The Unwed Father and the Right to Know of His Child's Existence," *Kentucky Law Journal* 76 (1987–88), pp. 949–1009; Jennifer J. Raab, "*Lehr v. Robertson*: Unwed Fathers and Adoption—How Much Process Is Due?" *Harvard Women's Law Journal* 7 (1984), pp. 265–287; Claudia Serviss, "*Lehr v. Robertson*'s 'Grasp the Opportunity:' For California's Natural Fathers, Custody May Be Beyond Their Grasp," *Western State University Law Review* 18 (1991), pp. 771–790; Rebecca L. Steward, "Constitutional Rights of Unwed Fathers: Is Equal Protection Equal for Unwed Fathers?" *Southwestern University Law Review* 19 (1990), pp. 1087–1111; Daniel C. Zinman, "Father Knows Best: The Unwed Father's Right to Raise his Infant Surrendered for Adoption," *Fordham Law Review* 60 (April 1992), pp. 971–1001. Wolfgang Hirczy argues that the law should insist that the paternity of every child be established at birth, a necessary prerequisite for an unwed father's assertion of paternal rights; see "The Politics of Illegitimacy: A Cross-National Comparison," paper presented at the Annual Meeting of the American Political Science Association, Chicago, Illinois, September 3–6, 1992.

3. Mary Becker, "The Rights of Unwed Parents: Feminist Approaches," *Social Service Review* 63 (December 1989), pp. 496–518; Nancy S. Erickson, "The Feminist Dilemma over Unwed Parents' Custody Rights: The Mother's Rights Must Take Priority," *Journal of Law and Inequality* 2 (1984), pp. 447–472; Nancy S. Erickson, "Neither Abortion nor Adoption: Women without Options," paper presented at the American Association of Law Schools (AALS), San Francisco, CA, January 6, 1990, p. 39, n. 22; Barbara Katz Rothman, *Recreating Motherhood: Ideology and Technology in a Patriarchal Society* (New York and London: W. W. Norton, 1989).

4. Martha Albertson Fineman, *The Illusion of Equality* (Chicago: University of Chicago, 1991), exposes the pernicious effects of false gender equality with respect to custody disputes when married couples divorce, but does not address the issue I examine here. She suggests making custody depend upon actual care given to a child.

5. I think that the situations of sperm donors and of gestational mothers ("surrogate" mothers) are distinguishable with respect to the enforceability of contracts made prior to conception, both because of the different

biological and social roles of each during pregnancy and because of the need to resist the tradition of male appropriation of women's reproductive labor. For an argument against the enforceability of pregnancy contracts see my " 'Surrogate Mothering' and Women's Freedom: A Critique of Contracts for Human Reproduction," *Signs* 18, 3 (Spring 1993), pp. 618–639.

6. Sally Johnson, "Helping Fathers Become Parents," *New York Times*, February 24, 1994, metropolitan edition, p. C1, discusses the very low day-to-day involvement of fathers with their children.

7. On this dilemma more generally, see Zillah Eisenstein, *The Female Body and the Law* (Berkeley: University of California Press, 1988).

8. On reconceptualizing the liberal individual, see Virginia Held, *Feminist Morality: Transforming Culture, Society, and Politics* (Chicago: University of Chicago Press, 1993), especially "Noncontractual Society: The Postpatriarchal Family as Model," pp. 192–214. On the concept of autonomy in liberal theory, see Jennifer Nedelsky, "Reconceiving Autonomy: Sources, Thoughts and Possibilities," *Yale Journal of Law and Feminism* 1:1 (Spring 1989), pp. 7–36, and "Law, Boundaries, and the Bounded Self," *Representations* 30 (Spring 1990), pp. 162–189. On some limitations of the legal concept of individual rights see Mary Ann Glendon, *Rights Talk* (New York: Free Press, 1991).

9. Hamilton, "The Unwed Father," pp. 949–950.

10. Elizabeth Rose Stanton, "The Rights of the Biological Father: From Adoption and Custody to Surrogate Motherhood," *Vermont Law Review* 12 (1987), pp. 87–121, 92. Stanton quotes Note, "Custody Rights of Unwed Fathers," *Pacific Law Journal* 4 (1973), p. 923:

> Various reasons have been proposed for considering the unwed mother a more natural guardian than the father. These include: (1) the mother is more easily identified than the father; (2) she is biologically better suited to care for and nurture the child; and (3) the natural bonds of love and affection for the child are stronger in the mother than in any other person.

11. Becker, "The Rights of Unwed Parents," p. 498.

12. William Blackstone, *Commentaries on the Laws of England*, 9th ed. (1783), ed. Berkowitz and Throne (1978), vol. 1, p. 453. On coverture in general see Mary L. Shanley, *Feminism, Marriage and the Law in Victorian England* (Princeton: Princeton University Press, 1989). On laws governing custody in the early United States, see Michael Grossberg, *Governing the Hearth: Law and the Family in Nineteenth-Century America* (Chapel Hill: University of North Carolina, 1985), and Hendrick Hartog, *Breaking the Bonds of Matrimony* (Princeton University, unpublished manuscript). See also Joan Mahoney, "Adoption as a Feminist Alternative to Reproductive Technology," in this volume.

13. Also important was the rise in both social and judicial attention to childhood and its particular needs. See Jamil S. Zainaldin, "The Emergence of a Modern American Family Law: Child Custody, Adoption, and the Courts, 1796–1851," *Northwestern University Law Review* 73 (1979), pp. 1038–1089; Grossberg; and Hartog.

14. *Weber v. Aetna Casualty & Surety Co.*, 406 U.S. 164 (1972); *Gomez v. Perez*, 409 U.S. 535 (1973); and *Trimble v. Gordon*, 430 U.S. 762 (1977).

15. *Stanley v. Illinois*, 405 U.S. 645 (1972) at 651.

16. *Caban v. Mohammed*, 441 U.S. 380 (1979) at 385.

17. 441 U.S. at 392, n. 11.

18. *Lehr v. Robertson*, 463 U.S. 248 (1983) at 268.

19. 463 U.S. at 272.

20. Justices O'Connor and Kennedy rejected Justice Scalia's assertion that the proper methodology for discerning what interests are protected by the due process clause is to look at "the most specific level at which a relevant tradition protecting, or denying protection to, the asserted right can be identified." Justice Stevens also concurred in the judgment, asserting without much apparent basis that because Michael could have obtained visitation rights as a "nonparent" he did not need further protection.

21. This issue was raised by Jonathan Lehr but was not definitively answered by the Court in *Lehr v. Robertson*, since the majority rejected evidence he offered in support of his contention that his efforts to know his daughter had been rebuffed by her mother.

22. 413 U.S. at 262.

23. Serviss, "*Lehr v. Robertson*'s 'Grasp the Opportunity,'" p. 788.

24. Hamilton, "The Unwed Father"; Zinman, "Father Knows Best."

25. "Having My Baby," *ABA Journal*, May 1992, pp. 84–86, 84.

26. Katharine Bartlett, "Re-Expressing Parenthood," *Yale Law Journal* 98 (1988), pp. 293–340, 303.

27. "Recent Developments: Family Law—Unwed Fathers' Rights—New York Court of Appeals Mandates Veto Power over Newborn's Adoption for Unwed Father Who Demonstrates Parental Responsibility—*In re Raquel Marie X. . . . ,*" *Harvard Law Review* 104 (January 1991), pp. 800–807, 807. Martha Albertson Fineman, "Dominant Discourse, Professional Language, and Legal Change in Child Custody Decisionmaking," *Harvard Law Review* 101 (1988), pp. 727–774, 770, and Eveleigh, "Certainly Not Child's Play," also express strong reservations about the best interest test in custody adjudication.

28. *In re Baby Girl Eason*, 257 Ga. 292 at 297, 358 S.E.2d 459 at 463 (1987), quoted in Zinman, pp. 993–994.

29. Eveleigh, "Certainly Not Child's Play," for example, writes as if the biological mother who has relinquished custody has no relevant interest; when

a biological father seeks custody of his newborn offspring, the relevant interests, she says, are those of the state, the biological father, and the child.

30. Maureen A. Sweeney, "Between Sorrow and Happy Endings: A New Paradigm of Adoption," *Yale Journal of Law and Feminism* (Spring 1990), pp. 329–370; Erickson, "The Feminist Dilemma," p. 459 and n. 65; Erickson, "Neither Abortion Nor Adoption," p. 39 and n. 22.

31. The uniqueness of pregnancy has implications for the custodial claims not only of unwed fathers but also for those of a lesbian partner who had planned to co-parent a child, as well as those of a genetic mother who might turn to a "surrogate" to bear a child on her behalf.

32. On the social construction of the experience of pregnancy and childbirth see Emily Martin, *The Woman in the Body: A Cultural Analysis of Reproduction* (Boston: Beacon Press, 1987), and Barbara Katz Rothman, *In Labor* (New York: Norton, 1982).

33. *Planned Parenthood of Southeastern Pennsylvania v. Casey*, 112 S. Ct. 2791 (1992).

34. Rothman, *Recreating Motherhood*, p. 254.

35. Rothman, *Recreating Motherhood*, p. 254.

36. Rothman, *Recreating Motherhood*, p. 255.

37. Rothman, *Recreating Motherhood*, p. 97.

38. Erickson, "The Feminist Dilemma," pp. 461–462.

39. Mary Becker, "Maternal Feelings: Myth, Taboo, and Child Custody," *Review of Law and Women's Studies* 1 (1992), pp. 901–992, 971.

40. Becker, "Maternal Feelings," p. 972.

41. Martha Albertson Fineman, *The Illusion of Equality*.

42. See, for this view, Catharine A. MacKinnon, *Toward a Feminist Theory of the State* (Cambridge: Harvard University Press, 1989), p. 174; see also her *Feminism Unmodified* (Cambridge: Harvard University Press, 1987), p. 88. For an opposing view see Katie Roiphe, *The Morning After* (Boston: Little, Brown, 1993), which sees many feminist challenges to social structures of inequality that affect relationships between men and women as contributions to an ideology not of female empowerment but of female weakness and need for protection.

43. Janet Farrell Smith, "Parenting and Property," in *Mothering: Essays in Feminist Theory*, ed. Joyce Treblicot (Totowa, NJ: Rowman & Allanheld, 1983), 199–212, argues against the "property model" of parenting and family relationships.

44. Excellent discussions of the ways in which classical liberal theory pays insufficient attention to the ways in which individuals are constituted in and by their relationships to others are found in Held, *Feminist Morality*, Nedelsky, "Reconceiving Autonomy" and "Law, Boundaries, and the Bounded Self," Sara Ruddick, *Maternal Thinking: Towards a Politics of Peace* (Boston: Beacon Press, 1989), and Joan C. Tronto, *Moral Boundaries: A Political Argument for an Ethic of Care* (New York: Routledge, 1993).

Issues involving children raise in a particularly acute manner the tension between protecting people as individuals and protecting family associations or family ties. On the dilemmas inherent in using privacy language to afford protection to both individuals and families see Kenneth L. Karst, "The Freedom of Intimate Association," *Yale Law Journal* 89 (1980), p. 624–692.

45. Although, see also cases that permitted sterilization of the mentally retarded, *Buck v. Bell*, 274 U.S. 200 (1927) and *Sterilization of Moore*, 289 N.C. 95, 221 S.E.2d 307 (1976).

46. See Susan M. Okin, *Justice, Gender, and the Family* (New York: Basic Books, 1989), and Frances Olsen, "The Myth of State Intervention in the Family," *University of Michigan Journal of Law Reform* 18: 4 (1985) for a clear analysis of the impossibility of complete state neutrality toward the family.

47. Bartlett, "Re-Expressing Parenthood," p. 295. For an interesting critique of Bartlett that is flawed by its failure to recognize the deeply individualistic as well as the patriarchal characteristics of contemporary family law, see Janet L. Dolgin, "Status and Contract in Feminist Legal Theory of the Family: A Reply to Bartlett," *Women's Rights Law Reporter* 12 (Summer 1990), 103–113. The idea that parental rights depend upon the fulfillment of parental duties receives one of its classic expressions in John Locke's argument against the patriarchal ideas of Sir Robert Filmer. Filmer held that the very act of begetting a child gave a father sovereignty over his offspring. By contrast, Locke asserts that not procreation, but only providing care for a child bestows parental authority, and that by nature (although not necessarily by law) mothers share such authority. But despite Locke's rejection of patriarchal reasoning with respect to both polity and family, patriarchal notions crept back into much liberal political theory and law because these used the language of the rights of autonomous individuals to talk about or characterize the relationship between parent and child. To some extent, when nineteenth-century feminists began their assault on the common-law doctrine of coverture, they used Lockean notions of individual freedom and equality to argue that mothers should have equal rights over marital children. Even these reforms, however, did not subvert the notion of parental autonomy or of parental rights to custody. See John Locke, *Second Treatise of Government*, II, vi, sec. 58. On patriarchalism see Gordon Schochet, *Patriarchalism in Political Thought* (New York: Basic Books, 1975); on Locke's antipatriarchalism see Mary L. Shanley, "Marriage Contract and Social Contract in Seventeenth Century English Political Thought," *Western Political Quarterly* 32, 1 (March 1979), pp. 79–91.

48. See Zillah Eisenstein, *The Female Body and the Law* (Berkeley: University of California Press, 1988).

49. As Cynthia Daniels has pointed out, the image of the pregnant drug addict is deeply disturbing, "representing as it does the paradox of a woman si-

multaneously engaged in the destruction of life (addiction) and the perpetuation of life (pregnancy)." Cynthia R. Daniels, *At Women's Expense: State Power and the Politics of Fetal Rights* (Cambridge: Harvard University Press, 1993), p. 98.

50. Daniels, *At Women's Expense*, p. 125.

51. See Iris Marion Young, "Punishment, Treatment, Empowerment: Three Approaches to Policy for Pregnant Addicts," *Feminist Studies* 20, 1 (Spring 1994), pp. 33–58.

52. "Recent Developments," *Harvard Law Review*, p. 805.

53. *In Matter of Raquel Marie X*, 76 N.Y.2d 387 (1990).

54. 76 N.Y.2d at 405, 559 N.E.2d at 426, 559 N.Y.S.2d at 863.

55. "Recent Developments," *Harvard Law Review*, p. 803.

56. 76 N.Y.2d at 428, 559 N.E.2d at 428, 559 N.Y.S.2d at 865.

57. New York State Legislature, Assembly, A. 8028, May 17, 1993; introduced by Member of the Assembly Vito Lopez and referred to the Committee on the Judiciary.

58. New York State Legislature, Senate, S. 3776-B, March 11, 1991; introduced by Senator Mary Goodhue.

59. New York State Legislature, Assembly, A. 8319A, June 4, 1993; introduced by Member of the Assembly Vito Lopez (at the request of the Governor) and referred to the Committee on Children and Families.

60. Nancy Erickson, "Proposal for a Model Law on Unwed Fathers' Adoption Rights," unpublished paper, Brooklyn, N.Y., 1991.

61. *Matter of Robert O. v. Russell K.* (80 N.Y.2d 252 [1992]) at 262.

62. Hamilton, "The Unwed Father," p. 1103, n. 406 ("Proposed Statute," § 0000 [b][a]). Less drastically, Justice Titone, concurring in *Robert O. v. Russell K.*, also felt it unreasonable to require that a man who wishes to assert paternal rights know of the pregnancy of his sexual partner.

63. See interesting suggestions for ways in which the law might recognize more than two parents in Katharine Bartlett, "Rethinking Parenthood as an Exclusive Status: The Need for Legal Alternatives When the Premise of the Nuclear Family Has Failed," *Virginia Law Review*, 70 (1984), pp. 879–963. See also Elizabeth Bartholet, *Family Bonds: Adoption and the Politics of Parenting* (Boston: Houghton Mifflin, 1993).

64. I leave aside in this chapter cases of contract parenthood, artificial insemination by donor, and embryo transfer, in all of which issues involving the distinctions between genetic, biological, and "intentional" parents arise, and in which there may be more than two adults claiming the status of "parent."

PART III:
ELECTING AND
PREVENTING BIRTH

Introduction[1]

Joan C. Callahan

The papers in this section by Joan C. Callahan, Janice G. Raymond, and Laura M. Purdy take up three questions pertaining to choices to have or not have children. My own paper focuses on the use of potassium chloride injection to ensure a stillborn in late abortion. Janice Raymond's paper focuses on a relatively recent development in birth control technology, RU 486, a preparation that effects birth control by inducing menstruation, thereby emptying the contents of a woman's uterus. Laura Purdy's paper focuses on the right to reproduce, particularly in regard to children who, it can be predicted, will have serious physical anomalies. Each of these papers raises the issue of abortion in general, which has been touched on along the way by several other authors in earlier papers. It is time to turn to some discussion of that issue.[2]

Controlling Birth

Abortion has always been practiced as a variant of birth control, and it may even be the preferred method of birth control in some societies— for example, those in which safe and reliable contraception is not readily available—or for certain women under certain circumstances. For example, it may be the method of choice for women in rigorously pronatalist societies or for a woman whose male partner is opposed to contraception, since abortion, whether self-induced or surreptitiously performed by someone else, can be disguised as illness.[3]

Primitive methods of self-induced abortion include jumping from great heights, having others jump up and down on a woman's abdomen, ingesting emetic and toxic substances, and using invasive probes (e.g., sticks, knitting needles, and, more recently, the infamous wire hangers). These obviously dangerous kinds of techniques have been used by women for centuries, despite public policies and public attitudes condemning abortion. For example, despite restrictive abortion laws, the dramatic increase in self-induced abortion in the nineteenth-century United States is well documented.[4] Worldwide estimates commonly put the occurrence of abortion prior to liberalization of abortion laws in the same range as postliberalization, suggesting that the legalization of elective abortion simply legitimizes actual practice. In the United States, *Roe v. Wade* legitimized a trend to relax restrictions on abortion that had already begun throughout the states as a result of popular support for elective abortion.[5] By 1973, the time of the decision in *Roe*, nearly a third of the states had liberalized their abortion laws, making them more coherent with the "demand" for abortion reflected in actual practice, including attempts to self-abort, the use of abortionists acting illegally, and elective abortion disguised as therapeutic abortion.[6]

The incidence of abortion to prevent unwanted births, then, seems not to be significantly affected by public policy restricting or permitting it. The legal protection of elective abortion seems not to increase the occurrence of elective abortion so much as it increases the safety of abortion for women. For example, when abortion laws were made less restrictive in Czechoslovakia in the 1950s, abortion-related deaths dropped by 56 percent between 1953 and 1957 and by an additional 38 percent between 1958 and 1962. Romania, on the other hand, enacted a restrictive abortion law in 1966, and abortion-related deaths of Romanian women aged fifteen to forty-four rose from 14.3 per million in 1965 to 97.5 per million by 1978.[7] Despite the fact that making elective abortion legal seems not to increase the number of abortions and clearly causes harm to women to skyrocket, there are increasingly militant forces on the right working to sustain restrictive abortion laws throughout the world and to replace more liberal policies with more restrictive ones. In recent years in the United States, increasingly well-organized and well-financed activism on the right has resulted in a number of legal attempts to limit women's access to abortion, harassment of women seeking abortions, and the assassination of physicians known for their abortion work. Despite the U.S. Supreme Court's clear articulation in *Roe* that even a viable fetus is not a person in the eyes of the law, those who oppose abortion for reasons less than preservation of a woman's life generally do so on the ground that, from the time of fertilization onward, genetically human beings are persons who have as compelling a right to life as have grown human persons.

My paper, which opens this section, focuses on the question of ensuring a stillborn in late abortion. The paper is structured to respond to the arguments that have been given in the medical and bioethics literature both against and for the moral acceptability ensuring a stillborn in late abortion. Among the arguments against doing this is the general so-called pro-life argument that all abortion for reasons less than self-defense is wrong because such abortions involve killing an innocent person. I address this position by suggesting that its common defense, which is a logical wedge argument, is wrongheaded insofar as it fails to recognize that the question of the morality of elective abortion is not one that can be settled by an argument that purports to prove on logical grounds alone that human fetuses are persons. I suggest that it is mistaken to think that the question of the morality of elective abortion is one that can be discovered, and we need to realize that this is a question that must be *decided*. That is, since human conceptuses, embryos, and fetuses are as much unlike paradigm cases of persons as acorns are unlike oak trees, and since the distinguishing features of paradigm cases of persons are properties that don't emerge until some time after birth, we need to *decide* when we shall begin to treat very young, genetically human beings as persons with the full protection of the law. That is, we need to decide when should we treat beings that do not yet have the characteristics of paradigm cases of persons as if they were persons already. My conclusion on this point is that we ought not to commence treating genetically human beings as persons until they are detached from women by birth, since deciding to treat them as persons any earlier than birth opens the door to morally unacceptable treatment of women who are, unquestionably, persons.

The paper deals with other objections to ensuring a stillborn in late abortion, including the less metaphysical objections that even if a woman has a right to the termination of a pregnancy, she has no right to the death of a fetus, and that late fetuses are relevantly like infants and are, therefore, entitled to the same protections that infants are commonly given. I agree with the claim that a woman's right to terminate a pregnancy does not entail or include a right to the death of her fetus. But I argue that since a woman does have a right to the safest abortion procedure possible, and since ensuring a stillborn in late abortion adds to the procedure's safety, a woman has a derivative right to seek fetal demise before an abortion procedure. I also argue that the interests of fetuses and the children they might become favor ensuring a stillborn in late abortion. To the objection that fetuses and infants should be treated analogously, I argue that insofar as this is plausible, the implication is that some infanticide is morally acceptable, rather than that the preservation of all late aborted fetuses is morally required. These responses to the common objections to ensuring a stillborn in late abortion are offered as correctives to the main replies that have previously been offered to them in the literature, since those replies, I argue, are inadequate.

Much of my position rests on a controversial view of what is in the interests of children in a society that, despite much rhetoric to the contrary, does not accommodate children well. That view has been seriously challenged by Christine Overall in a prepublication comment on the paper, who argues that "The argument appears to make it too easy to rationalize getting rid of certain children rather than mending our ways with respect to our treatment of them." This position anticipates the argument against abortion that feminist disability theorists have made against the kind of position Laura Purdy takes in her paper in this section.

As mentioned, part of my paper in this section deals with the arguments regarding fetal personhood. But it needs to be pointed out that there have been a number of attempts in the feminist literature to move away from consideration of the moral status of the fetus in discussions of abortion. Mary Mahowald's paper in part II is a recent example. A classic example of the attempt to set aside the question of fetal personhood in discussions of abortion was offered over twenty years ago by Judith Jarvis Thomson.[8] Thomson uses several analogies to argue that even if we understand pre-embryos or embryos or fetuses to be persons, that status is simply not relevant to a woman's right to abort a pregnancy and thereby kill her conceptus. Among the most memorable of these is her analogy of the fetus to a violinist who has been hooked up to a woman's kidneys and will need to stay hooked up to the woman for a significant amount of time if he is to survive. Thomson argues that even though the violinist is unquestionably a person and even though it would be admirable of a woman in this situation to offer her body as a temporary life support for him, the violinist has no right against her for use of her body, and she would not act unjustly if she unhooked him (or had him unhooked), which would kill him. Although Thomson doesn't argue this, she would likely say much the same if a woman who was the only one who could save the violinist had initially agreed to allow him to be hooked up to her but later changed her mind because of discomfort and/or threats to her own health in providing support for him in this way. Minimally, we could expect that Thomson would argue against the law's requiring her to stay hooked up to him, that is, against the law's requiring specific performance of what was initially agreed to in such a case. And it is likely that those who agree with Thomson's original argument from analogy regarding the violinist would agree, as well, that even if the woman were less than admirable for going back on her word (and she need *not* be considered this if the analogy to pregnancy is taken seriously, since pregnancy is an exquisitely intimate burden and it can gravely threaten a woman's health), she should not be required by law to remain hooked up to the violinist, even though she had once promised to do so. Indeed, many people who hold the position that elective abortion should be illegal would very likely reject requiring specific performance in either Thomson's violinist case as she originally articulated it or in the amended case I have suggested where a woman initially promises to serve as a life support.

But the problem is that those who are opposed to elective abortion on the ground that a genetically human being has the full rights of a person from fertilization onward simply reject such analogies as irrelevant to the question of abortion, and they insist that a pregnant woman has special duties toward the conceptus/person that she carries that morally preclude her aborting. Indeed, no matter how many arguments are put forward against the view that fetuses (or pre-embryos or embryos) should be recognized as having the rights of full persons and no matter how many Thomsonesque arguments for ignoring the question of prenatal personhood are put forward, the disagreement over the legal availability of elective abortion continues. No one seems to listen to the arguments, and the debate has become intractable. The debate is intractable for several reasons, including political, religious, economic, and eugenic reasons; but most important, it is intractable because of different metaphysical and normative views on the nature and value of women.

State Interest in the Regulation of Reproduction

The regulation of reproduction by the state is, historically, broad and deep. As Joan Mahoney and Mary Shanley have pointed out in their papers in parts I and II, respectively, the passage of property has been and continues to be tied to reproduction in most of the world. Further, political, various sorts of moral, religious, general economic, class, and eugenic considerations have all contributed to the state's interest in having a say about who will reproduce and how much they will reproduce.

For example, in response to the loss of French lives in World War I and the fear of Germany's greater population, the French in 1920 adopted the most restrictive laws in Europe in regard to abortion and the dissemination of contraceptive information.[9] Hermann Goering, founder of the Gestapo, made it clear that the Nazis intended to increase Germany's population from 66 million to 90 million, which would require more territory.[10] And Benito Mussolini held that if Italy were to amount to anything as a world power, it would need to enter the second half of the twentieth century with a population of 60 million.[11] Today in the Middle East, nations such as Israel, Iran, and Iraq, which are struggling to maintain political viability or seize political dominance, have stridently pronatalist policies. Political reasons for attending to reproduction, then, remain strong throughout much of the world.

Limiting birth has also been held to encourage sexual excesses, to lead to the decline of the family, and to increase greed and self-indulgence. The secular moralists of nineteenth-century France reasoned this way, as did turn-of-the-century English Anglicans, arguing that limiting births was bad for the public interest, since this contributes to lifestyles that make citizens physically and morally weak.[12]

Religion, of course, has played and continues to play a dominant role in state interest in reproduction, generally in the direction of supporting pronatalist policies. In the United States, for example, groups such as the Women's Christian Temperance Union and the New York Young Men's Christian Association were instrumental in getting passed the federal Comstock Law of 1873, which prohibited sending contraceptive information through the mails. The Comstock Law had a hundred-year legacy. It was not until 1965, in *Griswold v. Connecticut*, that the U.S. Supreme Court made it clear that states could not make it illegal for married couples to obtain and use contraceptives, and not until 1972, in *Eisenstadt v. Baird*, that the Court ensured that unmarried persons could not be prevented by law from obtaining and using contraceptives.[13] The Comstock Law itself was not repealed until 1971. Today in the United States, nearly all those who actively oppose elective abortion and the ready availability of safe and effective contraception are members of religious (generally Christian) groups.

On the other side of the coin, states also sometimes try to limit reproduction, either universally across the citizenry or selectively across certain groups. China serves as a prime example of a government's attempt to enforce a rigorous general antinatalist policy. Because of alarming increases in population and the concern to avoid famine in the future, the Chinese government in 1979 adopted a policy which forbade families to have more than one child unless special, clearly circumscribed conditions obtained. The result of the policy has been an extremely troubling set of coercive and risky practices, including unrelenting pressure on women to have abortions and sterilizations, and the indiscriminate application of potentially harmful contraceptive technologies, such as intrauterine devices.[14] Further, son preference remains strong in China, since ancestor worship must be carried on by sons. The one-child policy, combined with the culture's common religious commitment to ancestor worship, has led to a good deal of female infanticide in China, which continues to be overlooked by the state.[15] And, as Helen Bequaert Holmes has pointed out in her paper in part II, much the same is true in contemporary India, where the government continually overlooks the common practice of amniocentesis and abortion for sex selection and the killing and fatal neglect of female children.

States also get involved in reproduction for eugenic purposes, sometimes combining pro- and antinatalist policies. In Nazi Germany, for example, sterilization laws were adopted to help preclude reproduction by "inferiors," while tremendous pressure, including a full-blown propaganda campaign, was applied to women of the desired heritage, pressing them to leave the work force and return to the home to reproduce.[16] Unhappily, Margaret Sanger played an important part in U.S. eugenics practices in the 1930s by calling for "more children from the fit, less from the unfit," for limitation of reproduction of the illiterate and "degenerate" who threatened "our way of life," and for sterilization or segregation by sex of those whose offspring would be unfit—in her words, "the whole dysgenic population."[17] Sanger, who was so aware of the oppression of women caused by lack of individual reproductive control, could never quite see the racial and class biases that informed her eugenicism or the basic incoherence in a view calling for both reproductive freedom and eugenics.

Today, concerns about the same biases, as well as concerns about the treatment of women, inform the work of feminists dealing with so-called population problems. In developing nations, members of the racially or ethnically dominant classes are, as is common in so-called First World nations, much better situated in general than are the lower classes, which typically include high numbers of those of races or castes less valued in the society. Although oppression of women crosses all classes, women from lower classes and less esteemed races around the world are the primary targets for population control efforts by more developed nations. Thus, as Betsy Hartmann reports, there have been "Smiling Family Safaris" in Indonesia, where thousands of women have been brought together in a picniclike atmosphere to become *aspari* (angels) by accepting intrauterine devices; in Thailand, women have been required to accept the long-acting contraceptive, Depo-Provera, before being permitted to marry; in South Africa, adolescent black girls have been injected with Depo-Provera without their consent, and black women have been required to document their use of birth control as part of their applications for jobs.[18] Not only are such practices morally repugnant, they completely miss the usual causes of low quality life in developing nations, causes which generally do not include absolute scarcity in regions of the world where we see famine and destitution. For example, the Sahelian famine in the late 1960s and early 1970s, which resulted in hundreds of thousands of deaths and massive migrations southward, was not a result of inadequate resources in the region, since nearly all of the affected countries had enough food to feed their own people, as evidenced by the fact that agricultural exports from the region actually increased during the famine years.[19] The problem of poverty is virtually always not a matter of absolute scarcity, but is, rather, the result of the distribution of resources and services in a society. One only needs to consider the phenomenon of homelessness in the United States today to recognize this. The key to development and prosperity doesn't lie in attempting to control the reproduction of those considered least desirable and a burden in a society. Rather, it lies in reforming the social and economic conditions which breed destitution for segments of a society. The focus on directly controlling birth, particularly among the least well off and least valued in any given society, leads to completely overlooking the economic and social conditions which discourage people from limiting their own reproduction. Thus, in societies where there is no substantial social security system for aged persons and, therefore, where people must rely on their children for support in their later years, the incentive to reproduce is and will continue to be strong. And it is even stronger in such societies where there is a high child mortality rate. In societies or segments of societies where children are a primary source of social esteem, or where having children has deep religious meaning, or where children are otherwise needed to contribute to the economy of families, external attempts to control reproduction are simply bound to fail.[20]

Even more, as long as societies keep women in subordinate positions by tying women's worth to reproduction and by affording women no viable choices for meaningful work and social engagement unconnected to their reproductive roles, women will have little incentive to limit their reproduction. So-called population problems turn out not to be genuine population problems at all, but interlocking problems of sexual, racial or ethnic, and classist biases which governments are uniformly slow to rectify because states are commonly run by those of privileged sex, class, and race or ethnicity.

I said earlier that the intractability of the abortion debate is importantly related to views on the nature and value of women. In her autobiography, Margaret Sanger reports being told in 1918 by an unnamed

German gynecologist regarding abortion that "We will never give control of our numbers to the women themselves. What, let them control the future of the human race? With abortion, it is in our hands; we make the decisions and they must come to us." Traditionally, such decisions have not been afforded to women—in no small part because of a persistent view of human nature which stretches back to Aristotle and beyond and according to which women, in nature and value, are very different from men.[21] Kristin Luker has forcefully argued that this traditional view of women is intimately linked to the intractability of the contemporary abortion debate and the continuing opposition of many people to readily available birth control aids.[22]

According to this kind of view, the purported intrinsic differences between women and men make women and men naturally suited to different roles, which require different excellences or virtues. Women, on this view, are suited by nature to create and manage a home and to bear and rear children. A woman's value, then, lies in her being an excellent specimen of her kind—an excellent wife/manager and mother.[23] But the ready availability of abortion and contraceptive aids leaves women free to avoid their "natural" roles. When a society protects reproductive choice by accepting safe and readily available contraception and/or elective abortion, those who subscribe to this view of women are deeply disturbed to find the view rejected. The stakes are high for both women and men; but they are particularly high for women who consider their value to lie in what they take to be their "natural" roles as wives and mothers. When a society accepts widely practiced birth control, these women perceive the state to be devaluing their very lives. Legal restrictions on the availability of abortion and contraception shore up the social recognition of their lives' value. Thus, despite the heavy burdens women have had to bear and, in many parts of the world, continue to have to bear under coercive pronatalist policies, such policies serve to make women's place and value unambiguous, and for that reason many women have supported and continue to support such policies. Once one understands the metaphysics of woman that commonly lies behind the position that abortion should not be readily available to women, the fact that no one who is opposed to elective abortion really listens to the *arguments* for abortion's being available to women is not surprising. The arguments don't count because there is a whole worldview at stake. To support elective abortion is to support a view of women that allows us to be other than what we are believed to be destined by God and/or nature to be, namely, wives and mothers. Intimately connected to all of this is the current debate over the availability of RU 486.

RU 486

RU 486 (or mifepristone) is an antiprogesterone agent which interferes with the actions of progesterone that are necessary for a pregnancy to proceed. Basically, it "tricks" the uterus into doing what happens at the end of every menstrual cycle—sloughing off and expelling the uterine lining.[24] Because it can be taken orally and because of the way it acts, RU 486 has been widely touted as a method which demedicalizes abortion, putting it directly into the hands of women. As Janice Raymond points out in her paper in this section, this is a myth. Nevertheless, the popular perception of RU 486 is that it is a pill which a woman can take in the privacy of her home and effect a simple miscarriage with no special medical intervention. The popular argument commonly given against the availability of RU 486 in the United States and elsewhere rests on the claim that RU 486 is morally unacceptable because it causes abortion and because (the usual argument) all elective abortion unjustifiably kills innocent persons. There has been massive mobilization from the right to block the introduction of this drug in the United States and elsewhere. But it needs to be stressed that it is no small matter that RU 486 is popularly understood as a birth control methodology that can be easily and secretly taken by women—that is, that this perception of RU 486 largely accounts for the vehemence of the negative response to its availability. It is, in the popular imagination of those who continue to subscribe to what I've been calling an Aristotelian metaphysics of woman, the very worst kind of birth control methodology—a pill which not only allows women to avoid motherhood, it is a pill that allows women to kill their babies in secret. Insofar as this is the perception, it is a perception that this preparation will hide abortion away where its perpetrators cannot easily be identified.

But, as Raymond points out, this perception is based on a misunderstanding of what the administration of RU 486 involves. That is, unlike the perception that has been encouraged by the developers and producers of RU 486 (and that has been further encouraged by a number of feminist activists), application of this technology involves a woman's being examined for pregnancy and her being administered the preparation in a medical facility and attended in that facility for several hours, within which the drug should induce the expulsion of a woman's uterine contents. If that doesn't happen, the woman is sent home, and she must return to the medical facility for examination after the expulsion to ensure that all the products of conception have been expelled. If they have not been, she will need to undergo suction abortion. Thus, even though it is true that RU 486 can add to the privacy of abortion (since it can, in principle, be administered in any physician's office, and can provide "cover" for physicians who otherwise wouldn't do abortions), Raymond means to explode the myth that RU 486 virtually completely demedicalizes abortion and she means to alert us to the sorts of mystification that surround so many of the technologies that are applied to women's bodies.

"Strange Bedfellows" and Feminist Disagreement

Now, a number of feminists have argued stridently for the ready availability of RU 486 in the United States. It has been common for such feminists to argue not only that RU 486 should be available but, even more strongly, that government blocking of the availability of RU 486 is actually a violation of women's rights.[25] Raymond's paper is addressed primarily to this feminist audience, which, as mentioned in the introduction to this book, includes members of The Feminist Majority Foundation, a group founded by Eleanor Smeal, former director of the National Organization for Women. Unhappily, and as Raymond recounts in her paper here, Ellie Smeal has publicly attacked Raymond for her position on RU 486, charging Raymond with being anti-feminist and aligned with right-wing forces. But nothing could be further from the truth. As a member of FINRRAGE, the Feminist International Network of Resistance to Reproductive and Genetic Engineering, Janice Raymond has been, for many years, extremely active in the international women's health movement and one of feminism's most radical critics of various reproductive technologies and their negative implications for the well-being of women and children. She takes her place with critics such as Rita Arditti, Gena Corea, Mary Daly, Ruth Hubbard, Renate Klein, Christine Overall, Barbara Katz Rothman, Robyn Rowland, and others, who have made a life commitment to cautioning us about technologies applied to woman's bodies.[26] Certainly, committed feminists can disagree about the sorts of things that add to or take away from women's oppression. But Smeal makes a grave mistake in taking Raymond's position to be reflective in *any* way of right-wing thinking.

Smeal's charge against Raymond raises two critical issues for feminists. The first is what counts as a genuinely feminist position; the second is how disagreements between and among feminists should be handled. As I have said in the introduction, feminist views are those that begin with the observation that women, as a group, are oppressed, and they share the commitment to overcoming that oppression. These features set feminist views apart from antifeminist and nonfeminist views, and they bind all feminist views together. Feminists, however, often disagree on precisely what contributes to women's oppression, and with that, precisely how women's oppression will be overcome. The disagreement between Smeal and Raymond on the question of RU 486 is not a feminist/nonfeminist or feminist/antifeminist disagreement, but a disagreement between two committed feminists on how a technology does or does not contribute to the oppression of women. What is so very unfortunate in this case is Smeal's failure to see that, leading to her public discrediting of (rather than disagreeing with) Raymond's unequivocally feminist position on RU 486.

The Smeal/Raymond case is an interesting instance of what Helen Holmes calls "the strange bedfellows problem" in her contribution to part II. It has struck many feminist theorists and activists as more than a little ironic that they find themselves holding the same substantive positions as those with whom they are least ideologically aligned. Thus, Holmes finds herself in unfamiliar company as she takes her position opposing sex preselection. And Barbara Katz Rothman notes that she often finds herself on television programs, cast with priests or rabbis, included to provide a "balanced" view, only to find herself arguing (say) the same anti-surrogacy position as her interlocutor.[27] But, as both Holmes and Rothman point out, the crucial difference between these "strange bedfellows" lies in the paths they have taken to get to their conclusions, and where they are going with their positions. For feminists such as Holmes, Rothman, and Raymond, it is the perception of how these technologies disserve women and children that leads them to the same substantive conclusions as those who are motivated by far different concerns. And it is that perception, which is the very cornerstone of feminism, that Smeal manages to miss in discrediting Raymond.

There is, potentially, a similar problem that can arise between feminist theorists such as Laura Purdy, whose paper completes this section, and who argues against reproducing children who will have or have significant probability of having serious disabilities, and those feminists who are known as disability theorists, who argue that abortion for reasons of disability adds to an already troubling set of societal attitudes toward those with disabilities. Purdy's view is that doing the best for our children includes not having children who we know will have a definite or high probability of substantial suffering. Purdy mentions technical philosophical arguments for asserting that bringing a disabled child into the world does not count as harming that child. But she is most concerned to address the more meaningful arguments of disability theorists, such as Adrienne Asch.[28] Asch and other feminists are, for example, highly critical of prenatal screening because of its implications for pressure on women to produce the perfect child, its implications for the imposition of unwanted fetal therapy, and its implications for the social position of those with disabilities.[29] In taking such positions against prenatal screening and abortion because of disability, feminists again find themselves in odd company, such as the Vatican.[30]

But Purdy's view cannot be characterized as nonfeminist or as insensitive to the well-being of children. Indeed, the very heart of her position is that, given the choices that contemporary diagnostic resources and birth control technologies afford us, women, so far as they are able, should elect not to bring children into the world who will start out with very serious burdens. The tension here between a view such as Purdy's and that of feminist disability theorists is vexing, and reminiscent of Christine Overall's extremely sensitive objection to my own paper on ensuring a stillborn in late abortion. Whether such tensions can be resolved in ways that will satisfy the very serious concerns of feminists who find ourselves in troubling but respectful disagreement remains to be seen as the conversations on these issues continue among us.

Notes

1. Portions of the following discussion have been adapted with permission from James W. Knight and Joan C. Callahan, *Preventing Birth: Contemporary Methods and Related Moral Controversies* (Salt Lake City: University of Utah Press, 1989), chs. 2, 7, and 9. For a much more detailed and developed discussion of the issue of elective abortion, see *Preventing Birth*, ch. 7.

2. See, too, the introduction to Part IV.

3. See, e.g., Rosalind Pollack Petchesky, *Abortion and Women's Choice: The State, Sexuality, and Reproductive Freedom* (Boston: Northeastern University Press, 1985).

4. See, e.g., James C. Mohr, *Abortion in America: The Origins and Evolution of a National Policy, 1800–1900* (New York: Oxford University Press, 1978).

5. *Roe v. Wade*, 410 U.S. 113 (1973).

6. See, e.g., Kristin Luker, *Abortion and the Politics of Motherhood* (Berkeley: University of California Press, 1984), and Petchesky, *Abortion and Women's Choice*.

7. See, e.g., Stanley Henshaw, "Induced Abortion: A Worldwide Perspective," *International Family Planning Perspectives* 18 (1987): 250.

8. Judith Jarvis Thomson, "A Defense of Abortion," *Philosophy and Public Affairs* 1:1 (1971): 47–66.

9. See, e.g., Angus McLaren, *Sexuality and the Social Order: The Debate Over the Fertility of Women and Workers in France, 1770–1920* (New York: Holmes and Meier, 1983).

10. See, e.g., Margaret Sanger, *An Autobiography* (New York: Norton, 1938; reissued New York: Dover, 1971).

11. See, e.g., Sanger, *An Autobiography*, and Katherine Organski and A. F. K. Organski, *Population and World Power* (New York: Knopf, 1961).

12. See, e.g., McLaren, *Sexuality and the Social Order*, and Peter Fryer, *The Birth Controllers* (London: Seeker and Warburg, 1965).

13. *Griswold v. Connecticut*, 381 U.S. 479 (1965), and *Eisenstadt v. Baird*, 405 U.S. 438 (1972).

14. For a discussion of the risks to women associated with intrauterine devices, see Knight and Callahan, *Preventing Birth*, chs. 1 and 6.

15. See, e.g., Elizabeth Croll, Delia Davin, and Penny Kane, eds., *China's One-Child Family Policy* (New York: St. Martin's, 1985).

16. See, e.g., Marilyn Jane Field, *The Comparative Politics of Birth Control: Determinants of Policy Variation and Change in the Developed Nations* (New York: Praeger, 1983).

17. See Margaret Sanger, *An Autobiography*; "Why Not Birth Control in America?" *Birth Control Review*, May 1919, p. 10; *The Pivot of Civilization* (New York: Brentano, 1922); and "My Way to Peace," speech to the New York History Society, January 17, 1932, in Sanger Manuscripts, Sophia Smith Collection, Smith College, Northampton, Mass.

18. Betsy Hartmann, *Reproductive Rights and Wrongs: The Global Politics of Population Control and Contraceptive Choice* (New York: Harper and Row, 1987). With the fall of apartheid and South Africa's election of Nelson Mandela as president in May of 1994, we can hope, finally, to see the end of such practices.

19. See Hartmann, *Reproductive Rights and Wrongs*, and Amartya Sen, *Poverty and Famines: An Essay on Entitlement and Deprivation* (Oxford: Clarendon, 1981).

20. See, e.g., Donald Warwick, *Bitter Pills: Population Politics and Their Implications in Eight Developing Countries* (Cambridge: Cambridge University Press, 1982). See also Hartmann, *Reproductive Rights and Wrongs*.

21. For an especially illuminating discussion of the concept of "woman" in Aristotle, see Elizabeth V. Spelman, *Inessential Woman: Problems of Exclusion in Feminist Thought* (Boston: Beacon, 1988), ch. 2.

22. Kristin Luker, *Abortion and the Politics of Motherhood* (Berkeley: University of California Press, 1984).

23. See Patricia Smith's discussion of this metaphysics of woman in her contribution to part I.

24. See, e.g., Knight and Callahan, *Preventing Birth*, pp. 170–176.

25. See, e.g., Kathleen Marie Dixon, "Professional Responsibility, Reproductive Choice, and the Limits of Appropriate Intervention: The Battle Over RU 486," in Daniel E. Wueste, ed., *Professional Ethics and Social Responsibility* (Totowa, NJ: Rowman and Littlefield, 1994), pp. 175–204.

26. See, for example, Janice Raymond's latest contribution, *Women as Wombs: Reproductive Technologies and the Battle Over Women's Freedom* (New York: HarperCollins, 1993).

27. Barbara Katz Rothman, *Recreating Motherhood* (New York: Norton, 1989), p. 240.

28. See, for example, Adrienne Asch, "Reproductive Technology and Disability," in Sherrill Cohen and Nadine Taub, eds., *Reproductive Laws for the 1990s* (Clifton, NJ: Humana Press, 1989), pp. 69–124 (this selection also includes an extremely helpful bibliography on disability). For a focus on women with disabilities, see Martha Fine and Adrienne Asch, eds., *Women with Disabilities: Essays in Psychology, Culture, and Politics* (Philadelphia: Temple University Press, 1988).

29. See, for example, Mary Sue Henifin, Ruth Hubbard, and Judy Norsigian, "Prenatal Screening," in Cohen and Taub, eds., *Reproductive Laws for the 1990s*, pp. 155–183.

30. Congregation for the Doctrine of the Faith, Vatican Translation, *Instruction on Respect for Human Life in Its Origin and on the Dignity of Procreation: Replies to Certain Questions of the Day* (Boston: St. Paul Editions, 1987).

Ensuring a Stillborn:
The Ethics of
Lethal Injection
in Late Abortion

Joan C. Callahan

A rather daring article published in *Obstetrics and Gynecology* in 1992 has been stirring debate for some time.[1] The objective of the authors' study is stated at the paper's outset:

> With the intention of preventing the attendant medical, ethical, and legal problems arising from the birth of live-born, anomalous fetuses, we initiated a program offering fetal intracardiac potassium chloride injection as an adjunctive measure in the setting of genetically indicated second-trimester abortion (296).

The authors observe that "Direct fetal intracardiac potassium chloride injection effectively causes immediate fetal cardiac arrest" (296), and they suggest that this approach be adopted "in cases of abortion by labor-induction methods at advanced gestation to ensure that the abortus is stillborn" (296).

Although the authors mention only the "medical, ethical, and legal problems" that can arise when an abortus turns out to be liveborn, the economic and psychological burdens that can attend maintenance of an anomalous infant surviving abortion will also be avoided by fetal intracardiac potassium chloride (KCl) injection.[2] Moreover, although the authors limit themselves to a discussion of "genetically indicated second-trimester abortion," it is obvious that intracardiac KCl injection can be used just as effectively to avoid all these problems for late abortion of nonanomalous, but unwanted fetuses.

If the case for ensuring the death of a seriously anomalous second-trimester fetus is not plausible, then it is unlikely that a strong case can be made for using intracardiac KCl injection in late elective abortion of healthy fetuses. On the other hand, if the case for ensuring the death of a healthy second-trimester fetus is plausible, then a plausible case for ensuring the death of a seriously anomalous second-trimester fetus might flow from it. In this paper, I concur with these authors on the moral acceptability of using intracardiac KCl injection to ensure that a seriously anomalous fetus will not be liveborn following a late abortion procedure. But I go beyond so-called genetically indicated second-trimester abortion and address the even more controversial question of the moral acceptability of using this method for late elective abortion of nonanomalous fetuses.

I proceed by looking at the main moral arguments against and the main arguments supporting the use of intracardiac KCl injection for anomalous fetuses. These appear in a companion piece to the article in the same issue of *Obstetrics and Gynecology*, written by several of the same authors joined by bioethicist John Fletcher, which supports the use of intracardiac KCl injection for anomalous fetuses in cases where resuscitation and treatment of a infant might be imposed despite the dissent of parents.[3] In doing this, I argue that both the replies to the objections to KCl injection and the positive arguments for use of KCl injection that appear in Fletcher et al. are seriously flawed. Since their article captures the main lines of thinking on this question and since it will be widely read by practitioners, a detailed criticism of and correction to its arguments is important.

Fletcher et al. first consider three objections to the use of intracardiac KCl injection in late abortion, namely:

1) [a]ll abortions are unjust; 2) infants and second-trimester fetuses at similar weights with identical defects should be managed in like fashion; and 3) the patient is not entitled to the death of the fetus, only to evacuation of the uterine contents [that is, to the termination of the pregnancy, as opposed to the termination of the fetus] (summary, 310).

They argue for the use of fetal KCl injection on three grounds:

1) The woman's decision for abortion is protected because the practice assures her right to non-interference; 2) potential psychological harm to the patient and other family members is avoided; and 3) the potential for coercive intervention by other health care professionals is eliminated (summary, 310).

I'll adopt their ordering of the issue by first considering their replies to the objections.

The Objection from the Injustice of
Abortion in General

To the objection that all abortions are unjust, Fletcher et al. reply:

> Clearly, if this objection were morally valid and legally enforced,
> all abortions would be ruled out, at any stage of gestation, without
> respect to chromosomal or structural anomalies. In fact, this situa-
> tion does not exist. . . . A very wide majority of the American pub-
> lic supports a woman's right of choice about abortion, especially in
> cases of diagnosed fetal anomalies (311).

But as they articulate it, this reply to the argument for the injustice of
abortion in general rests on a simplistic sort of moral relativism which
just presumes that a cultural or societal majority has a corner on moral
judgment for members of that culture or society. I cannot present the
full case against this sort of cultural relativism here.[4] But it should suffice to point out that this sort of relativism makes meaningful moral
evaluation impossible since, on this view, whatever a majority thinks is
right *defines* the right, and therefore any moral criticism of the majority
position is necessarily wrong. Further, any change in the majority's view
is a correct change; yet until such a change, those in the minority *necessarily* hold the wrong moral position. A moral theory riddled with such
moral and logical paradoxes is too flawed to be even mildly attractive as
a serious theory to offer us guidance in morally dilemmatic situations.
Indeed, such a theory cannot even allow that there *are* moral dilemmas,
since all moral questions can be solved simply by taking a poll to find
out what those in the majority think is right. Now, Fletcher and his
coauthors might not mean to be appealing to such a simplistic and problematic doctrine here. But if they are not, then it needs to be said clearly
just what (other, more credible) argument they mean to be making.

What is really needed in response to the argument from the immorality of abortion in general is a careful, sustained consideration of the
reasons people have for holding that position. Those of us who are unequivocally supportive of a woman's entitlement to terminate a pregnancy often fail to see the genuine and important moral commitments
of those who oppose abortion. Those moral commitments merit sensitive consideration through careful argument rather than too quick and
fallacious dismissal.

That much said, however, careful consideration of the reasons people
have for holding that abortion is always (or nearly always) morally unjustified and should be prohibited shows that those reasons are unac-

ceptable, since they either rest on religious commitments that would be wrong to enforce in a pluralistic society, or they rest on an unsound philosophical argument for fetal rights.[5]

In brief, the philosophical argument given against abortion is a wedge argument, which rests on the assumption that unless beings are radically different, they may not be treated in radically different ways. If fetuses are persons, then they must be treated as we would treat any persons, acknowledging in custom and in law their powerful right to life. The argument proceeds by asking us to consider a being who is unequivocally a person—any ordinary person, say, at 25. There is no radical difference between a person at 25 and a person at 24 1/2, thus persons at these ages, the argument goes, must not be treated in radically different ways—if we cannot kill one for reasons less than self-defense, then we cannot kill the other for reasons less than self-defense. The argument then presses back through childhood and past birth, contending that change of place, from the womb to the wider world, is not a substantial change in a being itself. Thus, the fetus just before birth and the fetus just after birth are essentially the same, and they must be treated in the same ways. Finally, the argument passes back to conception. There is no "bright line" to be found during the prenatal stage which would justify allowing killing before that demarcation while requiring protection of fetal life beyond that point. Even if viability weren't a moving line, it is not sufficient of itself, it is argued, to mark a boundary between unjustified and justified killing, since we don't think that killing grown persons can be justified simply because they are dependent on others for their survival. Logic and fairness, then, are held to combine to cement the conclusion that abortion is unjust.

But the main problem with this wedge argument is its assumption that beings who are not radically different may never be treated in radically different ways, since this assumption entails that society cannot be justified in setting limits that must be set. The argument would entail that society must give the five-year-old the right to drive and the six-year-old the right to vote. The fact that there is no "bright line" separating the 20-year-old from the 21-year-old need not lead us to believe that setting a drinking age at 21 is not justified.[6]

The whole search for and failure to find a bright line separating beings that are intrinsically different rests on the erroneous assumption that the question of the morality of abortion is one that might (somehow) be settled by discovery, much as one might discover whether there is a person hiding in the bushes by going and taking a careful look. But the question of abortion cannot be settled by some sort of direct discovery, since prenatal human beings (particularly, very young ones) have none of the characteristics that compel a recognition of personhood.[7] The real question is this: When, all things considered, should very young human beings be treated as persons with the attendant moral and legal rights of persons? That is, when should beings that do not (yet) have the characteristics of paradigm cases of persons be treated as persons? This is a question that needs to be settled by *deciding* what convention it would be morally and legally best to adopt. If the proponent of the wedge argument is clear on the nature of the question and means to be presenting a case for setting a convention of recognizing personhood at fertilization, then the basic argument is that any other point for recognition of personhood is arbitrary from a moral point of view. But this is false. Birth is not, from the moral point of view, an arbitrary point for beginning to treat very young human beings as persons.

Although there are some fascinating physiological changes at birth, as L. W. Sumner points out, late fetuses and infants do have "the same size, shape, internal constitution, species membership, capacities, level of consciousness, and so forth."[8] They are, intrinsically, quite alike. But, as Mary Anne Warren has pointed out, at birth there are radically new conditions regarding what is involved in preserving the life of a very young human being. Most notably, preserving that life violates no right of the infant's biological mother. Adopting the convention of recognizing personhood at birth rather than at some earlier stage has the distinct moral advantage of respecting the unquestionable personhood of women. As Warren has argued,

> . . . pregnancy . . . is probably the *only* case in which the legal personhood of one human being is necessarily incompatible with that of another. . . . To try to "protect" the fetus other than through [the pregnant woman's] cooperation and consent is effectively to nullify her right to autonomy, and potentially to expose her to violent physical assaults such as would not be legally condoned in any other type of case. . . . *There is room for only one person with full and equal rights inside a single human skin.*[9]

Does it follow from all this, however, that there is *no* plausible objection to the use of intracardiac KCl injection in late abortion? I certainly don't think so. First, the fact that a being is not a person does not entail that just anything can be done to it. If a being is sentient, pain should not be inflicted on it without compelling moral justification. But this point, as we shall see shortly, *supports* using intracardiac KCl injection in late abortion.[10] Furthermore, the longer a healthy fetus develops, the closer it gets to becoming a paradigm case of a person, and even if potential personhood isn't sufficient to establish a strong right to life, the loss of that potential is appropriately regretted. Abortion and the death of a fetus is never a happy choice, since it does involve the sacrifice of human life, and this is always an important loss. And the more that life is developed and promising, the more deeply the loss is felt.

Still, it doesn't follow from grief that abortion involving the death of a fetus cannot be justified. Abortion and the loss of fetal life is always a choice that is thought to be the lesser of two evils; defenders of choice do not hold that abortion is an intrinsic good.[11] But the fact that a choice is not a happy one simply does not entail that it is an unjustified one.

The Objection from the Limits to a Woman's Rights

As mentioned, the other two objections Fletcher et al. raise are: 2) infants and second-trimester fetuses with identical defects should be managed in like fashion; and 3) a woman, though entitled to termination of a pregnancy, is not entitled to the death of her fetus. Let me take the second of these first.

That anyone would be morally *entitled to* the death of any living being is an idea which, frankly, I am unable to grasp. I am entitled to defend my life and if, under some set of unfortunate circumstances, the only way that I can accomplish that is by taking the life of another (human or nonhuman) being which threatens my life, I am, derivatively, entitled to take that life to remove the threat. That is, I am entitled to be free of the threat—if killing is the only way I can do this, then it is morally permissible for me to kill.

The fundamental right to autonomy entitles a woman to terminate a pregnancy. If pregnancy termination can be accomplished only by actions that will result in the fetus's death, a woman is entitled to take those actions. But it certainly does not follow from this that if a woman does not need to kill her fetus to exercise her autonomy right to be free of a pregnancy that she is still entitled to kill it. That is, her right to autonomy does not of itself include a right to the death of her fetus. If she has an autonomy right to kill her fetus, that right would be derivative from her right to terminate her pregnancy. But to say this is to argue for precisely what Fletcher et al. virtually dismiss by simply asserting that their

> . . . premise is that the autonomy of a woman (and the biological father, if available and involved) who decides for abortion of an affected fetus ought to be protected from interference by others. . . . If an act of direct killing of the affected fetus would, in fact, protect the choices of mother and father from interference and

coercive imposition of treatment, then the act would be justified on those grounds. . . . [Thus,] if interference by others not associated with the abortion procedure is likely, potassium chloride injection is justified to prevent interference and imposition of coercive treatment by assuring that the fetus is dead before completion of the abortion process (312).

This reply to the objection that a woman is not entitled to the death of her fetus simply seems to beg the question by merely asserting that her right to noninterference with abortion includes the right to the death of her fetus before the completion of the abortion process. But assertion is not argument; and in this case the assertion involves a critical conceptual mistake. For, again, if the right is to noninterference with termination of a pregnancy and if that can be accomplished without killing the fetus, then a right to noninterference with termination of pregnancy simply involves no right to kill the fetus. Thus, no right to the death of her fetus is contained within or follows from a woman's right to noninterference with abortion of her pregnancy.

I think, then, that the objection that a woman's right to autonomy does not entitle her to the death of her fetus stands. But does it follow from this that fetal intracardiac KCl injection cannot be justified? It doesn't follow, and I want to argue that it can be justified on the basis of considerations that will return us to the question of a woman's right to the death of her fetus. Before getting on to my positive argument for the justifiability of ensuring a stillborn in late abortion, though, let me first finish the discussion of Fletcher et al. by looking quickly at the final objection to using intracardiac KCl injection that they respond to and their positive arguments for using fetal intracardiac KCl.

The Objection from the Formal Principle of Justice

The final objection Fletcher et al. take up is captured in the claim that infants and second-trimester fetuses with identical defects should be managed in like fashion. The authors offer what seems to be an internally inconsistent response to this objection, which they interpret as an objection from infanticide. That is, they read this objection as contending that killing anomalous fetuses is wrong because it sets a precedent for killing anomalous infants. Initially, their response is limited to a brief discussion of Baby Theresa (an anencephalic infant born by cesarean section in Florida in March of 1992), followed by the assertion that the case "underscores the need to make difficult choices" (311) and the unanswered rhetorical question, "How far do the rights of the anencephalic neonate extend when compared to the normal neonate?" (311). The suggestion implicit here certainly seems to be that some infanticide is justifiable. But the authors neither say this explicitly nor offer any defense of that position. Later, they reconsider the objection and take a view much like the one I have offered above, namely, that there is a crucial moral difference between fetuses and infants, since infants are independently existing beings and fetuses are not (312). (I interpret this to be the view that infants are independent of women's bodies while fetuses are not.) Thus, the authors use this distinction between the circumstances of fetuses and the circumstances of infants to deny that their view sets any precedent for infanticide.

But this second discussion of the objection seems internally inconsistent in two ways. First, it conflicts with what seems to be the implicit suggestion behind the authors' rhetorical question in the first discussion of the objection, namely, that some infanticide (say, of anencephalic infants) might be justified. Second, and more importantly, it seems to conflict with the spirit of their argument from noninterference. That is, the argument from a woman's right to noninterference, as the authors present it, seems *really* to be an argument for a woman's right not to be a mother of a living child—a right to not have biological motherhood imposed upon her. The authors do not put their position this way; but given their inclusion of consideration of the autonomy of the genetic father, it seems that this is what they have in mind. If the authors really mean to champion a right to not be a biological mother of a surviving infant, however, the door is obviously wide open to the infanticide objection.[12]

A more credible response begins by recognizing that the objection under consideration may not be one from a precedent for infanticide at all, but a straightforward objection from justice that takes into account our current practices regarding infants and that rests on the formal principle of justice—that is, the principle that relevantly like cases, all else being equal, should be treated similarly. Insofar as late fetuses are not essentially different from infants, they therefore must be treated as infants with the same anomalies would be treated—that is, they should not be killed.

But if this is the objection, it may be a version of the first objection—which takes fetuses to be persons—and that objection has already been addressed. Further, (and here is where a mirror-image of the authors' response has force), there is the *crucial* moral difference between fetuses and liveborn infants that fetuses are, until they emerge, part of women's bodies, and anything that is done to or for them necessarily involves a woman's body. Thus, the case of the fetus and the infant are not like cases, *all* things considered, and the formal principle of justice applies to cases that are similar *all* morally relevant features considered, and therefore, it doesn't apply here. Thus, even if one accepts that infants should not be killed, one need not accept, on the basis of the formal principle of justice, the same for fetuses.

On the other hand, if the objection (or some other objection) is from a precedent for infanticide, I would want to argue that some infanticide *is* morally justifiable and I would ground that argument in two ways. First, even though I have argued that the convention of recognizing personhood should be set at birth, that view (when fully laid out) pertains to those infants with the capacities to develop into actual persons.[13]

If an infant will never have the capacities to develop the kinds of characteristics that define persons, then that infant is not even a potential person and, therefore, failure to treat it as a person can be justified. Thus, for example, I have argued elsewhere that transplants of vital organs from anencephalic infants can be justified.[14] Second, if it can be argued that infants with certain deficits may be killed, then the formal principle of justice would seem to allow killing fetuses with the same deficits. This, I think, amounts to the substantive position that Fletcher et al. hint at with the rhetorical question in their first discussion of the objection from the formal principle of justice. But if this *is* their position, it needs to be made explicit and defended.

To sum up so far: I have argued that the replies Fletcher et al. have offered to the main objections to ensuring a stillborn in late abortion are seriously inadequate. But I have also argued that the position that all abortions are unjust has not been defended adequately and that certain severely anomalous fetuses (and certain severely anomalous infants) need not be treated even as potential persons. Thus, I, too, have rejected two of the main objections to KCl injection that are raised and rejected by Fletcher et al. On the other hand, I have argued against Fletcher et al. that a woman's right to autonomy does not contain or of itself entail a right to the death of her fetus. It does not follow from this, however, that no other right or reason might justify ensuring a stillborn in late abortion. Let me finish by looking at Fletcher et al.'s positive arguments for the use of intracardiac KCl injection and a sketch of the argument that I believe justifies ensuring a stillborn in late abortion.

The Safety of Women and the Interests of Anomalous Fetuses

What the authors list as two of the arguments for the use of fetal intracardiac KCl injection emerge in their treatment of the objections they discuss. These are listed as (1) protection of a woman's right to non-interference and (2) prevention of coercive intervention by other health care personnel. But these really comprise a single argument, since a right to non-interference includes a right to be free of coercive intervention from others, and I have already argued that this right cannot provide an entitlement to the death of a fetus.

The final positive argument offered for ensuring a stillborn is the "avoidance of psychological harm to the woman and other family members if the neonate survives [the] abortion attempt" (311). Avoidance of any sort of harm is always a relevant moral reason for doing or not doing something. But since the other arguments the authors offer for ensuring a stillborn are so plainly unsound, the avoidance of psychological costs to the woman and other family members in the case of survival seems completely unlikely to convince anyone not already supportive of ensuring that a liveborn infant will not result from pregnancy abortion.

There are two crucial considerations lacking in this argument from harm (and from the authors' discussion in general): (1) a serious consideration of the safety of women and (2) the interests of fetuses and the children fetuses might become. And these, I want to suggest, are precisely the considerations that are the compelling ones in justifying ensuring a stillborn in late abortion.

A stillbirth in cases of late abortion is not only "easier" on a woman for all the reasons Fletcher et al. mention, it is safer as well. The most common and safest second trimester abortion procedure today is dilation and evacuation (D and E). In this procedure, laminaria tents are used to gently dilate the cervical canal over a period of hours. After sufficient cervical dilation is achieved, appropriate anesthesia is administered, and the products of conception are removed with forceps. It has been common to crush the fetus for removal.[15] But this involves risk to the woman, since tissue becomes separated, and one of the most common complications of abortion is septicemia resulting from retention of products of conception.[16] Thus, if the fetus can be removed intact, this is much safer for the woman. If fetal demise occurs some hours before a D and E, the fetal tissue will have softened considerably, making it possible for the fetus to be removed intact. In a living fetus, tissue does not collapse in this way, and removal of the fetus without crushing and tissue laceration is far more difficult. Furthermore, with fetal demise a woman's uterus is more likely to move naturally into contractions, aiding in inducing labor and (again) making the possibility of removing the fetus intact much more likely.[17] When a women chooses abortion (either because a fetus is anomalous or because she simply does not want to continue a pregnancy), she is entitled to the safest procedure possible. Attempting to ensure the survival of a fetus through a pregnancy abortion subjects a woman to increased risk. Although I have argued that a right to autonomy by itself does not entitle a woman to the death of her fetus, a woman has no obligation to assume risks to ensure its survival, and others are not entitled to impose risks on her in order to try to preserve her fetus. A woman's entitlement to the safest procedure available, then, is sufficient by itself to justify ensuring a stillborn in late abortion.

Dr. Warren Hern has pointed out to me that a number of practitioners attempt to ensure live fetuses after late abortions so that genetic tests can be conducted on them. It is his position (and I concur) that practitioners who do this without offering a woman the option of fetal demise before abortion act in a morally unacceptable manner, since they place research before the good of their patients.[18] This view, then, sets a presumption *in favor of* ensuring fetal demise before a late abortion, a presumption which can be overcome only by a woman's informed willingness to assume the additional risks that attend attempting to ensure a live abortus through the procedure.

It should be emphasized at this point that Fletcher et al. include the genetic father's views, as well as the woman's views, in their discussion. But this inclusion should be rejected, primarily on the ground that it can, too easily, lead to hazards for women. For example, it invites the possibility that a man might insist that an abortion be conducted in a way that maximizes a fetus's chances of survival, which, again, can subject a woman to a procedure not maximally safe for her. In order to ensure respect for a woman's right to elect a maximally safe procedure, *all* questions regarding abortion (or delivery in cases where a child is wanted by the woman) must be the exclusive province of the woman.

The second consideration that Fletcher et al. leave out in their discussion of avoiding harm is that in the case of seriously anomalous fetuses it is simply not in *their* interests to survive. Intracardiac KCl injection is painless or virtually so for the fetus, and one need not go through the conceptual contortions and moral distortions of arguments from rights to noninterference to defend a practice that can be defended straightforwardly on grounds of what is in the short-term interests of fetuses themselves and what is in the long-term interests the children they might become.

As regards short-term interests, insofar as a late fetus may be even moderately sentient, non-maleficence requires that its suffering should be minimized. That is, even though I have argued that fetuses should not be treated as persons, there are still duties of non-maleficence to sentient beings, and utilizing intracardiac KCl injection ensures the prevention of any pain that might otherwise be brought on the fetus during or shortly after an abortion procedure.[19] As regards long-term interests of the seriously anomalous children fetuses might become, I want to suggest that we need to be *acutely* aware of the fact that we have institutions that house thousands of individuals whose lives would be shocking to most of us, and that population ought not be increased. The reason analysts and commentators want to avoid relying on this sort of argument, of course, is that it involves judgments about so-called quality of life, and such judgments are contentious by their very nature. But, like it or not, such judgments are made every day. The familiar distinction between use of ordinary and extraordinary means in health care provision depends on judgments regarding quality of life—if no real benefit to an individual can be derived from a certain treatment, then the treatment gets labeled "extraordinary." Thus, what counts as ordinary or extraordinary varies from case to case, according to prior judgments regarding what sort of quality of life a certain treatment is likely to yield for a certain individual.[20] Judgments about quality of life, then, are made all the time, whether we are comfortable admitting that or not.

Late abortions of seriously anomalous fetuses are undertaken precisely *because* it is decided that if these fetuses were to survive, their lives would be of an unacceptably low quality. If a decision in favor of abortion of a pregnancy is made on this ground, then consistency in attending to the best interests of *this* fetus would seem to require that the suffering that would predictably or highly probably attend extended survival should be precluded. I want to suggest, then, that the short-term and long-term interests of seriously anomalous fetuses is each sufficient to justify ensuring a stillbirth in late abortion.

Late Elective Abortion of Healthy Fetuses

I said at the beginning of this discussion that I wanted to go further than cases of seriously anomalous fetuses and ask about the justifiability of using intracardiac KCl injection for late elective abortion. Let me finish with this question.

I believe that the short-term interest of nonanomalous fetuses in not having suffering caused to them in or after an abortion procedure is sufficient to justify using intracardiac KCl injection. But, it is likely to be argued, the long-term interests of the children nonanomalous fetuses could become can outweigh any temporary suffering they might experience during and/or shortly after an abortion procedure. Thus, it might be objected, one cannot argue from the either the short-term or the long-term interests of late nonanomalous fetuses to ensuring their deaths before an abortion procedure.

We need the option of abortion, not only to ensure the well-being of women, but also because parenting is *such* an important matter.[21] Women who do not want to be mothers of children should not be mothers. Being a parent is difficult enough for even those who are enthusiastic about the task, and it is too important a task to be left up to institutions or individuals who are not fully committed to doing it to the very best of their abilities. If we really care about the well-being of children, the last thing we want to do is in any way force women to have children or bring children into the world for whom we cannot reasonably assure loving homes.

But do we really care about children? Or is it more that we care about some *idea* of caring about children? Ours is not a society that accommodates children well. Certainly our workplaces are not designed to accommodate children. Nor are most of our shops or public spaces. Nor are women (who remain the primary caretakers of children) well rewarded in our society, let alone rewarded for taking care of children. Indeed, most of the persons below the poverty level in our society are women *and* their children.

I want to suggest that a critical question in deciding on the justifiability of using KCl injection in any late abortion is this: If this pregnancy yields an infant and that infant survives, what are its life prospects? That is, laying ideals aside and taking social realities into full and lucid account, what are *this* fetus's *real* life prospects?

I argued earlier that the convention of recognizing personhood should be set at birth because there are radical changes in what is involved in sustaining the life of an infant as opposed to the life of a fetus. In particular, sustaining an infant after birth, be it "natural" or induced premature birth in abortion, involves no violation of the rights of a woman to self-direction and bodily integrity. But it certainly does not follow from this that women should not elect stillbirth in late abortion. Nor does it follow that, without exception, infants (anomalous or not) that come into the world liveborn after abortion should be sustained.[22] To suggest that the recognition of personhood should be conventionally set at birth is to suggest that a strong right to life be recognized at birth, since the properties of persons emerge individually and over time, and there is no clear time when we can say for all human individuals they are now actual persons, much as there are no clear boundaries between where the Mississippi River ends and the Gulf of Mexico begins. The purpose of setting this convention at birth is to give us a place to begin with very young human beings that does not compromise the actual personhood of women. However, to say that recognition of personhood at birth should be set as a *convention* is also to say that infants are not yet actual persons. Thus, in cases involving departures from such a convention, actual persons are not wronged. My suggestion, then, is that if there is good reason to believe that it would not be in some particular infant's best interest to emerge as a person, either because of profound anomalies or because there is no one standing by who will see to that infant's flourishing, it would be wrong to bring that infant forward.

Whether infants surviving abortion procedures should be sustained, then, is a question to be answered in terms of the life prospects of each particular infant in its very real present social circumstances, and the crucial question here is whether there is someone who is fully prepared to care for it and fully prepared to see to its flourishing as it moves from personhood conventionally recognized to actual personhood. And *this* (along with considerations of safety for women) is the issue that consistently goes unconsidered by those who insist that late abortions must be conducted in ways that maximize the probability of survival of the abortus, and that everything possible must be done to sustain even the most seriously anomalous infants that survive an abortion procedure.

In closing, then, the view I want to forward is just the very simple one that every child should be a wanted child, and that it is wrong to bring a child into the world with no one standing by who is ready, willing, and able to assume responsibility for that child's flourishing. Unfortunately, our society has not provided this, even for those nonanomalous infants that are liveborn after late abortion. In short, then, until we, as a society, are prepared to take the parenting of these children seriously, they should not be brought forward on the basis of an appeal to some abstract right to life which serves to let us tell ourselves that we are good people who respect human life when, in fact, we neglect human life all around us.

The argument is all that much stronger for the justifiability of ensuring a stillborn in cases of serious fetal anomaly, since many of these infants, even if rigorously sustained, will have lives that are, at best, short and painful—lives that are no use to them at all. Others could survive longer; but it is all that much harder to find parents for these children than for nonanomalous infants.

The fault, then, is not so much in our lofty moral principles as in ourselves. Until we are a community that is *genuinely* committed to the flourishing of each child in our midst, rather than committed merely to the Quaylean rhetoric which serves to puff us up while so many of our children languish, we shall have a *duty to avoid* bringing unwanted children into the community, and that duty, I submit, is sufficient to justify ensuring a stillborn in any late abortion.

In an unpublished comment on an earlier version of this paper, Christine Overall made an objection to this argument, which I agree is extremely worrisome. She says:

> I find this view problematic precisely because it seems to cater to rather than criticize some of the worst characteristics of North American society. . . . Our failure to accommodate children well represents our moral failures as a culture, and I am uneasy about justifying actions or policies merely by drawing on our moral failures. The argument appears to make it too easy to rationalize getting rid of certain children rather than mending our ways with respect to our treatment of them. . . . the argument raises, or should raise, serious concerns about what kinds of infants are going to be killed or allowed to die. Persons with disabilities have rightly expressed strong moral reservations about any practices or policies that encourage us to decide the fate of human beings on the basis of our willingness to accommodate their differences. In short, I am unable to accept an argument that justifies forms of passive or active infanticide, even of so-called anomalous infants, primarily on the grounds of our failure to accommodate them.[23]

I am uneasy, too—very uneasy. But, in the end, I suppose I am even more uneasy about the realities of life for those children who, because of our moral failures, will not be well accommodated. Troubling as it might be, I find that I am unable to accept their suffering on the ground that we should do better. We *should* do better—much better. There is simply no question about that. But until we do better, the task is not to press for the preservation of these children by ensuring their survival through abortion procedures; it is rather to press unremittingly for those needed changes in individuals and our social institutions that will improve the prospects for *all* children.

Conclusion

To sum up: I have argued that the responses that Fletcher et al. offer to the objections to ensuring a stillborn in late abortion are seriously flawed, as are their positive arguments for the moral acceptability of ensuring a stillborn in late abortion. In place of the arguments offered by these authors I have suggested that each of two other considerations is sufficient by itself to justify ensuring a stillborn in late abortion.

These considerations are the safety of women and the interests of fetuses (anomalous or not) and the interests of children those fetuses might become.[24]

Notes

1. Nelson B. Isada, Peter G. Pryde, Mark P. Johnson, Mordechai Hallak, William B. Blessed, and Mark I. Evans, "Fetal Intracardiac Potassium Chloride Injection to Avoid the Hopeless Resuscitation of an Abnormal Abortus: I. Clinical Issues," *Obstetrics and Gynecology* 80:2 (August 1992): 296–299.

2. As we shall see momentarily, the issue of psychological burdens is raised in a companion piece to the article.

3. John C. Fletcher, Nelson B. Isada, Peter G. Pryde, Mark Paul Johnson, and Mark I. Evans, "Fetal Intracardiac Potassium Chloride Injection to Avoid the Hopeless Resuscitation of an Abnormal Abortus: II. Ethical Issues," *Obstetrics and Gynecology* 80:2 (August 1992): 310–313.

4. For helpful discussions of the problems with ethical relativism, see Paul W. Taylor, "Social Science and Ethical Relativism," *Journal of Philosophy* 55:1 (1958): 32–44; Carl Wellman, "The Ethical Implications of Cultural Relativity," *Journal of Philosophy* 60:7 (1963): 169–184; the discussion of relativism in Walter Terence Stace, *The Concept of Morals* (1937) (all reprinted in Paul W. Taylor, ed., *Problems of Moral Philosophy: An Introduction*, 3rd ed., [Belmont, CA: Wadsworth, 1978], ch. 2); and see the discussion of relativism in Paul W. Taylor, *Principles of Ethics: An Introduction* (Belmont, CA: Dickenson, 1975).

5. I have argued this more thoroughly elsewhere. See Joan C. Callahan, "*The Silent Scream*: A New, Conclusive Argument against Abortion?" *Philosophy Research Archives* 11 (1986): 181–195; Joan C. Callahan, "The Fetus and Fundamental Rights," in Patricia B. Jung and Thomas A. Shannon, eds., *Abortion and Catholicism: The American Debate* (New York: Crossroads, 1988), pp. 217–231; James W. Knight and Joan C. Callahan, *Preventing Birth: Contemporary Methods and Related Moral Controversies* (Salt Lake City: University of Utah Press, 1989), ch. 7; Joan C. Callahan and James W. Knight, "Women, Fetuses, Medicine, and the Law," in Helen Bequaert Holmes and Laura M. Purdy, eds., *Feminist Perspectives in Medical Ethics* (Bloomington: Indiana University Press, 1992), pp. 224–253. Longer versions of this last paper appear as Joan C. Callahan and James W. Knight, "Prenatal Harm as Child Abuse?" *Women and Criminal Justice* 3:2 (1992): 5–33, reprinted in Clarice Feinman, ed., *The Criminalization of a Woman's Body* (New York: Haworth, 1992), pp. 127–155; and Joan C. Callahan and James W. Knight, "On Treating Prenatal Harm as Child Abuse," in Diana Tietjens Meyers, Kenneth Kipnis, and Cornelius F. Murphy, Jr., eds., *Kin-*

dred Matters: Rethinking the Philosophy of the Family (Ithaca, NY: Cornell University Press, 1993), pp. 143–170.

6. Of course, setting certain limits might be unjustified vis-à-vis conventions governing other rights and responsibilities. Thus, for example, it is often argued that setting the drinking age at 21 cannot be justified when the military draft age is 18. But the point here is simply that society is justified in setting *some* limits, even though there may be nothing "in the nature of things" that picks out the precise limit set. As regards abortion: There must be *some* public policy governing it—i.e., all abortion is allowed, or all abortion is disallowed, or some abortion is allowed, some disallowed. The argument I am looking at contends that no (elective) abortion is morally permissible (and that policy should follow this moral prohibition). My point is that the argument most commonly given to justify the claim that elective abortion is immoral is unsound because it rests on an assumption that needs to be rejected.

7. I discuss these characteristics in more detail elsewhere. Again, see the pieces cited in note 5.

8. L. W. Sumner, *Abortion and Moral Theory* (Princeton, New Jersey: Princeton University Press, 1983), p. 53. Sumner erroneously concludes from this, however, that moral standing and a compelling right to life must be recognized earlier in development, and he takes sentience as this point, thereby drawing a moral distinction between early and late abortion. Although sentience seems, uncontroversially, to give a being some moral standing, it's not at all clear that sentience endows a being with a compelling right to life. For problems internal to Sumner's view, see Mary Anne Warren, "The Moral Significance of Birth," *Hypatia* 4:3 (1989): 46–65.

9. Warren, "The Moral Significance of Birth," pp. 61, 63, emphases in original.

10. For a fuller discussion of fetal sentience, see Callahan, "The Fetus and Fundamental Rights," and Callahan, *"The Silent Scream."*

11. For discussions of women's reluctance to choose abortion and postabortion depression, see, e.g., Magna Denes, *In Necessity and Sorrow* (New York: Penguin, 1977); Linda Bird Franke, *The Ambivalence of Abortion* (New York: Dell, 1978); Beverly Wildung Harrison, *Our Right to Choose: Toward a New Ethic of Abortion* (Boston: Beacon Press, 1983); Caroline Whitbeck, "The Moral Implications of Regarding Women as People," in William B. Bondeson et al., eds., *Abortion and the Status of the Fetus* (Boston: D. Reidel, 1983); Betsy Hartmann, *Reproductive Rights and Wrongs: The Politics of Population Control and Reproductive Choice* (New York: Harper & Row, 1987). Occasionally, however, it is argued that abortion is a positive good because it is crucial to the well-being of women. See, e.g., Rosalind Pollack Petchesky, *Abortion and Women's Choice: The State, Sexuality, and Women's Reproductive Freedom* (New York: Longman, 1984).

12. There are other problems with the view that people have a right to not be biological parents. For example, such a right could be called on to attempt

forcing women to have abortions in cases where men do not want to be biological parents. See Christine Overall's discussion of the right not to be a biological parent in her contribution to part 11.

13. For a discussion of the distinctions among actual, potential, and future persons, see the pieces by Callahan and Knight cited in note 5.

14. Or, at least, such transplants cannot be objected to on the ground that they involve violating the rights of a person. Again, see the pieces by Callahan and Knight cited in note 5.

15. See, e.g., Knight and Callahan, *Preventing Birth*, pp. 190–191.

16. See, e.g., Robert A. Hatcher, Felicia Stewart, James Trussell, et al., *Contraceptive Technology: 1990–1992* (New York: Irvington, 1992), ch. 21; and Paul D. Blumenthal, "Abortion: Epidemiology, Safety, and Technique," *Current Opinion in Obstetrics and Gynecology* 4 (1992): 506–512.

17. I am grateful to Warren M. Hern, M. D., for our conversations on safety in abortion techniques. On this and more generally, see his *Abortion Practice* (Boulder, CO: Alpenglo Graphics, 1984, pb. 1990).

18. Warren M. Hern, M.D., personal communication, September 1993.

19. I am grateful to Christine Overall for suggesting this articulation of the point.

20. See, e.g., James Rachels, "More Impertinent Distinctions and a Defense of Active Euthanasia," in Thomas A. Mappes and Jane S. Zembaty, eds., *Biomedical Ethics*, 1st ed. (New York: McGraw-Hill, 1981), pp. 355–359.

21. Barbara Katz Rothman argues this eloquently in *Recreating Motherhood: Ideology and Technology in a Patriarchal Society* (New York: Norton, 1989).

22. Again, see the pieces listed in note 5 on the distinctions between potential, future, conventional, and actual persons.

23. Christine Overall, "Commentary on Joan Callahan's 'Ensuring a Stillborn: The Ethics of Lethal Injection in Late Abortion,' " typescript, February 1993.

24. An earlier version of this paper was prepared at the invitation of the National Abortion Federation, for their conference, "Second Trimester Abortion—From Every Angle," Dallas, Texas, September 13–14, 1992. I am grateful to Michael Burnhill, M.D., for offering me the opportunity to discuss this issue with members of the NAF. I am also grateful to Warren Hern, M.D., Mary Mahowald, and the participants in the Philosophy Colloquium Series at Queens University for helpful comments on an earlier draft. I am especially indebted to Christine Overall for the astute and sensitive observations in her comment on the paper, delivered at Queens University in February of 1993. As we go to press, a slightly expanded version of this paper is scheduled to appear in the *Journal of Clinical Ethics*, accompanied by several commentaries, including one from John Fletcher.

RU 486:
Progress or Peril?

Janice G. Raymond

In 1988, two scientists and I undertook a study of RU 486, the new chemical abortifacient, which has been increasingly promoted as a safe, private abortion method for women. For many years, all of us had worked in the area of the ethics and politics of medical technologies or in primary medical research, and we came to this project fortified with a hope that RU 486 was a promising abortion method for women worldwide but also with a skepticism that was born out of a history of other proclaimed miraculous drugs and technologies that later proved perilous or ultimately ineffective.

The result of this investigation was a book-length report, published at the end of 1991, entitled *RU 486: Misconceptions, Myths and Morals.*[1] In this chapter, I summarize the findings of this study, noting especially the claims made for the drug, the short and potential long-term effects of the drug on women, and its proposed use in developing countries. Equally important, however, I use RU 486 as a case study in the ethics and politics of reproductive technologies to raise issues about choice, the politics of abortion, gender and the tolerance of pain, dissent, and the framework of medical fundamentalism in which many of these issues are crystallized.

In examining the existing medical literature on this drug, we became convinced that there is an urgent need for more critical discussion of RU 486. The discussion is needed *not* on the terms of the anti-abortionists who unfortunately have raised health and safety issues about the drug opportunistically, in service of their own campaign against abortion, but rather from a women's-health perspective. We also discovered that much of the positive reaction to RU 486 thus far has depended on studies done by affiliates of Roussel-Uclaf, the drug's developers, with 95 percent of the literature reiterating the Roussel-Uclaf findings.

What Is RU 486?

What exactly is RU 486? In most of the media reports, RU 486 (mifepristone) is described as an antihormone which blocks the action of progesterone in a woman's uterus. Progesterone is necessary to produce and sustain the lining of the uterus in order that a fertilized egg can implant and develop there. Thus, RU 486 prevents the maintenance of the uterine lining, and thereby terminates an ongoing pregnancy, if it is taken within 63 days after the last menstrual period in combination with prostaglandin, which causes contractions. Although this sounds like a simple and straightforward explanation, it suggests that the antiprogesterone activity of RU 486 is localized and does not affect other parts of the female body. This is not necessarily the case.

The most important center in the body for the production of hormones is the pituitary gland, which is located at the base of the brain. Together with the hypothalamus—the region in the brain that regulates the central nervous system, heart, abdominal organs, emotions, and mood—the pituitary controls other glands in the body. Some studies have shown that RU 486 interferes with this "hypothalamic-pituitary axis," and therefore may provoke unexpected, and thus unnoted, disturbances in the body's metabolism.[2] It may also interfere with future ovulation.[3]

Proponents of RU 486, such as Etienne Baulieu, its (disputed) inventor, admit that the function of progesterone, and thus of antiprogesterone chemicals such as RU 486, on other areas in the body "is not well understood."[4] Other researchers are concerned about progesterone's influence on the central nervous system, especially on cortical function.[5] When RU 486 blocks progesterone in one part of the body, the uterus, its effects on other parts of the body where progesterone is also found could be serious. Most significant, the full metabolic impact of the drug, by the researchers' own admission, is not well researched.

There are also the long-term effects of prostaglandin which, thus far, researchers have generally not spoken about. One of the members of our team, Lynette Dumble, is a prostaglandin expert and primary medical researcher who, for years, has used prostaglandins in the treatment of transplant patients. Her research, as well as that of others, reveals that even a short-term dose of prostaglandin can have an immunosuppressive effect, and that this may have serious consequences in the body's defense against disease.[6]

Claims for RU 486/PG Abortion

The major selling point of RU 486 has been that it will change the abortion experience fundamentally for women. Proponents assert it will 1) privatize abortion and allow women to control the experience; 2) de-medicalize abortion and prevent anti-abortion harassment of women at clinics since, they say, RU 486 can be taken in the privacy of one's own home; and 3) make abortion safe, effective, and non-invasive in contrast to so-called surgical abortion which, all of a sudden, is portrayed as not-so-safe, not-so-effective, and invasive. (The term "surgical" abortion is deceptive, since most first trimester abortions are *suction* abortions and require only a local anaesthetic.) As U.S. columnist Ellen Goodman wrote, "What could be more private than taking a pill? How could a state control swallowing?"[7]

The medical literature tells another story, belying the myth of the do-it-yourself abortion. Alan Templeton at the University of Aberdeen, who led the British trials, admits that "To maintain safety you require extremely close medical supervision."[8] No country that has used RU 486 thus far has allowed the drug to be taken at home. And most have limited, even more than for suction abortion, the number of hospitals and centers where RU 486 abortions can be delivered. Most researchers and clinicians agree that RU 486 will *never* be given without medical supervision, yet they speak out of both sides of their mouths in stating that RU 486 gives women more control of abortion. The kind of medical management that RU 486 requires is not physician oversight from afar, but a *highly medicalized treatment regimen* which is multi-stepped, time-consuming and, for many women, productive of pain and lengthy suffering.

First, a woman seeking a chemical abortion via RU 486 must undergo a physical exam and pregnancy test. Most centers now administering RU 486 use vaginal ultrasound to confirm the existence and age of a woman's pregnancy. This in itself is not a painful procedure, but it does refute the claims of proponents who, in comparing RU 486/PG to suction abortion, assert that no instruments are inserted into a woman's body.

After confirmation of pregnancy, a woman is then given RU 486 in tablet form and swallows them, not at home, but in the presence of a doctor or nurse *at the center*. As noted above, this directly contradicts one of the myths supporting the privacy argument—that it doesn't require going to a clinic.

As a third step, most centers now administer prostaglandins in concert with RU 486, hereafter referred to as RU 486/PG. The success rate when RU 486 was used alone varied from 60–90 percent. Prostaglandins are given to propel and strengthen the contractions which expel the embryo from the uterus. Thus women must return to the clinical center for either injectable, suppository, or oral prostaglandins, because these have to be given 36–48 hours after the RU 486 treatment. Increasingly, it is the prostaglandin which requires more medical oversight, especially to watch for possible cardiovascular complications.

Then the wait begins. Many clinics keep women prone for 3 to 4 hours after the RU 486/PG treatment, in the hope that the embryo will be expelled, before sending them home. Other women wait hours, days, and some even weeks. The only thing that is private about RU 486 is that the final stage of the abortion, the expulsion of the embryo, often happens at home. Calling this an "at-home abortion" is plainly deceptive, since most of the treatment transpires in the clinic or hospital under strict conditions of medical control and supervision. What does happen at home can be an excruciatingly long wait for the fetus to be expelled, often accompanied by pain, bleeding, vomiting, nausea, and other complications drawn out over a substantially lengthy period of time, particularly when compared to a conventional abortion.

Finally, a woman must return to the medical center for another doctor's exam to make sure the abortion is complete. Vaginal ultrasound is used again to ascertain termination of pregnancy and expulsion of remaining tissue. Five to seven percent of RU 486/PG abortions are incomplete, compared to a less than one percent incomplete rate for suction abortions. If a full abortion has not been achieved, a woman undergoes a conventional abortion procedure—thus a second abortion.[9]

The Use of RU 486/PG in Developing Countries

The problems connected with RU 486/PG abortions are magnified in developing countries. Yet many medical, population, and women's groups continue to promote the drug as a corrective to the 200,000 botched abortions that are reported yearly worldwide, most of which occur in developing countries. However, most of these problematic procedures take place in countries where abortion is illegal, and most involve women's failed attempts to self-abort or abortions done by untrained practitioners.[10] Given the mandatory medicalized setting which RU 486/PG administration requires, chemical abortion would do nothing to lessen the number of botched abortions that result from abortion being illegal.

Additionally, the implications for women regarding monitoring and access problems in developing countries is staggering. Many women would have to travel to a medical center several times, often from long distances, for the various stages of treatment and testing. The prostaglandin must also be refrigerated. Add to this the fact that many women do not seek, or have access to, medical treatment early enough for chemical abortion to work within the limited window of time within which RU 486/PG can be used. The same is true in western countries for many women of color, as well as for rural and poor women, who do not have access to the kind of sequential medical treatment needed for safe RU 486/PG abortions. For these and other reasons, the 6th International Women and Health Meeting, held in the Philippines in November, 1990, went on record as being opposed to trials and the introduction of RU 486, especially in developing countries. Additionally in white, middle-class, western contexts, there have been problems with compliance and follow-up in RU 486/PG administration. Many women, for example, do not return for the final exam to verify complete expulsion of the embryo and tissue.[11]

There are also many *contraindications* (conditions making the drug inadvisable) which, for many women, militate against taking RU 486/PG: "obesity"; heart disease and women at risk for it (heavy smokers); gynecological disorders such as uterine scars, fibroids, abnormal menstrual bleeding, pelvic inflammatory disease (PID), and even irregular menstrual cycles; a history of liver, gastrointestinal, or renal disease; intrauterine or oral contraceptives used up to the time that women become pregnant; asthma; hypertension; blood clotting problems; and anemia. Black women have a significantly higher incidence of fibroids than do white women; and many women of color, as well as poor women, have a high rate of anemia. It has been estimated, for example, that 64 percent of women in Bangladesh have preexisting anemia. In India, the situation is worse.[12] The results of pilot studies carried out among Chinese women in Hong Kong and Singapore suggest that the blood loss associated with RU 486/PG abortion is greater than that observed in European women.[13] This may be due to preexisting anemia.

The number of drugs that are now given as part of the RU 486 treatment regimen is tantamount to a *drug cocktail*.

1. First, it was only RU 486;
2. Then, RU 486 plus prostaglandins;

3. Then, RU 486 plus PGs plus narcotic or non-narcotic painkillers;

4. Then, RU 486 plus PGs plus painkillers plus pre-medication; and

5. Most recently, some clinicians are giving women antibiotics; and others have given women oral contraceptives to stop the bleeding. The claims for the simplicity of the RU 486 method continue to multiply, yet no clinician or researcher has addressed the steadily increasing melange of drugs added to the treatment regimen and the possible synergistic effects of this chemical cocktail.

At a time when public consciousness of chemicals used on crops and animals translates into people "eating organic," we see an enormous increase in the chemicals that are being prescribed for women, especially in the reproductive realm. From a young girl's birth to her old age, she may take fertility drugs, DES, Depo-Provera, the pill, a new generation of anti-pregnancy vaccines that are especially being promoted in Third World countries, tranquilizers, estrogen- (now hormone-) replacement therapy, Norplant (the new long-lasting contraceptive implant) and now RU 486/PG. While these drugs differ in their degree of possible harm to women, all of them have been recognized as problematic. The point is that more and more questionable drugs are being prescribed for women at the same time that warnings against exposure to synthetic chemicals, especially in food, are rising. Can we be disturbed about chemically fed plants and animals and remain unconcerned about chemically fed women? Can any genuine ecological movement ignore the increasing chemical contamination of women's bodies?

Medical Fundamentalism

We have generally used the term "fundamentalism" to refer to religious and political conservativism and to the reactionary, reductionistic, inhumane, and selective principles of the antiabortionists who campaign against women's right to abortion. But fundamentalism is not simply a historical conservatism; it can also be applied to liberal movements whose reactionary, reductionistic, inhumane, and selective principles militate against women's right to healthy and safe drugs and technologies.

Robert Jay Lifton first coined the term "medical fundamentalism" to illustrate fundamental beliefs and symbols that operated and were taken for granted in the Nazi medical context—what he also calls "totalizing features," exerting near-total control of the environment in which a medical technique is launched and accepted.[14] I have employed the term to discuss many of the beliefs and assumptions that are taken for granted within the context of technological reproduction, specifically with respect to new reproductive technologies, but also which apply in the RU 486 context. Many people are willing to question a fundamentalism that is overtly religious; yet when these same totalizing principles and practices appear in the guise of a secular science, they are not recognized as another brand of fundamentalism.

In the case of RU 486, one of the operating fundamentals is that *complications are minimal.* When we examined the primary medical literature on RU 486/PG, however, we found striking complications. In addition to the medical supervision and access problems, there are complications of incomplete abortions, continuing pregnancies, and residual tissue remaining in the uteri of 2–13 percent of women who undergo the combination treatment.[15] Bleeding is another complication. In the UK Multicentre studies, 5 out of 500 women required both blood transfusions and curettage.[16] Prolonged heavy bleeding is regarded as the chief problem and most serious side effect of chemical abortions. In studies where bleeding is reported, the range of heavy bleeding falls between 15 and 23 percent.[17] Many studies also report a significant drop in hemoglobin levels which could lead to low blood pressure and shock, often necessitating a blood transfusion.[18] Other studies report a high incidence of moderate bleeding. Still others discount the seriousness of such bleeding.[19]

Pain is insignificant. This is another unquestioned fundamental assumption operating generally in the context of reproductive technologies. Pain is increasingly minimized or relativized to the extent of dismissing it as a complication. Judgments about the intensity of pain women experience are often evaluated differently by researchers and by the women themselves. Studies state that "pain is a difficult parameter to compare," adding that "the perception of pain depends on personal, social and cultural factors."[20] Interestingly, medical sensitivity to these factors appears mostly in contexts where it is in the interests of the researchers to minimize women's pain. A more telling measurement of the pain women do experience is the amount and kind of analgesics that are given after RU 486/PG. In the UK Multicentre trials, 50 percent of 500 women received *narcotic* analgesics after RU 486/PG treatment; an additional 30 percent required non-narcotic analgesia.[21]

Other complications are mainly gastrointestinal. Vomiting, nausea and diarrhea are frequently reported by women. Additional immediate complications are fainting, fatigue, shift in mood, and thirst.

In evaluating the medical literature on complications, it became clear that some complications are accepted without comment or criticism. Others are reported as "minimal," "tolerable," and "acceptable." The medical literature on RU 486 would be an excellent arena for an exercise in hermeneutics—increasingly, in the minds and reports of the researchers and clinicians, more and more pain and bleeding are interpreted as less and less of a problem for women. Given the complications reported in the medical literature on RU 486/PG, the normative judgment in the same literature that complications are "minimal" not only contradicts the facts about the severity of complications but transforms women's pain into insignificance. Pain that would be intolerable for men becomes tolerable for women, the threshold for female pain is constantly raised, and the message, when all is said and done, is that female pain is expected so what's a little more?

Nineteenth- and early twentieth-century western sexologists promoted a theory of female masochism which collapsed sexual pain and sexual pleasure for women. Reproductive researchers and technologists commonly operate on the similar assumption that women will accept any pain or any procedure either to become pregnant, as in the case of in vitro fertilization, or to prevent pregnancy, as in the case of RU 486. There is a growing culture of medical exploitation of women's bodies based on the assumptions that pain is normal for women and that complications are insignificant. *That a woman will endure anything to become pregnant or to prevent pregnancy has become a fundamental assumption of modern reproductive medicine underlying standard medical practice and treatment.*

Liberal Fundamentalism

The vast public relations campaign of what has become the RU 486 lobby has brought together medical researchers, population groups, and women's groups to shape public perception of the drug by what Edward Herman and Noam Chomsky call "manufacturing consent." On the level of imagery, RU 486 is presented as a miracle technology which will create an abortion revolution for women. Metaphors of progress dominate the media coverage, and critical commentary is ignored, confined to capsulized space, or misrepresented. Promoters of RU 486 have gone even further and tried to silence critics.

Suppression of dissent is a characteristic of all fundamentalist movements. The RU 486 lobby has strategically attempted to stifle all critical evaluations of the drug, especially our study. In raising criticisms about

RU 486, we found that reproductive rights' and women's groups accused us of aiding and abetting anti-abortionists. We saw other researchers who were also indicting RU 486 silenced by the response from some proponents of the drug that any woman who registers objections or even concerns about RU 486 is playing into the hands of the right wing. Medical fundamentalism, even its liberal variety, dismisses the independence of women's critical judgment which, presumably, has been one of the vital legacies of this wave of feminism. Women have the right to safe and effective abortions; but women also have the right to question whether RU 486 fulfills those claims.

Instead of addressing the issues that we raise in our study of RU 486, several reproductive rights' and women's groups led a concerted campaign to attack our credentials, our feminism, and our persons. Eleanor Smeal, president of the Feminist Majority, which has mounted a major campaign to bring RU 486 into the United States, told *Science* magazine that "one reason for Raymond's attack on RU 486 is that . . . Raymond, a former nun, has links to organizations that have been critical of abortion in general."[22] As University of Illinois sociologist Pauline Bart has remarked about the smear campaign of Smeal and the Feminist Majority, "They have the morality of Chicago aldermen."

In addition to the Feminist Majority, the Reproductive Health Technologies Project, organized by the private consulting firm of Bass and Howe, has brought together women's health organizations, population groups, and medical researchers to promote RU 486. In attempting to discredit our work, their tactic has been to reassert the charge of right-wing affiliation and to represent our criticisms as anti-abortion. In a communique to members of their coalition implying that we were naive and/or dupes of the anti-abortion movement, they wrote:

> To those of us involved in the U.S. abortion rights battle on the political front, it is particularly troubling that . . . their alarmist rhetoric echoes the National Right to Life Committee and other anti-abortion groups who have made RU 486 a cornerstone of their activities. These women either do not understand, or do not care, how "heaven-sent" their actions are for the very opponents of a woman's right to reproductive control and autonomy. . . .[23]

It is significant that this warning was sounded on September 6, 1991, five days before our report was off the press!

It is remarkable that women who have long been active in and publicly identified with the women's movement and, more specifically, with the international women's and reproductive health movement, are now slandered by an organization that has no history of involvement in women's health issues (the Feminist Majority) and a private consulting firm (Bass and Howe) that is making a business out of coalition-building. What is more remarkable is that the women's groups in this coalition are permitting these falsehoods to stand.

Another tactic of both groups has been to misrepresent the source of our report on RU 486. While all three authors are members of the international feminist network FINRRAGE, which monitors the development and use of new reproductive technologies worldwide, and two are widely known as founders of this network, the report was commissioned by the Institute on Women and Technology. Yet both groups have chosen to misrepresent our work as FINRRAGE-generated, because in pro–reproductive technological U.S. circles, FINRRAGE is identified as "extremist" for taking many critical stands against techniques such as in vitro fertilization and surrogacy. And thus it is that we find the Reproductive Health Technologies Project writing that we use so-called alarmist words like "chemical" abortions! But RU 486 is just that—a chemical abortion. In fact, that is the terminology used by medical researchers themselves. "Chemical abortion" is hardly a loaded phrase and, for years, environmentalists have criticized "chemical" methods of agriculture. One purpose of the work that we do at the Institute on Women and Technology is to link a longstanding feminist critique of chemical methods of birth control, abortion, and reproduction—where they have held dangers for women—with a longstanding environmental critique of dangerous chemicals in agriculture.

The graphic consequence of attempting to suppress feminist dissent such as ours is that groups like the Feminist Majority and the Reproductive Health Technologies Project fortify the centrality of the right wing as the defenders of women's health and safety. By discrediting genuine feminist concerns about the complications of RU 486, they are allowing the right wing to co-opt issues of women's health and safety as an opportunistic policy handle for the right's own campaign against abortion. Thus any complications associated with RU 486 and injurious to women become the "moral property" of the anti-abortionists. In effect, the liberals are handing over *ownership* of the critique of RU 486 to the right wing by maligning and discrediting the feminist critique of groups such as ours, who have long campaigned for women's rights to reproductive self-determination and abortion.

The stifling of dissent has also been achieved by warning critics that if women continue to battle the drug companies and researchers, they will jeopardize the future of reproductive products. Shortly after the attacks on me by the Feminist Majority were published, Karen Hicks, co-chair of the Dalkon Shield Information Network, wrote to Eleanor

Smeal criticizing what she termed her "shameless and outrageous attack" on my person. She related the experience of the Dalkon Shield survivors who, in their struggle for justice and compensation from A. H. Robins, were "beat down" by well-known members of "the organized feminist movement."[24] Women who have had the courage to confront the pharmaceutical companies over products that have injured, maimed, and, in some cases, killed women are told by other feminists that they endanger further reproductive research, drugs, and technologies in a U.S. R & D climate that is already chilled by the political right wing.

Promoters of RU 486/PG and other reproductive drugs and technologies point to the dearth of birth control, abortion, and reproductive technology now being developed. What is more important, however, is that there is a lack of *appropriate technology* for women, and the researchers and pharmaceutical companies have little interest in developing such low-cost and low-tech options. There has been virtually no research on condom improvement, barrier methods, and menstrual extraction, in contrast to the enthusiasm for the pill, IUDs, injectables, and sterilization. Most of the available drugs and technologies have been attended by risk and by sometimes deadly harm to women. Only women bear the burden of these reproductive technologies and drugs. These are the reasons why women have fought to have victims compensated and to have these products removed from the market. This seems like such an obvious truth; but when truth is distorted and misrepresented by the very people who should recognize it, then we find ourselves uttering words in defense of statements which sound outrageously elementary to our own ears.

The Subverting of Choice

A final principle of medical fundamentalism is that *RU 486 enhances women's choice*. Choice so dominates the discussion of reproductive technologies in the west that it is almost impossible to recognize the injuries that are done to women. Thus, many harmful drugs and technologies are presented as a woman's private choice rather than as public violence against women. The right not to be harmed cannot be reduced to the instrumentality of individual choice alone, because individual choice can and does include the right to harm one's self or propagate harm on others. The fundamentalism of this individualized perspective, with its foregrounding of unconditioned free will on the part of women, functions as a smoke screen for what is really medical experimentation and medical abuse.

Choice has become so fundamental that when critics of reproductive drugs and technologies spotlight the ways in which women are abused by these products, we are accused of making women into victims and, supposedly, of denying that women are capable of choice. To expose the victimization of women is to be blamed for creating women as victims.

Furthermore, is choice the real issue, or is the issue *what* choices, and in what context, selective women's choices are fostered? Whose interests are most served by representing reproductive drugs and technologies as a woman's private choice while rendering invisible the force of institutionalized, male-dominant interests? The subverting of choice to promote medical and corporate interests in the realm of reproductive drugs and technologies has been largely unexamined. In the industrialized countries, RU 486 is promoted as "more choice" for women, but "more choice" may actually provide less choice for women and more choice for doctors.

Currently, only 25 percent of medical students in the United States are trained to perform abortions. Since the 1973 *Roe v. Wade* decision, abortion services have been steadily and drastically cut, especially in rural areas.[25] This is not only because legal and other roadblocks to elective abortion have been created by the anti-abortionists and right-wing politicians, but also because the medical profession has gradually retreated from performing conventional abortions. General reluctance to perform conventional abortions converts easily to general physician enthusiasm for the RU 486 method, since it is easier to pass out pills and let women take the consequences than to continue to perform distasteful, boring and socially controversial suction abortions. The RU 486 method makes the actual abortion less visible to the doctors but not to the women involved.

David Healey, a prominent Australian fertility specialist who is a proponent of RU 486, says that RU 486 makes conventional abortions obsolete.[26] This has become the fanciful and reckless conclusion of several RU 486 researchers. We expect that at some point in the future, as has happened with a number of reproductive drugs and technologies, the short- and long-term complications of RU 486 will become more widely known and publicized, lawsuits will follow, and the media will do its usual routine featuring progress turned into peril. And the tragic consequence may be that women will be unable to turn back to other conventional means of abortion if these services, to use David Healey's phrase, become "obsolete."

The right to choose is fast becoming the right to consume. Reducing choice to consumption is nothing new. Corporate and professional interests, for many years, have used the rhetoric of choice to sell their products. For years, against the tide of overwhelming evidence that silicone breast implants have caused untold damage to women, Dow Corning continued to defend them and to enlist women as spokepersons who argued that they must be preserved as a "choice" for women. In February 1992, just before the FDA issued its decision sharply restricting silicone implants to women undergoing reconstruction after breast cancer surgery and to women with serious breast deformities, *The Boston Globe* ran a point-counterpoint story on two women's breast implant experiences. Sallie Kate Park, a victim of breast cancer who chose breast reconstruction and silicone augmentation after a mastectomy, lamented that women would have this "choice" of implants yanked from them by the FDA. As the article reported, "To Park, it is simply a matter of choice . . . 'I didn't have a choice when I had cancer. But [FDA Commissioner Dr. David Kessler] is taking away my choices of how to deal with it and to heal. . . .' "[27]

The other woman interviewed, Teresa Whitehurst, who underwent breast implantation because she was flat-chested, reported suffering through a series of leaks, ruptures, hardenings, body aches, shrinking of the implants, and ultimate infection. After six operations, a loss of breast tissue, and numerous other problems, she had the implants removed. When asked about the argument made by Park that breast implants should be a matter of choice, Whitehurst called the choice argument a "red herring." " 'The FDA exists,' she said, 'to prevent us from making bad choices that should never have been allowed in the first place.' "[28] Simple, but very philosophically and politically astute. Yet corporate America continues to defend such products on grounds of a woman's right to choose while, at the same time, denying large numbers of female workers the jobs, promotions, and wages/salaries that would indeed give them real life choices.

It is not news that the rhetoric of choice has been used by corporate America to sell products. What is new is the way in which some progressive and feminist groups have taken up the language of the corporate world and become consumer movements for new technologies and drugs. We have a primary example of this in the selling of RU 486.

The liberal emphasis on choice has become so abstract that many accept the rhetoric without questioning the reality of what is promoted as choice. This consumer-oriented kind of choice subordinates women's right to be protected from harm to "the right to use any medically promoted drug or technology." Conveniently, the agent is deleted in the phrase, "the right to use any medically promoted drug or technology," collapsing her right to use it with their right to manufacture and sell it and effectively placing women's rights to physical and mental well-being, bodily integrity, and human dignity in the back seat.

Conclusion

We need a feminist reproductive politics that links why/how women get pregnant to the technologies of abortion, contraception, and reproduction. In other words, we need a reproductive politics that is connected to the sexual politics of women's lives. On a practical level, we need to de-medicalize abortion and not re-medicalize it with ever more questionable drugs that require medical control and supervision. First-trimester abortion is one of the simplest of gynecological procedures; trained paramedics in Third World countries perform them safely and competently. The Vermont Women's Health Center performs one-third of all abortions in that state, with all of them done by physicians' assistants who, as part of a two-year training program in women's health care, learn the procedure. Why, then, cannot trained lay women do abortion in other contexts, for example, in women's health centers in other states? Feminists must challenge the medical monopoly on abortion provision, a monopoly that lacks justification as fewer doctors want or are trained to perform abortions.

No procedure requiring the strict medical supervision and involving the risks and complications of RU 486/PG will provide reproductive self-determination for women. Women must challenge the physician monopoly of abortion, especially in the west. In doing so, we must advocate woman-controlled and woman-performed abortions rather than another medical/chemical solution that requires the degree and kind of medical control necessary to RU 486. Rather than depending on some alleged medical miracle to guarantee abortions for women, women should "seize the means of reproduction" and take back control of abortion.

Notes

1. Janice G. Raymond, Renate Klein, and Lynette J. Dumble, *RU 486: Misconceptions, Myths and Morals* (Cambridge, MA: Institute on Women and Technology, 1991). This book is obtainable for $10.95 from the Institute on Women and Technology, P. O. Box 9338, N. Amherst, MA 01059.

2. Lynnette K. Nieman et al., "Successful Treatment of Cushing's Syndrome with the Glucocorticoid Antagonist RU 486," *Journal of Clinical Endocrinology and Metabolism* 61: 1985, 536–40.

3. Gary D. Hodgen, "Pregnancy Prevention by Intravaginal Delivery of Progesterone Antagonist: RU 486 Tampon for Menstrual Induction and Absorption," *Fertility and Sterility* 44: 1985, 263–67. See also Etienne-Emile Baulieu, "RU 486: An Antiprogestin Steroid with Contragestive Activity in

Women," in Etienne-Emile Baulieu and Sheldon Segal (eds.), *The Antiprogestin Steroid RU 486 and Human Fertility Control* (New York: Plenum Press, 1985), pp. 1–27.

4. Etienne-Emile Baulieu, "Contragestion and Other Clinical Applications of RU 486: An Antiprogesterone at the Receptor," *Science* 245: 1989, 1351.

5. William Crowley, "Progesterone Antagonism," *The New England Journal of Medicine* 315 (25): 1986, 1607.

6. Raymond, Klein, and Dumble, pp. 80–111.

7. Ellen Goodman, "Abortion Pill: A Mix of Chemistry, Politics," *The Boston Globe*, July 17, 1989: 11.

8. Quoted in *Sunday Times Magazine* (UK), "French Abortion Pill on Sale Here in 1990," October 30, 1988.

9. Raymond, Klein, and Dumble, p. 38. Here we cite several of the studies reporting incomplete RU 486/PG abortions, with figures ranging from 13.4 percent (Gao et al., 1988) to the lowest of 2 percent (Rodger and Baird, 1989). See notes 13 and 15 for complete citations to these studies.

10. Jodi Jacobson, *The Global Politics of Abortion*, Worldwatch Paper 97 (Washington: Worldwatch Institute, July 1990), esp. pp. 38–45.

11. When asked whether there was any succeeding supervision of women who had undergone RU 486 abortions in the U.S. trials done in Southern California, Daniel Mishell responded: " . . . we cannot even get the patients to return to have their blood drawn." (Quoted in David Grimes et al., "Early Abortion with a Single Dose of the Antiprogestin RU 486," *American Journal of Obstetrics and Gynecology* 158: 1988, 1311.) Likewise, there have been difficulties in getting women to return for sequential treatments of RU 486 and prostaglandins, as well as final tests to determine complete termination of pregnancy. See, for example, Louise Silvestre et al., "Voluntary Interruption of Pregnancy with Mifepristone (RU 486) and a Prostaglandin Analogue," *The New England Journal of Medicine* 322, 1990, 646. In this study, which collected data from 73 RU 486/PG abortion centers in France, 75 out of 2115 women did not return for follow-up after they had received prostaglandin analogues. They were thus dropped out of the study. Numbers of dropouts are not reported in most of the studies and thus, as epidemiologists know, we lose much important documentation of possible complications, since women who drop out of trials are more likely to have problems than those who stay in. Any medical treatment involving multiple steps is fraught with non-compliance.

12. Amanda LeGrand, "Medical and Users' Aspects of RU 486 with Particular Emphasis on its Use in Third World Countries." In WEMOS, Women and Pharmaceuticals, *Proceedings of Seminar on RU 486: The Abortion Pill* (Amsterdam), 1990: 21.

13. Ji Gao et al., "Pregnancy Interruption with RU 486 in Combination with dl-15-methyl-prostaglandin-F_{2a}-methylester: The Chinese Experience," *Contraception* 38: 1988, 675–83.

14. See Robert Jay Lifton, *The Nazi Doctors: Medical Killing and the Psychology of Genocide* (New York: Basic Books, 1986), 472, 488.

15. A 2 percent incomplete abortion rate was reported in Mary W. Rodger and David T. Baird, "Blood Loss Following a Prostaglandin Analogue (Gemeprost)," *Contraception* 40: 1989, 439–47; the highest reported incomplete abortion rate comes from Gao et al., 1988.

16. UK Multicentre Trial, "The Efficacy and Tolerance of Mifepristone and Prostaglandin in First Trimester Termination of Pregnancy," *British Journal of Obstetrics and Gynaecology* 97: 1990, 480–86.

17. Gao et al. report the highest incidence of heavy bleeding, but in all studies where heavy bleeding was reported, the range was 15–23 percent.

18. Regine Sitruk-Ware et al. reported a 15.3 percent drop in hemoglobin. See "The Use of the Antiprogestin RU 486 (mifepristone) as an Abortifacient in Early Pregnancy—Clinical and Pathological Findings: Predictive Factors for Efficacy," *Contraception* 41: 1990, 221–43.

19. Rodger and Baird, for example, state quite baldly: "As we gained experience, we became more confident in disregarding minimum continued vaginal bleeding." The disregarding of these factors by researchers establishes a standard which determines the acceptability of different degrees of blood loss and judgments about heavy vs. moderate vs. minimal loss of blood. Judgments about the seriousness of blood loss are obviously in the eye of the beholder. See Mary W. Rodger and David T. Baird, "Induction of Therapeutic Abortion in Early Pregnancy with Mifepristone in Combination with Prostaglandin Pessary," *Lancet* ii: December 19, 1987, 1417.

20. Marja-Liisa Swahn and Marc Bydgeman, "Termination of Early Pregnancy with RU 486 (Mifepristone) in Combination with a Prostaglandin Analogue (Sulprostone)," *Acta Obstetrica et Gynecologica Scandinavica* 68: 1989, 298–99.

21. UK Multicentre Trial, p. 483.

22. Michelle Hoffman, *Science* 25: October 11, 1991, 199.

23. Reproductive Health Technologies Project, Communication from Marie Bass to Advisory and Working Group, Friends and Colleagues in the Pro-Choice Community, September 6, 1991, pp. 5–6.

24. Letter of Karen M. Hicks, Co-Chair of the Dalkon Shield Information Network, to Eleanor Smeal, Feminist Majority Foundation, November 7, 1991. Quoted with Dr. Hicks's permission.

25. The Guttmacher Institute, quoted in Ellen Goodman, "Year One after Webster," *The Boston Globe*, July 1, 1990: p. 91.

26. David Healey, quoted in Philip McIntosh, "Professor Urges Introduction of Abortion Pill," *The Age* (Australia), July 24, 1990: p. 5.

27. Quoted in Renee Graham, "Implants: Two Women's Stories," *The Boston Globe*, January 30, 1992: p. 53.

28. Quoted in Graham, p. 55.

Loving Future People

Laura M. Purdy

Moral philosophers often wonder what a better world would look like.[1] It seems clear that eradicating war and poverty and building ecologically sustainable economies, among other things, would improve life immensely for many people. Only achieving such goals will enable us to provide the clean water, nutritious food, safe shelter, education, and medical care essential for human welfare; by themselves, these goods would go far toward helping people fashion satisfying lives. We will not have a morally bearable world until everybody enjoys them.

In the United States and elsewhere, individuals in increasing numbers lack these basic prerequisites for a decent life, and our first priority should be to create a floor of well-being with respect to them below which no one would be allowed to fall.

Prominent among requisite policies would be promoting justice for women. Most, if not all societies, define women in such a way that it seems right to subordinate us to men; the resultant inequality of burdens and benefits is still being documented. A just society would get rid of this inequality. To recommend such a state of affairs is not to embrace a libertarian moral theory, but rather to assert the importance of women's equal autonomy within a more caring and egalitarian society.

Although many details of this just society remain to be worked out, feminists are sketching out its main lines. They include truly equal education that equips us to take up whatever work suits our talents and interests, sufficient compensation for all occupations to enable us to live independently of men if we wish, and the right to determine whether and when we will have children. They assume social support for those decisions, including the resources necessary for bearing and rearing healthy children. The gap between the conditions in which most women now live and this feminist utopia is huge. At present, many women lack the equal educational and work opportunities that would help guarantee decent living conditions—including a safe environment and appropriate medical care—for themselves and their children. Justice requires getting closer to this ideal.

Having reached this conclusion, the main work of the moral philosopher qua philosopher is done: moral or political exhortation is not part of the job description.[2] However, there remain a few problems to mop up. Among them is the question of possible moral limits on women's reproductive rights.[3]

The Right to Reproduce

Although there is no explicit constitutional right to procreate, it is generally assumed that such a right is implied by other fundamental constitutional rights. It is also assumed that it is, in any case, morally justifiable to assert such a right, and that this right should be protected by law. Certainly, the assumption that individuals have a right to control their own bodies is deeply embedded in the Anglo-American intellectual tradition, and that right, because of reproductive biology, might reasonably be taken to imply for women, if not for men, a moral right to reproduce that should be protected by law. At present there are significant legal limits on women's reproductive rights, and, given the contemporary political climate, more are likely to be forthcoming. I believe that such legal limitations are unjustifiable.[4] It does not follow, though, that there are no *moral* limits on reproduction.

The right to reproduce is one of those moral rights that has been more assumed than argued for; it could, no doubt, be traced back to earlier days when human existence was more threatened by underpopulation than overpopulation.[5] The whole network of expectations and assumptions about reproduction is usually taken for granted and viewed as obvious, natural, and legitimate. However, cultural changes and technological developments have begun to inspire more serious scrutiny of these issues, even if a good deal of it still seems to me to be tied to fairly parochial "popular wisdom."[6]

The most plausible case for recognizing a moral right to reproduce comes, it seems to me, from a utilitarian moral theory coupled with the desire for children.[7] As I have suggested elsewhere, it is good, other things being equal, for desires to be satisfied.[8] Unfortunately, the potential for harm via reproduction means that very often things are not equal. Seeking to satisfy the urge to reproduce may increase the suffering created by overpopulation, contribute to the failure to meet the needs of existing children, channel women into rigid and narrow social roles, promote technologies that harm women, and bring to existence children who are more likely than average to lead miserable lives.[9]

If we are consistent in our concern about human happiness, it seems clear that we must attend to the welfare of future people. For the most part, it is possible to envision social policies that will further the good of both existing persons and the interests of future ones[10]; but here, sharp conflicts may emerge between the desires of the former and the interests of the latter. Most people want children, and they want their own children—that is, children who carry their own genetic material.

Some 15 years ago, I began wondering whether it is ever wrong to have children and wrote a paper arguing that if you are at risk for a serious illness like Huntington's disease, a good case can be made against your procreating; that paper still provokes animated—and highly emotional—discussion. And, despite the proliferation of fascinating new questions in biomedical ethics, this core issue still haunts us, returning again and again in different guises; its most recent incarnations involve "fetal abuse," neonatal AIDS, and genetic therapy.[11]

I originally claimed that although there is good reason to reject legal interference in individual decisions about reproduction, we need much more open discussion of the ethical dimensions of such decisions, for exercising your legal rights can sometimes be morally wrong. Since we ought to try to provide every child with at least a normal opportunity for a good life, and since we do not harm possible people if we prevent them from existing, we ought to try to prevent the birth of those with a significant risk of living worse than normal lives. I then went on to argue that Huntington's disease presents such a risk.[12]

My argument has been attacked on various grounds connected with the particularities of Huntington's disease.[13] A second objection could be based on women's privacy rights: women have only just been achieving some measure of control over our bodies, and this control is by no means either secure or universal; we should therefore encourage society to keep its nose out of these matters, even to the point of withholding moral evaluation of the reproductive decisions women make. While this concern is extremely important, we should nonetheless be wary of asserting the necessity for such an extreme suspension of judgment where there is potential for serious harm to others.[14]

Two other objections have emerged against the position that procreation is sometimes irresponsible. One comes from philosophers who hold that it is morally permissible to create children unless there is reason to think that they would prefer death to the life they live. The other comes from disability rights activists who hold that it is, among other things, bias against disabled people, not well-grounded moral argument, which motivates such recommendations. I shall be concentrating here on the second case, except where the two intersect.[15]

Arguments from Disability

Marsha Saxton and Adrienne Asch argue against abortion for disability.[16] Both also distinguish between abortion for disability and the attempt to avoid conception on those grounds. Asch writes:

> Although I have serious moral qualms about selective abortion for sex or disability, I do not have moral objections—albeit social and psychological ones—to deciding not to conceive if one knows that one's offspring will be of one sex or will have a certain disability. I consider women who refrain from childbearing and rearing for these reasons to be misguided, possibly depriving themselves of the joys of parenthood by their unthinking acceptance of the values of a society still deeply sexist and ambivalent about people with disabilities (p. 321).

Neither Asch nor Saxton reject abortion in general, but they clearly think that aborting an existing fetus is morally worse than failing to conceive one.[17] Yet it seems to me that their arguments, if sound, are as telling against failing to conceive as against aborting. For this reason, and because more general questions about abortion would quickly obscure the specific question I want to consider here, my argument will focus simply on the question of what we want for future people.[18]

One of the clearest and most powerful messages to come from both Asch and Saxton is that much suffering of disabled persons arises not from their disabilities but from the social response to their disabilities. The United States is, in many ways, an uncaring society, which, despite its relative wealth, tolerates a great deal of preventable misery on the part of those who must depend more than normal on community resources. Support is often both miserly and, because of the influence of special interests and erroneous preconceptions about the needs of individuals with disabilities, not offered in the form that would be most useful to them.[19]

Asch and Saxton are certainly right here: it is clear that the plight of disabled persons would be much improved if each had all the help possible. And, such help should be available: we waste billions on the military and other boondoggles, whereas a fraction of that amount would enable us to create a society that would meet people's needs far better.

Quite apart from our evaluation of disabilities themselves, however, this nasty state of affairs raises the question of the extent to which we ought to take into account socially imposed obstacles to satisfying lives when we try to judge whether it is morally right to bring a particular child into the world. As a dyed-in-the-wool consequentialist, I cannot ignore the probable difficulties that await children with special problems. It seems to me that only the truly rich can secure the well-being of those with the most serious problems. Given the costs and other difficulties of guaranteeing good care, even very well-to-do individuals might well wonder whether their offspring will get the care they need after their own deaths. This question is still more acute for those who aren't so well off—the vast majority of the U.S. population. Furthermore, it would be unwise to forget that many women are at risk for divorce and its financial aftermath.[20] Although the solution is obvious—more social responsibility for individual needs—it's beginning to look as though none of us will see that come about in our lifetimes. It seems to me that this consideration should be, in the case of some decisions about future children, decisive.

Other facets of the inadequacy of the social response to disabled people involve common habits, attitudes, and values. Ignorance leads even basically nice people to behave in hurtful ways; less good-hearted ones may be thoughtless or cruelly unsympathetic. In addition, apparently innocent values we hold make life difficult. "[W]e, especially in the United States, live in a culture obsessed with health and well-being. We value rugged self-reliance, athletic prowess, and rigid standards of beauty. We incessantly pursue eternal youth," writes Saxton (p. 303). Certainly, excessive admiration for independence, along with athleticism and narrow conceptions of beauty, make life more painful than it need be for many; they are especially problematic for some disabled people. They constrict the range of prized achievement and characteristics in unjustifiable and harmful ways, and could often be traced, I suspect, to unexamined gender-, race-, or class-based prejudice. It would therefore be desirable to see much of the energy now directed toward promoting these values channeled instead toward others, such as intellectual or artistic achievement, creating warm and supportive emotional networks, and opening our eyes to the beauty of a wide variety of body types. Unfortunately, our culture doesn't seem to be moving in that direction. It's all very well to believe that such social values shouldn't count, but that doesn't do much to lessen their impact on our children.[21]

Furthermore, there are serious objections to lumping health and well-being together with these other suspect values. Good health and the feeling of well-being it helps engender are significant factors in a happy life. They enable people to engage in a wide variety of satisfying activities, and to feel good while they are doing them. When they are absent, our suffering is caused not by our consciousness of having failed to live up to some artificial social value but by the intrinsic pain or limitation caused by that absence.

Denigrating these values is doubly mistaken. First, denying the worth of goals that can be achieved only partially (if at all) by some people would seem to require us to exclude from the arena of desirable traits many otherwise plausible candidates.[22] Perhaps more importantly, it also denies the value of less-than-maximal achievement of such values, and hence undermines the primary argument in favor of allocating social resources to help people cope with special problems. If health and well-being aren't valuable, what moral case is there for eradicating the social obstacles Asch and Saxton complain of so bitterly? Surely it is just their importance that obligates us to provide the opportunity to help people reach the highest levels of which they are capable. If health and well-being are of no special value, what is wrong with letting people languish in pain, or sit in the street with a tin cup when a prosthetic leg or seeing-eye dog could make them independent?

Secondly, it is important to resist the temptation to identify with our every characteristic. Members of oppressed groups quite rightly want to change society's perception of the features that oppressors latch onto as the mark of their alleged inferiority.[23] Such is the source of such slogans as "Black is beautiful!", of the emphasis on gay pride, and of the valorizing of women's nurturing capacity. However fitting this approach may be in some cases, its appropriateness for every characteristic does not follow. Moral failings are one obvious example.

More generally, we need to think through more carefully any leap from qualities to persons. First, qualities must be evaluated on independent grounds, not on the basis of their connection with us. Then, it is important to keep in mind that to value some characteristic isn't necessarily to look with contempt upon those who lack it. Such an equation would suggest, among other things, that teachers always (ought to) have contempt for their pupils. And, on the one hand, we may admire diametrically opposed characteristics that could not, by their very nature, be found in a single individual. Consider your widely read couch potato friend: do you really have contempt for her because she isn't Mikhail Baryshnikov? Or the converse? On the other, our assessment of and liking for individuals is not determined in any obvious way by whether they exemplify our favorite traits. Don't we all know people who, given their characteristics, ought to be our dearest friends—yet we just don't click? And don't we all have friends who don't meet our "standards" at all?

None of this is to deny that it might be appropriate in some contexts for disability rights activists to downplay the effects of certain impairments. It might be helpful, for example, to forcefully remind able-bodied individuals that people with physical problems are people first and foremost. That would help reinforce the point that, like other citizens with special difficulties, their needs should be secured as unobtrusively and respectfully as possible, and that they ought not to be viewed as mere objects of pity.

The Demands of Love

Perhaps the worry here is that since some disabled people cannot become healthy or fully able no matter what we do, society will—in a fit of pique—declare that it is not worth doing anything at all. But that would be true only if the help were motivated by a quasi-aesthetic perfectionism.

Doubts and questions about the motivation of those who argue for preventing certain births lurk continuously in the wings here. There are indeed those who seek "perfection" in others. Their desire for it, their narrow and rigid standards, and their utter lack of human empathy with those who fail to "measure up" justifies wariness: it would be inexcusable to ignore the lessons of history or to allow ourselves to be taken in by those who seek to camouflage their bigotry with lofty rationalizations. However, it would be equally inexcusable to dismiss the possibility that a caring and coherent position can lead, by an altogether different route, to the same conclusion that it is wrong to knowingly bring some children into the world.[24]

When I look into my heart to see what it says about this matter I see, I admit, emotions I would rather not feel—reluctance to face the burdens society must bear, unease in the presence of some disabled persons. But most of all, what I see there are the demands of love: to love someone is to care desperately about their welfare and to want for them only good things. The thought that I might bring to life a child with serious physical or mental problems when I could, by doing something different, bring forth one without them, is utterly incomprehensible to me. Isn't that what love means?

Appeals to love in ethics generally are unhelpful. The exhortation to love or care for another doesn't usually tell you what to do: for example, it may be that the best way to help an alcoholic mate is to leave the relationship, even if that causes a lot of suffering. Nor does an appeal to love tell us how to resolve conflicts of interest: it suggests that even legitimate interests of our own must always be subordinated to those of others. Until everybody takes that approach, this leads to rather lopsided relationships.

Where the appeal to love and care does have enormous power, however, is in the quite common conflict between our own desires and the welfare of others, where those desires either fail to constitute a legitimate interest, or where the disparity between the two is clear. Thus, if your life could be saved by someone's pulling a hair from my head, love would dictate allowing the pulling, despite my legitimate interest in protecting my body from attack.

So to say that love is relevant here is to say that there is sometimes a disparity between a future person's interest in a healthy body and the interest in procreation. Defending that viewpoint requires showing that the moral right to reproduce is relatively weak and that the moral right to a healthy body is relatively strong.[25] Given the potential for harm to another that reproduction involves, it seems to me that the presumed right to reproduce one's genetically related offspring is indeed the weakest element in the right to control your body. Although this claim clearly needs more argument, I will concentrate here on the argument for healthy bodies—the claim that people are better off without disease or special limitation, and that this interest is sufficiently compelling in some cases to justify the judgment that reproducing would be wrong.

Disagreement about my claim could be about ends or means. That is, it could be about the value of health pure and simple, or it could be about its value in comparison to the means necessary to procure it. Surely, it is hard to disagree about the former: if you could ensure good health for everyone at no cost, say by pushing an easily accessible button, then failing to push it would be indefensible. But that doesn't, of course, determine the lengths to which we should be prepared to go if ensuring or trying to ensure good health takes more than that. It seems that Asch and Saxton are in the odd position of holding that it is generally questionable to try to avoid health problems by altering reproductive behavior, but that we should go to great lengths to repair or compensate for health problems once children with them are born.[26]

This position appropriately emphasizes how much suffering from disability and disease is unnecessary, arising as it does from our failure as individuals and as a society to take away their sting. Clearly, greater social responsibility would cause some health problems simply to dissolve, just as early surgery can repair a heart valve leaving no trace of disease, or wheelchair ramps can open up new worlds; others, like diabetes, once life-threatening, could become relatively minor irritations. Frustration at the blindness, inertia, and selfishness that now stand between those with certain disabilities and a satisfying life is understandable and activism to remove barriers and get needed support is justifiable and urgent.

However, it seems to me that some of the arguments intended to further that goal can be, as I suggested earlier, inadequate and counterproductive. Downplaying in every context the suffering that can be caused by disability itself as Saxton and Asch do, is, I think, an example. Thus Saxton, at one point, seems to claim that *all* suffering is social: "the 'suffering' we may experience is a result of not enough human caring, acceptance, and respect" (p. 308).

Suffering

I do not doubt that a great deal of the suffering caused by disease and disability does arise from that source. Perhaps all the suffering felt by some people is of this sort—people with minimal or cosmetic problems, or those who have been able to tailor their desires to their circumstances. But in other cases, even were every conceivable aid available, the disease or disability itself would remain and be itself the cause of limit or pain. Neither immense human caring nor the most sophisticated gadgetry will restore freedom of movement to the paraplegic, for example. And it is not only such major disability that can cause misery: I have both observed and felt it in connections that might well be dismissed as minor by those who are not experiencing them. In my own case, for example, my inability to see adequately at a crucial period in my development as a dancer was in part responsible for the failure to progress enough to make a career worthwhile. Yet that was a goal toward which I had worked since I was a small child, and for which both I and my parents had made major sacrifices.[27] Although I was able to make another satisfying life for myself, not everybody who has this kind of experience is so lucky.

That the degree of suffering may not be directly correlated with the apparent severity of disability may be taken as a reason for giving up on the idea of avoiding the birth of children at risk for serious health problems. After all, discussion of this issue always focuses on the most severe diseases and disabilities, assumes that these are the ones that cause the most suffering, and usually ends with what is taken as the trump question: where do we draw the line? But my guess is that it is true that the most severe disabilities do often cause great suffering; it is just that more minor ones can also do so more often than most of us suppose, and not just because the environment is so harsh. That seems to me to be good reason for being concerned about both kinds rather than grounds for throwing up our hands.

Of course it is necessary to draw some lines, since everybody carries deleterious genes, and hardly any of us are free of at least minor inadequacies in health functioning. Common sense would suggest some preliminary guidelines, however. Being a carrier, for example, is no problem unless the relevant gene is dominant and carries with it the threat of serious problems, or is recessive but your mate also carries it. Likewise decisions about what constitutes a major threat will depend to a considerable extent on the environment a child can reasonably be expected to live in. Demanding certainty in these judgments would be irrational, but that does not mean that we should ignore the probabilities. Different people obviously have different intuitions about such matters, but that does not mean that we should give up on attempting to achieve some consensus through discussion and debate.

Concern about the broader context of reproduction raises important questions here about the morality of creating children who will face other kinds of hardships. What, for instance, of those who by their very existence as females, or African Americans, can be expected to live especially difficult lives? It would be tempting to say that there is nothing intrinsically undesirable about such characteristics: whatever special difficulties such persons face are purely a social matter, and hence that my thesis about refraining from reproduction would not hold here. Unfortunately, however, that answer will not do. For my argument ultimately depends more upon the degree and inevitability of the suffering than its source. So, where we can be certain about these things, there is at least a prima facie case against reproduction in these cases, too.[28] If we want to reproduce in a situation of this sort, we need to ask ourselves whether we truly have the welfare of our possible offspring at heart, or are we merely gratifying a desire of our own. Dealing with situations of this kind in the detail they deserve is impossible here, but it does seem reasonable to point out one consequence of the purely social nature of the problem, namely that we might in general be both less certain of the drawbacks and that there is more possibility of unexpected social progress.

Before going any further here, it is important to note two points. First, discussion about what we owe others tends to stick with the minimum; second, what might be an appropriate moral framework for thinking about the present might not be adequate for thinking about the future.

Thinking in terms of the moral minimum seems both to keep us on the firmest moral ground and is consistent with the moral atmosphere we are most used to. It also closely resembles the legal definitions and principles that parallel our moral thinking, structures intended to facilitate legal decision-making. Such legal premises are in part, too, a legacy of the narrow classical liberalism that still colors our perceptions of what a good society should look like. Thus we tend quite naturally here to fall into talking in terms of "minimally bearable lives," rather than satisfying or even downright happy ones. And, while we may feel quite sure that it is wrong to bring into existence those whose lives will be truly miserable, there is a great deal more uneasiness about the judgment that we ought on moral grounds to refrain from bringing to existence those who, despite much legitimate dissatisfaction, can be expected to prefer life to the alternative.

This intellectual groove is seriously problematic, I believe, even for the garden-variety moral decisions that face us every day; however, it clearly fails to guide us in an intelligent and compassionate way when decisions affecting future people are at stake. If individuals can harm each other only by worsening their condition, then by definition, we cannot harm future people if avoiding the harm also means that a particular person will not be brought to existence.[29] According to your moral perspective, it becomes either supererogatory—or morally suspect.[30] In either case it undermines not only the kind of reproductive concerns discussed here, but also denies any moral urgency to more general attempts to improve the quality of future people's lives.[31] But it's not clear why we should accept a moral approach with such consequences. In particular, a few moments' reflection on the benefits many of us enjoy as a result of the efforts of previous generations should reinforce my point.[32]

There are, of course, other obstacles to the project of protecting future people from serious physical problems. We as yet know very little about genetic traits. Furthermore, there may be insuperable moral objections to the kind of research necessary to find out more, or to the procedures necessary to utilize that knowledge.[33] Still worse, it might turn out that some genes are inextricably linked with others that it may be important to keep in the gene pool; others may confer, like a single copy of the gene for sickle cell anemia, a benefit. However, none of these problems entail that we should not, other things being equal, do what we can here to avoid creating people with serious health problems. I think that ordinary decency would therefore suggest that we at least make the effort to investigate our genetic history and, if necessary, attempt to avoid transmitting serious conditions.

Arguing against this position, Saxton denies that the fact that disabled individuals suffer and even commit suicide is a reason to prevent their births: after all, she argues, non-disabled people commit suicide, too. That non-disabled people also commit suicide is irrelevant, however. A good society does what it can to prevent or alleviate suffering on the part of its members. That there are many and diverse causes of such suffering isn't a good reason to ignore any particular one. Her attitude toward some kinds of suffering seems oddly cavalier, almost as though it is good for us.

This question of morally appropriate challenges never seems far in the background here. Much of the writing about disability emphasizes the advantages of such challenge. For instance, Denise Karuth, in her moving and informative essay, "If I Were a Car, I Would Be a Lemon," writes that "the process of learning to live with a disability presents an opportunity to develop competencies in judgment, problem solving, and compassion that few of life's other experiences can equal" (p. 25). Perhaps. But as I read what it takes to manage her lot of blindness and MS—only some of which could be alleviated by maximal social support—I am skeptical about whether the lessons learned justify the suffering they require. Since wise and compassionate folk exist who have not had such difficulties, it would surely be good to reduce the number who do to a minimum; the experiences of those who suffer from health catastrophes after birth will surely suffice.[34]

There may well be compensations for some disabilities. In *Seeing Voices*, Oliver Sacks takes us on a "journey into the world of the deaf." American Sign Language, it turns out, is a powerful and elegant means of communication, one that might in the future help communication not only with deaf persons, but with chimps, babies and those who speak languages other than our own. The world would clearly be a poorer place without ASL; now that it is here, it can enrich the lives of both those who are hearing-impaired and those who are not. It seems nonetheless doubtful that many deaf persons would refuse new ears.[35]

A somewhat different, but related, cluster of worries about preventing the birth of disabled individuals centers on issues of control. Asch (1989) asks what will happen when women who abort fetuses with problems they do not think they can cope with, have other children who "develop characteristics [they] dislike or find overwhelming" (p. 320). She goes on to suggest that such women may not recognize or may refuse to accept that childbearing should be undertaken only if "we are willing to face what we cannot control and to seek resources in themselves and the world to master it" (p. 320). Now it may very well be that some women who knowingly choose to avoid bringing a child with a disability into the world have an unrealistic view of childrearing, as do, no doubt, many who go ahead. But the solution in both these cases is early and universal education to pierce the rosy haze pronatalism still wraps around babies and having babies.[36] There is no reason to slight or belittle the judgment of those who attempt to avoid foreseeable problems, nor to prejudge their ability to cope with unexpected ones.

It would be all too easy here to fall in line with the backlash's rejection of women's barely won right to control our bodies and lives. It is only lately that women have begun to be able to exert such control, and we should be wary of suggestions that there is something wrong with it—especially since it is still mostly women who are expected to sacrifice their other plans to care for others, and this without much support.[37] In any case, it is one thing to have to cope with difficulties that couldn't have been avoided; it is quite another when they could have been.[38] Given that difference, it in no way follows (or is even empirically likely) that by attempting to prevent the birth of children with disabilities we encourage the kind of self-indulgence that refuses to come to terms with the demands of life.

Despite the importance of questions about the social costs of certain decisions about reproduction, the main focus here still needs to be on what happens to children, not the attitudes of others. Thus I am deeply troubled by Saxton's comment that she would "like to welcome any child born to me. I believe that I have the emotional, financial, and other resources to effectively care for a child. I know I can be a good mother and my husband a good father to any child" (p. 310). Would that her warmth and generosity were more common! But although these traits would help children deal with their problems, wouldn't it be better to try to avoid the serious and foreseeable burdens in the first place?

Existing and Possible Persons

As I write these last paragraphs, I can hear in my mind's ear the angry reaction build: she wants to kill us off—she's talking about getting rid of persons who have a right to life just to get rid of their problems. That would be true if what were at issue was killing those with serious health problems; that would of course also be a ludicrous misunderstanding of my position, comparable to the reception of Peter Singer's views in Austria.[39]

One of the most common themes in writing on this topic is the distressing possibility that if we attempt to avoid the birth of children with disease or disability, we will harm those who already exist. At the most practical level, some believe that acting so as to avoid such births will lead us to reduce the social resources now allocated to the disabled. At a more theoretical level, the judgment that life is better without such problems is taken as an insult to those now facing them.[40]

The first worry would be legitimate if the only reason for attempting to prevent such births is the kind of aesthetic preference for perfection to which I objected earlier, an outlook that does indeed fail to see any morally significant difference between existing and possible persons. But I mean to make, maintain, and rely on this difference.

It *is* unreasonable, in a world of limited resources and great need, to be required to allocate resources for those who didn't have to need them. The obvious rejoinder is to point to the waste and corruption now apparent in the distribution of resources. Unfortunately, that does not make those resources available for human welfare. Even were such waste eradicated, it is quite likely that, given the overall world situation, every spare dime would be needed to avert the suffering of already existing persons. Isn't it immoral to knowingly act so as to increase the demands on these resources, resources that could otherwise be used for projects such as feeding the starving or averting environmental disaster? Isn't attempting to avoid the birth of those who are likely to require extra resources, other things being equal, on a par with other attempts to share resources more equally? But from none of this does it follow that we should reduce the concern for those who already exist: on the contrary, it is in part *their* welfare that dictates such careful use of resources. This is not to say, as I suggested earlier, that any and all measures should be used to achieve the goal I am recommending, for some may themselves be wasteful of resources or have other morally dubious consequences. Whereas it may be wrong to refuse to undergo relatively noninvasive testing when there is evidence that you are at risk of passing some serious problem on to your child,[41] it does not follow that you ought to be taking every conceivable step to avoid that outcome. Nor am I recommending anything like legally sanctioned invasions of women's bodies for prenatal testing or therapy.[42]

Asch (1989) warns of more subtle harm to the living from attempts to avoid the birth of disabled children. She asks whether "we want to send the message to all such people now living that there should be 'no more of your kind' in the future (p. 319)." This interpretation draws its force from the possibility that what is being said is that although you are a perfectly nice person, because of your imperfections and neediness, you still aren't worth the trouble and we don't want to repeat you. And that would be a devastating thing to hear. If this interpretation were correct, it would also reflect very badly on the speaker: one would hardly know where to start in on such a crude, instrumental view of human life.[43]

But I would dispute Asch's view that by attempting to avoid the birth of individuals with serious impairments that we either intend or in fact send such a message to the living. Wanting a world where fewer suffer implies doing what we can to alleviate the difficulties of those who now exist as well as doing what we can to relieve future people of them. This is an entirely different justification for the position in question, one that ought to be reassuring, not threatening. Too, it is surely important here once again to resist the identification of disability and the disabled. My disability is not me, no matter how much it may affect my choices.[44] With this point firmly in mind, it should be possible to mentally separate my existence from the existence of my disability. Thus, I could rejoice, for instance, at the goal of eradicating nearsightedness, without taking that aim as an attempt to eradicate *me*, or people like me—even if achieving it means avoiding the birth of certain children.[45] But it's not as if the world is to be cleansed of me or people relevantly like me: of, say, all future brown-eyed woman philosophers.

Contributing to the misunderstandings here is, I think, a fundamental uneasiness about our power to determine who shall be brought into being. Such uneasiness is, I think, an appropriate danger signal: it alerts us to the fact that we are embarking on a new and potentially harmful project. But we need to resist the urge to latch onto apparently plausible limits that may in fact be undesirable.[46]

I believe that such limits show up in the argument at the intersection of the philosopher's case against attempting to prevent the birth of unhealthy babies and the one advanced by disability rights activists. It is the claim that if potential individuals would judge their lives worth living, then bringing them to life is no injury, and thus that there are no grounds for asserting on their behalf that it is wrong to create them.[47]

Derek Parfit is one of the philosophers who has been considering this problem.[48] He supposes that a child will have some defect—say, a withered arm—if she is conceived now; in 3 months, her mother could instead conceive a sound child, since the teratogenic drug that would cause the problem will have passed out of her system. But waiting would mean that the child with a withered arm (let us call her Minnie) would not exist; the child who would be born 3 months later would be someone else. So the price of existence, for Minnie, is a withered arm. Consequently, unless she agrees that non-existence would be preferable to life with a bad arm, she is not wronged.

But this case rests in part on the assumption that a different egg and a different sperm necessarily produce a different person. And, of course, if we define ourselves as the product of a given egg and sperm, then it is indeed trivially true that different ones would not be us. We do know that some genetic rolls of the dice result in vastly different characteristics, but it seems quite likely that many would produce only tiny differences—grayish eyes instead of greenish, the ability to curl your tongue or not, a slightly bigger pancreas. On the other hand, however, nurture clearly plays a significant role in who we are. Not only does it affect our personality, it also affects the expression of physical traits.[49] So a given environment is quite likely to mold even somewhat genetically diverse children into similar patterns. Conversely, different environments help create different people out of those with similar genetic endowments. For example, a friend of mine was born to poor, uneducated Druse villagers, but adopted at birth by Scottish missionaries and is now a professor of literature. Is there any serious sense in which we could say she is the same person she would have been had she never left her original family? On a smaller scale, perhaps, we can be deeply changed by divorce, war, or accident. Thus the idea that the only significant determinant of who we are is the union of a particular egg and sperm seems rather unsatisfactory.

But even suppose that premise were true; does it necessarily have any significance, moral or otherwise? Consider Minnie, the child of the mother who didn't wait. She is quite happy with life, although she would prefer not to have a withered arm. Suppose we suggest to her that she could have been born whole only at the cost of being somebody else?

A rational Minnie would be aware of the odds against *any* of us having our particular genetic and environmental constitution. If mom had failed to ovulate in July, the August-conceived you might have had curly hair instead of straight. If there was a crisis at work and dad was too tired to make love on Friday night, the Saturday morning you might have a talent for running instead of race-walking. . . . In any case, the rational Minnie, although glad to be alive, would realize that if some other Minnie had been born instead, she herself wouldn't be looking enviously down from heaven saying "Drat, there, but for my mother's misplaced moral concern, would be me."[50]

Furthermore, let us imagine that Minnie's mother *had* waited, and that as a result, sound-bodied Minnie$_2$ was born instead of Minnie. Maybe Minnie$_2$ would have had other problems but let us suppose that all else is equal, so that the only difference between them is that the two Minnies are "different" people—that is, conceived of different eggs and sperm. Even assuming that they are quite different, if Minnie$_2$ had been born instead of Minnie, is there any reason for thinking that she would be any less attached to her particular self than the original Minnie? Is there any reason for her to regret not having been the bad-armed Minnie? In short, if Minnie$_2$ is brought to life, why should she be any less glad to be who she is than Minnie would have been had she existed? Furthermore, wouldn't she be delighted that her mother had been thoughtful and waited? Her delight at being alive is no less than Minnie's would have been, and she has two good arms to boot.

In short, if Minnie had been born instead, Minnie$_2$ wouldn't be here to be upset about that—and the converse. The other would just be one of trillions of unconceived possibilities out there. Furthermore, the realization that we ourselves might have been one of them seems to me to demand some detachment from the conditions that led us to be here. Saxton asks whether she could in good conscience have a medical test that would, if her mother had had access to it, have led to her being aborted. Not only would that reasoning militate against legal abortion in general, but it would demand that we commend fruitful acts of rape or incest. I myself would never have been born had World War II not occurred. Was it therefore a good thing?

The conclusion to be drawn from this thought exercise is surely that there is no good reason to conceive a child at special risk for disability when you could with little effort conceive one at only the usual odds. There are, additionally, good reasons for not doing so, based on the welfare of future persons. Parfit himself cannot, given his premises, find any way out of the dilemma he has described, and concludes that we need to change the focus of our moral concern: "our reasons for acting should become *more impersonal*. Greater impersonality may seem threatening. But it would often be better for everyone" (1984, p. 443). By this he means that we ought to be more willing to judge that the prospect of people living in a harmed state should deter us from bringing it about, even if, according to the usual criteria, no one has been harmed.[51] That conclusion is compatible with a utilitarian approach that seeks greater happiness for each individual, rather than a highly populated world where individual lives are barely worth living.

Although Parfit's conclusion that we should lessen our fixation on individual rights and be more attentive to the overall picture is attractive, I am not quite ready to concede it as the whole story. Can it really be true that we do not wrong a child with serious impairments when we knowingly bring it into the world?[52] There is no space here for a full analysis of the issue, but one promising avenue would be further questioning the extreme abstraction of some of the premises Parfit uses to generate his paradoxes, an abstraction that sometimes beguiles us into accepting implausible assumptions.[53] Reasoning with such bare-boned instruments denies us the context essential for developing livable moral views.

In general, the conjunction of abstract method and focus on harming individuals (as opposed to states of harm) in the way Parfit poses the question is most unfortunate, since it implicitly promotes an unattractive ethic of moral minimalism that could hardly be distinguished from libertarianism. The underlying moral principle here seems to be that it is morally permissible to bring you to life so long as you can be expected to find your life worth living, because you are not thereby harmed (even if you have been born in a harmed state) and it is permissible to do anything that does not harm you.[54] What we owe others is thus reduced to not harming them, and the standard for not having harmed them is set very low. Generalizing these principles to other cases would lead to a great deal of misery. Why couldn't a government refuse to fund polio vaccination programs, for instance, on the grounds that even if a certain percentage of babies become paralyzed, they'll still be glad to be alive? Why pay for good schools when poor ones won't make kids wish they were dead?

Preventable and Unpreventable Harms

The stopper is supposed to be the morally relevant distinction between preventable harms and unpreventable ones. In this situation, unpreventable harm is one that couldn't have been avoided without precluding your existence. But there is no particular reason for thinking that such a stringent criterion would be required in other cases. For instance, there might be no way for manufacturers to make "satisfactory" profits and reduce occupational hazards, and so the harm to workers would be neither preventable, nor, if their subsequent life still is worth living, a wrong done to them. Moreover, a different (and I think more realistic) view of personal identity, one that views some life experiences as constitutive of who you are, could undermine the crucial stopper effect still more. For if we recognize that some experiences can make you a different person, the impetus for social intervention, especially in children's lives, would be seriously undermined. At risk would be such desirable enterprises as Head Start and early nutrition programs.

However, my worry here goes still deeper. Although facts and logic constrain possible moral theories, they do not by themselves determine the values inherent in them. Thus how we approach ethics reflects our more general attitudes and dispositions. A narrow focus on not harming others, rather than enthusiasm for flourishing and happiness, will therefore both arise from—but also help perpetuate—the relevant attitudes. Yet it is not from such a narrow, almost legalistic conception of morality that flows the kind of generosity that will *of course* do everything to dissolve the effects of disability and disease: it flows, instead, from a utilitarian preoccupation with doing whatever good one can. So to the extent that disability rights activists borrow the morally minimalistic terms of Parfit's dilemma, they implicitly work against their own moral interests.

Conclusion

As I suggested earlier, it is good, other things being equal, for desires to be satisfied. It does not follow from this that we should accept desires uncritically, but merely that there is a prima facie case for satisfying them, other things being equal. In the case of the desire for genetically related children, however, other things are often not equal. It has in the past led to a great deal of misery when, for instance, a couple could not produce an appropriate heir, or when an inappropriate ("illegitimate") one was instead produced. Today, the first problem is leading women to try dangerous and expensive reproductive technologies in the search for a genetically related child when they could instead adopt a child in need of a good home. It can also motivate people to risk the health of their future children, even though they could still enjoy the other aspects of having children by sacrificing all or part of the genetic link.

It is true that providing a decent quality of life for each of us would, by itself, go far toward avoiding the birth of children with serious health problems, and is, for this and other reasons, morally obligatory. Since efforts in this direction are not even on the political horizon, and since they will not by themselves make every problematic case go away, how are we to face these issues in the meantime?

Having said that there is a serious strike against bringing certain children to life does not give us much specific guidance, and there is no space here to consider that issue in the detail it deserves.[55] It is well known that a variety of options now exist for those who want to refrain from producing children with their own genetic material. Among them are AID and egg donation, as well as contract pregnancy and adoption. Although AID is widely used and, for the most part regarded as uncontroversial, egg donation and contract pregnancy are not.[56] The last word on these remains to be said; I have argued elsewhere at length that contract pregnancy, if stringently regulated, could be made a morally acceptable alternative to the usual method of childbearing.[57] Adoption, although more morally problematic and practically difficult than is often thought, may also be in many cases a reasonable option.

Unfortunately these compromises have only limited utility for some, most notably the poor. Not only do the poor face more than their share of the kinds of health problems that create risk for babies, but they get less help with them. And the reproductive risk now posed for them by the AIDS epidemic is making their lives still more difficult. Given society's responsibility for so much of their plight, it hardly seems tenable to argue that they are now to forego one of their only sources of satisfaction, reproducing "their own" genetically related children. Yet, that does not protect their children. As John Arras points out in his sensitive paper on the topic, "the reproductive decisions of infected women have serious and problematic ethical implications for their offspring. . . . "[58] The interplay of social and individual responsibility here creates moral problems that cannot be adequately resolved by pointing the finger solely at individuals, even if doing that seems to be the only way to prevent immediate harm. However, the unfair price such individuals pay for stopping it underlines once again our ultimate social responsibility in many of these matters.

Notes

1. Thanks to Joan Callahan and Dorothy Wertz for their helpful comments on this paper.

2. Working for change is the job of political activists. Of course, moral philosophers can be activists, too; in fact, given our positions of moral authority, we may well have a moral duty in this regard.

3. This lengthy preface is intended to emphasize the priority of fighting both for human welfare and especially for women's basic welfare—a priority that may well seem to disappear in any treatment of a limited and problematic area. (I am not excluding in the scope of my concern here the welfare of other sentient creatures; however, in this paper I will be concentrating on human welfare.)

4. Even if there is no clear constitutional right to procreate, the consequences of failing to act as if there is one would be at present very harmful to women. See my "Are Pregnant Women Fetal Containers?" *Bioethics* 4, 4 (Oct. 1990), 273-91.

5. My position that it is sometimes wrong to reproduce in the usual way does not require any prior showing that there is such a right. For if there is, it doesn't follow that it can always be morally exercised; if there isn't, it is still necessary to lay out the conditions for morally acceptable reproduction.

6. Consider, for example, the recent debate about the nature and justification of the desire for children that is emerging in the feminist debate about artificial reproductive technologies. For further readings see *Reproductive Technologies: Gender, Motherhood and Medicine*, ed. Michelle Stanworth (Minneapolis: University of Minnesota Press, 1987), and *Feminist Perspectives in Medical Ethics*, ed. Helen Bequaert Holmes and Laura M. Purdy (Bloomington: Indiana University Press, 1992).

7. For an examination of other possibilities, see Ruth F. Chadwick, "Having Children: An Introduction," *Ethics, Reproduction and Genetic Control*, ed. Ruth F. Chadwick (London: Croom Helm, 1987), pp. 3-10. The status of the desire for children needs more work; in particular, its sources and consequences need much more thorough scrutiny.

8. See "Genetic Disease: Can Having Children Be Immoral?" *Genetics Now*, ed. John L. Buckley (Washington D.C.: University Press of America, 1978); reprinted in *Biomedical Ethics*, ed. Thomas A. Mappes and Jane S. Zembaty, 3rd ed. (New York: McGraw-Hill, 1991).

9. This last is not entirely unconnected with the others, of course.

10. It may not be possible to reconcile the two if either the population grows too large or if the definition of basic welfare is too inclusive, so that acute conflicts arise between present needs and future ones.

11. See, for example, my "Are Pregnant Women Fetal Containers?"; John D. Arras, "AIDS and Reproductive Decisions: Having Children in Fear and Trembling," *The Milbank Quarterly* 68, 3 (1990), 353–82; and Noam Zohar, "Prospects for 'Genetic Therapy'—Can a Person Benefit from Being Altered?" and Jeffrey P. Kahn, "Genetic Harm: Bitten by the Body That Keeps You?" both in *Bioethics* 5, 4 (October 1991), 275–308.

12. Robert Simon has pointed out to me that there are good reasons for thinking in terms of a more objective criterion than "opportunity for a normal life." They center on the otherwise difficult-to-manage relativistic element in judgments about what is "normal."

13. The main objection has been that HD doesn't require such moral restraint. It is argued that potential parents are usually going ahead without knowing for sure whether they have the disease. If they don't, then their children are not really at risk. Even if they do, there is only a fifty percent chance that each child will be afflicted with the disease. And, even if a child turns out to have the disease, he or she will have between twenty and fifty years of good life. My evaluation of these factors has not changed in the time since I wrote the paper; they seem to me, if anything, to increase the horror of the disease. In particular, the prospect of a short life seems to me especially tragic, not only because of the depression quite likely to be caused by knowledge of it, but because of the loss to all those (like women) whose early lives are often taken up with the demands of others. It takes many women well into middle age to overcome the sexist upbringing that deprives them of the self-confidence to make more choices based on their own interests. Deaths of people in their prime also deprives society of some of its best and wisest members. In case such considerations don't move you, it is always possible to find still more dreadful diseases, like Tay-Sachs, where they don't apply.

14. I argued in an earlier paper that although it would not be reasonable at this point to make prenatal harm a crime, it is still wrong for women to act in ways that are likely to harm their fetuses. Among other things, most of such harm arises because of factors beyond women's control and that could be remedied if society made avoiding it a priority. So unless society does what it can, it is hypocritical and unjust to blame women for causing prenatal harms. ("Are Pregnant Women Fetal Containers?")

15. Two points about my focus here. First, I am uneasy about contributing to

the balkanization of progressive political movements that arises from criticizing our allies rather than those with whom we have far more basic disagreements. However, it also seems important to try to develop the strongest positions possible in order to facilitate social change. Second, because I am considering primarily arguments of disability rights writers, the following discussion is centered on the question of disability. It should be understood that concern for painful or limiting disease is not thereby excluded.

16. Marsha Saxton, "Born and Unborn: The Implications of Reproductive Technologies for People with Disabilities," *Test-Tube Women: What Future for Motherhood?* ed. Rita Arditti, Renate Duelli-Klein, and Shelley Minden (London: Pandora, 1984); Adrienne Asch, "Can Aborting 'Imperfect' Children Be Immoral?" *Ethical Issues in Modern Medicine*, ed. John Arras and Nancy Rhoden (Mountain View, CA: Mayfield Press, 1989).

17. Asch writes in support of abortion because of women's right to control their bodies; she also asserts that because newborns are legally persons, it is wrong to deprive them of medical care unless they are dying. She does not discuss the philosophical assumptions underlying these positions (Adrienne Asch, "Real Moral Dilemmas," *Christianity and Crisis* 46, 10 [July 14, 1986], 237–40).

18. My arguments also hold for those who regard the relevant kinds of abortions as no more morally significant than failing to conceive.

19. For a recent, moving discussion, see a series of articles in *The Progressive*, August 1991 (Mary Johnson, "Disabled Americans Push for Access," Laura Hershey, "Exit the Nursing Home," and Joseph P. Shapiro, " 'I Can Do Things for Myself Now," pp. 21–29). These articles highlight both the ignorance and the bad faith involved in much current practice.

20. The recent (1991–92) recession, which included widespread unemployment, cuts in federal and state welfare programs, and the increasingly serious health insurance crisis, should give pause to those of modest means who assume that they will be able to make sure their children's needs will be met. Furthermore, it is by now generally known that women usually fare poorly after divorce, especially if they have stayed at home to take care of children. Alimony is now rare, and they must now earn a living (with non-existent or rusty job skills). Since they are usually granted custody of the children, and are given only the inadequate child support offered by most fathers, they must somehow cover childcare expenses, too. With a divorce rate of 50 percent, no married woman can be sure that she will not find herself trapped in such difficult circumstances.

21. Anybody who has tried to raise thoughtful and caring children knows how difficult it is to teach them these values, as well as the hostility they face if they accept them. It does not follow that we should give up on such projects, but we need to be realistic about their toll. Therefore, we should think twice about imposing such burdens on children.

22. This approach to grading values might lead to a *reductio ad absurdum* rejection of any value, even that of life itself, since, after all, not everybody can live.

23. Thanks to Dianne Romain for helping me think more clearly about this issue.

24. For a paper on a closely related example, see Janice G. Raymond, "Fetalists Are Not Feminists: They Are Not the Same," *Made To Order: The Myth of Reproductive and Genetic Progress*, ed. Patricia Spallone and Deborah Lynn Steinberg (Oxford: Pergamon, 1987).

25. If ought implies can, we don't, strictly speaking, have a right to a healthy body. But that is not to say that we ought not to be trying to do the best we can.

26. Asch does make some distinction between problems for which changes in reproductive behavior are appropriate, and lesser ones for which they are not. She asks whether "we wish to abort for disability that will not cause great physical pain or death in early childhood" (Adrienne Asch, "Reproductive Technology and Disability," *Reproductive Laws for the 1990s*, ed. Sherrill Cohen and Nadine Taub [Clifton, N.J.: Humana Press, 1988], pp. 88–89). I would include chronic pain, serious physical or mental limitation, and mental suffering (including the prospect of an early but not imminent death) to the list of conditions to which people shouldn't be subjected.

27. The ease with which some dismiss the pains of others is unnerving; some of this arises no doubt from mere thoughtlessness, lack of experience, or the attempt to "cheer up." It hurts nonetheless. I was struck by a letter to Ann Landers that reads in part:

> I, too, have suffered because some people have no idea what living with a handicap is like.
>
> I am 33 years old and have multiple sclerosis. I have been told countless times how lucky I am to be able to park in a special place, work only half days, etc. I try to explain calmly that I'd gladly park anywhere and work all day in exchange for the privilege of good health. Surprisingly, that doesn't make an impression. I've been told, "I could handle that," and "It's no big deal," or "They'll find a cure soon."
>
> . . . I pray a cure will be found soon, but in the meantime it is a VERY big deal to those of us who have it. Anyone who doubts that can speak to my children. We used to live in Montana and climb mountains. Now my life is completely different. We can't even walk around the zoo because Mom has MS . . . (*The Ithaca Journal*, Friday, December 6, 1991).

28. Consider Joel Feinberg's comments on this question:
> " . . . if before the child has been born, we *know* that the conditions for the fulfillment of his most basic interests have already been destroyed, and

we permit him nevertheless to be born, we become a party to the violation of his rights. It bears repeating that not all interests of the newborn child should or can qualify for prenatal legal protection, but only those very basic ones whose satisfaction is known to be indispensable to a decent life. The state cannot insure all or even many of its citizens against bad luck in the lottery of life. . . . On the other hand, to be dealt severe mental retardation, congenital syphilis, blindness, deafness, advanced heroin addiction, permanent paralysis or incontinence, guaranteed malnutrition, and economic deprivation so far below a reasonable minimum as to be inescapably degrading and sordid, is not merely to have 'bad luck' " (*Harm to Others* [Oxford: Oxford University Press, 1984], p. 99).

29. See Feinberg, ch. 1, and ch. 2, section 8.

30. Those who imagine future people waiting in line to be born, where the relevant moral rule presumably ought to be first come, first served, will be most apt to see the effort to prefer the birth of those more likely to live more satisfying lives as morally evil.

31. For example, to the extent that women now have babies because of lack of access to contraception and abortion, or even, more broadly, because of the lack of satisfying alternative social roles, achieving women's equality will alter who gets born. Derek Parfit also points out the counterintuitive consequences with respect to pollution. See his *Reasons and Persons* (Oxford: Oxford University Press, 1984), pt. IV

32. For example, good social arrangements could now provide everyone with a kind of security and well-being that was unavailable to anybody just a few generations ago. No longer must we bear child after child only to watch them die, no longer need we fear such diseases as polio or smallpox. Although many scientific advances have proved to be mixed blessings, there is no doubt that many of us now have lives of unprecedented satisfaction and that many more could do so if we cared to make it a social priority.

33. Thus, for example, it may be inappropriate to spend such a large proportion of the science research budget on the human genome project, for it may open up possibilities too dangerous to handle at present. Even if it is successful, there may be good reasons to refrain from instituting the kind of mandatory screening programs that would capitalize most effectively on the knowledge gained by it. They might, for example, involve racism or other harmful stereotyped assumptions.

34. It should not be inferred that what I say here implies that children grow best when everything is made easy for them, and that is not, in any case, a situation we are in danger of providing for most of them. See my book *In Their Best Interest? The Case against Equal Rights for Children* (Ithaca: Cornell University Press, 1992).

One might argue that reducing the number of people with disabilities would weaken the disability rights movement, since advocates tend to have personal links with impaired individuals. That wouldn't be a very appealing objection, since it would be a paradigm case of using people as mere means. It's also dubious from a consequentialist viewpoint, since it will be all that most families can do to cope with their own child's immediate needs. The most promising development would be recruiting energetic workers who are free to devote themselves wholeheartedly to advancing the interests of people with impairments, much as the civil rights movement recruited students.

35. The debate about cochlear implants erupted after this piece was written. Some deaf people have refused cochlear implants that could restore hearing for themselves or their children. They do so in part because they do not see deafness as a disability, and in part because they fear that the deaf community will be impoverished if there are fewer young people entering it. The latter concern is understandable and one would think that it would be possible to ensure that hearing children of the deaf would be taught to sign; it would be better still if signing came to be more universal among hearing people. The claim that deafness is not a disability is less appealing. Resolving this question is a delicate matter, but I would be inclined to defer to John Stuart Mill's test for deciding which of two states of affairs is more desirable, namely, consultation with those who have experienced both. I suspect that such persons would not choose to be deaf. (Edward Dolnick, "Deafness as Culture," *The Atlantic* 272, 3 [September 1993], 37–51; John Stuart Mill, "Utilitarianism," *The Utilitarians* [NY: Dolphin Books, 1961], p. 401.)

36. It is sad (and instructive) that anybody who tries to get childless students to think in realistic terms about children is immediately plastered with the reputation of "baby-basher," just as those who attempt to get them to think realistically about women's place in society become "male-bashers."

37. Good parenting is by itself a demanding enterprise, one that is barely compatible under present circumstances with many jobs. Adding special needs to that mix will be, in the case of many women, the straw that breaks the camel's back.

38. Asch agrees that elective abortion should remain a legal option for women, even where she doubts the morality of abortion for disability. However, I fear that her position about the wrongness of most abortions for disability will cause some women to feel that they should not abort in that case, even where they would prefer to do so. That is why I think it is important to address this issue head on. See, for example, her article, "Real Moral Dilemmas," and "Shared Dreams: A Left Perspective on Disability Rights and Reproductive Rights," by Adrienne Asch and Michelle Fine, in Asch and Fine's *Women with Disabilities: Essays in Psychology, Culture, and Politics* (Philadelphia: Temple University Press, 1988).

39. See Helga Kuhse and Peter Singer, "From the Editors," *Bioethics* 5, 4 (October 1991), iv–v, for a brief account. A major conference at which he was

to speak was threatened with disruption, on the grounds that he and others who have argued in favor of euthanasia were "preparing the way for a re-surgence of Nazi-style mass killing" (p. iv). Rejecting a proposal to with-draw its invitation to Singer, the conference's organizing committee in-stead canceled the conference.

40. See, for example, Adrienne Asch, who writes in *Reproductive Laws* apropos of suits for wrongful birth and wrongful life: "claiming that life with dis-ability is worse than no life at all offends self-respecting disabled people and represents the extreme of what is dangerous about testing, diagnosing, and suing" (p. 95).

41. If *knowing* that you will most likely come down with something dreadful like Huntington's Disease is too much for you to bear, then how can you impose such risk on your children?

42. See my "Are Pregnant Women Fetal Containers?"

43. The beginning of a proper response would be to deny the moral framework that judges people according to a crude cost-benefit analysis, one that would conclude that some people don't "pay off." A livable moral frame-work must, on the contrary, concentrate on each person's opportunity to live a satisfying life; it recognizes our interdependence and takes for granted that we will all be helping each other at different times and in dif-ferent ways. This way of looking at things leaves judgments about whether one's life is worth living to the individuals in question. However, it would not necessarily preclude an effort at avoiding some births for the kinds of reasons proposed here. This effort would be precluded by the response that virtually every possible life is worth living. However, that position might have some trouble showing why, other things being equal, we should not prefer to bring a non-disabled rather than a disabled individual into existence.

44. Certain mental disabilities might be an exception to this claim.

45. Since the advent of effective, comfortable, safe, and cheap contact lenses, simple nearsightedness is no longer a persuasive example for the middle-class in Western industrialized nations. In other circumstances such as non-technological societies where keen eyesight is essential for survival, it could still be a ghastly problem.

46. Our reluctance to deliberately monkey with the future in certain ways (to-gether with our apparently foolhardy willingness to do so in others) seems as yet inadequately explored. Bringing these fears out into the open would probably help us make wiser choices. See, for example, Jonathan Glover, *What Sort of People Should There Be?* (Middlesex, England: Penguin Books, 1984).

47. This argument assumes that the only reason for refraining from bringing someone into existence is that it would wrong them; however, if who we bring to existence is neutral—that is, there is no reason for preferring one

possible future person over another—then we could still argue against bringing the unhealthy one into existence on the grounds of unnecessary burden to others, which tips the case against the unhealthy.

48. Derek Parfit, "On Doing the Best for Our Children," in *Ethics and Population*, ed. M. D. Bayles (Cambridge, MA: Schenkman, 1976); see also his *Reasons and Persons* (Oxford: Oxford University Press, 1984), pt. 4.

49. Alison Jaggar points out that athletic girls tend to grow taller than non-athletic ones, since being physically active retards the onset of puberty, when growth slows ("Sex Inequality and Bias in Sex Differences Research," *Science, Morality and Feminist Theory*, ed. Marsha Hanen and Kai Nielsen [*Canadian Journal of Philosophy*, supp. vol. 13, 1987], p. 34).

50. It is enormously important to recognize the limits of our thought experiments. As we try to think through the implications of various choices, we almost necessarily attribute to the "players" a kind of ghostly existence, as if they were waiting in the wings to be called out on stage. This conception tends to lead us astray, causing us to think inappropriately in terms of discrimination, hard feelings and so forth.

51. This distinction is Feinberg's. (See *Harm to Others*, ch. 1, section 1.) Feinberg implicitly agrees with Parfit when he asserts that "It is, of course, possible to be wronged without being harmed . . . and it is possible to blame *A* for bringing *B* into existence in an initially harmful condition, but that is still another thing than *A* harming *B*, which as we have seen . . . requires worsening a person's prior condition, or at least making it worse than it would otherwise have been . . . " (p. 99).

52. This line of argument seems worth pursuing in part because of how odd it is to have to say that it would be wrong to inflict a given problem on an existing person, but not wrong to bring others to life if having it is the condition of their existence—when there is otherwise no particular good reason for "choosing" them. So if I failed to inoculate my child against, say, a bacterial version of Huntington's disease, I would be considered an irresponsible parent, even though the arguments in favor of conception of a child at risk for it downplay the misery of the disease. The differences in these two cases just seem insufficient to bear the moral weight required of them. That anybody has the disease is what's bad, not who they are or why they have it.

53. Thus, for example, he says that his Wide Average Principle "could imply that, in the best possible history, only two people ever live" (p. 416). He comments that: "most of us find this view too extreme. Most of us believe that there is value in quantity, but that this value has, in any period, an upper limit." Because the whole approach is so abstract, adding yet another abstract principle to counteract the counterintuitive consequence of the first becomes necessary. However, it would not be necessary if we thought seriously about what it would mean to imagine a two-person world. This rumination would, by itself, show that the Wide Average Principle could

never imply that a two-person history would be best. And so forth. His descriptions of human interactions remind us uncomfortably of billiard balls.

54. There are also difficult epistemological problems, since different people have different thresholds for suffering. Mistaken guesses about a given situation may reap truly dreadful suffering as the individual comes to the conclusion that her life is not worth living, both on her part and that of those who love her.

55. I discussed some of these, such as the question of risk, in "Genetic Disease: Can Having Children Be Immoral?"

56. For views on these issues see Holmes and Purdy, *Issues in Reproductive Technology I: An Anthology*, ed. Helen Bequaert Holmes (New York: Garland, 1992); and Richard Hull, *Ethical Issues in the New Reproductive Technologies* (Belmont, CA: Wadsworth, 1990).

57. See "Surrogate Mothering: Exploitation or Empowerment?" *Bioethics* 3, 1 (January 1989), 18–34; "Another Look at Contract Pregnancy," *Issues in Reproductive Technology I: An Anthology*, ed. Helen Bequaert Holmes (New York: Garland, 1992).

58. Arras, "AIDS and Reproductive Decisions."

PART IV:
PRENATAL AND
PRECONCEPTIVE HARM

Introduction[1]

Joan C. Callahan

In January of 1994, the U.S. Supreme Court ruled that organized groups protesting abortion can be prosecuted under federal racketeering laws.[2] In May of 1994, Roussel Uclaf, manufacturer of RU 486, agreed to give the American patent rights for the drug to the Population Council. The Population Council will begin clinical trials of the drug as they look for a U.S. manufacturer to make RU 486 available in the United States as a birth control method. It is not surprising that as opponents of elective abortion in the United States find their cause faltering in the face of (1) the enforcement of laws proscribing any coercive attempts at preventing women from seeking elective abortions and (2) the prospect of wide availability of RU 486 in the foreseeable future, we continue to see a number of court cases involving women and prenatal harm. If it is true, as suggested in the introduction to part III, that much of what makes the abortion debate intractable is an underlying metaphysics of woman which grounds the nature and value of women in our reproductive capacities, and if precluding elective abortion is (at least in part) an attempt to keep women tied to their "natural" roles as wives and mothers, then as those with this metaphysics lose ground in the abortion debate, we can expect them to find other ways to try to ensure that women are "good mothers." Attempting to control the behavior of fertile and pregnant women is one very promising way to do this. The papers in this section by Janet Gallagher, Joan E. Bertin, and Uma Narayan address the question of controlling women, ostensibly in order to prevent preconceptive and prenatal harm.

331

332

Preconceptive and Prenatal Harm
and the Abortion Debate

In the introduction to part III and in my paper there, I argued that human conceptuses, embryos, and fetuses are not persons and should not be recognized as persons by the law.[3] This position is consistent with the U.S. Supreme Court's 1973 decision in *Roe v. Wade*, which did *not* hold that a fetus is to be recognized as a person at viability.[4] Indeed, in writing for the Court, Justice Harry Blackmun explicitly refuses to take up the moral question of prenatal personhood and he makes clear that there is no precedent in the law for recognizing prenatal human beings as legal persons. What the Court did rule, however, is that the state has a compelling interest in human fetuses once they have reached viability. The *Roe* decision contains three major conclusions, based on three interests taken by the Court to be compelling—namely, the safety of women, the privacy of women as citizens, and the viable fetus as a "potential human life."[5] The Court's conclusions parallel the trimesters of pregnancy:

(1) Abortion decisions during the first trimester of pregnancy must be left up to the woman and her physician. Blackmun argues this by pointing out that prior to the development of antiseptic techniques, surgical abortion at any stage was seriously dangerous for a woman. However, antiseptic techniques now make it safer for a woman to undergo early abortion than to continue a pregnancy to term. Since a crucial part of the rationale for the earliest U.S. anti-abortion statutes was protecting the health of women, prohibiting early abortion can no longer be justified by an appeal to the safety of women.[6] Combined with the interest in women's safety, the Court leans on a series of decisions, going back to *Union Pacific R. Co. v. Botsford* (1891),[7] that recognize a constitutional right of citizens to make decisions within certain "zones of personal privacy." Included here are decisions regarding reproduction. Thus, the Court takes the health of a woman and her right to privacy to be the compelling interests to be protected during the first trimester of pregnancy.

(2) The same interests remain compelling during the second trimester; but because of increased risks of abortion as a pregnancy proceeds, the Court allows that protection of women's health makes it permissible for jurisdictions to regulate abortion after the first trimester in certain ways, for example, by requiring that they be performed in certain kinds of facilities by personnel with certain kinds of credentials.

(3) After the second trimester, a woman's health is still considered a compelling interest. But since abortion is now generally more dangerous for a woman than is continuing a pregnancy to term, this interest now justifies a jurisdiction's prohibiting elective abortion in the third trimester. Also, the State's interest in protecting women's privacy gives way at this point to the State's interest in what Blackmun calls "the potentiality of human life," which, again, is the presumptively viable fetus. Thus, in the third trimester, jurisdictions may prohibit abortion unless the life or health of a woman is threatened by continuation of her pregnancy.

According to the *Roe* decision, then, a woman in the United States has a right to elective abortion through the end of the second trimester of pregnancy, and a right to abortion even later than that if her life or health would be endangered by continuing the pregnancy. Given that "health" is a very vague term, and that it can be taken to refer to a woman's mental health as well as her physical health, the decision in *Roe* is extremely liberal, allowing, in principle, jurisdictions to permit abortions through the third trimester of pregnancy.

On the other hand, the decision in *Roe* pertains to the legal right to terminate a pregnancy. It does not contend that the state has no interest in protecting even previable conceptuses, embryos, or fetuses from injury. In particular, the decision says nothing about potential prenatal injury in cases where a pregnancy will be continued to term. This, added to *Roe*'s expression of compelling interest in the "potentiality of human life," has been used to shore up other arguments for expanding liability for prenatal harm, for restricting the behaviors of pregnant women, and for imposing medical and surgical interventions on women to prevent prenatal harm.[8]

Thus, although the *Roe* decision guarantees U.S. women the right to elective abortion through the end of the second trimester of pregnancy and allows the legality of abortion even later than this, commentators rightly point out that a very different issue regarding protection of the prenatal human being arises when a woman does not abort a pregnancy, and her actions (or the actions of another) result in the birth of a damaged child. It is true that at least some of these commentators may be unhappy with the *Roe* decision's refusal to recognize prenatal human beings as persons in either the moral or legal sense. However, it may be perfectly consistent for a person to take a moral position which holds (1) that elective abortion is acceptable, yet (2) that people may be held legally liable for or may be prevented by the law from contributing to nonfatal prenatal harm because such harms (ultimately) involve persons, insofar as a distinction is made between those conceptuses, embryos, and fetuses that will be aborted and those that will be liveborn. That is, there is no inconsistency in holding that prenatal human beings are not persons and that even very late elective abortion is morally permissible and, at the same time, holding that when a pregnancy will be brought to term, prenatal injury should be avoided.

But the crucial questions here are (1) whether it is acceptable to use the impositional, restraining, and criminal powers of the law against pregnant women to attempt to ensure that they do not harm their fetuses by their actions or allow harm to their fetuses by their refusals of medical and/or surgical interventions thought by practitioners to be helpful to fetuses, and (2) whether the law should allow exclusions of women from certain contexts because of concerns about prenatal and preconceptive harm. Janet Gallagher's paper takes up the first of these questions; the papers by Joan E. Bertin and Uma Narayan take up the second.

Pregnant Women and Prenatal Harm

Janet Gallagher traces the history of the recent "fetal rights movement," and even though she is well aware of the harm that (say) certain forms of drug use can cause to fetuses and which will later be manifest in the children those fetuses will become, Gallagher points out how deeply issues of race, ethnicity, and class figure into purported concerns about fetal protection. For example, she notes that a 1980s review of the cases of Caesarean sections ordered by courts to protect fetuses showed that 81 percent of the women subjected to such orders were African-American, Asian, or Hispanic, and that none were private patients; a 1992 review of the prosecutions for drug use during pregnancy showed that 70 percent of the women prosecuted whose race could be ascertained were women of color; and another study showed that despite comparable drug use among non-Hispanic whites and minority women, African-American women were nearly 10 times more likely to be reported to authorities for drug use than were other women.

Gallagher is also concerned to illuminate the gendered dimensions of so-called fetal protection. Not only has the rush to protect fetuses from the women who bear them taken place within a new cultural emphasis on father's rights; the focus on pregnant women has proceeded with no attention to male behaviors, including male substance abuse, and their effects on reproduction. Indeed, as Gallagher notes, in one nearly unbelievable case, a pregnant woman who fled to a hospital emergency room after being beaten by her husband was arrested when it was ascertained that she had been drinking.

In addition to making the dimensions of gender, race, ethnicity, and class transparent in the purported concerns about fetuses, Gallagher wants to make clear that using the strong arm of the law to interfere with and/or punish women for causing prenatal harm to their offspring is a species of collective bad faith. Dealing with prenatal harm this way allows society to continue to fail to assume responsibility for the social conditions that encourage behaviors such as drug use among pregnant women. She ends her paper calling for a more productive use of social resources—for a variety of positive programs that will not only help pregnant women, but will help women, particularly poor women, and children generally.

Workplace Harms and "Fetal Protection" Policies

In the papers that complete this section and the book, Joan E. Bertin and Uma Narayan take a careful look at so-called fetal protection policies in the U.S. workplace. Like Gallagher, they focus on the gender, racial, ethnic, and class biases that underpin policies that exclude fertile and/or pregnant women from taking certain jobs. Bertin argues that these exclusionary policies gained credence because of their reliance on ostensibly objective reproductive science. But that science, like so much of our science, she argues, has a long history of bias which continues into the present. Among the gender biases in contemporary reproductive science Bertin points out is the continuing overstatement of women's biological and behavioral responsibility for the well-being of the next generation. Women are held to be almost exclusively responsible for the outcomes of their pregnancies, while progenerating men and the men who create environments that involve reproductive hazards are seldom, if ever, even considered as contributing causal factors to prenatal or pre-conceptive harm (i.e., harm to gametes). Bertin also points out that these policies rely on an assumption that women's gametes and fetuses are hypersusceptible to harm from workplace toxins. But the same sort of evidence that is given to justify this assumption (animal data, historical and anecdotal data, and methodologically flawed studies) is taken to be inconclusive when male susceptibility to workplace toxins is considered. In considering such facts, Bertin concludes that culturally assigned sex roles, rather than good science, underpin the assumption that women and fetuses are uniquely vulnerable in the workplace. In short, the subtext is that women and "unborn children" do not belong in the workplace—at least not in positions that are thought to be the proper province of men.

It is precisely this line of thought that Uma Narayan takes up and emphasizes in her consideration of whether such policies are likely to be found in the Third World. As does Bertin, Narayan makes it clear that many jobs traditionally held by women workers in the West (e.g., jobs in laundries, dry-cleaning facilities, pottery- and jewelry-making industries, and x-ray technology) deploy substances that are associated with reproductive damage. Women are also the primary workers in early childhood care settings, pediatric offices, and other environments which commonly expose them to viral infections that can be dangerous to fetuses. Yet these industries and fields have not developed "fetal protection" policies that would exclude women from these jobs. Narayan asks why this is so, and she concludes that it simply would be unthinkable in our culture to exclude women from these positions—women are central to these inevitably low-paying occupations. In other U.S. industries, however, the workforce has customarily been largely male. Women are perceived as marginal in these contexts, and the jobs associated with potential harm to fetuses (and/or women's gametes) are among the more lucrative industrial positions. When these facts are combined, purported concerns about fetal protection tend to arise. But, as Narayan points out, it is precisely when these facts combine that claims about concern for fetuses, and even claims about fear of tort liability for fetal harm, are at their most incredible. The most plausible explanation for the development of these policies under these conditions is a gendered one—these policies can keep women out of jobs that men want. Further, Narayan argues, the current public discourse about fetuses, and the intense interest in fetuses that is characteristic of the United States but not common in Third World societies, create an atmosphere that invites such policies. Narayan suggests that these features of U.S. culture explain why work-related "fetal protection" policies have appeared in the United States; but they also explain why such policies are very unlikely to appear in nations that either need or prefer women in precisely the kinds of jobs from which "fetal protection" policies would exclude them.

In a recent landmark case, however, the U.S. Supreme Court has held that one of the country's paradigm "fetal protection" policies will not bear constitutional scrutiny, raising questions about the legal validity of any such policies in the United States in the future, but also raising questions about women's legal liability for causing prenatal harm by taking positions in workplaces that they have been warned contain reproductive hazards.

"Fetal Protection" in the Wake of *Johnson Controls*[9]

In 1982, Johnson Controls, Inc., adopted a policy which held that

> . . . women who are pregnant or who are capable of bearing children will not be placed into jobs involving lead exposure or which could expose them [ultimately] to lead . . . through transfer or promotion rights.[10]

Thus, the Johnson Controls policy barred fertile women even from positions that might lead, through transfer or the normal course of promotion, to jobs that would put them in lead-contaminated environments. The policy defined "women . . . capable of bearing children" as "[a]ll women except those whose inability to bear children is medically documented."[11] In March of 1991, the U.S. Supreme Court held that Title VII of the Civil Rights Act of 1964[12] precluded the Johnson Controls policy. Writing for the Court, now-retired Justice Harry Blackmun uses language that is strong and memorable. He says, for example, that

> . . . women as capable of doing their jobs as their male counterparts may not be forced to choose between having a child and having a job[13];

that

> [w]ith the Pregnancy Discrimination Act, Congress made clear that the decision to become pregnant or work while being either pregnant or capable of becoming pregnant [is] reserved for each individual woman for herself[14];

that

> [d]ecisions about the welfare of future children must be left to the parents who conceive, bear, support and raise them rather than to the employers who hire those parents[15];

that

> . . . it is no more appropriate for the courts than it is for individual

employers to decide whether a woman's reproductive role is more important to herself and her family than her economic role;[16]

and that

[the Court does] no more than hold that the Pregnancy Discrimination Act means what it says.[17]

These are powerful and unequivocal contentions, and with them Blackmun gives us a decision that makes clear that women will no longer be selected for exclusion from positions in the workforce because of our reproductive capacities alone. But there are some troubling features of the decision, too.

A close look at the decision and concurrences in *Johnson Controls* reveals an interplay between Blackmun and other justices, particularly Justices Byron White and Antonin Scalia, which forces Blackmun into dicta that set the stage for exempting businesses such as Johnson Controls from any liability for preconceptive or prenatal harm that might be caused by hazards in their workplaces. For example, in his concurrence, White expresses his concern about the potential tort liability of businesses that admit women into work environments thought to be reproductively hazardous: " 'An increasing number of courts," says White, "have recognized the right to recover for prenatal injuries caused by torts committed [even] prior to conception."[18] Blackmun responds to this concern in the decision, asserting that

[w]ithout negligence, it would be difficult for a court to find liability on the part of an employer. If, under general tort principles, Title VII bans sex-specific fetal-protection policies, the employer fully informs the woman of the risk, and the employer has not acted negligently, the basis for holding an employer liable seems remote at best. . . . [T]he tort liability that the concurrence fears [would] punish employers for *complying* with Title VII's clear command. When it is impossible for an employer to comply with both state [tort] and federal requirements, this Court has ruled that federal law pre-empts that of the States.[19]

Indeed, Blackmun says explicitly that "concerns about the welfare of the next generation [cannot] be considered a part of the 'essence' of Johnson Controls' business."[20] Now, although this is really a technical point, having to do with a legal notion of what counts as the "essence" of a business, it gives away a good deal, since it suggests that businesses need not operate in a way which takes into central account the welfare of the next generation—a message to business that is hardly comforting. White's concurrence, then, leads Blackmun to make explicit in the decision the Court's position that (absent negligence) employers who are precluded by federal law from excluding fertile women from the workplace will not be liable for torts if hazards in those workplaces do, in fact, cause prenatal (or preconceptive) harm, just as long as women have been warned of the hazards. This is seriously troubling in at least two ways.

First, it sets the stage for securing immunity for businesses that, though short of acting negligently, have not done all they can to clean up their workplaces. Second, with all the attempts we have recently seen to hold women liable for prenatal harm to their offspring, the decision does not bode well for fertile or pregnant women who take positions in potentially hazardous environments. Should a woman who takes a position in one of these environments give birth to a child who seems to have been harmed prenatally or preconceptively by a substance in her work environment of which she was warned, the recent history of holding women liable for causing prenatal harm, coupled with employer immunity, leave a chilling opening for the state to punish women for "opting" to put their future children at risk, much as women are currently being punished for subjecting their future children to the risks of other teratogenic substances, such as cocaine and alcohol.

A far more attractive decision would have been one with dicta explicitly pressing businesses to do everything they can to rid their workplaces of toxins that might cause reproductive and other harms. Or, minimally, a more attractive decision would have made explicit that potential parents (female and male) who take positions in potentially hazardous environments would enjoy the same immunity from prosecution as this decision virtually promises business.

But the complexion of the Court on which Blackmun sat during his final years as a Supreme Court Justice was such as to make it very unlikely that any such dicta would have been supported by his colleagues, and it can be surmised that the attorneys who represented the plaintiffs and Blackmun did what was necessary to ensure that Johnson Controls' policy was struck down. We are now seeing some important changes in the complexion of the U.S. Supreme Court; but those changes are still not likely to be sufficient to create a Court that is as mindful as it needs to be of the position of women and others whose real lives and interests have been and continue to be subordinated within a complex system of oppression that continues to thrive.

Although it is true, as Patricia Smith argues in her contribution to part I of this volume, that the world many of us live in today would be unrecognizable to our grandmothers, it is also true that the interlocking systems of racial, ethnic, classist, sexist, heterosexist, ageist, and ableist oppression are far from being overcome in virtually all of the world as we know it, and they are certainly not overcome in the United States. Thus (again), given continuing attempts to control women to prevent prenatal harm and continuing prosecutions of women for causing prenatal harm, the *Johnson Controls* decision leaves women vulnerable to legal consequences if they should have children who are damaged by their "choices" to work in hazardous workplaces.

In large measure, that vulnerability rests on the sort of individualism that remains ideologically dominant in Western culture today—an ideology that lets us hold individuals (and often the least powerful and least well-off individuals among us) responsible for problems for which we are collectively responsible.[21] Janet Gallagher admonishes us, as a society, to finally address the conditions of life that encourage pregnant women to seek the illusory refuge of drugs. In the same way, we, as a society, need to finally realize that our collective interests in certain products and services, and our willingness to have those products produced and services rendered in ways that may lead to reproductive harm, make us collectively responsible for such harms.[22] As Joan Bertin and Uma Narayan point out, "fetal protection" policies shift the responsibility for reproductive safety to individual women, relieving men of any share in that responsibility. And, as Bertin emphasizes, this leaves employers free to maintain reproductively hazardous workplaces.

Simply removing or precluding those policies is not enough to ensure that responsibility for reproductive safety (and with it, liability for reproductive harm) will not continue to fall on individual women. If we are, collectively, willing to allow businesses to produce products and render services in reproductively hazardous workplaces, we must be equally willing to assume responsibility for the harms that result, making it a matter of clear policy that any such harms will not be ascribed to individual parents (female or male) who take positions in those workplaces, but will be assumed by the social *system* that allows the continuation of product production and service provision in hazardous workplaces. Such a policy can serve as an important step out of the extreme ideological individualism that leads to the collective bad faith that Gallagher illuminates. This bad faith, which contributes so substantially to any number of social problems, ensures that such problems will not be resolved as long as they are simplistically and falsely approached as questions of purely individual responsibility.

Notes

1. Portions of the following discussion have been adapted with permission from James W. Knight and Joan C. Callahan, *Preventing Birth: Contemporary Methods and Related Moral Controversies* (Salt Lake City: University of Utah Press, 1989), chs. 7 and 9; and Joan C. Callahan, "Let's Get the Lead Out: Or Why *Johnson Controls* Is Not an Unequivocal Victory for Women," *Journal of Social Philosophy* 25:3 (1994): 65–75. See also Joan C. Callahan and James W. Knight, "On Treating Prenatal Harm as Child Abuse," in Diana Meyers, Kenneth Kipnis, and Cornelius Murphy, eds., *Kindred Matters: Rethinking the Philosophy of the Family* (New York: Cornell University Press, 1993), pp. 143–170; Joan C. Callahan and James W. Knight, "Prenatal Harm as Child Abuse?" in *Women and Criminal Justice* 3:1/2 (1992): 5–33, reprinted in Clarice Feinman, ed., *The Criminalization of a Woman's Body* (Binghamton, NY: Haworth Press, 1992), pp. 127–155; and Joan C. Callahan and James W. Knight, "Women, Fetuses, Medicine, and the Law," in Helen Bequaert Holmes and Laura M. Purdy, eds., *Feminist Perspectives on Medical Ethics* (Bloomington: Indiana University Press, 1992), pp. 224–239.

2. *National Organization for Women v. Scheidler et al.*, Cert. to the U.S. Court of Appeals for the Seventh Circuit, No. 92–780, argued December 8, 1993, dec'd. January 24, 1994.

3. Hereafter, I shall sometimes use the term "fetus" and its cognates to refer to the developing human being at all prenatal stages. Technically, the appropriate terms are "conceptus" through the first two weeks of gestation, "embryo" between weeks two and six of gestation, and "fetus" from week six onward. Gestational stages are also commonly calculated from the first day of a pregnant woman's last menstrual period, which adds about two weeks to the calculation. When I use "fetus" or one of its cognates alone, it is simply for the sake of efficiency; but I do mean to be talking about all of these prenatal developmental stages.

4. *Roe v. Wade*, 410 U.S. 113 (1973).

5. For a discussion of the problems with this language, as well as other problems with the structure of Blackmun's argument in *Roe*, see Knight and Callahan, *Preventing Birth*, ch. 7.

6. In 1800, no American jurisdictions had statutes prohibiting abortion. The first U.S. anti-abortion laws, which appeared between 1821 and 1841, were enacted (initially) to protect women from poisoning and (a little later) from surgical injury resulting from the "rashness of young practitioners" attempting to distinguish themselves. See, e.g., *Revised Statutes of New York, 1828–1835 Inclusive*, vol. I (Albany, 1983); and James C. Mohr, *Abortion in America: The Origins and Evolution of a National Policy, 1800–1900* (New York: Oxford University Press, 1978).

7. *Union Pacific R. Co. v. Botsford*, 141 U.S. 250 (1891).

8. See, for example, *Jefferson v. Griffin Spalding County Hospital Authority*, 247 Ga. 86, 274 S.E.2d 457 (1981); Watson A. Bowes, Jr., and Brad Selgestad, "Fetal v. Maternal Rights: Medical and Legal Perspectives," *Obstetrics and Gynecology* 58 (1981): 209–214; Jeffrey A. Parness and Susan K. Pritchard, "To Be or Not to Be: Protecting the Unborn's Potentiality of Life," *University of Cincinnati Law Review* 51 (1982): 257–298; John A. Robertson, "The Right to Procreate and In Utero Fetal Therapy," *Journal of Legal Medicine* 3 (1982): 333–366; Jeffrey L. Lenow, "The Fetus as a Patient: Emerging Rights as a Person?" *American Journal of Law and Medicine* 9 (1983): 1–29; Jeffrey A. Parness, "The Duty to Prevent Handicaps: Laws Promoting the Prevention of Handicaps to Newborns," *Western New England Law Review* 5 (1983): 431–464; Charles J. Dougherty, "The Right to Begin Life with Sound Body and Mind: Fetal Patients and Conflicts with Their Mothers," *University of Detroit Law Review* 63 (1985): 89–117; Deborah Mathieu, "Respecting Liberty and Preventing Harm: Limits of State Intervention in Prenatal Choice," *Harvard Journal of Law and Public Policy* 8 (1985): 19–55; Jeffrey A. Parness, "Crimes against the Unborn: Protecting and Respecting the Potentiality of Human Life," *Harvard Journal on Legislation* 22 (1985): 97–172; John A. Robertson, "Legal Issues in Fetal Therapy," *Seminars in Perinatology* 9 (1985): 136–142; John A. Robertson, "Legal Issues in Prenatal Therapy," *Clinical Obstetrics and Gynecology* 29 (1986): 603–611; Jeffrey A. Parness, "Letter," *Hastings Center Report* 17:3 (1987): 26; Willard Green and Charles Brill, "Letter," *Hastings Center Report* 17:3 (1987): 25.

9. *International Union, UAW, v. Johnson Controls*, SC 113 L. ed (1991) 158. For a more detailed discussion of this case, see Callahan, "Let's Get the Lead Out."

10. *Johnson Controls*, p. 189.

11. *Johnson Controls*, p. 169.

12. 42 USCS (1964) Sect. 2000e et seq.

13. *Johnson Controls*, p. 178.

14. *Johnson Controls*, p. 178.

15. *Johnson Controls*, p. 178.

16. *Johnson Controls*, p. 181.

17. *Johnson Controls*, p. 181.

18. *Johnson Controls*, Justice White concurring, p. 182.

19. *Johnson Controls*, pp. 179, 180.

20. *Johnson Controls*, p. 178.

21. Cf. Laura Purdy's discussion of social responsibility in her paper in part III.

22. See the substances, products, and services listed by Uma Narayan in her paper in this section.

Collective Bad Faith: "Protecting" the Fetus

Janet Gallagher

Fetal Rights and Gendered Wrongs

Between 1986 and 1992, over 160 women were arrested for the use of drugs while pregnant.[1] Hundreds more were threatened with the loss of custody of their children.[2]

> In Charleston, women who come into the public hospital for prenatal care or delivery are selectively tested for drugs: those who test positive have their names turned over to the police. The police then go to the hospital. The women, who are still recovering from the delivery, are handcuffed and taken to jail and stay there until they can make bail. At least one woman arrived at the jail still bleeding from the delivery; she was told to sit on a towel.[3]

Judges throughout the country have been asked, or have tried on their own initiative, to subject pregnant women to involuntary commitment to hospitals or to home arrest or to drug treatment centers.[4]

Still other pregnant women, picked up on minor criminal charges which would ordinarily draw little or no prison time, have found themselves sentenced to jail for the duration of their pregnancies by judges determined to ensure a drug-free "maternal environment." Brenda Vaughan, a first offender convicted on a check fraud charge in Washington, D.C., in 1988, was sentenced to 180 days in jail even though the prosecutor had agreed to the probation customary for first offenses. The judge based the harsh sentence on Vaughan's pregnancy and her having tested positive for cocaine. "I'm going to keep her locked up until the baby is born," declared the judge.[5]

Vaughan's sentence, although disproportionate to the offense with which she was charged, was nothing compared to sentences confronting women arrested specifically for drug use during pregnancy. Jennifer Johnson, a Florida woman, was threatened with 30 years in jail. Prosecutors could seek such draconian sentences in the pregnancy cases because they charged women, not with drug use or possession itself, but with much graver crimes like child endangerment or distributing drugs to a minor, or even assault with a deadly weapon.[6] And their rationale for the charges' applicability was grotesque. Johnson, for example, was specifically charged with delivery of an illegal substance to a minor, based on the sixty-second period during which the child had been delivered but the umbilical cord had not yet been cut.[7]

Vigorous assertions of "fetal rights" are not new, nor are they confined to cases of drug use. In late 1986, a San Diego woman was arrested and jailed for six days on charges of "medical neglect" of her fetus. Prosecutors alleged that her disregard of doctors' instructions had caused the brain-death of her newborn son. In addition to alleging that Pamela Stewart Monson (Pamela Rae Stewart) had ingested street drugs, prosecutors also charged that she had had sexual intercourse with her husband, and had failed to report promptly to the hospital when she began bleeding.[8] A municipal court judge dismissed the charges, holding that the legislature had never intended the parental support statute under which prosecutors brought the case to be used for such purposes.[9] An incensed state legislator promptly introduced legislation applying existing child-endangerment statutes to fetuses.[10]

Although the Pamela Rae Stewart case was heavily publicized, it was not the first time that women had been subjected to special scrutiny or penalties for their behavior while pregnant.[11] Just a year before the Stewart case hit the headlines, a pregnant Wisconsin teenager had been confined in a secure facility, not because of drug use, but " . . . because of her alleged tendencies 'to be on the run' and 'to lack motivation' to seek prenatal care."[12]

The late 1970s and early 1980s had seen the emergence of a new set of legal theories arguing for the recognition of "fetal rights." Law review articles,[13] medical journals,[14] and scattered judicial decisions[15] called for curbs on pregnant women's medical decision-making rights and behaviors in the name of a child's "right to be born healthy."[16] Doctors sought judicial approval for forced cesarean sections,[17] blood transfusions,[18] or even hospital detentions[19] of pregnant women whose choices or behavior they viewed as medically threatening to fetuses.

There were demands, and even some judicial orders, that comatose or brain-dead pregnant women be maintained on life support so that attempts to deliver their fetuses safely could be made.[20]

Scholarly commentators called for the prosecution of women giving birth to babies that showed signs of maternal drug or alcohol use.[21] Signs were posted in restaurants and bars warning pregnant women that alcohol might harm their unborn children.[22] Michigan's highest court allowed a son to sue his mother for having used a medicine during pregnancy that discolored his teeth.[23]

The "fetal rights" phenomenon can be properly understood only in its social and political context. It emerges from a glorification of medical technology resulting in a distorted public view of it, combined with a sharp backlash against the women's movement, especially against the claim to reproductive freedom symbolized by the *Roe v. Wade* abortion decision.[24] The drive to assert legal rights for fetuses reflects a broader attempt to reassert male control over women and over reproduction itself. It is part of a furious reaction against those changes in women's role and status that *Roe* exemplified.[25] Men experiencing a loss of control over the individual women in their lives attempted to reassert it through the courts, urging judges to assert *their* power as *parens patriae* ("father[s] of the country") or to invoke a "state interest" in the fetus.

The fetus's emergence as patient, plaintiff, and even quasi-religious icon serves as a vehicle for efforts to reinforce the claims of traditional maternal norms and gender roles on white, Anglo women. And, as Professor Dorothy Roberts has persuasively argued, glorification of fetal rights also serves a recurrent eugenic and racist impulse to deter and punish childbearing by women of color.[26] Casting the pregnant woman as a threat to her fetus who must be restrained or punished by doctors or prosecutors serves these larger political themes.

This attempt to reassert male and medical power is not without precedent. Nor is the sometimes apocalyptic language of anti-abortionists who equate women's demand for reproductive self-determination with the fall of Western civilization.[27] There is, for example, a striking parallel between the way the current alleged epidemic of infertility is blamed on women[28] and the rhetoric of nineteenth century "regular" doctors pressing for anti-abortion laws.[29] Then as now, white, non-immigrant women were blamed for evading their reproductive duty and their God-given, natural lot in life. In both eras, champions of more traditional women's roles linked the falling birthrates of *their* women to race suicide and national decline.[30]

Today, infertility is blamed on women's selfishly deferring childbirth for careerist reasons, or having abortions, or being sexually promiscuous.[31] Little or no attention is paid to environmental poisons or work-place hazards affecting both men and women, except when efforts are made to ban women from high-paying blue-collar jobs under the guise of "fetal protection" policies.[32] Nor is much public attention focused on infertility caused by poor or non-existent medical care.[33]

Skidding Down the Slippery Slope: Forced Cesareans

The most draconian expression of this none-too-subtle gender warfare is the court-ordered cesarean section. While there have never been more than a scattered handful of these cases around the country,[34] they are symbolically significant and have generated much comment in professional and scholarly journals.[35]

A 1981 Georgia court order for a cesarean section, the first of only three appellate decisions formally reported in the casebooks, arose from a pregnant woman's religious objection to surgery and blood transfusions. The Atlanta hospital sought court intervention. Doctors testified that the woman had a complete placenta previa, a condition in which the placenta blocks the birth canal. They claimed that there was a 99% certainty that the fetus would die in a vaginal delivery and, indeed, a 50% chance that the woman herself would die. The court, convinced by the doctors' presentations, declared the fetus "a human being fully capable of sustaining life independent of the mother" lacking "proper parental care and subsistence." Citing *Roe v. Wade* as authority for state protection of a viable, unborn child,[36] the judges granted temporary custody of the fetus to the social service agency and gave it "full authority to make all decisions, including giving consent to the surgical delivery."[37] The procedure never actually took place. In a development the Georgia medical society journal labeled "Mother Nature Reverses on Appeal," the woman's placenta shifted and she gave vaginal birth to a healthy 7 lb., 2 oz. baby girl.[38]

But other cases ended tragically. In 1984, a Nigerian woman in Chicago, expecting triplets, was hospitalized for the final stage of her pregnancy. The woman and her husband steadfastly reiterated their unwillingness to consent to the cesarean section that doctors regarded as necessary for a safe multiple birth. As the woman's due date approached, doctors and hospital legal counsel obtained a court order granting the hospital administrator temporary custody of the triplets and authorizing a cesarean section as soon as the woman went into labor. Dr. Veronika Kolder reports:

Although this plan was known to all the residents, it was never presented to the patient. She was not given the opportunity to seek care elsewhere. . . . Confronted with the doctor's intentions, the woman and her husband became irate. The husband was asked to leave, refused, and was forcibly removed from the hospital by seven security officers. The woman became combative and was placed in full leathers, a term that refers to leather wrist and ankle cuffs that are attached to the four corners of a bed to prevent the patient from moving. Despite her restraints, the woman continued to scream for help and bit through her intravenous tubing in an attempt to get free. . . . Some days later, the hospital newsletter published a photograph of the woman and her three children, making no mention of the violent melee attending the birth. Months later still, hospital staff learned that the woman's husband had killed himself, leaving her and the children utterly destitute.[39]

A 1987 case in Washington, D.C., dramatically illustrated just how easily judges can careen out of control once launched on the "slippery slope" of enforcing the patienthood of the fetus. In a nightmarish drama, a gravely ill pregnant woman was literally sacrificed in order to give her 26-week fetus a "better though slim chance."[40] The fetus, drastically premature and already compromised by the woman's ill health, "survived" for two hours on life-support. Twenty-eight-year-old Angela Carder survived for two more days; her death certificate listed the cesarean as a contributing cause of death.[41]

New Visibility, Claims of New Status

The claims of "fetal rights" became imaginable only when it became possible to see and think of the fetus as separate from the woman within whose body it is carried. Ultrasound,[42] color photographs like the famous Nilson photos printed by *Life*,[43] and dramatic television footage all combine to portray a fetus as a free-floating entity engaging our fascinated attention.

See the egg as it is released by the ovary and follow the sperm from its early development through ejaculation and then on its perilous journey toward the egg. With magnification of up to half a million times the actual size, you can see exactly what happens at the moment of conception. After the sperm fertilizes the egg, the camera follows the development of the single new cell into an embryo, then a fetus, until finally, a baby is born.[44]

Antiabortionists strove to " . . . [M]ake fetal personhood a self-ful-filling prophecy by making the fetus a *public presence*. . . . "[45] Dr. Ber-nard Nathanson, a prominent Right to Life spokesman, created the 1985 film, *The Silent Scream*, in which he claimed that the "dazzling" new "science of fetology" creates an irrebuttable argument against abor-tion.[46] This reliance upon scientific knowledge, notes political scientist Rosalind Petchesky, represents a "conscious strategic shift" by leaders of the antiabortion movement "from religious discourses and authorities to medicotechnical ones."[47]

The news media's fascination with medical technology helped rein-force controlling, punitive attitudes toward pregnant women. By the early 1980s, neonatal intensive care units enabled the survival of such very premature babies that it seemed to some that the viability line drawn in *Roe v. Wade*—the boundary beyond which states could bar any abortions not necessary for the life or health of the woman—was mov-ing inexorably back into ever earlier stages of pregnancy, and that the *Roe* formulation itself would collapse.[48]

The emergence of fetal surgery, first extensively publicized in the early 1980s,[49] promised to provide therapeutic interventions in the womb itself, and gave rise to claims that the fetus was now a patient in its own right.[50] The advent of fetal surgery incited a veritable explosion of articles in law reviews, medical journals, and the popular press fo-cused on whether and how hypothetically unwilling pregnant women could be *forced* to undergo the procedures.[51]

Popular perceptions of technological advances and their implications were often wildly exaggerated. The allegedly inexorable reduction in the number of weeks of pregnancy required for viability, for example, rep-resented a profound, ideologically driven misunderstanding of the data. In reality, while there has been a significant improvement in the capac-ity of medicine to support the survival of young preemies born at 23 and 24 weeks' gestation, there has been little appreciable success in aiding survival for fetuses born earlier in a pregnancy.[52] While the recent de-velopment of an artificial substitute for surfactant (a liquid that helps keep lungs inflated) may promise relief for one major threat to prema-ture infants, other serious problems remain.[53] And even those preemies who survive delivery at 23 and 24 weeks often sustain catastrophic brain damage.[54]

Despite the medical realities, the seeming erosion of *Roe*'s viability line was seized upon to further "blur the boundary between fetus and baby."[55] Nathanson exulted,

. . . from the moment we are set in motion with the penetration of the egg by the sperm we are an unstoppable continuum. . . . No

more trimesters, no more embryo or fetus, just as there are no junior children or senior children, no major adolescents and minor
adolescents; it is simply one seamless continuum of prenatality,
with no Bar Mitzvahs in the uterus.[56]

Pregnancy, Paternity, and the Rescue of the Icon

Contributing to the demands that pregnant women be punished and
controlled in the late 1970s and early 1980s was, ironically enough, the
very success of the movement for access to birth control and legal abortion. Pregnancy and birth became, at least for the medically advantaged,
a chosen and cherished experience. Relieved of the constant anxiety of
unintended pregnancy, the opinion-making classes embraced parenthood with a vengeance. And it wasn't just appreciation of pregnancy
that was heightened. Anxiety had risen, too. The availability of new
tests and procedures to detect anomalies[57] before birth, along with
new devices to monitor "distress" or potential problems during labor,
freighted prospective parenthood with ever greater apprehension and
made the development and well being of the fetus an obsessive preoccupation.[58]

All of this took place in a time of bewildering, stressful changes in
gender power relations. While the pitched, ongoing battle over abortion
has held center stage at least since the Supreme Court decision in *Roe*,
there have been other, somewhat less publicized fronts in the war to control " . . . a most precious human resource—the power to reproduce the
species."[59] The increased incidence of divorce gave rise to a "Fathers'
Rights Movement," which won major victories in the legislatures and
the courts,[60] and to an epidemic of child snatchings. Even unwed fathers
demanded and gained the power to block adoptions.[61] The emergence of
"surrogate" or "contract" motherhood led to a renewed emphasis on
genetic fatherhood and a burst of legal rhetoric and lower court decisions reaffirming the ancient, "sire-centered" view of children as " . . .
really the fruit, even the possession of men."[62] In one California case,
for example, a young black woman agreed to carry the IVF embryo of
a co-worker and her husband for $10,000. A month or so before the
birth, she moved in court for custody, arguing that she had bonded with
the fetus and that she questioned the genetic parents' commitment to
the coming child. The couple's attorney's closing statement maintained
that the gestational mother had no more rights "than a day school or
baby sitter." The trial court judge agreed, ruling that the birth mother
was "a genetic stranger," not a parent.[63] In yet another bizarre case of

judicial deference to the primacy of the genetic (and especially male genetic) link, a sperm donor was allowed parental rights and access to the child born as a result of his sperm having been used to inseminate one member of a lesbian couple. The court reasoned that since the women had employed self-insemination they were not entitled to the protection of the California statute which cuts off the parental rights of sperm donors when a physician performs the actual insemination.[64]

Male Primacy

The theme of the primacy of the male "seed" intertwines with another theme of contemporary gender warfare: the vision of the male as the rescuer of the child from the dangerous or criminally negligent mother. The surgeon invades the womb to remedy a defect that menaces the well-being of the child-to-be; the obstetrician performs a crash cesarean in response to a monitor's warning of "fetal distress"; Operation "Rescue"ers blockade an abortion clinic.

♀ image

Pregnant women's bodies thus become stage sets in a powerful psychodrama, simultaneously idealized as havens and feared as scenes of deadly peril. Anti-abortion rhetoric presents us with alternating imagery of woman as harbor and woman as threat. Nathanson's film, for example, proposes that we envision a fetus first "moving rather serenely in the uterus . . . moving quietly in its sanctuary" and then emitting " . . . the silent scream of a child threatened imminently with extinction."[65]

To the extent that we feel besieged and menaced in a world of ambiguity and danger and chaos, the fetus becomes a stand-in for us and for those we love.[66] Like us, it is at risk. And frightened people are offered a delusory assurance that they can somehow make the world safer by imposing legal restraints and controls on pregnant women, by enforcing a new norm of motherhood through criminal sanction, civil lawsuits, and naked physical violence.[67]

The fetus becomes an icon, the object of a quasi-religious cult.[68] And the woman within whose body that new object of devotion exists drops out of sight as an individual with hopes and plans and choices. She becomes instead the environment of the fetus, "the mother ship," or the "uterine capsule."[69]

The compelling new visual images of the fetus play powerfully on deeply rooted patriarchal attitudes in which pregnant women are viewed as vessels, fields, or gardens in which the male seed is temporarily planted.[70] It has become too easy for us to think of the fetus as something quite distinct from the body and life of the woman who carries it, to ignore the ethical and legal significance of the real geography of pregnancy.

In such a cultural context, it became easier to claim that the fact that medical technology now allows us to view and even to treat the fetus challenges the permissibility of abortion and authorizes civil and criminal sanctions against pregnant women who deviate from prescribed maternal norms. The allegedly neutral language of science appears to justify reassertion of male control over women and over reproduction itself.[71]

And reports of a "Maternal-Fetal Conflict" seem made to order for the sort of media coverage that stimulates and feeds the public's emotional appetite for rescues, miracles, and punishment. A market-hungry media aggravates public anxieties and confusion by presenting new medical technologies and dilemmas as psychodramas to be milked for cheap thrills of hope or horror. Hope is exemplified by the "miracle" IVF child; or the "brave" little preemie in a neonatal intensive care unit—small as a robin, yet fighting for life; or the baby harvested from the body of a brain-dead woman maintained for months on life support to enable doctors to bring "life out of death." The "evil scientist" thawing frozen embryos or throwing them down the sink makes a satisfying villain.[72] So does the hugely pregnant woman in a public service ad, looking defiantly into the camera and hoisting a wine glass above a caption that exclaims, "Here's to birth defects."[73]

In a time of genuine, agonizing dilemmas in individual lives and in public policy, the news media has fed us a marketable and ideologically charged mix of easily recognizable stock victims, villains, and heroes. A front page tabloid headline labels "crack babies" as the "CHILDREN OF THE DAMNED."[74] Good fathers rescue their own and other children. Eric Poole, a young black man from Oakland, is featured in *People* after having publicly insisted that the fetus he had fathered be carried to term in the body of its brain-dead mother.[75] The young man then turned the child over to his own mother to be raised. A television ad for a men's clothing company features a young man protectively holding a toddler and inveighing against pregnant women's abuse of drugs.[76] Michael Dorris, a Native American scholar and novelist who wrote a bestselling book about his adopted son's affliction with fetal alcohol syndrome as a result of his birth mother's heavy drinking during pregnancy, is featured embracing his small adopted son on the front page of the *New York Times Book Review*.[77]

In an era of little public appetite for complexity and ambiguity, policy discussion yields to the use of stock figures and sound bites. Stories that confirm people's biases or fears strike chords of response and belief. Television news coverage cultivates and then caters to its audience's short attention span and its appetite for the same "stars, conflict, [and] emotional kick" provided in prime time entertainment shows.[78]

The figure of the drunken or drug-using pregnant woman becomes a villainess as satisfying as any in a soap opera. She bears the charge of all the anger and anxiety aroused by women's "abandonment" of a traditional nurturing role.[79] She becomes the scapegoat for the anger of men and the ambivalence of women over their own deviation from an idealized maternal norm. And the fetus plays the role of the innocent victim to be rescued and celebrated.

Discrimination: Race and Class

While certainly not a new problem,[80] drug use during pregnancy took on "crisis" proportions with the onslaught of crack—a cheap, smokable form of cocaine—in the mid-1980s.[81] Estimates are that as many as 375,000 children may be born each year to women who have used illegal drugs while pregnant,[82] and that up to 11% of pregnant women have used drugs at some point during their pregnancies.[83] Some 75 percent of those women are thought to have used cocaine.[84] A 1992 survey by the Child Welfare League of America revealed that hospitals in 12 cities were caring for 7000 "boarder babies," infants healthy enough to be discharged but who were held after birth because of family abandonment or alleged inability to care. According to the study, 85 percent of those infants held had been exposed to drugs or alcohol before birth.[85] There is, undeniably, legitimate cause for serious concern about the impact of such drug use on children. Cocaine consumption during pregnancy has been linked to prematurity, low birthweight, neurobehavioral problems, and developmental abnormalities.[86] At the same time, press coverage has been unabashedly sensationalist, may have exaggerated the actual damage done by drug use during pregnancy,[87] and has lent itself to appropriation in the service of other agendas.

effect of coke

"Keeping Baby Safe from Mom"[88] became a rallying cry for conservative politicians and prosecutors. It not only played upon the fears and resentments set loose by the women's movement, it also served to divert attention from the drastic shift of federal funds and attention away from the needs of poor women and children. As Katha Pollitt points out, "The focus on maternal behavior allows the government to appear to be concerned about babies without having to spend any money, change any priorities, or challenge any vested interests."[89] But this insistence on pointing the finger of blame at individual women is an exercise in collective bad faith, a social self-deception which rationalizes our passivity toward the genuinely horrifying living conditions confronting many poor women.

It is no coincidence that we are obsessed with pregnant women's behavior at the same time that children's health is declining, by virtually any yardstick one chooses. Take general well-being: In constant dollars, welfare payments are now about two-thirds the 1965 level. Take housing: Thousands of children are now growing up in homeless shelters and welfare hotels. Even profoundly alcoholic women bear healthy babies two-thirds of the time. Will two-thirds of today's homeless kids emerge unscathed from their dangerous and lead-permeated environments? Take access to medical care: Inner-city hospitals are closing all over the country, millions of kids have no health insurance, and most doctors refuse uninsured or Medicaid patients. Even immunization rates are down: Whooping cough and measles are on the rise.[90]

Governmental reaction to the crisis took three main forms. There were criminal prosecutions, employing charges such as delivering drugs to a minor, child endangerment, or drug trafficking.[91] Social service agencies around the country used positive drug tests on newborn infants' urine as grounds for moving to take custody of the babies.[92] And there were scattered instances of "preventative prenatal detentions" intended to protect the fetuses of women alleged to be substance abusers or posing some other risk to the pregnancy.[93]

The prosecutions were the most dramatic and heavily publicized. In Butte County, California, the local district attorney called a news conference to announce that positive toxicology tests on newborns would trigger prosecutions for illegal drug use.[94] The D.A. touted the program as an effort " . . . to protect the newest and most innocent of our citizens."[95] But, as Susan Faludi reports:

The first woman snared in Ramsey's dragnet was an impoverished twenty-seven-year-old heroin addict. For the prosecutor's purposes, however, she proved to be less than the ideal first criminal. The young woman had, in fact, been traveling 130 miles round trip to the nearest methadone clinic, a $200-a-month private program in Sacramento. When her car broke down, she had hitchhiked. When her funds ran out, the program had discharged her, even knowing that she was pregnant. Two months from her due date, she appealed to several medical providers in the area—without success. None of these mitigating circumstances, however, deterred Ramsey and his pregnancy police squad. When her newborn tested positive for heroin, his team descended on her hospital room less than twenty-four hours after she had given birth, interrogated her, and took away her baby.[96]

Although it has been far less publicized than the criminal cases, child welfare agencies throughout the nation have seized custody of thousands of infants born with positive toxicologies. A number of states make indications of maternal drug use subject to mandatory reporting as child abuse.[97] In some jurisdictions, legislatures or courts have defined prenatal drug exposure as child neglect or abuse on the theory that it poses actual or potential harm to the child.[98]

The prosecutions, custody deprivations, and detention threats zeroed in on poor women, especially African American and Hispanic women. In fact, a 1992 review of the prosecutions revealed that 70 percent of the women prosecuted whose race could be ascertained were women of color.[99] One Florida study showed that, despite the fact that drug use was equally prevalent among non-Hispanic whites and minority women, African American women were almost 10 times more likely to be reported to the authorities.[100] (The court-ordered cesarean section cases had reflected similar racial disparity: 81 percent of the women subjected to such treatment had been African American, Asian, or Hispanic; none had been private patients.)[101] Professor Dorothy Roberts notes that such disparities arise not just out of racist attitudes on the part of health professionals, but also out of the simple reality that poor women of color are dependent on public clinics and hospitals and are therefore more vulnerable to governmental surveillance and control.[102]

Indeed, the campaign for "fetal rights" displays very different aspects as it affects different groups of women. It may be viewed as part of a more general, ideological effort to reassert male control over women and over reproduction that encourages, even mandates motherhood among white, non-immigrant women,[103] while attempting to recontain it within heterosexual, husband-headed families.[104] When the focus shifts to women of color, however, "fetal rights" plays out a different— although equally traditional—theme: discouraging and devaluing maternity.[105]

There are racist, eugenicist, and nativist echoes to the drumbeat of invective against welfare mothers who threaten society by giving birth to a "bio-underclass" of crack babies.[106] One bill, introduced in the Ohio legislature in 1989, reflected that heritage, providing that women who use "a drug of abuse" during pregnancy resulting in a baby being "addicted at birth" could be prosecuted on felony charges.[107]

A repeat offender must elect either to undergo tubal ligation or to participate in a five-year contraception program. If she fails to remain drug-free during the five-year program, the judge must sentence her to be sterilized.[108]

While that bill failed to pass in Ohio, bills and policies encouraging the use of Norplant, a long-term contraceptive, by low-income women have shown up throughout the country.[109] And judges in several states have imposed birth control requirements on women accused of child abuse.[110] Such policies are reminiscent of Colonial-era "bastardy" laws in that they are clearly more geared toward preventing economic burdens on the taxpayers than toward child protection.[111] The Washington, D.C., judge who sentenced Brenda Vaughan to jail time, for example, expressed a determination to protect the fetus and the "taxpaying public."[112]

The Courts

The prosecutions of drug-using pregnant women tapped into those deep misogynist and racist undercurrents, generating front-page headlines for "tough" D.A.s and politicians. They fared less well when subjected to legal review. In fact, not one of the drug prosecutions challenged in court[113] has been able to withstand judicial scrutiny.[114]

The Jennifer Johnson case went all the way to the Florida Supreme Court before being unanimously reversed.[115] The court rejected the prosecutor's use of a criminal statute against delivering drugs to minors, ruling that the legislature had never intended the law to apply to "delivery" of drugs through the umbilical cord in the moments just after birth. Criminal statutes are to be construed strictly and, when there is doubt as to their meaning, viewed in the light most favorable to the accused. In determining whether a penal statute applies to a particular set of facts, the court must consider the legislative purpose and goals. The Florida court found that the legislature had expressly rejected criminal prosecution as a means of dealing with substance abuse by pregnant women.[116]

Most of the courts rejecting the "drug baby" prosecutions have relied on similar statutory interpretation, including arguments that a fetus is not legally a person or child as defined in the criminal statute at issue.[117] Courts have emphasized that women accused under distorted applications of criminal drug laws can scarcely be said to have been afforded the notice or warning of the legal consequences of their action mandated by constitutional due process.[118]

The Florida decision also cited an American Medical Association report pointing out that addicted women never "intended" a harmful act to their fetus.[119] The American Public Health Association amicus brief had urged the court to bar prosecution on the grounds that it was based upon Johnson's status as an addict and would thus punish her for a disease, not a crime, but the state Supreme Court did not address that argument.[120] In fact, the *Johnson* court—like most of the other courts ruling on these cases—found it unnecessary to reach many of the constitutional arguments raised by critics of prosecution.[121]

Courts traditionally refrain from declaring a law, or its application to a specific situation, unconstitutional when the task can be accomplished through statutory construction. This more narrow approach conserves judicial resources and prevents unnecessarily direct clashes with the other branches of government. It can also be frustrating to those preoccupied with the deeper, more resonant constitutional issues.

Few of the courts urged to review the discrimination or privacy arguments against prosecution or loss of parental rights in the drug cases have done so—on the record. Those arguments, while seldom explicitly reached, have been made in the legal briefs and in the public policy debates and they have proved compelling. In fact, the legal and medical/public policy critiques of the punitive approach to substance abuse by pregnant women are inextricably interwoven.

Privacy

Critics have also pointed out that the prosecutions violate women's constitutional rights of privacy, self-determination, and autonomy in making reproductive decisions. Criminal law enforcement of a "duty to care" for the fetus could subject women of childbearing capacity to sweeping, heavily burdensome restrictions:

> At all stages of pregnancy, the fetus is completely, biologically dependent on the woman, and thus virtually everything she does could have some effect on the fetus. No criminal statute could be tailored enough to protect women's right to privacy or due process; 900,000 women each year suffer miscarriages and stillbirths—every one of them could theoretically be dragged into court and be required to prove that their prenatal care was adequate. Women who have diabetes or who are obese, women with cancer or epilepsy who need drugs that could harm the fetus, and women who are too poor to eat adequately could all be characterized as fetal abusers. Allowing criminal sanctions or state intervention moves us toward turning pregnancy itself into a crime, since no woman can provide the perfect womb.[122]

Massachusetts Judge Suzanne DelVecchio cited privacy grounds in dismissing prosecution of a woman on charges of distributing cocaine to a person under eighteen (her fetus), noting, " . . . [T]he level of state intervention and control over a woman's body required by this prosecution could open the door to many other arbitrary restrictions on a woman's pregnancy."[123]

And there is a far more specific right at stake: the right to choose to bear a child.[124] Professor Dorothy Roberts contends, as did the lawyers for Jennifer Johnson, that it was Johnson's choice to give birth that subjected her to the risk of thirty years in jail. As the prosecutor had summed it up, "[W]hen she delivered that baby, she broke the law in the state," and the trial judge declared that the defendant "made a choice to become pregnant and to allow those pregnancies to come to term."[125]

Even worse, in some ways, than reducing pregnant women to the status of fetal containers is this singling out of poor, substance-abusing (primarily African American) women and criminalizing carrying their pregnancies to term. This, argues Roberts, leads to "an invidious government standard for childbearing" and violates rights both of equal protection and of autonomy over reproductive decisions.[126] It "perpetuates the historic devaluation of Black women as mothers"[127] reflected in the reproductive commodification of black women during slavery, the coercive sterilization of African American and other women of color in the twentieth century,[128] and the continuing "disproportionate removal of Black children from their families."[129]

Under the "fundamental rights" analysis employed by federal courts in the privacy cases of the 1970s and 1980s, government action that infringes upon an individual's fundamental rights of personal decision making or bodily integrity is constitutionally permissible only if it serves a compelling state interest and, even then, only if there is no less drastic alternative.[130] Judge DelVecchio found that the prosecution in *Pellegrini* could not withstand this "strict scrutiny."[131] While agreeing that Massachusetts had a compelling state interest in the health and welfare of a viable fetus, the judge found that since no actual harm to the infant had been shown, mere speculation about possible harm could not outweigh the woman's privacy interests.[132] Moreover, the state's proposed means of furthering the interest in the potential health of a future child was not "narrowly tailored" enough.[133] Instead, "The Commonwealth may effectuate its stated interest in protecting viable fetuses through less restrictive means, such as education and making available medical care and drug treatment centers for pregnant women."[134]

The Florida Supreme Court went even further in *Johnson*, adopting Judge Winifred Sharp's dissent in the intermediate appellate court condemning the prosecution as counterproductive, "the least effective response to this crisis."[135] It has been the public-policy and medical objections to the punitive approach that have proved most effective in halting the movement toward criminalization. Virtually every medical organization has condemned the prosecutions as likely to deter poor women from seeking out needed prenatal care and to chill patient-physician communication.[136] Fear of prosecution could lead women to abort their pregnancies, withhold important information from health care workers, or even avoid hospital birth altogether.[137] "Yet," wrote Judge Sharp, "the infants of these women are, as a group, the most fragile and sick, and most in need of hospital neonatal care."[138]

Discrimination Revisited: Women

The courts, however, have generally chosen not to explicitly tackle any of the discrimination issues created by the legal rush to protect fetuses. The *Johnson* court, for example, did not address claims that the drug prosecutions were racially discriminatory, although such charges have occasioned much public notice and criticism.[139] Even the presiding justice of one New York appellate court has observed:

> . . . [P]ress reports to the contrary, cocaine-exposed infants are not mainly the children of racial or ethnic minorities. In fact, available studies show that cocaine use is slightly higher among white, middle class women than in other groups. However, as medical authorities admit, the middle class mother is less likely to be tested for evidence of the drug.[140]

There has also been criticism of the glaring gender discrimination inherent in focusing "fetal protection" measures on pregnant women while ignoring male behavior and substance abuse.[141] Pamela Rae Stewart, for example, was charged with having disregarded doctors' orders by having sexual intercourse with her husband. No charges were ever brought against the husband, even though he had also been aware of the doctor's instructions.[142] In one Wyoming case, a pregnant woman who had fled to a hospital emergency room after being beaten by her husband was arrested and jailed on child endangerment charges when tests revealed that she'd been drinking.[143]

Critics of the widespread use of drug screening tests on newborns to seize custody of children on the grounds of maternal neglect or abuse point out that reliance on such tests fails to identify drug use by fathers. The insistent emphasis on individual maternal responsibility for fetal and child well-being is not only sexist, but ineffective public policy. It ignores the reality that men have an impact on the well-being of their children—before, during, and after pregnancy. Male drug use, smoking, drinking, and exposure to workplace toxins harms both future offspring and the children with whom men live.[144] But men's deviations from the parental ideal are largely ignored by officials and by the media, while pregnant women, in contrast, are confronted constantly with signs, pamphlets, and scolding strangers warning them not to drink alcoholic beverages[145] or to smoke.[146]

Progress: The Impact of *A. C.*

The unanimous *Johnson* opinion reflected development of a strong national consensus among doctors, ethicists, and lawyers that criminalization of pregnant women's substance abuse was counter-productive. The grounds for that consensus had been prepared by earlier national debates over the Pamela Rae Stewart prosecution in California[147] and over court-ordered cesarean sections.

Stewart's 1986 arrest for "medical neglect" of her fetus had triggered alarm not only among feminists and civil libertarians, but also from medical organizations who viewed criminal prosecutions as likely to frighten away precisely those pregnant women who most needed prenatal care. Health care workers made their position known in friend-of-court briefs, public statements, and press releases. Their organizations were to be called upon again all too soon.

Less than a year after *Stewart* came *A.C.*,[148] the Washington D.C. case in which a young woman dying of cancer was forced to undergo a cesarean in a futile effort to "rescue" her 26-week fetus. The incident aroused widespread revulsion and helped spur emergence of a strong consensus against the much-touted "trend" toward fetal rights.[149] As long as the fetal rights proposals had been confined to the tidy theoretical abstractions of law reviews and speculative discussions at bioethics conferences, they seemed plausible—even compelling. But *A.C.* played out that theorizing in all its concrete brutality. And people—especially health care workers—were appalled. The case set off a firestorm of opposition. Unlike most of the other women subjected to court-ordered surgery, Angela Carder was white and middle class.[150] Her angry and articulate parents called in the ACLU and made the rounds of the tv talk shows. *A.C.* created a remarkable coalition among feminists, doctors, bioethicists, and legal scholars.[151] The American College of Obstetricians and Gynecologists (ACOG) roundly condemned the court's action as a violation of the woman's autonomy and a threat to the doctor-patient relationship.[152]

Although the trial judge's decision had initially been upheld in a telephone hearing by a hastily convened appeals panel, the public uproar forced reconsideration by the full D. C. Court of Appeals. Significantly enough, among those arguing against the forced surgery were the ACOG and the AMA.[153]

After well over a year of consideration, the highest appeals court in the District of Columbia ruled 7–1 that Angela Carder should not have been forced to undergo surgery against her will: not even if she was dying, not even if her fetus were viable. The woman, held the court, is the one to make decisions for herself and for the fetus. And if she is not herself competent to make a decision, then a court should employ "substituted judgement" and decide—as best it can—as she would likely decide if she *were* competent.[154] The court based its ruling on both common law and constitutional rights. Noting that our legal tradition will not compel one person to undergo significant health risk or bodily invasion to benefit another,[155] the court declared, "Surely . . . a fetus cannot have rights in this respect superior to those of a person who has already been born."[156]

While technically binding only in the District of Columbia, the opinion had major national impact. As the first appellate decision developed through written briefs, full oral argument, and time for reflective deliberations, *A.C.* undercut the authority of all earlier court opinions on the topic.[157] The hospital subsequently entered into a ground-breaking settlement with Angela Carders's parents under which it publicly committed itself to respect the autonomy of pregnant patients, declaring, "We strongly believe that difficult medical decisions should be made within the doctor–patient relationship and not by the courts."[158]

The "fetal rights" movement was halted on other fronts, too. The Illinois Supreme Court eloquently rejected a claim that lawsuits could be brought by a child against her mother for negligent infliction of prenatal injuries.[159] The court declared:

A legal right of a fetus to begin life with a sound mind and body assertable against a mother would make a pregnant woman the guarantor of the mind and body of her child at birth. A legal duty to guarantee the mental and physical health of another has never before been recognized in law. Any action that negatively impacted on fetal development would be a breach of the pregnant woman's duty to her developing fetus. Mother and child would be legal adversaries from the moment of conception until birth. Holding a third person liable for prenatal injuries furthers the interests of both the mother and the subsequently born child and does not interfere with the defendant's right to control his or her own life.

Holding a mother liable for the unintentional infliction of prenatal injuries subjects to state scrutiny all the decisions a woman must make in attempting to carry a pregnancy to term, and infringes on her right to privacy and bodily autonomy. Logic does not demand that a pregnant woman be treated in a court of law as a stranger to her developing fetus.[160]

And, in a landmark decision for women's employment rights, the U.S. Supreme Court sharply rejected efforts by large industrial companies to deal with reproductive hazards in the workplace by simply excluding women of childbearing capacity.[161]

Communal Good Faith:
"It Takes a Whole Village to Raise a Child"

The substance abuse issue is more challenging to feminists than the earlier debate over forced medical treatment. We cannot legitimately invoke the rights of bodily integrity, medical self-determination, and religious liberty—so starkly at issue in the court-ordered cesarean cases—in connection with a pregnant woman's addiction to crack. The constitutional analysis is different, and the realities of addiction demand that we go beyond sheerly civil libertarian protest if we are to be taken seriously by beleaguered and anguished health care workers, family court judges, and foster parents. We must grapple honestly with the costs—to the individual child and to the community—of a pregnant woman's addiction.

Still, I would argue that thoughtful analysis and reflection on the "fetal rights" issues in the area of child neglect and abuse cases yields results very similar to the national consensus achieved in the debates over forced cesarean sections and criminal prosecution for substance abuse. Automatically seizing babies who test positive for maternal drug use is bad law and worse public policy: not only because it impinges upon the fundamental right to parent one's children[162] and raises serious issues of due process[163] and equal protection,[164] but because it's simply not the best solution for the children.

Here, too, less drastic alternatives are not just constitutional mandates; they make good public policy sense. Giving fetuses rights and lawyers, while failing to provide accessible prenatal care and drug treatment on demand for the women who carry them, is mere posturing—a paradigm of societal bad faith. It is a refusal to shoulder our own social burden, a self-indulgent unwillingness to confront the urgent and very difficult task of healing the shattered lives of so many poor women among us.

Society may have a compelling interest, even a duty as *parens patriae*, toward the children of substance-abusing women. It is much less clear that we have the communal capacity or willingness to undertake the role of parent once we seize a child, whatever our verbal pieties. This, too, is collective bad faith. Court determinations of neglect and abuse are of little assistance amid the virtual collapse of the child welfare and foster care systems in many areas. The influx of children during the height of the crack epidemic overwhelmed many local systems, causing burnout and high turnover rates among social workers and judges alike.[165] A 1991 study by the National Commission on Family Foster Care estimated that by 1995 the number of children being raised outside the home of their natural parents (in foster care families, institutions, halfway houses, and so on) would rise to over 500,000.[166]

While it is clear that leaving a child in the natural parents' custody can sometimes result in tragedy, the alternative is not always assuredly better.[167] Although the law requires diligent efforts by foster care agencies to strengthen family ties before there can be proceedings to terminate the parental rights of birth parents,[168] all too often children are caught up in a sort of legal limbo, deprived of secure and permanent homes, "hostages of a system that has substituted government neglect for parental neglect."[169] One federal judge condemned the Washington, D.C. foster care system, citing an 11-year-old boy who had spent his entire life in foster care—in 11 different placements. The judge decried the mistreatment of "children relegated to entire childhoods spent in foster care drift . . . a lost generation. . . ."[170]

There are less drastic—and more productive—means by which the community can intervene in the problem of substance abuse by pregnant women. The most obvious is development of drug treatment on demand that is both appropriate for and accessible to pregnant women. Treatment programs are in disgracefully short supply for all drug abusers, but particularly for women who are pregnant or responsible for children.

Less than one percent of federal anti-drug funding was aimed at treatment for women—and even less for pregnant women. A survey of seventy-eight drug-treatment programs in New York City found that the vast majority of them refused treatment to poor pregnant women on drugs; 87 percent denied treatment to pregnant women on Medicaid who were addicted to crack. Across the country, two-thirds of hospitals reported that they had no place to refer drug-addicted pregnant women for treatment.[171]

Much of this reluctance to care for pregnant substance abusers is attributable to treatment providers' fears about potentially catastrophic lawsuits that may be brought on behalf of children with injuries that sympathetic juries might be persuaded to blame on their mother's care during pregnancy.[172] A similar (and, unfortunately, all too realistic) fear about potential malpractice liability had been a significant factor in hospitals' attempts to force court-ordered cesareans on women.[173]

And even when drug and alcohol treatment programs *are* nominally available to pregnant women, their lack of child care effectively bars women's participation. Moreover, researchers report, "[p]redominantly male staffs and clients are often hostile to female clients and employ a confrontational style of therapy that makes many women uncomfortable."[174]

Many women's needs go well beyond drug treatment. They also require housing and physical safety—havens from a street culture of sexism, drugs, and violence. Studies of substance-abusing women reveal a startlingly high incidence of rape, incest, and physical battering.[175] Many are trapped in relationships with battering men who themselves abuse drugs or alcohol. Indeed, substance abuse may represent an attempt at self-medication, a response to unbearable anxiety and physical violence.[176] We need to provide a range of treatment models: residential "rehab" in therapeutic communities with stays of varying lengths, neighborhood-based outpatient clinics, 12-step groups, acupuncture. Individuals find sobriety by different routes, often only after a series of attempts. But drug treatment alone, even if designed for women, will not necessarily suffice. It should be coordinated with comprehensive programs which provide women with accessible and user-friendly medical and social services: prenatal care, therapeutic day care, parenting classes, family planning, and adult education.

Several successful programs include continuing contact with a consistently available case manager, advocate, or community intervenor. Harbor Clinic at UCLA, for example, provides prenatal, obstetric, and pediatric care as well as a case manager to serve as an advocate for women with social service agencies and the criminal justice system.[177] Martin Luther King Hospital, also in Los Angeles, provides a home-intervention program for families with babies up to 18 months old. Community intervention workers intensively trained in mothering techniques for drug-exposed babies visit the home twice a week to work with the family. Project Futures in Chicago runs a neighborhood center offering prenatal and postpartum medical care, group therapy, drug treatment, education, and parenting classes. Particularly high-risk families may be placed in a structured residential setting. Trained mothers from the community make three home visits a week during early stages of parent drug treatment, then once a week, with daily phone calls. The outreach worker mothers also help participating adults form support groups.[178]

These are labor-intensive programs. In a sense, they attempt to furnish surrogate aunts and grandmothers who can both nurture and scold young mothers into turning around their lives. These programs not only provide women with support; they pose an insistent demand for self-transformation, for taking responsibility for one's children and for oneself.

Pregnancy can be a window of opportunity for a substance-abusing woman, providing a vital impetus for change. But the wider community has to go beyond developing and funding programs designed for pregnant drug users. We have to begin, as a society, to address, finally and fully, the brutal, seemingly hopeless conditions of life that have led so many poor women to seek such an illusory and destructive refuge.

Notes

1. Lynn Paltrow, "Criminal Prosecutions against Pregnant Women: National Update and Overview," *ACLU Reproductive Freedom Project*, April 1992, p. i.

2. Kevin B. Zeese, *Drug Testing Legal Manual* (New York: Clark Boardman, 1990), Sect. 8.09.

3. Lynn Paltrow, "When Becoming Pregnant Is a Crime," *Criminal Justice Ethics*, Winter/Spring 1990, p. 41.

4. See, e.g., *State v. Young*, No. C569593 (Charleston Ct. Gen. Sess. Nov. 15, 1989). One of the most bizarre cases involved a pregnant Native American woman jailed in Fargo, N.D., for reckless endangerment of her fetus because she was addicted to paint sniffing. Hearing that the woman was considering an abortion, an anti-abortion group styling itself the "Lambs of Christ" offered her up to $10,000 to carry the pregnancy to term. The woman, whose six children had been taken away from her, ultimately did have an abortion. See Gina Kolata, "Woman in Abortion Dispute Ends Her Pregnancy," *New York Times*, Feb. 26, 1992, p. A10, col. 4.

5. Victoria Churchville, "D.C. Judge Jails Woman as Protection for Fetus," *Washington Post*, July 23, 1988, p. A1. The judge's action was particularly ironic in light of the scandalously bad conditions for pregnant women in jail. Prison systems throughout the country have been sued; lawyers for incarcerated women blame inadequate medical care for the large number of miscarriages and poor birth outcomes. "A California study in 1983 found that less than half of prison pregnancies ended in live births and 30 percent of them suffered miscarriages. In Alameda County's Santa Rita Jail, 73 percent of the pregnant women were miscarrying, fifty times the state

average" (Ellen Barry, "Quality of Prenatal Care for Incarcerated Women Challenged," *Youth Law News*, National Center for Youth Law, 6: 6 [Nov.-Dec. 1985], cited in Susan Faludi, *Backlash: The Undeclared War against American Women* [New York: Crown, 1991], notes for p. 426, p. 537).

6. See *State v. Inzar*, No. 90CRS6960–61, Robeson Cty., N.C., April 9, 1991.

7. *Johnson v. State*, 578 So. 2d 419 (Fla. 5th DCA 1991), rev'd 602 So. 2d 1288 (Fla. 1992).

8. Jennifer Warren, "Woman Is Acquitted in Test of Obligation to an Unborn Child," *Los Angeles Times*, Feb. 27, 1987, p. 1.

9. "Doctors Aren't Policemen . . . ," *San Diego Tribune*, Feb. 28, 1987, p. C3, col. 1.

10. Daniel C. Carson, "Bill Offered—Based on Pamela Rae Stewart Case," *San Diego Union*, Mar. 7, 1987, p. A3, col. 1. The legislation was not adopted.

11. I have discussed these earlier cases in Janet Gallagher, "The Fetus and the Law: Whose Life Is It Anyway?" *Ms.* 62 (Sept. 1984); Janet Gallagher, "Prenatal Invasions and Interventions: What's Wrong With Fetal Rights," 10 *Harvard Women's Law Journal* 9 (Spring 1987); and Janet Gallagher, "Fetus As Patient," in Sherrill Cohen and Nadine Taub, eds., *Reproductive Laws for the 1990s* (Clifton, NJ: Humana Press, 1991), pp. 155–206.

12. "Girl Detained to Protect Fetus," *Wisconsin State Journal*, Aug. 16, 1985, p. 2, cited in Faludi, *Backlash*, p. 425.

13. See, e.g., Jeffrey A. Parness and Susan K. Pritchard, "To Be or Not to Be: Protecting the Unborn's Potentiality of Life," 51 *University of Cincinnati Law Review* 257 (1982); John A. Robertson, "Procreative Liberty and the Control of Conception, Pregnancy, and Childbirth," 69 *Virginia Law Review* 405 (1983).

14. See, e.g., Watson A. Bowes Jr. and Brad Selgestad, 59 *Obstetrics and Gynecology* 209 (1981); Ronna Jurow and Richard H. Paul, "Cesarean Delivery without Maternal Consent," 63 *Obstetrics and Gynecology* 596 (1984).

15. See, e.g., *Jefferson v. Griffin Spalding County Hospital Authority*, 247 Ga. 86, 274 S.E.2d 457 (1981); "*In re Madyun Fetus*," *Daily Washington Law Reporter*, Oct. 29, 1986, p. 2233, col. 3.

16. *Smith v. Brennan*, 157 A.2d 497 (N.J. 1960).

17. Veronika E. B. Kolder, Janet Gallagher, and Michael T. Parsons, "Court-Ordered Obstetrical Interventions," 316 *New England Journal of Medicine* 1192 (May 7, 1987).

18. Kolder, Gallagher, and Parsons, "Court-Ordered Obstetrical Interventions."

19. P. Soloff, S. Jewell, and L. Roth, "Civil Commitment and the Rights of the Unborn," 136 *American Journal of Psychiatry* 114 (1979).

20. For a discussion of several "coma baby" cases and of the pregnancy excep-

tion imposed on state living-will statutes by Right to Life lobbying, see Gallagher, "Fetus as Patient," pp. 168–70.

21. See, e.g., John E. B. Meyers, "Abuse and Neglect of the Unborn: Can the State Intervene?" 23 *Duquesne Law Review* 1 (Fall 1984).

22. "Healthy Fetal Signs," *New York Times*, April 22, 1991, p. 16, col. 1.

23. *Grodin v. Grodin*, 102 Mich. App. 396, 301 N.W.2d 869 (1980).

24. *Roe v. Wade*, 410 U.S. 113 (1973).

25. See Kristin Luker, *Abortion and the Politics of Motherhood* (Berkeley: University of California Press, 1984), pp. 158–192; and Faludi, *Backlash*, pp. 400–453.

26. Dorothy Roberts, "Punishing Drug Addicts Who Have Babies: Women of Color, Equality, and the Right of Privacy," 104 *Harvard Law Review* 1419 (May 1991).

27. Historian Carroll Smith-Rosenberg has pointed out that the Victorian discussion of sex and reproduction functioned as a "metaphoric discourse in which the physical body symbolized the social body and physical and sexual disorder stood for social discord and danger" (Smith-Rosenberg, *Disorderly Conduct: Visions of Gender in Victorian America* [New York: Knopf, 1985], p. 40). In the mid-nineteenth century, men "molded the twin themes of birth control and abortion (always defining them as women's decisions) into condensed symbols of national danger and decay" (Smith-Rosenberg, *Disorderly Conduct*, p. 180).

28. See, e.g., Faludi, *Backlash*, pp. 27–29.

29. See, e.g., Smith-Rosenberg, *Disorderly Conduct*, pp. 217–244.

30. See, e.g., Smith-Rosenberg, *Disorderly Conduct*, pp. 238–239; Tamar Jacoby, "Be Fruitful or Be Sorry" (review of Ben J. Wattenberg's *The Birth Dearth*), *New York Times Book Review*, July 13, 1987, p. 9; and Wayne King, "Robertson Urges New U.S. Policy to Increase U.S. Birth Rate," *New York Times*, Oct. 24, 1987, p. A9, col. 1.

31. See Faludi, *Backlash*, pp. 27–35.

32. See Joan Bertin, "Regulating Reproduction," and Uma Narayan, "The Discriminatory Nature of Industrial Health-Hazard Policies and Some Implications for Third World Women," both in this volume.

33. For an excellent discussion, see Laurie Nsiah-Jefferson, "Reproductive Laws, Women of Color, and Low-Income Women," in Cohen and Taub, eds., *Reproductive Laws for the 1990s*, pp. 23–67.

34. I examined eleven cases in Gallagher, "Prenatal Invasions."

35. See, e.g., Gallagher, "Prenatal Invasions"; Nancy K. Rhoden, "The Judge in the Delivery Room: The Emergence of Court-Ordered Caesareans," 74 *University of California Law Review* 701 (1987); Lawrence J. Nelson, Brian P. Buggy, and Carol J. Weil, "Forced Medical Treatment of Pregnant Women: Compelling Each to Live As Seems Good to the Rest," 37 *Hastings Law Journal* 703 (1986); Dawn Johnsen, "The Creation of Fetal

Rights: Conflicts with Women's Constitutional Rights: Liberty, Privacy, and Equal Protection," 95 *Yale Law Journal* 599 (1986); Note, "Recovery for Prenatal Injuries: The Right of a Child against Its Mother," 10 *Suffolk University Law Review* 582 (1986); Note, "Parental Liability for Prenatal Injury," 14 *Columbia Journal of Law and Social Problems* 47 (1978); Jeffrey A. Parness, "The Duty to Prevent Handicaps: Laws Promoting the Prevention of Handicaps to Newborns," 5 *Western New England Law Review* 431 (1983); Parness and Pritchard, " 'To Be or Not to Be' "; Note, "The Fetal Patient and the Unwilling Mother: A Standard for Judicial Intervention," 14 *Pacific Law Journal* 1065 (1983); John A. Robertson, "The Right to Procreate and In Utero Fetal Therapy," 3 *Journal of Legal Medicine* 333 (1982); Note, "Constitutional Limitations on State Intervention in Prenatal Care," 67 *Virginia Law Review* 1051 (1981).

36. In its 1973 opinion recognizing a woman's right to choose abortion, the Supreme Court had laid out a three-part scheme of pregnancy. In the first trimester, the woman could—in consultation with her doctor—freely choose to terminate her pregnancy. In the constitutional balance established by the Court, during the early stage of pregnancy a woman's right to privacy outweighs any possible state interest in regulating abortion. In the second stage of pregnancy, the government could impose certain regulations on abortion, but only those "reasonably related" to the protection of the woman's health. In the third stage of pregnancy, described by the court as following "viability," the government is permitted to make regulations protective of its "compelling state interest" in the "potential human life" and may even forbid those abortions not necessary to preserve the life or health of the woman (*Roe v. Wade* at 164–165). For a detailed examination of viability, see Nan Hunter, "Time Limits on Abortion," in Cohen and Taub, eds., *Reproductive Laws for the 1990s*, pp. 129–154.

37. *Jefferson v. Griffin Spalding County Hospital Authority*, 247 Ga. 86, 274 S.E.2d 457 (1981). Ironically, before *Jefferson*, *Roe* had been cited frequently as a patient's rights case. See Gallagher, "Prenatal Invasions," pp. 17–21.

38. "Mother Nature Reverses on Appeal," 70 *Medical Association of Georgia* 451 (1981). For descriptions of five other cases where doctors proved wrong and for discussion of overreliance on C-sections, see Gallagher, "Fetus as Patient."

39. Veronika E. B. Kolder, "Women's Health Law: A Feminist Perspective" (Aug. 1985, unpublished manuscript), cited in Gallagher, "Prenatal Invasions," pp. 9–10.

40. *In re A.C.*, 533 A.2d 611 (D.C. App. 1987) at 613, rev'd 573 A.2d 1235 (D.C. App. 1990).

41. Faludi, *Backlash*, p. 436.

42. "In this technique, a transducer sends sound waves through the amniotic fluid so they bounce off fetal structures and are reflected back, either as a still

image (scan) or, more frequently, as real-time moving images. . . ."(Rosalind Petchesky, "Fetal Images: The Power of Visual Culture in the Politics of Reproduction," 13 *Feminist Studies* 263, p. 273 [Summer 1987]).

43. "Life Before Birth," *Life*, April 30, 1965.

44. Video jacket blurb, "The Miracle of Life," Swedish TV Corp./WGBH, 1982.

45. Petchesky, "Fetal Images," p. 264.

46. Bernard Nathanson, *The Silent Scream* (Anaheim, CA: American Portrait Films, 1985), videotape.

47. Petchesky, "Fetal Images," p. 264.

48. Sandra J. O'Connor, dissenting, in *Akron v. Akron Center for Reproductive Health*, 462 U.S. 416 (1983).

49. See, e.g., W. H. Clewell et al., "A Surgical Approach to the Treatment of Fetal Hydrocephalus," 306 *New England Journal of Medicine* 1320 (1982).

50. "Treating the Unborn: Surgical Miracles inside the Womb," *Life*, April 1983, cover story.

51. See, e.g., Robertson, "The Right to Procreate and In Utero Fetal Therapy" (in note 35, above).

52. In the months after Justice O'Connor's heavily publicized dissent in the 1983 Supreme Court case, *Akron v. Akron Center for Reproductive Health*, in which she declared that advances in medical technology had placed *Roe* on a "collision course" with itself, two prominent neonatal specialists cited in her opinion wrote to an ACLU attorney to deny that their writings would support such a conclusion. See Nan Hunter, "Time Limits on Abortion," in Cohen and Taub, eds., *Reproductive Laws for the 1990s*.

53. "Lung Illness Curbed in Babies," *New York Times*, Aug. 9, 1990, p. B8, col. 3.

54. Elisabeth Rosenthal, "As More Tiny Infants Live, Choices and Burdens Grow," *New York Times*, Sept. 29, 1991, p. A1, col. 1.

55. Petchesky, "Fetal Images," p. 272.

56. Bernard Nathanson, *The Abortion Papers: Inside the Abortion Mentality* (New York: Fell, 1983), pp. 154–157.

57. The disability rights movement has created a new consciousness about too casual a resort to the language of "defect." See, e.g., Adrienne Asch, "Reproductive Technology and Disability," in Cohen and Taub, eds., *Reproductive Laws for the 1990s*, pp. 69–124; and Anne Finger, *Past Due: A Story of Disability, Pregnancy and Birth* (Seattle: Seal Press, 1990).

58. For a sobering examination of the impact of these new techniques, see Barbara Katz Rothman, *The Tentative Pregnancy: Prenatal Diagnosis and the Future of Motherhood* (New York: Viking Press, 1986).

59. Beverly W. Harrison, *Our Right to Choose: Toward a New Ethic of Abortion* (Boston: Beacon Press, 1983), p. 2.

60. See Laura Sack, "Women and Children First: A Feminist Analysis of the

Primary Caretaker Standard in Child Custody Cases," 4 *Yale Journal of Law and Feminism* 291 (1992).

61. *Stanley v. Illinois* 405 U.S 645 (1972); *Raquel Marie X*, 76 N.Y.2d 387, 559 N.Y.S.2d 588, cert. denied 111 S. Ct. 517 (1990).

62. Harrison, *Our Right to Choose*, p. 145. See also Barbara Katz Rothman, *Recreating Motherhood: Ideology and Technology in a Patriarchal Society* (New York: Norton, 1989).

63. *Johnson v. Calvert*, No. 63-31-90 (Orange County Sup. Ct., Nov. 21, 1990) superseded 851 P.2d 776 (1993).

64. *Jhordan C. v. Mary K.*, 179 Cal. App. 3d 386, 224 Cal. Rptr. 530 (1986).

65. The film features a highly magnified ultrasound image of a 12-week-old fetus during an abortion. Nathanson's narration claims, "Now, for the first time we have the technology to see abortion from the victim's vantage point." Medical experts joined pro-choice spokeswomen in condemning the film as sheer propaganda, pointing out that at 12 weeks, the fetus has no cerebral cortex to receive pain impulses; that no 'scream' is possible without air in the lungs; that fetal movements at this stage are reflexive and without purpose; that the image we see on the screen, along with the model that is continually displayed in front of the screen, is nearly twice the size of a normal 12-week fetus, and so forth. See Petchesky, "Fetal Images," p. 267.

66. So-called right-to-life propaganda invites and plays upon individual, fearful identification with the fetus. See, e.g., Gary Bergel, *When You Were Formed in Secret/Abortion in America*, a double "Intercessors for America" booklet (Reston, VA, 1986), which gives readers a grotesquely personalized version of conception and fetal development: "This is an account about you and your life before birth. . . . [In week one,] your mother had no idea you had 'nested' in her womb. . . . [By week two,] . . . you were able to move with a delightfully easy grace in your buoyant world. By the end of the month you could swim."

67. Faludi quotes "Operation Rescue" leader Randall Terry: "I was conceived out of wedlock. I could've been aborted. I hope and think that my parents wouldn't have, but I'm just real glad they didn't even have the choice" (cited in *Backlash*, p. 407).

68. There have been a number of disturbing manifestations of cult-like treatment of the fetus: a Connecticut clergyman erected a 30-foot poster of a fetus atop his church and marched it through the streets as part of a local parade; another clergyman carries an aborted fetus about the country in a small coffin, displaying it as "Baby Choice"; an artist creates a "reliquary" of fetal remains in formaldehyde.

In fact, the so-called right-to-life movement within the Catholic Church might be most usefully analyzed as a powerful heretical sect which the hierarchy has tried frantically to preempt. "Catholics United for Life" distributes a poster of a bloody fetus grotesquely displayed in a Christ-like pose on a white cross. New York's Cardinal John O'Connor's request that the Knights of Columbus (a Catholic fraternal organization) construct a "Tomb of the Unborn," complete with perpetual gas flame, in every Catholic cemetery was particularly startling to Catholics who know that even full-term infants who die shortly after birth are generally not accorded funeral masses or burial rites by the Church. See Tracy Early, "Cardinal to Knights: Build Tombs for the Unborn," *The Brooklyn Tablet*, Aug. 8, 1992, p. 4.

69. Nathanson, *The Abortion Papers*, pp. 124, 123. Barbara Katz Rothman suggests that the fetus has come to symbolize the solitary individual, "a . . . metaphor for 'man' in space . . . " (*The Tentative Pregnancy*, p. 114). Nathanson, in fact, wrote of the fetus as "the little aquanaut," in "intra-uterine exile" from the human community, "[f]loating in its internal sea. . . . " (*The Abortion Papers*, pp. 119, 117, 120).

70. A 1977 study of Roman Catholic teaching on sexuality notes the shaping influence of the view of the male seed as the "active principle" and of women as "receptacles, or the seed-gardens as it were," for human reproduction (A. Kosnik, W. Carroll, A. Cunningham, R. Modras, and J. Schulte, *Human Sexuality: New Directions in Catholic Thought* [London: Search Press, 1977], p. 59).

71. See, e.g., Bertin, "Regulating Reproduction."

72. For an actual 1973 incident, see Lori B. Andrews, *New Conceptions* (New York: St. Martin's Press, 1984), pp. 155–57.

73. Political fundraisers have found that targeting individual villains in direct mail solicitations generate more contributions than any discussion of issues. They use focus groups to identify such "devil figures." Jesse Helms is a proven fundraising villain for liberal causes or candidates, and Edward Kennedy is a star of solicitations to the right. See Richard L. Berke, "Democrats Try to Find New Crop of Villains," *New York Times*, March 26, 1990, p. A12, col. 6. The evil mother figure serves similar marketing needs for the news media, lending herself to eye- and emotion-catching headlines such as: "Crack Babies: The Worst Threat Is Mom Herself" (*Washington Post*, Aug. 6, 1989, Outlook, p. 1).

74. *New York Post*, May 8, 1990, p. 1.

75. William Plummer, "A Mother's Death, A Baby's Birth," *People*, Aug. 18, 1986, pp. 32–35.

76. "Members Only" ad, broadcast in New York City, 1989.

77. Announcing Michael Dorris, *The Broken Cord* (New York: Harper & Row, 1989). In an illustration emblematic of the blurred line between news and drama, the *Times* television guide later featured a photo of actor Jimmy Smits holding a young boy in the ABC docudrama on Dorris. The photo is captioned "Sins of the Mothers" (*New York Times Television Guide*, Feb. 2–8, 1992, cover).

78. Walter Goodman, "When the Public Business Is the Stuff of Mini-Series," *New York Times*, November 25, 1991, p. C18, col. 5.

79. Dr. George Gerbner, dean of the Annenberg School of Communications at the University of Pennsylvania, was asked about the disproportionately heavy television news coverage of the 1989 attack by a band of black teenagers on a white woman jogger in New York City's Central Park. "[N]ightly news tends to focus on items that satisfy the emotional needs of the audience," said Gerbner, noting that the coverage fed the desire of middle-class viewers "for incidents in the real world that would justify our fears" (quoted in Walter Goodman, "Television and the Attack in Central Park," in "Critic's Notebook," *New York Times*, May 2, 1989, p. C20, col. 1).

80. See, e.g., *In re Baby X*, 293 N.W.2d 736 (Mich. Ct. App. 1980).

81. Crack attracted many more female users than had ever been the case with heroin. Gina Kolata, "On Streets Ruled by Crack, Families Die," *New York Times*, Aug. 11, 1989, p. A13, col. 3.; Elisabeth Wynhausen, "Cracked Out," *Ms.*, Sept. 1988, p. 69.

82. National Association for Perinatal Addiction, Research and Education, *NAPARE: Perinatal Research and Addiction Update: A First National Hospital Incidence Survey* (NAPARE, Chicago: 1988).

83. Committee on Substance Abuse, 1989–90, American Academy of Pediatrics, 86 *Pediatrics* 639 (October 1990).

84. Report of the American Medical Association Board of Trustees, "Legal Interventions during Pregnancy," 264 *Journal of the American Medical Association* 2663 (Nov. 28, 1990).

85. J. C. Barden, "Hospitals Housing Healthy Infants," *New York Times*, July 26, 1992, p. 20, col. 3.

86. Still, it is difficult to sort out the impact of cocaine or other drugs from the effects of other risk factors: the woman and child's low socioeconomic status also usually means inadequate or no prenatal care, poor nutrition, exposure to environmental hazards, etc. See, e.g., Joan Bertin, "Regulating Reproduction," this volume; Sheigla Murphy and Marsha Rosenbaum, "Blame Poverty for Their Learning Disabilities," *New York Times*, Feb. 27, 1991, p. A26, col. 3.

87. Recent reports indicate that the adverse impact of cocaine may have been exaggerated. See, e.g., Linda C. Mayes et al., "The Problem of Prenatal Cocaine Exposure," 267 *Journal of the American Medical Association* 406 (Jan. 15, 1992); Gideon Koren et al., "Bias Against the Null Hypothesis: The Reproductive Hazards of Cocaine," *Lancet* 1440 (Dec. 16, 1989).

88. Rorie Sherman, "Keeping Baby Safe from Mom," *National Law Journal*, Oct. 3, 1988, p. 1.

89. Katha Pollitt, "Fetal Rights: A New Assault on Feminism," *The Nation*, March 26, 1990, p. 1.

90. Pollitt, "Fetal Rights," pp. 414–415. See also Faludi, *Backlash*, pp. 426–

428. And see Rothman: "One New York City subway ad series shows two newborn footprints, one from a full-term and one from a premature infant. The ads read, 'Guess which baby's mother smoked while pregnant?' Another asks, 'Guess which baby's mother drank while pregnant?' And yet another: 'Guess which baby's mother didn't get prenatal care?' I look in vain for the ad that says, 'Guess which baby's mother tried to get by on welfare?'; 'Guess which baby's mother had to live on the streets?'; or 'Guess which baby's mother was beaten by her husband?' " (*Recreating Motherhood*, p. 21).

91. See Paltrow, "Criminal Prosecutions."

92. See, e.g., *In re Stefanel Tyesha C.*, 157 A.D.2d 322 (N.Y. App. Div. 1990).

93. *Cox v. Court of Common Pleas*, No. 88AP856 (Ct. App. for Franklin County [Ohio], Dec. 13, 1988); *State v. Young*, No. C569593 (Charleston Ct. Gen. Sess., Nov. 15, 1989).

94. Terry Van Dell, "D. A. to Prosecute Moms of Addicted Newborns," *Chico Enterprise Record*, Oct. 28, 1988, p. 1A.

95. Mark Swendra, "Drug-Addicted Babies Problem," *Oroville Mercury Register*, Oct. 28, 1988, p. A1.

96. Faludi, *Backlash*, pp. 429–30.

97. For detailed discussion of state drug-testing and child abuse–reporting statutes, see Gloria M. Dabiri and George Bundy Smith, "Prenatal Drug Exposure: The Constitutional Implications of Three Governmental Approaches," 2 *Seton Hall Constitutional Law Journal* 53, 88–100 (1991).

98. See, e.g., *In re Stefanel Tyesha C.*

99. Paltrow, "Criminal Prosecutions," p. iv.

100. Ira Chasnoff et al., "Illicit Drug and Alcohol Use during Pregnancy," 322 *New England Journal of Medicine* 17 (April 26, 1990).

101. Kolder, Gallagher, and Parsons, "Court-Ordered Obstetrical Interventions."

102. Roberts, "Punishing Drug Addicts," p. 1432. She points out that the realities of race create a different perspective on the feminist legal debate over "rights" and "privacy" (pp. 1464–81). For an early and vividly useful discussion of privacy, class, and race, see Mary C. Dunlap, "Where the Person Ends, Does the Government Begin? An Exploration of Present Controversies Concerning 'The Right to Privacy,' " 12 *Lincoln Law Review* 47 (1981).

103. See, e.g., Faludi, *Backlash*.

104. The push to reassert and recontain motherhood can be seen in the anti-abortion drive and its insistence on husband/father notification, the disproportionate media focus on female infertility, the push for father's custody rights, and even Vice President Dan Quayle's attack on television character Murphy Brown's choice to become a single mother—" . . . the anarchy and lack of structure in our inner cities are testament to

how quickly civilization falls apart when the family foundation cracks" (Michael Wines, "Views on Single Motherhood Are Multiple at White House," *New York Times*, May 21, 1992, pp. A1, B16).

105. Roberts, "Punishing Drug Addicts," recounts the history of America's disdain for the motherhood of black women from slavery, through sterilization abuse, to the current disproportionate removal of black children from their mothers' custody. Her critique predates legislative initiatives to cut off any boost in welfare payments to women who bear additional children. See, e.g., Wayne King, "U.S. Approves Trenton Plan for Welfare," *New York Times*, July 21, 1992, p. B1, col. 6.

106. Charles Krauthammer, a syndicated columnist, urged detention of substance-abusing pregnant women in "We Can't Cancel Crack Babies' Futures," *New York Daily News*, Aug. 7, 1989, p. 26.

107. S. 324, Sect. 2919, 118th Ohio General Assembly, Reg. Sess. 1989–90.

108. Roberts, "Punishing Drug Addicts," n. 217.

109. Louisiana State Representative David Duke introduced a bill providing a $100 bonus to women on public assistance who had themselves implanted with Norplant. And, in an editorial that triggered rage among its black staff members and was ultimately retracted, the *Philadelphia Inquirer* asked, "Poverty and Norplant: Can Contraception Reduce the Underclass?" (Dec. 12, 1990, p. A18, col. 1).

110. See, e.g., "Birth Control Penalty Broken," *New York Times*, Aug. 31, 1988, p. A24, col. 5.

111. On "bastardy" laws, see Ann Jones, *Women Who Kill* (New York: Holt, Rinehart, and Winston, 1980), pp. 42–62; and Peter Hoffer and N. E. H. Hull, *Murdering Mothers* (New York: New York University Press, 1981), pp. 13–14.

112. Churchville, "D.C. Judge Jails Woman," p. C8, col. 1.

113. As in the overwhelming majority of criminal cases, most "drug baby" charges were resolved through plea bargains of some sort. See, e.g., *State v. Dawson*, discussed in Paltrow, "Criminal Prosecutions," p. 5.

114. *People v. Hardy*, 188 Mich. App. 305, 469 N.W.2d 50 (Mich. App. 1991); *People v. Bremer*, No. 90-32227-FH (Mich. Cir. Ct. Jan. 3, 1991); *State v. Gray*, 598 N.E.2d 710 (Ohio 1992); *Commonwealth v. Pellegrini*, No. 87970 (Mass. Sup. Ct. Oct. 15, 1990); *State v. Gethers*, 585 So. 2d 1140 (Fla. 4th DCA 1991); *People v. Morabito*, 580 N.Y.S. 2d 843 (N.Y. City Ct. 1992); *Welch v. Commonwealth*, No. 90-CA-1189-MR, (Ky. Ct. App. Feb. 7, 1992); *Commonwealth v. Kemp*, No. 2707 C 1991, Pa. Ct. of Common Pleas, Westmoreland Cy., Dec. 16, 1992).

115. *Johnson v. State*, 578 So. 2d 419 (Fla. 5th DCA 1991), rev'd, 602 So. 2d 1288, 1290 (1992).

116. *Johnson*, pp. 1293–1294, referring to Sect. 415.503(9)(a) 2. ch. 87–90 Sect. 1, Laws of Fla.

117. See, e.g., *Commonwealth v. Welch.* I would argue that reliance on the argument that fetuses have not been defined as children or persons in the law is inadequate. First, statutory definitions are all too easily changed by legislatures. (See, e.g., New Jersey's Child Abuse statute defining children so as to include fetuses: N.J. STAT. ANN. Sect. 30:4c-11 [West 1991].) But beyond that, insistence on a public dismissal of fetal status needlessly offends people of differing beliefs. For most people, it simply will not carry the ethical, emotional, and political weight of the debate. Opposition to "fetal rights"—whether in the forced medical treatment of pregnant women or in punishment of women for their conduct during pregnancy—is better grounded in appeals to women's rights of moral agency, equality, and non-subordination and to the sorts of public policy arguments advanced here.

118. See, e.g., *Commonwealth v. Pellegrini.* While it has not developed as an issue in the cases thus far, the procedural demands that bringing criminal charges against new mothers would place (or should, if constitutional standards were to be observed) upon the already strained resources of hospitals and social service agencies pose powerful public policy arguments against prosecution. For example, there would be significant costs and difficulties associated with securing and maintaining a proper "chain of custody" for the urine samples needed in evidence; doctors and nurses would be required to keep even more detailed and extensive notes of their discussions with women under their care; copies of those medical records would have to be provided to both prosecutors and defense attorneys before any court proceedings; and health care workers would undoubtedly have to spend whole days waiting to testify in overcrowded, backlogged criminal and family courts.

119. "AMA Board of Trustees Report: Legal Interventions During Pregnancy," 264 *Journal of the American Medical Association* 2663 (Nov. 28, 1990), pp. 2667–2668.

120. Under some Supreme Court precedents, prosecution in such a case might be barred by the Eighth Amendment's ban on cruel and unusual punishment.

121. Both criminal prosecutions and neglect or abuse proceedings, for example, raise Fourth Amendment issues of search and seizure, as well as privacy-rights issues involving informed consent to medical treatment. Evidentiary use of women's admissions of drug use or of medical records indicating such use implicate privacy rights to medical confidentiality and physician-patient privilege. For detailed discussion of these concerns, see Dabiri and Smith, "Prenatal Drug Exposure."

122. Lynn Paltrow, "Case Update and Overview of the Arguments against Permitting Forced Surgery, Prosecutions of Pregnant Women, or Civil Sanctions against Them for Their Conduct or Status during Pregnancy" *American Civil Liberties Union Reproductive Freedom Project* (ACLU: New York, 1992), p. 4.

123. *Commonwealth v. Pellegrini*, p. 9.

124. I have argued elsewhere that *Roe* includes a complementary right to choose to give birth. See Janet Gallagher, "*Right to Choose v. Byrne*: Brief Amicus Curiae," 7 *Women's Rights Law Reporter* 285 (1982), pp. 293–296; and Gallagher, "Prenatal Interventions and Invasions," pp. 38–40. The majority opinion in the U.S. Supreme Court's 1992 abortion case, *Planned Parenthood v. Casey*, has made that complementarity of rights explicit: "If indeed the woman's interest in deciding whether to bear and beget a child had not been recognized in *Roe*, the State might as readily restrict a woman's right to choose to carry a pregnancy to term as to terminate it, to further asserted state interests in population control, or eugenics, for example. Yet *Roe* has been sensibly relied upon to counter any such suggestions" (120 L.Ed. 2d 674, 112 S.Ct. 2791, 2811 [1992]).

125. Quoted in Lynn Paltrow, "When Becoming Pregnant Is a Crime," *Criminal Justice Ethics*, Winter/Spring 1990, pp. 41, 42.

126. Roberts, "Punishing Drug Addicts," p. 1427.

127. Roberts, "Punishing Drug Addicts," p. 1423.

128. See Rosalind Petchesky, *Abortion and Women's Choice: The State, Sexuality and Reproductive Freedom*, rev. ed. (Boston: Northeastern University Press, 1990), pp. 84–100.

129. Roberts, "Punishing Drug Addicts," p. 1427.

130. See, e.g., *Carey v. Population Services Int'l.*, 431 U.S. 678 (1977).

131. *Pellegrini* was decided before the U.S. Supreme Court decision in *Planned Parenthood v. Casey*, which substituted the "undue burden" test for the strict scrutiny originally applied in reviewing government restrictions on abortion. It is unclear as yet whether other reproductive privacy rights will be subjected to similar erosion in the federal courts. A growing number of state courts now afford individual rights of privacy greater protection than the federal courts do, relying on state constitutional grounds. See, e.g., *Right to Choose v. Byrne*, 91 N.J. 287, 450 A.2d 925 (1982) (State constitution mandates Medicaid funding for abortion). In any case, Lynn Paltrow (who served as Jennifer Johnson's lawyer in the successful challenge to the Florida prosecution) suggests that the drug prosecutions are so counterproductive that they cannot even withstand the "rational" standard of review, the least stringent level of judicial scrutiny (personal interview, September, 1992).

132. Some fetal rights advocates, like Professor John Robertson, have argued that whatever rights a pregnant woman might have are "waived" by her continuing the pregnancy past viability. See Robertson, "Procreative Liberty and the Control of Conception, Pregnancy, and Childbirth," 69 *Virginia Law Review* 405, 438, and 442. Such an analysis, dubious under any circumstances, makes no sense at all in the substance-abuse context, where "the most severe neurological damage can occur when the mother ingests drugs between the 13th and 52nd day of conception—often before a woman knows she is pregnant" (Judith Larsen, ed., *Drug-Exposed Infants and Their Families: Coordinating Responses of the Legal, Medical and*

Child Protection System [American Bar Association Center on Children and the Law: Washington, D.C. (1990), p. 58]). See also Note, "Maternal Rights and Fetal Wrongs: The Case against the Criminalization of Fetal Abuse," 101 *Harvard Law Review* 974, 998 (1988).

133. *Commonwealth v. Pellegrini*, p. 8.

134. *Commonwealth v. Pellegrini*, p. 8.

135. *Johnson*, p. 1295.

136. See, e.g., "Board of Trustees Report, Law and Medicine: Legal Interventions During Pregnancy," *Journal of the American Medical Association*, November 28, 1990, p. 2663.

137. While it has not been explored in the literature, I think it likely that the harshly punitive attitudes toward pregnant substance abusers create an incentive for abandonment and even infanticide. It is my impression, based on a close reading of the news coverage in one major metropolitan area, that such incidents had already increased due to the anti-abortion movement's success in reducing the social acceptability of, and access to, abortion. See, e.g., "Baby Left in Brooklyn Trash," *New York Times*, Feb. 16, 1991, p. 31, col. 1; "Mom Charged in Baby's Death," *New York Newsday*, Aug. 14, 1990, p. 20; "Dead Baby in Garbage," *New York Newsday*, Aug. 13, 1991, p. 32.

138. *Johnson*, p. 1296.

139. See, e.g., Gina Kolata, "Racial Bias Seen on Pregnant Addicts," *New York Times*, July 20, 1990, p. A-13, col. 1. Some critics note that most of the pregnancy prosecutions have been for the use of crack, a drug most frequently associated with urban African Americans. Prof. Roberts suggests that if "prosecutors had instead chosen to prosecute women addicted to alcohol or prescription medication, the policy of criminalizing prenatal conduct very likely would have suffered a hasty demise" (Roberts, "Punishing Drug Addicts," p. 1436). At least one judge found the racial discrimination argument persuasive, striking as unconstitutional a Minnesota state law which punished the possession of crack more harshly than possession of an equivalent amount of powdered cocaine. See Robb London, "Judge's Overruling of Crack Law Brings Turmoil," *New York Times*, Jan. 11, 1991, p. B5, col. 3.

140. Hon. Francis T. Murphy, "Prejudice Attacks Victims of Prenatal Drug Abuse," *New York Law Journal*, Jan. 29, 1992, p. 37, col. 5.

141. See, e.g., Bertin, "Regulating Reproduction."

142. Angela Bongavoglia, "The Ordeal of Pamela Rae Stewart," *Ms.*, July/August 1987, pp. 92, 201.

143. *State v. Pfannenstiel*, No.1-90-8CR (County Ct. of Laramie, Wy., complaint filed Jan. 5, 1990). The charges were later dismissed.

144. "Father's Cocaine Use May Raise His Child's Risk of Birth Defects," *Boston Globe*, Oct. 14, 1991, p. 36, col.1; "Study Links Cancer in Young

to Fathers' Smoking," *New York Times*, Jan. 24, 1991, p. B8, col. 3; Devra Lee Davis, "Fathers and Fetuses," *New York Times* Op-Ed, Mar. 1, 1991, p. A27, col. 1; Bertin, "Regulating Reproduction"; and Uma Narayan, "The Discriminatory Nature of Industrial Health-Hazard Policies and Some Implications for Third World Women Workers."

145. There have been several arrests for drinking during pregnancy. A Missouri woman was charged with child endangerment and assault after her son allegedly showed signs of fetal alcohol syndrome (Paltrow, "Criminal Prosecutions Against Pregnant Women," p. iii). A Massachusetts woman was prosecuted for motor vehicle homicide when she miscarried after an accident police attributed to her having been driving while intoxicated (*Commonwealth v. Levey*, No. 89-2725-2729 [Super. Ct. Mass. Dec. 4, 1989]). Charges were dropped upon her completion of a treatment program.

146. Headlines shriek " 'Bad' Child Linked to Mom Smoking"—"The more cigarettes a mother smokes, the more behavior problems her children are likely to have, researchers say" (*New York Newsday*, Sept. 4, 1992, p. 4, col. 1 ["The survey didn't ask about fathers' smoking"]); ABC has run anti-smoking spots presenting a ghostly fetus puffing on a cigarette as a deep-voiced narrator intones, "Would you give a cigarette to your unborn child? You do, every time you smoke when you're pregnant" (Fred Rothenberg, "Two Networks Reject Antismoking Spot," *Boston Globe*, Jan. 18, 1985, p. 3, col. 4); Brooklyn's Roman Catholic Diocesan paper features ads warning, "Babies Don't Thrive in Smoke-filled Wombs" (*The Tablet*, June 20, 1987, p. 15). This scolding of pregnant women for smoking, of course, takes place in a country that spends five times as much taxpayer money to subsidize the tobacco industry as to wean smokers from their addiction (Anna Quindlen, "Smoking and Politics," *New York Times*, Aug. 5, 1992, p. A23, col. 1).

147. *People v. Stewart*, No. M508197 (San Diego Mun. Ct., February 26, 1987).

148. *In re A.C.*

149. By 1987, a number of forceful articles opposing the court-ordered cesareans had appeared in legal and medical journals. See, e.g., George Annas, "Forced Caesareans: The Most Unkindest Cut of All," *Hastings Center Report*, June 1982, p. 16; Dawn Johnsen, "The Creation of Fetal Rights: Conflicts with Women's Constitutional Rights: Liberty, Privacy, and Equal Protection," 95 *Yale Law Journal* 599 (1986); Nelson, Buggy, and Weil, "Forced Medical Treatment of Pregnant Women: Compelling Each to Live as Seems Good to the Rest"; Gallagher, "Prenatal Invasions and Interventions"; Nancy Rhoden, "The Judge in the Delivery Room: The Emergence of Court-Ordered Caesareans," 74 *California Law Review* 1951 (1987).

150. A 1986 survey of hospitals revealed that 81 percent of the pregnant women subjected to court-ordered interventions were black, Asian, or

Hispanic; 44 percent were unmarried; 24 percent did not speak English as their primary language; and none were private patients (see Kolder, Gallagher, and Parsons, "Court-Ordered Obstetrical Interventions").

151. It is no coincidence that Lynn Paltrow, formerly of the ACLU Reproductive Freedom Project and now with the Center for Reproductive Law and Policy, served as a lawyer for Pamela Rae Stewart, the Carder family, and Jennifer Johnson. Paltrow marshalled legal arguments, press coverage, and friends of court into an effective tide of outrage.

152. American College of Obstetricians and Gynecologists Committee on Ethics, "Statement on Court-Ordered Cesarean Section for Dying Woman," ACOG: Washington, D.C., Nov. 24, 1987.

153. Some eighty of the most prominent legal, medical, and bioethics scholars and commentators in the country signed an amicus brief filed by the American Society of Law and Medicine.

154. The sole dissenter argued essentially that pregnant women cannot be treated like other persons because " . . . [U]niquely, the viable unborn child is literally captive within the mother's body" (*In re A.C.*, p. 1256).

155. See Gallagher, "Prenatal Invasions," pp. 23–28.

156. *In re A.C.*, p. 1244.

157. See also *In Re Baby Boy Doe*, 632 N.E.2d 326 (Ill. App. 1st Dist. 1994).

158. Statement by Christine St. Andre, administrator of the George Washington University Medical Center, November 28, 1990.

159. *Stallman v. Youngquist*, 531 N.E.2d 355 (Ill. 1988).

160. *Stallman v. Youngquist*, p. 360.

161. *International Union, UAW v. Johnson Controls, Inc.*, 111 S. Ct. 1196 (1991).

162. See, e.g., *Santosky v. Kramer* 455 U.S. 745 (1981).

163. See Dabiri and Smith, "Prenatal Drug Exposure."

164. Here, as in the criminal prosecutions, the realities of class and race mean that poor women of color will be disproportionately subject to testing and to the possible loss of their children by comparison with white women substance abusers. And (again) there are also gender disparities. A father arrested for possession of marijuana or driving while intoxicated (or beating the mother of his child) is not reported to neglect and abuse authorities (Panel presentation by Lynn Paltrow, Bar Association of the City of New York, Jan. 28, 1992).

165. In New York state, the turnover rate at private agencies in 1988 was 48 percent (See Michael Winerip, "A Child's Cry Goes Unheard: 'Tess is Dead,' " *New York Times*, March 24, 1989, B1, col. 1). Family Court judges were sometimes reduced to spending less than five minutes on a case (See Clara Hemphill, "The Numbing Caseload of Family Court," *New York Newsday*, March 9, 1989, p. 6). The caseload had increased by 50 percent in five years, noted one legal newspaper, and, "Since 1985, 40

percent of the bench—17 of 42 judges—have departed . . . " (Edward A. Adams, "Report Assails Family Courts' Physical Plants," *New York Law Journal*, May 8, 1989, p. 1, col. 5).

166. Martin Tolchin, "Panel Seeks Foster Care Reform," *New York Times*, Feb. 27, 1991, p. B3, col. 5.

167. James C. McKinley, "Foster Child Declared Brain Dead; Police Investigate Possible Abuse," *New York Times*, Sept. 14, 1989, p. B13, col. 3; "Bronx Woman Held in Death of a Foster Child, 22 Months," *New York Times*, July 4, 1990, p. 35, col. 6; Thomas Morgan, "Brooklyn Woman and Boyfriend Charged in Sex Abuse of 4 Sisters," *New York Times*, Nov. 21, 1990, p. B1, col. 4. While my own clipping file on such incidents is drawn only from New York City newspapers, I regard these as symptomatic of conditions in many foster care systems around the country staggering under the impact of the crack epidemic.

168. See, e.g., N.Y. Social Services Law Sect. 384 (b) 7.

169. A spokeswoman for the North American Coalition on Adoptable Children, quoted in J. C. Barden, "Counselling to Keep Families Together," *New York Times*, Sept. 21, 1991, p. A18, col. 1.

170. Neil A. Lewis, "U.S. Judge Rules District of Columbia Is Abusing Rights of Foster Children," *New York Times*, April 19, 1991, p. A10, col. 1.

171. Faludi, *Backlash*, p. 429.

172. "Most centers worry about the liability, so as soon as they discover a woman is pregnant, they refuse her or throw her out of the program. . . . Even emergency detoxification programs don't want pregnant women" (Molly McNulty, "Pregnancy Police: The Health Policy and Legal Implications of Punishing Pregnant Women for Harm to Their Fetuses," 16 *New York University Review of Law and Social Change* 277 [1988], n. 167, p. 301). See also Dr. Wendy Chavkin, Testimony Before House Select Committee on Children, Youth and Families, April 27, 1989.

173. See Gallagher, "Fetus as Patient," pp. 191–193.

174. Roberts, "Punishing Drug Addicts," p. 1449, citing Dr. Wendy Chavkin, "Drug Addiction and Pregnancy: Policy Crossroads," 80 *American Journal of Public Health* 483, 485 (1990).

175. " . . . 80 to 90 percent of female drug addicts and alcoholics have been victims of rape or incest" (Paltrow, "Pregnancy as a Crime," p. 45). See also Paltrow, "Criminal Prosecutions," p. iv, n. 13.

176. Hortensia Amaro et al., "Violence During Pregnancy and Substance Abuse," 80 *American Journal of Public Health* 575, 578 (1990).

177. Judith Larsen, "Creative Community Programs in Miami, Los Angeles and Chicago," in Larsen, ed., *Drug Exposed Infants and Their Families*, pp. 51–62, 56–57.

178. Larsen, "Creative Community Programs," p. 60.

Regulating Reproduction

Joan E. Bertin

A few years ago the Supreme Court decided that women who are fertile can work in jobs that may pose a risk to a fetus, and that employers may not deny them good employment, or require them to be sterilized, to promote "fetal safety."[1] The employer's "fetal protection" policy was purportedly designed to protect fetal health, but it failed to protect men from reproductive and other health risks. Protection for the fetus under such policies, moreover, extracted a high price from women workers— sterility or loss of access to potentially "more than 20 million jobs."[2]

The Court's decision recognized that laws requiring employers to maintain safe conditions are intended to protect women as well as men, and that women are entitled to make their own decisions about the possible effects of their employment on the health of a potential or actual fetus: "It is no more appropriate for the courts than it is for individual employers to decide whether a woman's reproductive role is more important to herself and her family than her economic role."

Medical ethicist Thomas Murray proposes a useful analogy to dramatize a basic defect in fetal protection policies. He compares the fertile woman working in a battery plant to the farmer who loses his farm and decides to move to an industrial area where employment opportunities are better:

Taking the job means a low, but genuine threat of cancer to his children. It also means better food, housing, clothing and health care, as well as greater peace of mind for him. Would he be morally wrong in taking the job—and the risk it entails . . . ? Or is he making a reasonable judgment?[3]

380

Corporate "fetal protectionism," Murray observes, deprives women of the opportunity to make "reasonable judgments" of this kind, and "sentimentalizes women and oversimplifies their moral choices . . . as if their only important moral attribute were pregnancy or pregnancy potential." As Murray's analogy reveals, fetal protection policies reduce women to single-dimension beings with limited and closely defined roles.

These policies reflect the assumption that fetal well-being will be enhanced if fertile women just stay home, thereby eliminating work-related risks of undefined probability and severity. This approach discounts or disregards the positive effects of women's employment, along with the risk that families of women displaced from their jobs by the policies will lose insurance benefits and fall into poverty. The policies adopt a "zero risk" approach to pregnancy, but only when the perceived risk derives from certain types of employment. The implementation of these policies primarily in male-intensive industries, but not in jobs with similar risks where women have traditionally worked,[4] suggests that it is women that do not conform to an idealized and sentimentalized female image who are most likely to be identified as needing involuntary "protection." "Fetal protection" mirrors traditional social conventions and expectations defining how women should fulfill their maternal duties and valuing women for their procreative activities, but not their economic contributions to family welfare.

Such policies gained credibility and respectability, however, because they were supported by reference to an ostensibly objective body of scientific data on reproductive risk. As Irving K. Zola noted more than 20 years ago:

> . . . medicine is becoming a major institution of social control, nudging aside, if not incorporating, the more traditional institutions of religion and law. It is becoming the new repository of truth, the place where absolute and often final judgments are made by supposedly morally neutral and objective experts. And these judgments are made not in the name of virtue or legitimacy, but in the name of health. . . . [T]oday the prestige of *any* proposal is immensely enhanced, if not justified, when it is expressed in the idiom of medical science.[5]

Because of this power, science—especially in the form of biological determinism—has often been used to advance social goals.[6] Social arrangements between the sexes have historically influenced scientific thought and inquiry in ways that facilitate the continuation of those arrangements, by suggesting or "proving" that they are biologically predetermined. Or are they?

Some Historical Background on Gender
Bias in Science

The way in which we perceive the world is shaped by our experiences, and this is no less true of scientists than others. The framing of questions for research, the conduct of investigations, the interpretation of data, the language employed, and other aspects of scientific inquiry are all influenced by societal premises. Cultural attitudes about women may thus find expression in scientific conclusions, which in turn serve to reinforce the original premise, along with social policy and legal relationships that are an integral part of the cultural arrangements.

Stephen Jay Gould speaks authoritatively and eloquently about cultural influence on the scientific process:

> Science, since people must do it, is a socially embedded activity. It progresses by hunch, vision, and intuition. . . . Facts are not pure and unsullied bits of information; culture also influences what we see and how we see it. . . . [S]ome topics are invested with enormous social importance but blessed with very little reliable information. When the ratio of data to social impact is so low, a history of scientific attitudes may be little more than an oblique record of social change.[7]

Gould documents at length the process by which the "science" of intelligence testing and quantification was used "invariably to find that oppressed and disadvantaged groups—races, classes or sexes—are innately inferior and deserve their status."[8] Other, more mundane, examples abound. For example, Darwin asserted that animals mated for life and that most female animals were monogamous. Recent field studies employing sophisticated methods for observing animal behavior have shown, however, that in most animal species, "infidelity is rife and females often have the wandering eye."[9] It probably is not a coincidence that Darwin's observations of animals match the idealized (but inaccurate) image of the marital relationship in Victorian society.[10]

The "craniology" movement of the nineteenth century sought to prove that intelligence was a function of brain size and to establish thereby male intellectual preeminence over women.[11] Darwin sought to "prove" the point through different logic, but with the same result:

> The chief distinction in the intellectual powers of the two sexes is shown in man's attaining to a higher eminence, in whatever he takes up, than can woman. . . . if men are capable of a decided pre-

Darwin

eminence over women in many subjects, the average of mental power in man must be above that of woman. . . . [12]

At the end of the nineteenth century, the United States Surgeon General asserted that "the brain of a woman [is] inferior in at least nineteen different ways to the brain of a man."[13]

The premise of women's intellectual inferiority served to rationalize women's exclusion from intellectual endeavors, so that they could devote themselves to the domestic activities to which they were said to be naturally suited. It was postulated as a scientific fact that education and intellectual activity physically undermined women's reproductive capacities.[14] This conclusion derived from a theory that the brain and the reproductive system were in competition in the body, and that one was used only at the expense of the other.[15] Because women were assumed to be intellectually inferior anyway, the medical advice to them was almost a foregone conclusion:

> Because reproduction was women's grand purpose in life, doctors agreed that women had to concentrate all their energy downward toward the womb. . . . At puberty, girls were advised to take a great deal of bed rest in order to help focus their strength on regulating their periods—though this might take years. Too much reading or intellectual stimulation in the fragile stage of adolescence could result in permanent damage to the reproductive organs, and sickly, irritable babies. . . . Every mental effort of the mother-to-be could deprive the unborn child of [phosphates, a] vital nutrient, or would so overtax the woman's own system that she would be driven to insanity.[16]

Medical science, in the person of a Harvard professor, declared that "higher education would cause women's uteruses to atrophy."[17]

In the nineteenth century, specific attitudes about women—their "natural" tendencies to nurture and tend to others, their self-sacrificing nature, their inability to compete with men in intellectual endeavors, their physical weakness, their dependence on men—were all supported by reference to medical science.[18] That these contentions now seem silly does not address the seriousness with which the assertions were accepted as scientifically valid at the time, nor does it suggest that we are any less susceptible to the influences of our own cultural arrangements and expectations:

> The leaders of craniometry were not conscious political ideologues. They regarded themselves as servants of their numbers, apostles of objectivity. And they confirmed all the common prejudices of com-

fortable white males—that blacks, women, and poor people occupy their subordinate roles by the harsh dictates of nature. Shall we believe that science is different today simply because we share the cultural context of most practicing scientists and mistake its influence for objective truth? . . . By what right, other than our own biases, can we . . . hold that science now operates independently of culture and class?[19]

Current Evidence of Bias in Science

As these historical examples demonstrate, social and cultural arrangements and expectations plainly can and do affect the questions that scientists ask and how they interpret information. Science is sometimes used to support existing arrangements or understandings, by demonstrating their inevitability. Culturally created expectations may preclude certain questions from being asked in the first place, and may cause discordant (but accurate) information to be disregarded. Historical examples are particularly useful because 20/20 hindsight permits us to discern biases that no longer exist, while contemporary assumptions that influence scientific inquiry are sometimes almost invisible because they are so widely shared—they are "cultural background noise."

In scientific research on reproduction and childrearing, gender-based stereotypes and norms are particularly entrenched. As a result, certain tendencies are apparent in both the way in which research is designed and the way in which the results are interpreted. These are some principal themes: (1) overstatement of women's responsibility (both biological and behavioral) for the well-being of the next generation; (2) underestimation of the significance of paternal factors (both biological and behavioral) that influence the well-being of the next generation; and (3) the use of scientific maxims to reinforce social behavioral norms, particularly the definition of appropriate maternal behavior. These tendencies derive from some of the same stereotypes that were prevalent in Darwin's day but have been transformed by contemporary life. For example, while women are not expected to engage exclusively in childbearing and childrearing activities, there is still the assumption that such responsibilities have primacy over others for women, and that women are more gratified by those activities than by other activities in their lives. A corresponding stereotype relegates women, but not men, to self-sacrificing behavior to advance the interests of children and spouses even at their own expense. Women are still viewed as being more skilled and "natural" caregivers, tending more towards helping and nurturing professions such as teaching, nursing, secretarial, and social work jobs.[20]

The sight of a woman in a pigments factory or a battery plant still poses problems of "cognitive dissonance," as is apparent from corporate medical policies discussed below.

How the Process Works: A Case Study

Overstatement of maternal responsibility for pregnancy outcome is nowhere more apparent than in corporate "fetal protection" policies that assume that all fertile women are equally (and always) likely to be pregnant, and that the fetus is always hypersusceptible to the effects of toxic agents. These policies became prevalent in the late 1970s and 1980s, particularly in lucrative industrial jobs and occupations that had recently become available to women as a result of non-discrimination laws. As a result, women of childbearing age were excluded from numerous employment opportunities unless they could prove their sterility, and some women did submit to surgical sterilization in order to qualify for full employment rights.[21] The policies apparently developed at the direction of corporate medical departments.[22]

An example drawn from the 1991 Supreme Court case displays the logic that led to the formulation of one such policy.[23] The medical expert who took credit for initiating that company's fetal protection policy relied specifically on historical experimental evidence and anecdotal data to support his view that the fetus is hypersensitive to the effects of lead. He discounted reports of health effects in the wives and children of male lead workers, however, on the ground that they were from "older literature," and said that the animal studies demonstrating a male-mediated effect on offspring from paternal lead exposure were "not significant." As to paternally mediated effects from lead, he conceded that "it has been reported"; but he concluded that there is no "great risk of any potential damage . . . to the germ cell."[24] He supported his opinion that exposed males and their children are not at risk with testimony that he had "seen a gentleman with chronic lead poisoning and renal failure conceive children and they're quite normal."[25] Asked to explain why he did not counsel men to reduce their lead levels when they were planning to have children, he answered: "Because I can't control that situation."[26] The plain implication is that women alone can and should be controlled to promote reproductive health.

The same expert testified that prenatal lead exposure can cause hyperactivity in a later born child. This was based on his experience with a single case. He attributed the hyperactivity to prenatal exposure even though he knew of no measurements of blood lead until the child, who had also been exposed to lead after birth, was at least a year old. He further conceded that there were other causes of hyperactivity in children that, in this case, had not been excluded.[27]

A research scientist involved in the same case described the various sources of lead to which children may be exposed, including lead in house dust and lead brought home on clothing or personal articles, but then cautioned:

> So much depends on the cleanliness of the house, so much depends on the care-giving characteristics of the *mother*, does she keep the child clean, does she keep the house clean.[28]

This expert also acknowledged the evidence of paternally mediated effects of lead in experimental data, but did not think that data merited cautionary employment policies because, although "suggestive," there were too many "uncertainties" over dosages, study design, etc.[29] He likewise acknowledged the possibility of chromosomal damage. As to the possibility of an effect on offspring from paternal exposure, he said, "I don't know. It's a good question."[30]

These excerpts are representative of the arguments propounded in support of the premise of fetal hypersusceptibility to toxic agents. First, inferences are permitted in favor of a finding of fetal risk. This includes the use of animal data, anecdotal and historical information, studies with poor methodology or inadequate control of confounders (paternal factors are rarely controlled for in studies of maternally mediated effects of toxic agents), and studies extrapolating from high dose to low dose. In contrast, the same research limitations are said to render data demonstrating male-mediated risk to pregnancy outcome unreliable or inconclusive—far too inadequate a basis to justify policy formulation or even precautionary warnings. Notwithstanding evidence of genetic, chromosomal, or other mechanisms by which heritable effects could occur as a result of exposure of either parent, the prevailing assumption is that women's exposure is what counts: "Because after all, the fetus is in the woman's body. And it is the transfer of the lead through her body across the placenta to the fetus that is what is having the direct effect."[31]

Researchers whose findings were cited by witnesses for Johnson Controls published a commentary that demonstrates the flaws in this logic:

> Considerable attention has been given to characterizing the impact of intrauterine exposure to lead on children's growth and development. Much less investigative effort has been devoted to assessing the effect of paternal exposure to lead on infant outcome. In our studies, we did not measure paternal exposure and *therefore cannot rule this out* as a contributing factor in our findings. . . . The posi-

tion that a given level of paternal but not maternal exposure is acceptable is without logical foundation and unsupportable on empirical grounds.[32]

Evidence of any fetal risk, even if inconclusive or poorly documented, has in the past ordinarily been sufficient to trigger corporate "protective" responses based on the assumption that there is no safe level of exposure. The premise of fetal hypersusceptibility, essential to such policies, is unproven in virtually every case.[33] The male (and his offspring) are presumed safe from the effects of toxic agents, until risk is conclusively demonstrated. Thus, with women there is often no inquiry into the extent or probability of risk at a given level of exposure, nor is there a consideration of comparative risks—for example, the risk associated with working as opposed to the risks associated with unemployment and poverty. This massive oversimplification of research reflects the fundamental assumption that the choices involved are simple for women. Between working at a job that involves exposure to some fetal risk, and not working; between exposure to some potentially hazardous agent and avoiding exposure, the decisions are expected to be foregone conclusions. This philosophy is stated plainly by the editor of the medical journal *Reproductive Toxicology*, Anthony Scialli, M. D., regarding the exclusion of women from jobs involving exposure to lead. Although he concedes that "this agent remains one of the most dangerous elements to which we expose workers of both sexes," removal of all fertile women is justified because of the "absolute need to protect the fetus."[34] This may be a personal article of faith, but it plainly is not a conclusion compelled by science.

Overestimation of Maternal Risk Factors

The foregoing examples demonstrate some of the forces at work in the effort to identify and quantify occupational reproductive health risks. Because women are assumed to have the option *not* to work, and the duty to put the interests of children and family ahead of their own interests, evidence of maternally mediated reproductive risk has led to different conclusions and policies than evidence of paternally mediated risks or any other kind of risk. Culturally assigned sex roles make it possible to view women as uniquely vulnerable at work, while a recognition of male vulnerability, in this area as in many others, is resisted.

When women engage in behavior that is not only potentially harmful, but socially undesirable as well, there is an even greater tendency to acknowledge and perhaps exaggerate the risk. Recent evidence comes from a study comparing the publication rate for positive and negative studies on the prenatal effects of cocaine:

> of 9 negative abstracts (showing no adverse effect) only 1 (11%) was accepted, whereas 28 of the 49 positive abstracts were accepted (57%). This difference was significant. Negative studies tended to verify cocaine use more often and to have more cocaine and control cases. . . . This bias against the null hypothesis may lead to distorted estimation of the teratogenic risk of cocaine.[35]

The authors concluded that "most negative studies were not rejected because of scientific flaws, but rather because of bias against their non-adverse message. The subconscious message may be that if a study did not detect an adverse effect of cocaine, when the common knowledge is that this is a 'bad drug,' then the study must be flawed."[36]

This study suggests that the assumption that cocaine is harmful during pregnancy and the belief that pregnant women should adjust their conduct to reduce all possible fetal risks may combine to create an exaggerated estimate of the actual risk. A 1992 review of the literature in this area concluded:

> [A]vailable evidence from the newborn period is far too slim and fragmented to allow any clear predictions about the effects of intrauterine exposure to cocaine on the course and outcome of child growth and development.[37]

Overstating the danger to induce or persuade pregnant women to abstain from cocaine use, which almost certainly does pose health risks to pregnant woman and others, has some appeal, although an accurate appraisal has obvious virtues lacking in a more manipulative and less honest approach. This dilemma has been addressed in a 1992 article on the effects of low to moderate alcohol consumption during pregnancy. The authors concluded that "there is no measurable or documented risk . . . for the well-nourished woman who drinks two or less alcoholic beverages per day while pregnant."[38] They then pose this important question:

> Why not accept the admonition not to drink during pregnancy? Is this not the safest course? A number of arguments may be offered against this course. First, there is no scientific evidence to support the recommendation not to drink. Second, based on the warning, women may consider (or have) an abortion if they consumed alcohol prior to realizing they were pregnant. Third, women may experience unnecessary anxiety during the pregnancy. Fourth, the emphasis on small amounts of alcohol consumption may detract from other and more harmful health behaviors (such as cigarette

smoking or poor nutrition). Fifth, should an infant be born with a problem (or develop one) from any cause, however unrelated, parents may experience unnecessary feelings of guilt. Sixth, because the claims about small amounts of alcohol may seem exaggerated, heavy drinkers may disregard the risk. Finally, development of any policy based upon uncertain grounds may decrease the effectiveness of sound recommendations.[39]

Another reason to avoid manipulation of data to serve apparently salutary goals of influencing maternal behavior relates to the distortion that occurs in public policy formulation as a result. In the employment context, efforts to reduce fetal risk by controlling women's access to employment made the risks to the remaining workers seem less significant and relieved the pressure to improve workplace conditions. A different but related kind of distortion in perception occurs in the discussion of prenatal drug and alcohol use, where the focus on socially disapproved behavior deflects attention from factors that are essential to rational public policy formulation.

For example, a comparison of upper-middle-class *alcoholic* women with impoverished *alcoholic* women revealed that the incidence of fetal alcohol syndrome among their children was highly correlated with socioeconomic factors: the incidence was 70.9 percent for impoverished mothers and 4.5 percent for upper-middle-class mothers.[40] Similarly, among women (47 subjects) who drank *more* than three drinks a day, a statistically significant effect was seen on childhood IQ at age four, but it was not as influential as maternal and paternal education (strong socioeconomic indicators) and various other factors, including birth order.[41]

Here, the focus on alcohol use in pregnancy obscured the critical significance of socioeconomic factors, such as parental education, and other postnatal influences on childhood growth and development. Greater attention to the significance of these factors might stimulate adoption of programs to improve nutrition, education, and economic conditions for infants and parents, which would more effectively promote fetal health and early childhood development than warning signs in subways and bars telling women not to drink at all when they are pregnant. The message is directed not only at women with a dependency they may be unable to control without treatment (which may not even be available), but also at healthy, well-nourished pregnant women who have an occasional drink or glass of wine, a habit that poses no documented risk.[42]

Some of the same confounding variables make it extremely difficult to assess the risks of prenatal cocaine exposure:

high-risk factors [include] low birth weight, prematurity, mothers who are frequently poor, malnourished, underprivileged, homeless, battered, lacking prenatal care, alcoholic, and HIV positive. Since each of these factors is known to be associated with poor infant outcome, it becomes extremely difficult to identify a mother's cocaine use as a single variable which might adversely affect her child.[43]

The public policy implications of misunderstandings or distortions about the nature of this risk are particularly dramatic:

Infants exposed to cocaine in utero are often represented as severely or even irrevocably brain damaged. . . . [A] social sentiment has arisen that the loss of these children is entirely attributable to the prenatal effects of cocaine (a permanent biological factor). Such a conviction works toward exempting society from having to face other possible explanations of the children's plight—explanations such as poverty, community violence, inadequate education, and diminishing employment opportunities that require deeper understanding of wider social values.[44]

These commentators present a compelling argument for insistence on scientific accuracy and resistance to hyperbole with regard to reproductive risk assessments. Their concerns are fully justified, as evidenced by the following excerpt from a court decision holding that a positive urine drug toxicology test on a newborn justified charges that the mother had engaged in "child abuse or neglect" by virtue of her prenatal drug use:

The presence of cocaine in the newborns' urine sufficiently established . . . that the children did in fact suffer such impaired condition, as every human being has the legal right to begin life unimpaired by physical or mental defects resulting from the negligence of another. . . . When women use cocaine while pregnant, the blood vessels in the placenta and fetus constrict, cutting off the flow of oxygen and nutrients.[45] The prenatal use of cocaine often causes miscarriages, stillbirths, premature, low-weight births or leaves the cocaine-exposed babies with various physical and neurological malfunctions. . . . [46]

As this opinion demonstrates, profoundly important legal rights and relationships are affected—in this case, whether a woman will have custody of her child or whether the child will be placed in foster care (an uncertain fate, at best) on the basis of a body of scientific evidence that is conceded to be incomplete and inconclusive, and that has almost certainly been tainted by cultural expectations and sex-based stereotypes.

Oversimplification, a feature of fetal protection policies, is likewise a hallmark of many official responses to prenatal drug use. The popular perception, shared by some judges and legislators, is that, since cocaine is a "bad" drug, any woman who uses any amount of it while pregnant must be a "bad" mother. This ignores not only the scientific uncertainties already noted, but other considerations that are essential to constructive responses to women's substance abuse.

For example, addiction treatment services fall far behind the demand for them, and women are especially underserved. In 1989, approximately four million women needed treatment, but only about 550,000 received it. A quarter-million of those needing treatment were pregnant, and only 30,000 of those received it.[47] The AMA's report on prenatal drug use concludes that female substance abusers "have high levels of depression, anxiety, sense of powerlessness, and low levels of self-esteem and self-confidence." Their drug use is not "a failure of individual willpower," and it is not "meant to harm the fetus but to satisfy an acute psychological and physical need."[48] These symptoms require specialized medical services, which are in scarce supply.

The AMA also reports that many women who abuse drugs are themselves the victims of sexual or physical abuse:

> seventy percent of women [in one treatment program] were sexually abused as children, as compared with 15% of non-substance abusers. . . . Seventy percent of female substance abusers report being beaten. . . .

Other data confirm the associations between male substance abuse, violence against pregnant women, and subsequent substance abuse by physically abused women:

> among men who batter their female partners, substance abuse has been found to frequently accompany battering. . . . [M]ultiple drug use among male partners is independently associated with over a two-fold increase in women's experience of violence during pregnancy.

The study also noted that "women who are abused may self-medicate with alcohol, illicit drugs, and prescription medication in order to cope with the violence. [In one study,] increased alcohol and drug use followed the first incident of abuse."[49] These data suggest that the problem of prenatal substance abuse cannot be addressed outside of the context in which it occurs, in which male substance abuse and violence is heavily implicated. Treatment must be geared to these complex realities of women's lives, if it is to be effective.

Underestimation of Paternal Risk Factors

This latter point demonstrates only one of several ways in which the focus on maternal responsibility and conduct deflects attention from the significant role men play in reproduction and the well-being of children. As evidenced in the data amassed in opposition to corporate fetal protection policies, male exposures to chemicals, drugs, alcohol, and other substances can substantially influence the course of pregnancy—and potentially the health of a future child—because of the potential for toxic agents to alter genetic material or damage sperm in other ways.[50] Paternal preconception exposures have been associated with childhood cancers,[51] reduced birth weights,[52] and other adverse pregnancy outcomes.[53] The risk of adverse pregnancy outcome may be increased when both parents are exposed to certain chemicals.[54]

In studies of children with fetal alcohol syndrome, "[a] possible risk factor that has received relatively little attention thus far is paternal alcohol consumption."[55] An example is the set of dietary guidelines issued by the Departments of Agriculture and Health and Human Services in 1990, which confined its recommendations about the effects of alcohol on reproduction to pregnant women.[56] Bias is apparent in the report's reference to an unconfirmed study on the effects of alcohol on lactation,[57] while omitting mention of a study *by the same author* reporting an association between fathers' preconception drinking and reduced birth weight.[58] Once again, men were led to believe that their behavior is irrelevant, and women were told that taking even the slightest risk is unacceptable.

Conclusion

The point is not to suggest that cocaine or alcohol use during pregnancy is risk free, which is plainly not true, or that workplace toxins are not hazardous to fetuses. The intent of this chapter is twofold: first, to demonstrate the way social arrangements and expectations about women infiltrate the scientific process; and secondly, to show how this yields incomplete and inadequate information that ultimately results in distorted and counterproductive legal and policy determinations. Women have been the principal victims of this process, but not the only ones.

The focus on individual women's behavior and responsibility overstates what women can and should do to act responsibly towards the next generation, and it may fail to address the real problems and their likely cures. One further consequence of assigning women sole responsibility for childbearing and childrearing is that everyone else is relieved of those responsibilities. For example, employers with fetal protection policies did not have to improve workplace conditions—they had successfully shifted the responsibility to women to insure reproductive safety, by sacrificing either their fertility or their jobs. Public officials may hope to avoid their responsibility to provide access to effective drug treatment, prenatal care, and other essential services by shifting attention away from the inadequacies of medical care and governmental programs and focusing instead on the culpability of the pregnant drug user.

Only by sentimentalizing women and by oversimplifying their lives and choices is it possible to relieve society of its responsibility to protect the next generation from the hazards created by the current one, be they toxic work environments or drug addiction. The incentive to maintain the fiction that this is women's work is powerful. No wonder that so much energy has gone into doing so.[59]

Notes

1. *International Union, UAW v. Johnson Controls*, 499 U.S. 187, (1991).

2. Frank Easterbrook, dissenting opinion, *International Union, UAW v. Johnson Controls*, 886 F.2d 871, 914 (7th Cir. 1989) (*en banc*).

3. Thomas Murray, "Are Fetal Protection Policies Ethical?" *Health and Environmental Digest* 4 (6): 6 (1990).

4. Maureen Paul, "Reproductive Fitness and Risk," *Occupational Medicine: State of the Art Reviews* 3 (2): 323–40 (1988); Mary S. Becker, "From *Muller v. Oregon* to Fetal Vulnerability Policies," *University of Chicago Law Review* 53:1219 (1986).

5. Irving K. Zola, "Medicine As An Institution of Social Control," *Sociological Review* 20:487–504 (1972).

6. Stephen Jay Gould, *The Mismeasure of Man* (New York; W. W. Norton, 1981); Ruth Hubbard, Mary Sue Henifin, and Barbara Fried, eds., *Biological Woman: The Convenient Myth* (Cambridge, MA: Schenkman, 1982); B. Ehrenreich and D. English, *For Her Own Good: 150 Years of the Experts' Advice to Women* (Garden City, NY: Doubleday, 1979).

7. Gould, 1981, pp. 21–2.

8. Gould, 1981, p. 25.

9. Natalie Angier, "Mating For Life? It's Not for the Birds or the Bees," *New York Times*, Aug. 21, 1990, C1.

10. Phyllis Rose, *Parallel Lives* (New York: Vintage, 1984).

11. M. Lowe, "Social Bodies: The Interaction of Culture and Women's Biology," in Hubbard et al., 1982, pp. 100–101.

12. Quoted in Hubbard et al., 1982, p. 29.

13. Quoted in Wendy Kaminer, *A Fearful Freedom: Women's Flight From Equality* (New York: Addison-Wesley, 1990), p. xiv.

14. Louise Michelle Newman, *Men's Ideas/Women's Realities: Popular Science 1870-1915* (New York: Pergamon Press, 1985).

15. Ehrenreich and English, 1979, pp. 125–28.

16. Ehrenreich and English, 1979, p. 127.

17. Ehrenreich and English, 1979, p. 128.

18. Newman, 1985.

19. Gould, 1981, p. 74.

20. A dispute in some sex discrimination cases is whether women "want" non-traditional jobs, such as truck driving or sales jobs. Witnesses for employers have asserted that the small numbers of women applicants or employees reflects women's disinterest in certain non-traditional jobs. This argument has been accepted in some cases, *e.g.*, *EEOC v. Sears, Roebuck & Co.*, 839 F.2d 302 (7th Cir. 1988) and rejected in others, e.g., *Kilgo v. Bowman Transportation Co.*, 789 F.2d 859 (11th Cir. 1986). Some feminist theorists postulate different developmental patterns and psychological characteristics for males and females, in the context of a larger discussion of the ways in which scientific theory and investigation have been oriented toward, and have reflected, male experiences and perspectives, e.g., Carol Gilligan, *In a Different Voice* (Cambridge, MA: Harvard University Press, 1982). Ironically, these arguments have been used to rationalize discrimination *against* women, on the theory that males and females need not be treated the same under law if they are not similarly situated. See Transcript of Proceedings, *United States v. Commonwealth of Virginia*, 766 F. Supp. 1407 (W.D. Va. 1991), affirmed in part, reversed in part and remanded, 976 F.2d 890 (4th Cir. 1992). For a discussion of this paradox, see, e.g., Rachel T. Hare-Mustin and Jeanne Marecek, *Making a Difference: Psychology and the Construction of Gender* (New Haven: Yale University Press, 1990).

21. Joan E. Bertin, "Women's Health and Women's Rights: Reproductive Health Hazards in the Workplace." In K. S. Ratcliffe, et al., eds., *Healing Technology: Feminist Perspectives* (Ann Arbor: U. Mich. Press, 1989) pp. 289–303.

22. In every reported case on this subject, corporate medical personnel have taken credit for instigating such policies. This fact is apparent in the court records of cases against the American Cyanamid Co., Olin Corp., Johnson

Controls Co., and other employers who have been involved in lawsuits challenging their practices as sex discrimination. These records are on file in the author's office.

23. *International Union, UAW v. Johnson Controls*, 1991.

24. Charles W. Fishburn, Transcript of Deposition, *International Union, UAW v. Johnson Controls* (E.D. Wis., No. 84-C-0472), June 13, 1985, pp. 73-4.

25. Fishburn, 1985, p. 85.

26. Fishburn, 1985, p. 85.

27. Fishburn, 1985, p. 37.

28. Paul A. Hammond, Transcript of Deposition, *International Union, UAW v. Johnson Controls* (E. D. Wis., No. 84-C-0472), June 18, 1986, p. 42, emphasis added.

29. Hammond, 1986, p. 71.

30. Hammond, 1986, p. 76.

31. J. Julian Chisolm, Transcript of Deposition, *International Union, UAW v. Johnson Controls* (E. D. Wis., No. 84-C-0472), June 19, 1986, p. 33.

32. Herbert L. Needleman and David Bellinger, "Commentary: Recent Developments," *Environmental Research* 46:190-91 (1989), pp. 190-91 (emphasis added).

33. D. R. Mattison, "Exclusion of Fertile Women from the Workplace: Bad Medicine, Worse Law," *Journal of the Arkansas Medical Society* 86(12):491-92 [1990]; Bertin, 1989.

34. Anthony R. Scialli, "Sexism In Toxicology," *Reproductive Toxicology* 3:219-220 (1989).

35. Koren et al., "Bias Against the Null Hypothesis: The Reproductive Hazards of Cocaine," *Lancet* 2 (8677): 1440-42, p. 1440 (1989).

36. Koren et al., 1989, p. 1441.

37. Mayes et al., "The Problem of Prenatal Cocaine Exposure," *Journal of the American Medical Ass'n*, 267 (3): 406-408, p. 406. (1992)

38. Joel J. Alpert and Barry Zuckerman, "Alcohol Use During Pregnancy: What Is the Risk?" *Pediatrics In Review* 12:375-79 (1992).

39. Alpert and Zuckerman, 1992.

40. Nesrin Bingol et al., "The Influence of Socioeconomic Factors on the Occurrence of Fetal Alcohol Syndrome," *Advances in Alcohol and Substance Abuse*, 105-18 (1987).

41. Ann P. Streissguth et al., "IQ at Age 4 In Relation to Maternal Alcohol Use and Smoking During Pregnancy," *Developmental Psychology* 25 (1): 3-11 (1989).

42. Alpert and Zuckerman, 1992; Genevieve Knupfer, "Abstaining for Foetal Health: The Fiction That Even Light Drinking is Dangerous," *British Journal of Addiction* (1991); Ernest Abel and Robert J. Sokol, "Is Occa-

sional Light Drinking during Pregnancy Harmful?" in Ruth Engs, ed., *Controversies in the Addiction Field*, 158–64 (1990).

43. Stephen Kandall, "Physician Dispels Myths About Drug-Exposed Infants," *American Academy of Pediatrics News* 7(1), p. 11 (1991).

44. Mayes et al., 1992, pp. 406, 408.

45. Besharov, "Let's Give Crack Babies a Way Out of Addict Families," *Newsday*, Sept. 3, 1989, p. 4.

46. *Matter of re Stefanel Tyesha*, 157 App. Div. 2d 322, 556 N.Y.S. 2d 280 (1990).

47. National Association of State Alcohol and Drug Abuse Directors, "Highlights of Results from Recent NASADAD Survey on State Alcohol and Drug Agency Use of FY 1989 Federal and State Funds" (1990).

48. American Medical Association, Report of the Board of Trustees, "Legal Interventions during Pregnancy: Court-Ordered Medical Treatments and Legal Penalties for Potentially Harmful Behavior By Pregnant Women," *Journal of The American Medical Association* 264(20) :2663–70 (1990), pp. 2667–68.

49. Hortensia Amaro et al., "Violence During Pregnancy and Substance Use," *American Journal of Public Health* 80 (5): 575–79, p. 578 (1990).

50. Paul, 1988.

51. E.g., John R. Wilkins and Ruth A. Koutras, "Paternal Occupation and Brain Cancer in Offspring: A Mortality-Based Case-Control Study," *American Journal of Industrial Medicine* 14: 299–318 (1988); Martin J. Gardner et al., "Results of Case-Control Study of Leukaemia and Lymphoma Among Young People near Sellafield Nuclear Plant in West Cumbria," *British Medical Journal* 300: 423–29 (1990).

52. Ruth E. Little and Charles F. Sing, "Father's Drinking and Infant Birth Weight: Report of an Association," *Teratology* 36: 59–65 (1987).

53. David A. Savitz, et al., "Effects of Parents' Occupational Exposures on Risk of Stillbirth, Preterm Delivery, and Small-for-Gestational-Age Infants," *American Journal of Epidemiology* 129 (6): 1201–18 (1989).

54. Kari Hemminki, et al., "Spontaneous Abortions in an Industrialized Community in Finland," *American Journal of Public Health* 73 (1): 32–37 (1983).

55. Ernest Abel and Julia A. Lee, "Paternal Alcohol Exposure Affects Offspring Behavior but not Body or Organ Weights in Mice," *Alcoholism: Clinical and Experimental Research* 12 (3): 349–55, p. 349 (1988).

56. Dietary Guidelines Advisory Committee, "Report on the Dietary Guidelines for Americans To the Secretary of Agriculture and the Secretary of Health and Human Services" (1990).

57. Ruth E. Little, et al., "Maternal Alcohol Use During Breastfeeding and Mental and Motor Development at One Year," *New England Journal of Medicine* 321:425–30 (1989).

58. Little and Sing, 1987.

59. For their research assistance and thought-provoking comments and discussion, I want especially to thank Laurie Beck, Mary Sue Henifin, Maureen Paul, Isabelle Katz Pinzler, Ellen Silbergeld, Jeanne Stellman, and Liz Werby, among others. Portions of this essay are adapted with permission from Joan E. Bertin, "Pregnancy and Social Control," in B. K. Rothman, ed., *Encyclopedia of Childbearing* (New York: Oryx Press, 1993), and Joan E. Bertin, "Reproductive Hazards in The Workplace: Lessons from *UAW v. Johnson Controls*," in H. L. Needleman and D. Bellinger, eds., *Prenatal Exposure to Toxicants: Developmental Consequences* (Baltimore: Johns Hopkins University Press) (1994) pp. 297–316. The author expresses her thanks to The Herman Goldman Foundation, The General Service Foundation, The Moriah Fund, and The Jessie Smith Noyes Foundation, for their support of this work.

The Discriminatory Nature of Industrial Health-Hazard Policies and Some Implications for Third World Women Workers

Uma Narayan

The policy of excluding fertile women from jobs, on the grounds that, were they to become pregnant, the work environment would pose unacceptable health hazards to their fetuses, has received wide public attention in the light of the *Johnson Controls* case in 1991. However, such policies have had a longer history in the United States than many people realize. In 1979, over 100,000 jobs were closed to women of childbearing capacity on the grounds of fetal protection.[1] The number could grow to a frightening extent, given estimates that roughly 20 million jobs involve exposure to potential reproductive hazards.[2]

I wish to suggest that we have reasons to be extremely suspicious about what has gone on in the development and implementation of such policies. Much of the debate surrounding them either takes for granted, or fails to question, two central assumptions, namely that

(1) women workers' exposure to toxins poses risks to offspring, while the exposure of male workers to the same toxins does not, and

(2) the motivation for these policies is rooted either in a concern for the welfare of offspring, or in a desire on the part of employers to avoid tort-liability lawsuits from children prenatally damaged because of maternal exposure.[3]

I believe there are substantial reasons for skepticism about both these claims. I shall develop an account of these reasons, and shall suggest that such claims serve as a cover for discriminatory attempts to exclude women from some well-paying industrial jobs. I shall further argue that

why policies are implemented

398

there are reasons to believe that exclusionary policies that take this particular form are unlikely to develop in most Third World contexts.

Are Industrial Reproductive Hazards a "Women's Problem"?

Two frequent arguments against these exclusionary policies have taken the following forms. One argument points out that excluding women from jobs involving toxic exposure might have more detrimental effects on offspring than permitting the exposure.[4] Another argument contends that individual women can make better decisions about their reproductive and work future than can employers. This argument accuses employers of a misplaced paternalism that is based on the assumption that women cannot be trusted to act responsibly.[5]

These arguments, as well as others, and discussions on this issue generally, fail to question the assumption that industrial reproductive hazards pose a "special" problem for women. The underlying idea seems to be that pregnant women working in certain toxic work environments could put their offspring at risk, and that, since men do not become pregnant, their exposure to these hazards does not put their offspring at risk.

However, there is substantial scientific evidence that suggests that offspring can be harmed by paternal exposure to toxic working conditions, and that paternal exposure is often equally dangerous to offspring. Nothstein and Ayres argue that the negative effects of exposure to a variety of toxic substances varies very little between men and women, and they conclude that the general "hypothesis of special susceptibility because of sex is largely without basis."[6]

Lead, which was the substance at issue in Johnson Controls, is harmful to both male and female reproductive systems. In men, it can cause impotence, sterility, and decreased sperm production. Studies show that unexposed wives of exposed men have more spontaneous abortions and stillbirths and that fetal abnormalities are greater in children of men exposed to lead. Both findings suggest that lead causes mutagenic changes in sperm. Studies also show that lead, like several other toxins to which male workers are exposed, can be transmitted to a fetus during intercourse, *after* conception has occurred.[7] Hence, preconceptive and prenatal harm can result from *either* parent's exposure to any of a variety of substances at the workplace.[8] Why, then, the focus on excluding women?

It seems more than likely that our deeply gendered views of women's reproductive and parenting roles influence the plausibility of the assumption that the *sole* pathway to the fetus is through the mother. The fact that a large proportion of studies on potential reproductive hazards in toxic work environments focus on women undoubtedly reinforces the tendencies of companies to institute policies that exclude only women. These studies further add to the pervasive assumption that fetuses are uniquely susceptible to harm through the mother.

However, that much of such research focuses on women cannot completely explain this phenomenon. There is a growing body of research demonstrating the harmful preconceptual and prenatal effects of *both* male and female parental exposure to substances such as lead. Still, the harmful effects to offspring via the mother tend to be emphasized, while harmful effects via the father tend to be systematically ignored, reinforcing the view that women alone bear the burden for the preconceptive and prenatal well-being of offspring.

Patricia Vawter Klein surveys over a century of this practice of using "scientific evidence" to exclude women from jobs, while ignoring dangers to men. She points out that recent scientific findings on the crossover of substances through the placenta has strengthened exclusionary policies towards fertile women, but that new and growing evidence on male contribution to chromosomal and mutagenic changes in fetuses has not once resulted in the exclusion of fertile men.[9] There is ample evidence for the pervasiveness and persistence of this tendency to one-sidedly use scientific data to exclude women from employment.

Joan Bertin succinctly summarizes the ways in which gender assumptions underlie what she calls a "selective vision in acknowledging workplace hazards." She points out that:

> hazards are often ignored or minimized, except when they involve female aspects of reproduction. Then employers act quickly to exclude fertile or pregnant women workers on the basis of preliminary, inconclusive, and sometimes speculative information. . . . Once the proof is in, chemicals that are particularly harmful to men (i.e., DBCP, kepone) have been banned, while women have been barred from working around chemicals suspected to cause fetal harm. These patterns once again reinforce the notion that the workplace must accommodate the needs of men, but not of women. . . .[10]

This evidence should give us pause in adding to a discourse on industrial health-hazards in a manner that reinforces the view that toxic substances in the workplace pose a special problem for women.[11]

Fetal Harms and Fear of Tort Liability

If both male and female parents can harm their future offspring as a result of exposure to toxic substances in the workplace, it would follow that any institution or policy that is *genuinely* concerned with preventing harms to future generations would try to exclude both men and women from such jobs, before and/or during the years when they planned to have children. Such a policy has never been implemented. The focus on dangers in the workplace to fetuses thus seems to divert attention from the real problem—how to protect men, women, and their potential offspring from hazardous working conditions, and the question of whether companies are doing enough to minimize worker exposure to mutagenic and teratogenic hazards. It also raises the concern that the welfare of fetuses is taken more seriously than the welfare of the workers themselves.

A close analysis of the types of jobs in which "fetal protection" policies have been implemented suggests that this is a suspiciously discriminatory phenomenon. Employers do not suggest excluding women to protect fetuses in occupations that are dominated by women. Over 97 percent of nurses are female, and nurses are routinely exposed to ionizing radiation from x-rays, ethylene oxide, and anaesthetic gases, all of which are suspected to cause reproductive damage. Working in laundries and dry-cleaning shops, in pottery and jewelry making, in the electronics industry, as dental technicians—all expose women in these predominantly female occupations to substances potentially hazardous to fetuses. Elementary school teachers, child care workers, and receptionists in pediatric offices are often exposed to viral infections that are dangerous to fetuses. But there have been no moves to bar women from these occupations in order to protect their fetuses. This suggests that there are reasons for skepticism regarding the claim that the welfare of fetuses is the driving force behind these policies.

Are employers who implement Johnson-type policies motivated by fear of tort liability from the offspring of workers who suffer harm as a result of their parents' exposure to mutagenic or teratogenic substances in the workplace? Two reasons to doubt this present themselves immediately:

(1) if offspring can be harmed by the exposure of *either* parent, employers could face lawsuits from the children of exposed male workers. However, there is no apparent concern over this possibility, which is hard to explain, given that it is well known

that men's exposure to toxins can result in preconceptive and prenatal harm;

(2) employers do not seem to be losing sleep over the possibility of lawsuits from affected children of exposed workers in the female-dominated occupations I just mentioned. If the concern were *really* to prevent preconceptive and prenatal harm in order to avoid tort liability, then we should see exclusions of men in the first case and exclusions of women in the second. But we do not see this.

The lack of concern about lawsuits from children of male workers on the part of employers who are purportedly worried about tort liability is even harder to explain when we realize that more men than women are employed in these industries, that male workers experience greater cumulative exposure per child born than do women,[12] and that widely publicized lawsuits have been brought by male workers who claimed that their workplace exposure resulted in injury to their children.[13]

There are additional reasons for rejecting claims that fear of liability is the motivating factor behind policies that exclude fertile women from certain jobs. Despite employers' alleged fears over the proliferation of such lawsuits, there has not yet been a single award based on prenatal injuries from maternal exposure in the workplace.[14] Several authors have pointed out that it would be very difficult to establish the causation necessary for such suits to be successful. Many of the birth defects associated with exposure to workplace toxins also occur in children whose parents have not been exposed to toxic substances in the workplace, though exposure may increase the probability of the defect. In such cases there would be little way to prove that the defect is the result of exposure to some particular toxin.[15]

In many instances it would also be difficult to prove that the defect resulted from exposure at the workplace. For instance, even if it could be shown that a defect is the result of prenatal exposure to lead, it would be difficult to show that the lead came from parental exposure in a workplace, since lead is found in paint, cooking and eating utensils, and water.[16] Even where prenatal risks from workplace chemicals have been extensively studied and proven, there are few documented cases of actual harm.[17] The existence of such difficulties in establishing liability further suggests that purported employer concerns about tort liability may only be a pretext for sex discrimination.[18]

There are other factors that, though not necessarily conclusive, tend to increase skepticism about purported employer fears of tort liability. Many legal questions concerning tort liability in this area remain unanswered. It is unclear whether the standard of liability in such cases is negligence or strict liability, and whether employer compliance with OSHA standards is a defense. While it is difficult to estimate employer risk of tort liability under such conditions of uncertainty, it is also far from obvious that employers are at risk of significant tort liability.[19]

The suspicion that employer fear of tort liability has little to do with these exclusionary policies is only reinforced when we consider the fact that, as mentioned earlier, there are hardly any attempts to exclude women from jobs involving exposure to hazardous substances where such jobs rely heavily on a female labor force.[20] No exclusionary policies have been adopted, for instance, in female-dominated industries such as agriculture and textiles, where substantial numbers of women are exposed to reproductive hazards, such as pesticides and hydrocarbons. Undoubtedly, one reason is that it would be impossible to find male workers who would replace these women in jobs that characteristically command low wages and lack benefits.

Women are excluded primarily from jobs where the workforce is largely male, where women are perceived as marginal members of the workforce, and where the jobs are among the higher-paying industrial jobs. When we put all these facts together, claims that the kinds of policies in question are motivated by concern for fetal health or by fear of tort liability lose whatever initial plausibility they may have.

Health-Hazard Policies and Third World Women Workers

Are policies like that at Johnson Controls likely to turn up in Third World contexts? It is difficult to generalize about the Third World, but I shall suggest that there are reasons to believe that such policies are *very* unlikely to appear there.

Third World women who are employed in what are traditionally regarded as "women's occupations" are unlikely to be targeted for exclusion from such jobs for the same sorts of reasons that we have already seen are relevant in the United States. That is, it is unlikely that employers would find men to replace them. Furthermore, with exceptions such as Southeast Asia, most Third World women are economically dependent on agriculture and the informal sectors,[21] areas where exclusionary policies seem unlikely. Women are often employed in these sectors because they work for lower wages than men, and as employment in these sectors is not effectively regulated, employers can hire whom they choose without attempting to use exclusionary policies as justifications.[22]

Women who are employed in more "modern" industrial occupations in women-dominated sectors of employment are also unlikely to be targeted for exclusion for a number of reasons. They are cheaper to hire than men and are considered to be a more docile labor force, while their "delicate fingers" and supposedly greater toleration for tedious routine are seen as making them more suitable for many of the assembly-line occupations they tend to be hired into.[23] Many of these assembly-line jobs do pose dangers both to women workers and their potential offspring, information about which is frequently available to their employers. Given that these employers still find it in their interests to hire women, much like employers in reproductively hazardous female-dominated occupations in Western industrialized countries, I see no reason to believe that things will change.

Given that the health and safety of workers is protected even less in many Third World contexts than in industrialized Western countries, employers in the Third World could hardly make a plausible claim that they are concerned about being on the receiving end of lawsuits, especially from their workers' offspring.[24] In fact, there is reason to speculate that, were fears of possible litigation here to become real, many employers would shift production overseas, to Third World countries where labor costs would be cheaper and where they could function without regard either for fetal safety or women's welfare.[25]

I believe that our finding the expressed concern about future tort liability plausible is largely a function of our perception of ourselves. The United States is one of the most litigious societies in the world, and it is this fact of our culture that leads many of us to find the claim that employers are motivated by fear of tort liability so convincing, even in the face of substantial reason for skepticism.

There is also an animated and pervasive public discourse about fetuses and fetal rights in the United States, with links to the so-called pro-life or anti-abortion movement. This discourse makes the type of policies in question more credible and helps them win public support. With few exceptions, neither broad public debate about fetal rights nor widespread anti-abortion movements exist in Third World countries.[26] The legal systems of most Third World countries do not recognize the "strong state interest in protecting the potential life of the fetus" that our Supreme Court has recognized repeatedly.[27] Judge Posner frankly admits that this recognition is "the product of a groundswell of powerful emotion by a significant part of the community."[28] There is, as of now, no such emotional groundswell in most Third World countries.

In fact, with a few exceptions, most Third World governments are preoccupied with overpopulation, which is widely (if questionably) perceived as the primary factor underlying poverty and underdevelopment. Fetal-protection issues are not likely to receive much attention in such contexts. Hence, moves to curtail employment opportunities for women on the grounds of fetal protection are also unlikely to arise in these contexts.

I do not wish to rule out the possibility that exclusionary policies might be instituted in Third World contexts if, for whatever reason, it was felt to be more expedient to reserve some range of jobs entirely for men. I just think it is unlikely, not only for the reasons I have given, but also because I believe employers would probably have been hiring only men all along for such jobs, with less of a problem than they might face here were they to do this.

While I believe that the exclusionary policies in question function to preserve a certain range of jobs for men in the United States, there are different patterns of women losing jobs to men in some Third World countries. For example, with shrinking agricultural employment in many parts of India, as much as 60 percent of the agricultural work traditionally performed by women has been taken over by men.[29] Where enough men are willing to do "women's work" at "women's wages," it seems that the gendered assumptions of the employers as to who "needs" the work suffice to make these jobs go to men. The joint lesson I am inclined to learn from the conjunction of such patterns, combined with my analysis of what is going on with Johnson-type policies, is that women seem likely to lose employment opportunities to men both when there are enough men willing to work those jobs at "women's wages" or when there are enough men who want to hold on to "men's work" that pays good "men's wages."

There are a variety of policies and practices that have worked to successfully marginalize women from employment in many Third World countries. These include "development policies" that are often entirely directed towards male workers and that often end up marginalizing women from a variety of traditional occupations; lack of education and skills; sexist hiring practices on the part of employers, and so on.[30] However, I am aware of no attempts in Third World contexts to exclude women from jobs that involve exposure to hazardous substances and, as I have argued, I think it is very unlikely that there will be any such attempts.

Conclusions

While it is clear that modern production techniques expose many workers to hazardous substances, and that protecting the health of workers and their future offspring raise many interesting ethical and legal questions, I am convinced that women in particular have good reasons to be cautious about the ways in which such issues are formulated and dealt with. While there may be contexts that genuinely raise issues about balancing the rights of women against the interests of fetuses and corporations, it seems clear that in many other cases, articulating the issues this way is itself sexist and detrimental to the interests of women.

I think that women need to have a shrewd perspective on what is going on beneath certain proposals and policies that affect them, refusing to accept at face value the reasons given in support of policies that are detrimental to their interests. It is not always sufficient that we are able to come up with countervailing reasons; we must be willing to question the prevalent descriptions of such policies, and point out the implausibility of their alleged rationales whenever necessary.

Specifically, I believe women have good reason to cultivate skepticism about the objectivity of scientific data, about the rationality of the ways in which scientific data is interpreted and put to legal use, and about the rationality of corporations and corporate policies, especially where the interests of women are at stake. I am not advocating a commitment to the view that science, business, and the law are deliberately "out to get" women, or are consciously engaged in conspiracies to discriminate against women, or even that such discrimination clearly serves the interests of those who engage in the discrimination. Deeply held views about gender help to generate and to perpetuate what superficially seem to be rational justifications for gender-based discrimination, even in contexts where it is unclear what specific interests are served by the discrimination. It takes critical and comprehensive attention to a variety of details in order to convince ourselves and others that these justifications are not as rational as they claim to be.

I would argue that, both ethically and legally, Johnson-type policies are best opposed (1) by pointing out that it is profoundly discriminatory to exclude only women from jobs that pose reproductive hazards to both women and men, and (2) by explicitly questioning the cogency and consistency of the fetal protection and tort liability avoidance rationales that are put forward in support of these policies. Women's position in the workforce, as in most parts of the world, remains sufficiently precarious and marginal to make vigilance absolutely necessary where any policies limiting women's workforce participation are concerned.

Notes

1. Bill Richards, "Faceoff on Hazardous Jobs: Women's Rights, Fetus Safety," *Washington Post*, November 3, 1979, p. 11.

2. Alison E. Grossman, "Striking Down Fetal Protection Policies: A Feminist Victory?" *Virginia Law Review* 77 (December 1991): 1607.

3. An example: "Motivated both by concern over tort-liability and concern for the health of future generations, employers opt to close doors to women workers rather than face liability for future injuries," in Pendleton E. Hamlet, "Fetal Protection Policies: A Statutory Proposal in the Wake of *International Union, UAW, v. Johnson Controls, Inc.*," *Cornell Law Review* 75 (July 1990): 1110.

4. Judge Cudahy, in his dissent in the Seventh Circuit Court of Appeals decision on *International Union, UAW, v. Johnson Controls*, argued, " . . . what is the situation of the pregnant woman, unemployed or working for the minimum wage and unprotected by health insurance, in relation to her pregnant sister, exposed to an indeterminate lead risk but well-fed, housed and doctored? Whose fetus is at greater risk?" 886 F.2d. at 902.

5. See, for instance, Alan C. Blanco, "Fetal Protection Programs Under Title VII—Rebutting the Procreative Presumption," *University of Pittsburgh Law Review* 46 (1985): 755–766.

6. Gary Z. Nothstein and Jeffrey P. Ayres, "Sex-Based Considerations of Differentiation in the Workplace: Exploring the Biomedical Interface between OSHA and Title VII," *Villanova Law Review* 26 (1980–81): 243–248.

7. Nothstein and Ayres, p. 239.

8. Such substances include lead (used in gasoline, bullets, batteries, pigments, pipe, and roofing materials); vinyl chloride (used in plastics and rubbers); benzene (used in paints, nylons, tires, and detergents); mercury (used in thermometers, dental fillings, mirrors, dyes); ionizing radiation; anaesthetic gases; carbon monoxide and pesticides (see Nothstein and Ayres, p. 247).

9. Patricia V. Klein, " 'For the Good of the Race': Reproductive Hazards from Lead and the Persistence of Exclusionary Policies Towards Women." In *Women, Work and Technology*, ed. Barbara D. Wright, Myra M. Ferree, et al. (Ann Arbor: University of Michigan Press, 1987), pp. 101–117. Klein also cites a 1969 study by Baltrop that suggests that placental transfer of lead occurs only after the fourteenth week of gestation, and that the fetus may not be contaminated by lead during the first trimester (p. 110).

10. Joan E. Bertin, "Reproductive Hazards in the Workplace," in *Reproductive Laws for the 1990s*, ed. Sherill Cohen and Nadine Taub (Clifton, NJ: Humana Press, 1989), pp. 281–82.

11. It is possible that there are substances that only affect fetuses via maternal exposure. However, I believe we should make very sure that such is in fact the case, no matter what we propose to do about it.

12. Bertin, p. 294.

13. For examples, see "Five Makers of Agent Orange Charge U.S. Misused Chemical in Vietnam: Companies Replying to Suit, Say Federal Negligence is Responsible for Any Harm to Veterans and Kin," *New York Times*,

Jan. 7, 1980, p. A14; and "Union, Citing Birth Defects, Asks Ban on a Herbicide," *New York Times*, Nov. 9, 1979, p. 16.

14. Hamlet, p. 1110. As of this writing, there has been only one reported case of a tort suit against a battery manufacturer brought by a female employee for lead injury to her child. The plaintiff got to a jury, but lost. See *Security National Bank v. Chloride, Inc.*, 602 F. Supp. 294 (D. Kan. 1985).

15. Hannah A. Furnish, "Prenatal Exposure to Fetally Toxic Work Environments: The Dilemma of the 1978 Pregnancy Amendment to Title VII of the Civil Rights Act," *Iowa Law Review* 63 (October 1980): 63–129.

16. Lucinda M. Finley, "The Exclusion of Fertile Women from the Hazardous Workplace: The Latest Example of Discriminatory Protective Policies, or a Legitimate, Neutral Response to an Emerging Social Problem?" *N.Y.U. Annual National Conference on Labor* 38 (1985): 16–39.

17. Grossman, p. 1621. It is also interesting to note that none of the babies born to female employees who were exposed to lead at Johnson Controls had birth defects or abnormalities.

18. This position is defended by Wendy W. Williams, "Firing the Woman to Protect the Fetus: The Reconciliation of Fetal Protection with Employment Opportunity Goals Under Title VII," *Georgetown Law Journal* 69 (February 1981): 641–704.

19. In his dissenting opinion in the Seventh Circuit Court of Appeals decision on *International Union, UAW, v. Johnson Controls*, Judge Posner remarks that Johnson Controls had not yet attempted to document its liability concerns (886 F.2d 871 at 904). He also points out that while eight women employed in battery production had become pregnant in eight years, "the only warning that was in effect during that period was one more likely to allay than to arouse concern. It compared the fetal hazards of airborne lead to those of cigarette smoking, and many women do not believe smoking is highly hazardous to the fetus" (886 F.2d 871 at 906). It stands to reason that employers genuinely worried about tort liability would have paid more attention to the efficacy of their warning.

20. Bertin cites one example of a 1987 case where "some manufacturers of semiconductor chips announced an intention to limit employment of women workers in response to a study purportedly showing an increased risk of miscarriage in such employment." She points out that, unlike earlier cases, this "involved an industry substantially populated by women" (Bertin, "Reproductive Hazards," p. 278). However, since this policy was only intended to exclude pregnant women, it is unlikely that the employers would have found it difficult to replace them.

21. Bina Agarwal, "Patriarchy and the 'Modernising' State," in *Structures of Patriarchy*, ed. Bina Agarwal (Atlantic Highlands, NJ: Zed Books, 1989), pp. 1–28.

22. The situation of women workers in these sectors in the Third World is analogous to their situation in the United States. Joan Bertin points out

that the most vulnerable and least powerful segment of workers in the United States—household and agricultural workers, disabled workers in sheltered workshops and institutions, etc.—are not even covered by the OSHA regulations, despite evidence that these workers might encounter substantial occupational health risks (Bertin, "Reproductive Hazards," p. 293).

23. Diane Elson and Ruth Pearson, "The Subordination of Women and the Internationalisation of Factory Production," in *Of Marriage and the Market: Subordination of Women in International Perspective*, ed. Kate Young et al., (London: CSE Books, 1981).

24. In the "export processing zones" or "free trade zones," where most women who work in "assembly line" industrial jobs are concentrated, industries and government often cooperate in banning unions and in dispensing with many existing labor laws. Countries where this has been documented include Korea, Singapore, Malaysia, the Philippines, and Sri Lanka. See Pasuk Phongpaichit, "Two Roads to the Factory," in Agarwal, pp. 151–163.

25. 28 U.S.C.A. § 1332(a)(2) extends the jurisdiction of federal courts to actions by aliens against a U.S. citizen or corporation, so long as the amount in controversy is greater than $50,000. However, an alien not living in the United States would face enormous practical difficulties in bringing a suit, and there would be a danger of prejudice against the alien in U.S. courts. See Charles Wright, *Federal Courts*, 4th ed., § 24 (St. Paul, MN: West Publishing Co., 1983). These corporations are therefore unlikely to be deterred by worries about lawsuits by Third World employees or their offspring.

26. Most Third World contexts also lack the fairly prevalent American interest in having a "perfect child."

27. See, e.g., *Maher v. Roe*, 432 U.S. 464, 478 (1977).

28. See his dissent in the Seventh Circuit Court of Appeals decision on *International Union, UAW, v. Johnson Controls*, 886 F.2d 871 at 905.

29. See Agarwal, "Patriarchy and the 'Modernising' State."

30. For details on the economic marginalization of women in the Third World, see some of the articles in Agarwal.

Contributors

Barbara J. Berg (1958–1995) was a clinical psychologist working as Assistant Professor in the Department of Psychology at Washington State University. She published numerous articles in the area of infertility.

Joan E. Bertin, an attorney, is Co-Director of the Program on Gender, Science and Law at Columbia University School of Public Health. Previously, she was Associate Director of the Women's Rights Project of the American Civil Liberties Union. She has litigated extensively on behalf of women's rights in a variety of areas and has written widely on these issues.

Joan C. Callahan is Professor of Philosophy at the University of Kentucky. She is editor of *Menopause: A Midlife Passage* and co-author with James W. Knight of *Preventing Birth: Contemporary Methods and Related Moral Controversies,* and has written numerous articles on ethics and social philosophy. She is at work on a second edition of her *Ethical Issues in Professional Life.*

Julie Crossen, an artist, is currently completing her studies in nursing. She lives in Cincinnati.

Janet Gallagher is Assistant Corporation Counsel, Torts Division, in the New York City Department of Law.

Helen Bequaert Holmes has a Ph.D. in genetics and is Coordinator,

Center for Genetics, Ethics, and Women. She is also co-founder of the international network Feminist Approaches to Bioethics. She is editor of *Issues in Reproductive Technology* and co-editor of *Feminist Perspectives in Medical Ethics*.

Joan Mahoney is Dean of The School of Law at Western New England College.

Mary B. Mahowald is Professor in the Department of Obstetrics and Gynecology, and Assistant Director of the Center for Clinical Medical Ethics at the University of Chicago College of Medicine. Her most recent books are *Women and Children in Health Care: An Unequal Majority* and the third revision of her *Philosophy of Woman*.

Uma Narayan is Assistant Professor in the Department of Philosophy at Vassar College. She writes and teaches in the areas of philosophy of law, social and political philosophy, ethics, and feminist issues in philosophy. She is co-editing a volume (with Mary L. Shanley) entitled *Reconstructing Political Theory: Feminist Perspectives*.

Christine Overall is Professor of Philosophy at Queen's University. She is the author of *Ethics and Human Reproduction: A Feminist Analysis* and *Human Reproduction: Principles, Practices, Policies*, and editor of *The Future of Human Reproduction*. She is co-editor of *Feminist Perspectives: Philosophical Essays on Method and Morals* and *Perspectives on AIDS: Ethical and Social Issues*.

Laura M. Purdy, Associate Professor of Philosophy at Wells College, is the author of *In Their Best Interest? The Case against Equal Rights for Children* and co-editor (with Helen Bequaert Holmes) of *Feminist Perspectives in Medical Ethics*.

Janice G. Raymond is Professor of Women's Studies and Medical Ethics at the University of Massachusetts, Amherst. She is the author of *The Transsexual Empire: The Making of the She-Male*; *A Passion for Friends: A Philosophy of Female Affection*; *The Sexual Liberals and the Attack on Feminism*; and *Women as Wombs: Reproductive Technologies and the Battle Over Women's Freedom*.

Mary L. (Molly) Shanley is Professor of Political Science on the Margaret Stiles Halleck Chair at Vassar College. She is author of *Femi-

nism, Marriage and the Law in Victorian England (Princeton: Princeton University Press, 1989) and editor, with Carole Pateman, of *Feminist Interpretations and Political Theory* (Cambridge: Polity Press; and State College, Penn State University Press, 1990). She is currently working, with Uma Narayan, on an anthology of essays reinterpreting central concepts in western political theory, and on a book on ethical issues in contemporary family law.

Patricia Smith is Associate Professor of Philosophy at the University of Kentucky, where she teaches social philosophy and jurisprudence. Her recent publications include *The Nature and Process of Law* and *Feminist Jurisprudence*.

Rosemarie Tong is Thatcher Professor in Medical Humanities and Philosophy at Davidson College. She is the author of *Women, Sex and the Law, Controlling Our Reproductive Destiny; Feminist Thought: A Comprehensive Introduction;* and *Feminine and Feminist Ethics.*

Index

415

Index